LEARNING FOR LIFE
CANADIAN READINGS IN ADULT EDUCATION

Learning for Life

Canadian Readings in Adult Education

SUE M. SCOTT
University of Alberta

BRUCE SPENCER
Athabasca University

ALAN M. THOMAS
Ontario Institute for Studies in Education

THOMPSON EDUCATIONAL PUBLISHING, INC.
Toronto

Canadian Cataloguing in Publication Data

Main entry under title:

Learning for life : Canadian readings in adult education

Includes bibliographical references
ISBN 1-55077-085-3

1. Adult education — Canada. I. Scott, Sue. II Spencer, Bruce. III. Thomas, Alan
M. (Alan Miller), 1928-

LC5254.L42 1998   374'.971   C97-932729-6

Cover photo:
Bookkeeping students at St. Francis Xavier Extension Department (date unknown).
Courtesy of St. Francis Xavier University Archives.

ISBN 1-55077-085-3
Printed in Canada.

Table of Contents

SECTION 2: PURPOSES

Part 1: Education for Economy

Part 2: Education for Transformation

Part 3: Education for Diversity

SECTION 3: CHALLENGES AND FUTURE VISIONS

Part 1: Current Challenges

Part 2: Future Visions

List of Contributors

- **Paul Bouchard** is Assistant Professor at Concordia University (Montreal). His research interests are in workplace learning, self-directed learning strategies and distance learning environments.

- **Barbara Burnaby** is a Professor in the Modern Language Centre and the Department of Curriculum, Teaching, and Learning at the Ontario Institute for Studies in Education at the University of Toronto. Her research and teaching areas include language education for adult immigrants, language in education for Canadian aboriginal peoples and adult literacy.

- **Donna M. Chovanec** is a Ph.D. student in International Education at the University of Alberta. She is a researcher, social worker and educator with a critical/feminist orientation. Her main area of interest is grassroots women's movements with a current focus on Latin America.

- **Darlene E. Clover** is a Senior Researcher at the Ontario Institute for Studies in Education at the University of Toronto. She is also the International Coordinator of the global adult education program, Learning for Environmental Action Programme (LEAP). Her areas of research include environmental adult education, feminist and popular education and community development. She is currently working on her doctorate at OISE.

- **Michael Collins** is Professor of Adult and Continuing Education and Coordinator of the Graduate Program at the University of Saskatchewan. He has worked as an adult educator in the United States and Great Britain as well as in Canada.

- **Patricia Cranton**, formerly Professor of Adult Education at Brock University in St. Catharines, Ontario, is now an independent educator and consultant. She specializes in transformative learning and psychological type theory.

- **Howard S. Davidson** is Assistant Professor in Continuing Education at the University of Manitoba. He recently edited *Schooling in a Total Institution: Critical Perspectives on Prison Education* (Bergin & Garvey, 1995).

- **Tara Fenwick** is an Adjunct Professor in the Department of Secondary Education at the University of Alberta. She specializes in organizational learning and adult education.

- **Marie A. Gillen** is Professor of Adult Education at St. Francis Xavier University in Antigonish, Nova Scotia. One of her interests is adult spirituality and ways that this particular aspect of adult development can be fostered.

- **André P. Grace** is a SSHRC Postdoctoral fellow at Pennsylvania State University. His interests include cultural studies, inclusion education and the history of adult education.

- **Denis Haughey** is Executive Director of the Parkland Institute, an Alberta research network. The Parkland Institute conducts and publishes research on progressive public policy alternatives in Canada.

- **Dorothy MacKeracher** is Professor of Adult Education in the Faculty of Education at the University of New Brunswick. She is author of *Making Sense of Adult Learning* (Culture Concepts, 1996).

- **D'Arcy Martin** has worked as an educator in the Canadian labour movement since 1978. He teaches a course in labour education at OISE/University of Toronto and is an active participant in the Canadian Association for the Study of Adult Education, the Canadian Network for Democratic Learning and the Ontario Workers Arts and Heritage Centre.

- **Susan May** is a projects coordinator with the Community Education Division of Grant MacEwan Community College in Edmonton, Alberta. Previously she worked for many years as a distance educator at both Athabasca University and St. Francis Xavier University.

- **Angela Miles** is a Professor in the Department of Adult Education, Community Development and Counselling Psychology at OISE. She teaches in the areas of community education and development and social movements, including Canadian and global feminist education and learning.

- **Marie-Thérèse Morin** is Professor in Andragogy in the Department of Education at the Université du Québec à Rimouski.

- **Geoff Peruniak** is Associate Professor in the Centre for Psychology at Athabasca University. His interests involve experiential learning including prior learning assessment, community education and career development.

- **Sue M. Scott** is Associate Professor in the Adult and Higher Education Program in the Department of Educational Policy Studies at the University of Alberta. She served as President of the Canadian Association for the Studies of Adult Education for two years. Her interests include community development and action, transformation in education and international development.

- **Gordon Selman** is Professor Emeritus at the University of British Columbia. His field of research and publication is the history and development of adult education in Canada and British Columbia. He is a Past President of the CAAE and CAUCE and chaired the organizing committee for CASAE. He is a co-author of *The Foundations of Adult Education in Canada* (Second Edition) (Thompson Educational, 1998) and author of *Adult Education in Canada: Historical Essays* (Thompson Educational, 1995), among other works.

- **Claudie Solar** is Associate Professor in the Department of Psychopédagogie and Andragogie at the Université de Montréal. Her interests are in feminism, transformation and math education.

- **Bruce Spencer** is Chair of the Centre for Work and Community Studies, Athabasca University, Alberta. He has written widely on workers' education, adult education and labour unions.

- **Joyce Stalker** is Senior Lecturer in the Department of Education Studies at the University of Waikato, Hamilton, New Zealand/Aotearoa. She balances her research interests in women, sociology and adult education with running, hiking, sewing and boogie boarding.

- **Alan M. Thomas** is Professor of Adult Education at the Ontario Institute for Studies in Education at the University of Toronto. He is the author of *Beyond Education: A New Perspective on Society's Management of Learning* (Jossey-Bass, 1991).

- **Michael R. Welton** is Professor of Adult Education at Mount Saint Vincent University in Halifax, Nova Scotia. He coordinates the graduate program in adult education.

Acknowledgements

We would like to acknowledge the most able assistance and professional editing of Naomi Frankel—who is also a University of Saskatchewan adult education graduate student—and thank Athabasca University for funding her editing. Many thanks go to the graduate students at the University of Alberta who helped by reading chapters and dialoguing on the contents. Particular thanks are due to Donna Chovanec, Colleen Ryan and Kevin Hood, graduate students in adult education, who gave assistance through different stages of the project and to the University of Alberta, Department of Educational Policy Studies, for financial support. Technical assistance was received from Athabasca University computer Help Desk and from Chris Prokop, systems analyst, and Georgie Kwan, secretary, Educational Policy Studies, University of Alberta. We would also like to thank Elizabeth Phinney for her copyediting.

The support of the leadership of the Canadian Association for the Study of Adult Education/l'Association canadienne pour l'éducation des adults (CASAE/ACEEA), particularly Michael Welton and Michael Collins, has been especially important, as we see this book as definitive for the field and want it to be as representative as possible. For the group of five academics (meeting at the 1994 CASAE/ACEEA conference on Sunday morning at Simon Fraser University on the Harbour Front in Vancouver), who committed CASAE/ACEEA to proceed, it is gratifying to see the plans for this book come to fruition. All proceeds from this book will go to support CASAE/ACEEA, the academic association that supports scholarship in adult education. CASAE/ACEEA publishes the *Canadian Journal for the Study of Adult Education/la Revue canadienne pour l'étude de l'éducation des adults*, a scholarly journal for those in the field.

We would also like to thank Keith Thompson for his support for this project and for his promotion of Canadian adult education literature.

Complementary Texts

This book is published along with two recommended companion volumes (1) *The Foundations of Adult Education in Canada, Second Edition* (by Gordon Selman, Michael Cooke, Mark Selman and Paul Dampier) and (2) *The Purposes of Adult Education: A Guide for Students* (by Bruce Spencer). The latter is intended as a companion to both this volume and to the *Foundations* book.

Bookkeeping students at St. Francis Xavier Extension Department (date unknown). *Courtesy of St. Francis Xavier University Archives.*

Preface

When minds were gripped by clearer visions and hearts were more certain,
the dialogue was barely audible. Now it approaches its proper volume.
— Alan Thomas, "Learning Our Way Out," p. 354.

Adult education in Canada has changed as the country has developed. Today adult education is at a crossroads, in danger of becoming directed only by the demands for vocational training, credentialism and the general requirement to prepare Canadians to meet the needs of the global economy. The temptation is to ignore the more diverse roadways established by adult education pioneers. With the lure of technology and expanded access to information—which often parades as education—we tend to forget our social roots and emancipatory aims as adult educators. All adult educators, including those primarily engaged in vocational training, need to be competent practitioners and aware of Canadian traditions in adult education.

This book, sponsored by the Canadian Association for the Study of Adult Education/l'Association canadienne pour l'éducation des adults (CASAE/ACEEA), is about recovering our origins. It is inspired by the great tradition of progressive adult education in Canada and those who contributed to the liberal movement that formed Canadian and international adult education. This tradition provides us with a lens with which to take a snapshot of the current Canadian field of adult education and a panoramic view of the issues and concerns facing us today. In short, the book is a contemporary guide to the condition of adult education which should be of value to citizens, policy makers and students.

Traditionally, adult educators have been in the forefront of policy making and education formation in Canada. The ideals and values revolving around social equity, democracy and social transformation have guided adult students' learning, research and actions and these have in turn influenced the goals set by policy makers. CASAE/ACEEA members pride themselves on educating adults who are, or will become, leaders in adult education, for example, in the fields of nursing, government, community, counselling, higher education, international education and development, human resource management, English and French as a second language, training and labour education.

As adult education moves into the twenty-first century we find ourselves engaging with new developments driven essentially by global market forces. The imperative becomes skills training, a technological focus and a capitalist competitive market economy. The danger is that the social agenda, which was historically supported by Canadian adult education—advocating equality, co-operation and universality in such fields as welfare, health care, higher education and co-operative enterprise—is being displaced. The neo-liberal market economic agenda also supports those who have resources such as computer skills and a good education and disadvantages further the have-nots who are excluded from knowledge-based jobs and the social and economic benefits that flow from them. The question is, given this framework, how can adult education recover its sense of social purpose as well as meet the individual aspirations of Canadians?

Outline of the Book

The chapters in this book represent the state of thinking in adult education today. The authors are Canadian practitioners, researchers and professors of adult education. The book is organized into three major sections: "Context and Aims," "Purposes" and "Challenges and Future Visions." These major sections are subdivided into parts—for example in part 1 of section 1 an attempt is made to articulate the current context as it relates to adult education and, in part 2, to reflect on our aims. Next, in section 2, we highlight some issues grouped under the major purposes—adult education for economy, transformation and diversity—and then end, in section 3, with a discussion of current challenges and future visions. There are holes, we know, but for a first edition we feel confident we have begun the dialogue necessary to provide a foundational focus on current happenings and competing interests in the field.

The rationale for section 1, "Context and Aims," is in understanding as to where we have come from; what current models or paradigms apply; what it is that scholars and practitioners in the field are writing about and doing. Section 2 is a consideration of the more philosophical aims of adult education: What is the intention of adult education activity and what is the stance of practitioners?

While there are various purposes for adult education that can be considered from a personal or social perspective, we have chosen, in section 2, to group chapters according to three essentially social criteria: education for "economy," "transformation" and "diversity." No one can doubt that the general provision of post-secondary and adult education is geared towards meeting economic objectives (the rhetoric is of "a skilled workforce," "knowledge-based economy," "knowledge-workers" and "workplace learning"). Part 1 of section 2 examines some of the issues arising from this focus.

Education for transformation (including such areas as social and community education, personal transformation and new social movements) contradicts the adaptive and/or accommodative purpose of education for economy, and it is therefore not surprising to find that social transformative education, which historically played such an important role in Canada, receives little public funding today. There is however increasing interest in adult education for personal and social transformation. Part 2 of section 2 discusses transformative learning, including tangential issues raised by ecological and prison education.

Part 3 of the "Purposes" section recognizes that adult education in Canada serves diverse audiences and purposes. It also draws inspiration from diverse sources. Given Canada's mosaic of cultural heritages, this could be an expansive sub-section; however, for this edition we have chosen to focus on women, seniors, the role of spirituality and religious activism and English as a second language (ESL).

There are a number of challenges facing adult educators, challenges which pose problems and possibilities for our conception of "learning for life." While we have discussed many of them in the first two parts of the book, we have chosen to separate four (self-directed learning, competence-based learning, prior learning assessment and distance education) for consideration in section 3, part 1. The final part 2, "Future Visions," provides two different views of the future of adult learning and education in Canada.

While we could have placed several chapters in various sections, we chose to sort them as we did because we read the central argument as contributing most to that particular theme. You, of course, are free to read them otherwise, and may choose to read chapters according to some other schema.

Chapter Synopses

Section 1—Historical and Current Contents

A brief synopsis of the various chapters follows as we try to show the threads that weave throughout the book. In section 1, six chapters contain a discussion of the historical and current contexts of adult education in the late twentieth century. Gordon Selman, one of our leading historians in the field, focuses on what some think is the hallmark of adult education in Canada, "citizenship education." Selman highlights Frontier College, the Antigonish Movement, National Farm Radio Forum and Citizens' Forum, the National Film Board, and other voluntary organizations such as the Women's Institutes, which have historically provided interpretation and direction for Canadian democracy. While these voluntary and semi-governmental organizations have served to ground Canadians in a vision for society improvement, Selman sees adult education moving to providing services to individuals today.

Michael Welton, in designing an adult education history course, a "Struggle of Memory against Forgetting," reminds us of the folk wisdom of practitioners in our history. He asks such poignant questions as, What are we forgetting that our forebears remembered? Why can't we initiate bold projects like the Antigonish Movement or the Citizens' Forum? A look at the 1950s, a chilly time for adult education, shows adult educators receiving criticism for their commitment to democracy. It was the beginning of an uneasiness with the narrow professional identity of adult educators as "learning experts."

Michael Collins's "Critical Returns: From Andragogy to Lifelong Education" provides an overview and critique of adult education. He focuses on the tradition of emancipatory pedagogy and critical education which prefigures the preoccupation with the recent lifelong learning/education concept. He calls for a reconstruction of modern adult education as a significant, moral and political emancipatory force within a system of lifelong education. Collins also increases our understanding of the theories of Habermas which appear in several chapters in this book (Welton, Cranton, Fenwick and Scott).

Marie-Thérèse Morin attempts a monumental task in documenting the shift in paradigms at the end of the twentieth century. Focusing on the dominant Newtonian paradigm and its implications for the social and the educational, Morin contrasts a new paradigm emerging from a major capitalist restructuring of our planet. Morin ends with a set of trends for adult educators based on this emerging paradigm.

Claudie Solar, in an extensive survey of the articles in seven adult education journals over a four-year period (1990-94), sets out a series of trends, one of which is a shift away from the behaviourist/humanist approaches based on Knowles. The view of adults is shifting away from that of learner to that of worker which reflects the economic emphasis on employability. She also notes substantial writing on education for transformation and for diversity.

Susan May's chapter, "Confronting Issues Affecting Adult Educators," is a survey of 149 adult education graduates from a Canadian university on the issues confronting them as adult education practitioners in the field. Adult educators fell on a continuum around the seven emergent issues; they either position themselves as advocating for the status quo or as social activists, as learning oriented or as education concerned; as situated on the margins or in a mainstream position in the field. A final section to May's chapter is on the future directions for the field.

Part 2, "Aims of Adult Education," is an important sub-section as it sets up the intentions of the field and of the practitioners within it. Sue Scott recognizes the diversity in the adult education field, and offers five possible philosophical orientations, each with corresponding aims for adult education. Clarifying one's philosophical orientation to teaching and learning serves as a guide to action in adult education. Comparing and contrasting the various frameworks shows the distinctions between each orientation as to its view of the learner, the role of the teacher, what strategies best facilitate teaching and how it evaluates if students have learned something.

Michael Collins builds a case to support his assertion that the aim of lifelong education is emancipatory pedagogy. Informed by critical theory and "reasoned" thought in opposition to postmodern deconstructionism, Collins argues that the aim of university-based adult education is to provide opportunities for students and professors to politicize their work off campus, on campus, in teacher preparation, in worksites and in global concerns where social justice is given the highest priority.

André Grace, in contradiction to Collins, argues that there is a place for postmodern discourse in adult education. He introduces a critical postmodern "theory of adult learning community" (TALC) which he suggests, in part, can contribute to a merging of the social reform orientation of critical adult education with the instrumental rationality of modernization. Thus, the aim of adult education for Grace is to re-integrate practical skills of teaching and learning with the public questions about the future of society to create a more holistic learning process.

Section 2—Purposes

In part 1, "Education for Economy," Paul Bouchard begins with an examination of the myths surrounding Human Capital Theory. Bouchard explains that arguments about human capital underpin the discourse on training and education for work but laments that most advocates and practitioners are not aware of the limitations of the concept. His chapter provides a clear guide to the assumptions made about human capital and is vital reading for trainers and other adult educators in the field.

Tara Fenwick challenges the notion of a "learning organization" which is a commonly held direction that organizations today are considering. She explores the contradictions and problems within organizations today and tries to clarify such terms as critical reflection, dialogue, problem solving and continuous learning.

D'Arcy Martin, a labour educator, provides a practitioner's view of recent developments in workplace training in Canada. He focuses on the experience of the Ontario Training and Adjustment Board and discusses their impact from a workers' perspective. While many of the training objectives of organized labour chime with those of employers, workers are particularly interested in the national recognition of generic, transportable skills and in issues of equity and fairness within the context of freely negotiated collective agreements.

Although labour education in Canada is the most prolific form of contemporary non-formal adult education, catering for some 120,000 Canadians a year, it is often overlooked in the literature. The chapter by Bruce Spencer serves to correct this omission. It explains current provision, how that fits with Canadian labour unions' organizational needs, and (drawing on examples from Canada and abroad, particularly Britain and Australia) speculates on new models in "Workers' Education for the Twenty-First Century."

In part 2, "Education for Transformation," of the "Purposes" section, Sue Scott leads off with "An Overview of Transformation Theory in Adult Education." Scott attempts to show that transformation is a theoretical term and provides a criteria for assessing if something actually transforms or simply changes. She systematically begins with social theorists, moves to personal theorists and ends with a merging of the two in Freire's theory of society and theory of self. While some of the theorists are discussed in other chapters in this book in more detail, the aim of the chapter is to foreshadow the other chapters in the transformation section.

Patricia Cranton focuses on transformative learning and summarizes a comprehensive number of theories in the area of personal transformative learning. She compares and contrasts the concepts and elements beginning with the perspective transformation of Jack Mezirow, and progressing to Habermas, Dewey, Schon, Freire and Tennant. She then proceeds to discuss individual differences, group processes and the educator's role in bringing about adult education.

At a time when Canadians are grappling with some of the most pressing questions concerning the crises in our society, Denis Haughey admonishes university adult education, university extension in particular, in his chapter "From Passion to Passivity: The Decline of University Extension for Social Change." Haughey suggests that the long history of extension personnel willing to take risks to advocate taking decision making from government and resting it with the people has dissipated over the years, beginning with the 1970s and the rise of adult education as a profession. The Canadian adult education movement sprang from social gospel roots and emphasized social change, which today is more prevalent in the voluntary sector. Haughey outlines why political inaction, professionalism, new sites for action and intellectual passivity are reasons adult educators are no longer socially active. His concern is that the university is being weakened as a credible force for social change in society.

Darlene Clover explicates the environmental themes and issues that are embedded but not made necessarily explicit in the adult education tradition of the past fifty years. Clover draws examples from non-formal educational endeavours, such as naturalist societies, organizations, clubs and outdoor education institutions, that continue today to educate adults on environmental issues, calling for a transformation of planet consciousness.

Howard Davidson takes a critical look at prison education and shows that, while the prison population is rising in Canada, the social and political forces point to limitations for alternative adult education inside prisons. Davidson discusses what prison education is and suggests that we look at the contradictions in the limitations for openings for more progressive adult education to exist.

In part 3, "Education for Diversity," Joyce Stalker's chapter examines women's participation in educational organizations, agencies and social movements. She explores the nature of misogyny that flows from macro-level factors related to gender and suggests that this barrier to participation is a daily practice in adult education institutions.

Angela Miles examines the current neo-liberal economic context of adult education and argues that adult education should maintain a broad, heterogeneous, multi-centred orientation rather than be seduced into commodification. She acknowledges that knowledge is creatively constructed in non-formal arenas such as social movements and is essential for the livelihood of the field.

Dorothy MacKeracher shows us that by the year 2031 there will be one in four Canadians over the age of sixty-five. This is a potentially large cohort of adult learners. Canadian government programs are shifting to a partnership-based paradigm in delivering programs that are more conducive to senior learners' styles, characteristics and needs.

Using the Antigonish Movement and particularly Moses Coady's philosophy and beliefs, Marie Gillen illustrates a vision for adult educators that is based in the spiritual dimensions of a full and abundant life for everyone. Her thesis is that the material as well as the spiritual, and the individual as well as the social, needs attending to for a holistic approach to adult education.

As immigrants and refugees are welcomed into Canada, English (and French) as a second language programs continue as important adult education for citizenship. Barbara Burnaby gives us a historical sketch of the major periods in Canadian ESL and discusses ESL in adult education as it relates to content, the learners' perspectives and mainstream agendas.

Section 3—Challenges and Future Visions

This final section highlights some of the new thinking and projection into the future about the field of adult education. Donna Chovanec begins part 1 by challenging one of the canons of adult education, self-directed learning (SDL), with a critical review of the concept's usefulness within adult education. Her extensive literature search highlights the contradictions and problems of using SDL approaches without carefully scrutinizing the philosophical premises, definitions, assumptions and procedures.

Competence-based learning, and its derivative, outcomes-based learning, is prominent in adult education practice, particularly in vocational education.

Geoff Peruniak, in a detailed and skilfully crafted chapter, provides a critical examination of the assumptions and practices of competence-based learning. One of his main conclusions is for "heart" to be placed at the centre of learning.

In the next chapter, Alan Thomas discusses his enthusiastic commitment to "prior learning assessment and recognition" (PLAR) and its potential for liberation of teaching from certification and, secondly, learning from instruction. He suggests that PLAR is potentially the most radical innovation since the introduction of mass formal education for children and youth! Fraught with problems and contradictions, however, PLAR is still in its early stages of development.

Bruce Spencer covers most of the arguments for and against distance education as adult education. While research is still needed on the medium, he maintains a social purpose education can be fostered and promoted at a distance when it is conducted in collaboration with established social movements. The addition of on-line technology (creating a "virtual classroom") changes individualized distance education from essentially private study to a social process, one more capable of promoting social purpose adult education.

Part 2 of section 3, "Challenges and Future Visions," concludes the book with two chapters that "sum it up" and project the future. Alan Thomas draws a distinction between learning and education. Education is seen as a system of learning increasingly more organized in the formal setting. Canadian adult education in the past has regarded social education as occurring primarily in the non-formal arena. Learning, he argues, is more individual, process oriented, an "outcome" of education, which has taken a more prominent position in the lexicon of educationalists in the last twenty years. Thomas outlines some of the goals and initiatives that need to occur in the future and compliments the authors in this book as approaching "the proper volume" of dialogue and differences of opinion necessary in a collection on the foundations of adult education in Canada.

Michael Welton suggests that there is a core value structure for socially responsible adult education that should guide our actions. The lifeworld in civil society provides the foundations for meaning, solidarity and stable personalities. Our commitment must be to the enlightened, relatively autonomous and reflective learner. He argues that the centrality of social learning processes is the formation of the active citizen, and that the fostering of discussion, debate and dialogue among citizens is compatible with "deliberative" democracy, a Twenty-First Century version of Canada's historic commitment to citizenship education.

SECTION 1
CONTEXT AND AIMS

Instructor D.L. McDougal and a class of Scandinavians, Mond Nickel Mine, Larchwood, Ontario, 1913. *Courtesy of Frontier College.*

Part 1

Historical and Current Contexts

1

The Imaginative Training for Citizenship

Gordon Selman

Citizenship education for adults is not the most important part of the field in Canada, nor the largest sector, but, for a variety of reasons, certain programs in the field of citizenship education have brought Canada into greater prominence in the international community of adult educators than has any other part of the field. The term *citizenship education* as used here, and generally in the adult education movement, refers to educational activities aimed at encouraging adults to feel a responsibility for playing an active part in the decision-making processes of their society and equipping them with political and social information and skills so that they might play such a role effectively.

For several decades of this century when the adult education movement was gaining visibility, several of the leading figures in the field believed, in the words of the 1946 Declaration of the Canadian Association for Adult Education, that the central task of adult education was "the imaginative training for citizenship" (cited in Kidd, 1963, pp. 9-10).

It is not surprising that Canadians have devoted so much time, energy and imagination to citizenship education. We are, after all, mainly a nation of immigrants and, as a result of our geography, have been relatively sparsely settled across a huge territory. The task of nation building in Canada has been a complicated one because of these and other factors, including the existence of the two dominant language communities (English and French), the concentration of other ethnic language groups in pockets across the country and the presence on Canada's southern boundary of a society (the United States) that has exercised a strong economic, social and cultural influence throughout the period of Canadian development. Canadians, of necessity, have had to turn to citizenship education to achieve a viable sense of community.

This chapter describes several Canadian programs in the field of citizenship education that have been considered both here and abroad to be outstanding projects, ones which have contributed to our understanding of both adult education and the relationship between adult education and social development. The descriptions which follow are necessarily quite brief, but the better-known projects are more fully described elsewhere in the literature.

Frontier College

Frontier College was established in 1899 by the efforts of Alfred Fitzpatrick, a Presbyterian minister. At first called the Reading Camps Association, the college soon specialized in sending "worker-teachers" to isolated bush camps on the Canadian frontier—mining, forestry, road and railway construction camps and the like. According to Cook (1987), by 1918 there were 3,700 such camps in Canada containing from 200,000 to 250,000 men. It was arranged with the employer that a job in the camp would be reserved for the person provided by Frontier College. This person would do a regular day's work alongside the other men (a feature which the college thought to be vitally important) and then in the evenings, on weekends and on other days off would teach classes to any who were interested in attending. Most of the men in the camps (the "bunkhouse men" as they were described in a well-known 1928 sociological study by E.W. Bradwin) were recent immigrants to Canada, and the educational work was usually in English as a second language, or what today we would term Adult Basic Education. This included as well a great deal of activity for the purpose of helping the immigrants learn about the nature of Canadian society. This citizenship education was used as the content of much of the language and basic education instruction (Cook 1987). Most of the teachers were recruited from the universities across Canada, and did this work as a summer job.

Frontier College has the longest continuous history of any adult education organization in Canada and for much of its life has specialized in the work of such worker-teachers. It has never been a large organization, having a small administrative and supervisory staff in Toronto and a modest number of teachers in the field. The number of teachers reached a peak of 208 in 1937, when the organization had been invited to provide teachers to a series of work camps for unemployed men developed by the Federal Department of National Defence (Thompson & Seager, 1985; Morrison, 1989).

For most of its history, Frontier College, a small organization, was not well known, even in educational circles. It came into greater prominence in the 1960s, however, when Canadians began to realize the extent of illiteracy and undereducation in Canada. As literacy and other basic education programs were mounted under the general umbrella of the government's various "War on Poverty" programs, Frontier College was the one Canadian organization which had extensive experience with this type of adult education and its personnel played a prominent part in the early training of staff for this work (Brooke, 1972).

The number of worker-teachers had fallen to 72 by 1972, and with the serious economic recession which set in the early 1980s, it became increasingly difficult to find job placements. Frontier College responded to these changed circumstances by moving into community development work (the personnel it provided usually serving under contract to provincial governments) and, increasingly since the mid-1980s, conducting literacy and other basic education work among persons with special needs (for example, First Nations groups, former prison inmates, the unemployed, and street kids) in the inner-city areas of some of the larger population centres in Canada (Morrison, 1989). The college also developed extensive curriculum and other teaching materials for literacy work. It was mainly in recognition of its more recent work in the inner cities that Frontier College received a UNESCO award for literacy work in 1977 (perhaps the only project in the more industrialized countries which had been so honoured). At the Education for All international conference in Bangkok in 1990, which was sponsored by several of the largest international aid agencies, Frontier College was selected as one of the highlighted projects.

The Antigonish Movement

Perhaps the single most famous adult education project developed in Canada is the Antigonish Movement, the name given to certain economic and social development extension activity conducted by St. Francis Xavier University, located in the city of Antigonish, Nova Scotia. The Antigonish Movement is the subject of a separate chapter in this book, so the description provided here will be very brief.

St. Francis Xavier's program was based on a "call to arms" which the university issued to the people of its Depression-ridden area. It began with "consciousness raising" activity. Father Moses M. Coady referred in his oratory at community meetings and in his writings to "the default of the people" (Coady, 1939; Laidlaw, 1971) whereby citizens had allowed control of their economic destiny to slip out of their own hands and into those of private enterprise entrepreneurs. The people of the region were urged and assisted to adopt the means provided by co-operative organizations to recover control of their livelihoods. Coady and the other leaders of the movement saw clearly that what began on the basis of an economic approach would soon move as well into other aspects of life; what began with empowerment in the economic sphere would inevitably permeate the cultural, social and political areas of life (Coady, 1939). It was essentially a community development movement that began with the economic but affected people's whole lives, not only as consumers and producers, but also as citizens.

Responding to the economically depressed conditions of its region and the plight of many fishermen, farmers, miners and other industrial workers, and taking inspiration from the ideas of Father Jimmy Tompkins and consultations with representative people of the region, St. Francis Xavier University created an extension department in 1928 and placed Father Moses M. Coady in charge of the work. Under the remarkable leadership of Coady and others, St. Francis Xavier mounted a program of education about co-operative organizations and credit unions through which the people of the region could, by working together, improve their economic and general living conditions (Coady, 1939; Laidlaw, 1961; Lotz & Welton, 1987; Stabler, 1987). This work was extremely successful, based as it was on leadership, organization and study materials from the university and the study, activity and commitment of the people in the region. In his study of the project, Stabler states that in the 1930s—the period of its most rapid growth—the number of study clubs involved in the work increased from 179 to 1,300, the number of members of these groups from 1,500 to 11,000, the number of credit unions from 8 to 170, and the number of other co-operative organizations from 2 to 85 (Stabler, 1987).

The success of the Antigonish Movement soon came to the attention of the world through the channels of the Catholic Church and the United Nations and its agencies. It was soon realized that the methodologies that had been developed to serve the needs of a disadvantaged and impoverished population in northern Nova Scotia had great potential for the developing nations of the world. Many hundreds of educators and other development workers from Third World countries came to Antigonish to study its extension methods. After Coady's death in 1959, the university created the Coady International Institute, which offered programs of varying lengths for students from abroad. Stabler has stated that within twenty-one years, the Institute had served 2,500 students from 111 countries, who came to take diploma or other courses (Stabler, 1987).

There has been considerable discussion in the literature as to the extent to which the Antigonish Movement may properly be seen as one which brought about significant social change. The early writers, such as Coady himself (1939) and Laidlaw (1961; 1971), saw the movement as a change agent, helping the people of the region to take their economic welfare into their own hands through their co-operative organizations, rather than remaining subservient to the major private enterprise entrepreneurs of the region.

In more recent years, a revisionist point of view has come increasingly to the fore, which contends that the movement had the effect of ameliorating the conditions under the then-existing capitalistic system, thus heading off efforts to change the system in any basic way (Lotz, 1977; Baum, 1980). Whatever the judgment, the Antigonish Movement has been widely recognized as an innovative adult education program and as an agent of social change. The leading student of Coady's work has stated that it was Coady's view that any adult educator worth his salt was "an aggressive agent of change" (Laidlaw, 1971, p. 57). Coady was a vocal critic of political philosophies of the extreme right and the extreme left. The Antigonish Movement promoted change, but it is fair to state that the changes envisaged were within the context of a liberal democratic society.

National Farm Radio Forum and Citizens' Forum

These two programs were joint ventures between the Canadian Association for Adult Education (CAAE) and the Canadian Broadcasting Corporation (CBC) (and in the case of Farm Forum, the Canadian Federation of Agriculture as well). They used the same educational methodologies but were aimed at different audiences. E.A. Corbett, the first and long-time director of the CAAE, was the creator of these projects, though he drew on experience in Britain and elsewhere where radio had been used as a stimulus for local discussion groups. Corbett was a Canadian nationalist and was strongly committed to educating and promoting communication among Canadians about matters of social, political and cultural significance (Armstrong, 1968; Corbett, 1957; Faris, 1975; Selman, 1981, 1991; Young, 1978). The two projects were designed to promote these goals and—especially in the case of the former—became models for citizenship and development education in many countries (Selman, 1991).

National Farm Radio Forum was launched on a regional basis in 1940 and went on the full national network the following year. The program, as the name suggests, was addressed mainly to Canadians living in small towns and rural areas of the country. The program used four main elements or methods: a pamphlet published by the CAAE on the topic for the week, which participants received a week or so before the topic was to be discussed; a weekly radio broadcast on the CBC designed to convey information and provoke discussion on the topic or issue of the week; local discussion groups (forums) organized by the CAAE, through provincial partners, in which members listened to the broadcasts each week and then discussed the subject among themselves; and a "feedback" mechanism through which the groups reported their views about the subject to a provincial secretary, who in turn briefly summarized on the air each week the nature of the groups' reactions to the previous week's topic. This feedback mechanism was also used for other purposes, including soliciting suggestions from participants about topics to be included in the series.

The topics the series covered ranged widely and included issues related to family and community life, production and marketing concerns and a variety of political, economic, social and cultural issues. Several of the groups that participated in Farm Forum took on separate lives of their own and carried out community improvement projects (Selman, 1991).

Farm Forum continued for approximately twenty-five years. Participation in the program peaked during the 1940s, with 1,600 groups containing approximately 30,000 members in 1949-50. From that point on there was a gradual decline, to about 500 groups by 1958. In spite of various efforts to bolster participation, there was a slow but continuing falling off until the mid-1960s, and the sponsoring bodies decided to bring the program to an end at the conclusion of the 1965 broadcast season.

Citizens' Forum was built on a similar methodology but was aimed at a wider audience. It dealt with social, cultural and political issues and was directed to all citizens, though most listening groups were in cities and medium-sized towns across the country. Citizens' Forum began operation in 1943 and continued until 1967. It never attained the level of participation of Farm Forum, attracting 1,215 groups in its first year of operation but never attaining that figure again. There was an attempt to convert it to television in the early 1960s, but this did not prove successful; the project was brought to an end in 1967.

Farm Forum attracted a great deal of international attention, and its methodologies were considered to have application to the needs of developing countries in particular. When Corbett attended the first UNESCO World Conference on Adult Education in Denmark in 1949, he found that "every English-speaking delegate" at the conference was familiar with the contributions of the project to the field of adult education (Kidd 1950, p. xi). UNESCO commissioned a study of the project in the early 1950s in order to make its methodologies better known in other countries (Sim, 1954). It has been estimated that at least forty-four other countries adopted aspects of the program for their own use (Cochrane et al., 1986), India being the leading example. Other adult education scholars have also paid tribute to Farm Forum's contributions to the methodology of adult education (e.g., Ohliger, 1967; Lowe, 1975). It is fair to say that Farm Forum stands with the Antigonish Movement as one of the best-known contributions made by Canada to the development of methodologies in adult education.

The NFB: Film Circuits and Challenge for Change

The National Film Board of Canada (NFB) has a worldwide reputation for the excellence of the films it has produced over the years, particularly its documentaries. At least two aspects of its work have a particularly prominent place in the field of adult education, and both may be seen as a contribution to citizenship education. The NFB was established in 1939. One of its chief purposes, according to the legislation that created it, was to "produce and distribute films designed to interpret Canada to Canadians" (cited in Jones,

1981). With the outbreak of World War II, a further purpose was added, that of rallying the Canadian people behind the war effort. In its annual report in 1942, the board specified its purpose. Its films had been "designed deliberately to promote a sense of national unity and national understanding between the many groups which go to make the Canadian nation" (in Evans, 1984, p. 117). Under the leadership initially of John Grierson, a recognized genius in the art of the film documentary, the NFB went on to make a noteworthy contribution to this end. The National Film Board has made a sustained and successful contribution to the development of Canada since its creation. Many aspects of its work could appropriately be singled out for attention, but this account will focus on two, its film distribution circuits during the immediate post-war years and its Challenge for Change project of the late 1960s.

John Grierson believed that the documentary film could be a powerful tool in shaping public opinion and beliefs. As one of his biographers has stated, "Grierson wanted to organize a movement to preach, spread and maintain the democratic faith" (Evans, 1984, p. 36). He saw himself as a propagandist, in the best sense of the term, seeing propaganda as "education given the punch that it needs to be effective in a mass society" (Lockerbie in John Grierson Project, 1984, p. 97). As Grierson put it, "I have been a propagandist all my working life because I believe that we have to do our democratic mind over if we are going to save democracy" (Hardy, in John Grierson Project, 1984, p. 108).

The NFB soon gained a reputation as a maker of excellent documentary films. It is one thing to make fine non-commercial films, however, and quite another to get people to watch them. To this end, during the war, the NFB organized a system of film circuits—rural film circuits, industrial circuits and trade union circuits—through which films on subjects vital to the war effort were taken by field staff to business and industrial sites, union meetings and many rural communities, and shown to local audiences. Thus in the first full year of operation, a quarter of a million people a month, or four million in the year, saw NFB productions (Buchanan, 1944; Evans, 1984).

In the years following the war, funds were not available to maintain the large number of field staff employed earlier. The Film Board hit upon the concept of establishing community-based "film councils" across Canada, organizations that would receive an assortment of films at the local level and take responsibility for showing them or arranging for them to be shown by other organizations within the community. The NFB set up film repositories and distribution centres in each province or region, usually in university extension departments, which took responsibility for managing the distribution of films to the film councils in its area. The board also loaned a great deal of projection equipment to the film councils. By the early 1950s there were 4,900 non-theatrical "viewing points" for NFB films in Canada and approximately one million people a month were viewing NFB films outside the regular theatres (Kidd, 1953). This work declined by the mid-1950s, however, as the effects of the new television networks in Canada brought other forms of entertainment into people's homes (Gray, 1973). By devising a distribution system that relied essentially on the efforts of local people and organizations, the board was able for a time to make a contribution of outstanding quality to citizenship education in Canada that reached into virtually every community in the country.

Challenge for Change was a product of the turbulent late 1960s. Since its earliest days under Grierson, the NFB had seen itself as being in the social change business, and it responded to the "War on Poverty" spirit of the 1960s by approaching several government departments and inviting them to join in the sponsorship of a special project "designed to improve communications, create greater understanding, promote new ideas, and provoke social change" (*Challenge for Change,* 1968). After securing the co-operation of several departments, the NFB proceeded with the new project, which provided equipment and technical advice to local communities, making it possible for them to use film making (and as the technology developed, videotape) in the community-development process. It was used both in the early stages of the development process, when the community was required to take stock of itself and increase communication among the various interest groups which had a stake in community affairs, and at the point when the community wished to communicate its opinions to appropriate outside authorities (usually government departments in a position to help). The first project took place on Fogo Island, off the east coast of Newfoundland, and was a joint effort between the NFB, the extension department of Memorial University of Newfoundland and the people of the area. This initial experiment was remarkably successful and the Film Board went on to develop such work in many centres across Canada.

The Fogo Island experiment attracted a great deal of publicity and "almost instant fame" (Jones 1981, p. 157). Foreign observers were quick to see that the project had potential for use in their countries as well. Observers from many countries came to Canada to examine the project, and leaders of the work in Canada, especially Colin Lowe of the Film Board and Donald Snowden of Memorial University, were in great demand as advisors in other countries. As one writer has stated, observers in other countries were interested in the unique combination of film making and community development, but as well, frequently registered surprise over "how these strange Canadians managed to create what seemed like a socially revolutionary program with money provided by governments for which they were making trouble" (Richardson, 1981, p. 7). The same thought occurred to people in government, of course, particularly as neo-conservative forces came to the fore by the end of the 1970s. By 1978, the number of government departments willing to co-sponsor the work fell to two; in the following year, the project was closed down.

The foregoing brief accounts of several of the best-known Canadian programs in citizenship education merely scratch the surface of such work in this
country.

Voluntary Organizations and Citizenship Education

A great deal of what may appropriately be termed citizenship education has
been carried out over the decades by voluntary organizations. This work has
taken many forms, including leadership training and development, social action and advocacy and training in the processes of government. The range of
voluntary groups is enormous, including service clubs, women's associations,
churches, unions and professional associations, co-operative organizations
and groups devoted to study and action in particular areas of concern such as
foreign policy. The Women's Institutes, an organization "invented" in Canada
that has since become a worldwide movement, is an outstanding example of
such organizations. The first institute was formed in Stoney Creek, Ontario, in
1897, and the movement spread rapidly to other communities across Canada.
The institutes were located mainly in rural areas and small towns. Supported
by provincial departments of agriculture, they performed both a social function, by bringing rural women together, and also a study group and advocacy
function, as the members sought to improve the quality of life for rural
women and their families (see Witter, 1979; Dennison, 1987).

The role of social movements over the years in citizenship education has
been extensive. The temperance and the suffragette movements are prominent
examples of earlier efforts that involved a great deal of educational work to
bring about social change. In recent decades, social movements conducting
educational work aimed at social change have abounded in areas including
ecological concerns, human rights, peace and disarmament, the role of women
in society and the welfare of various groups such as older persons, the handi-
capped, illiterate persons and First Nations' groups.

Particularly since the creation of the Canadian Citizenship Branch by the
federal government in 1945, government has played an active part in education related to citizenship, especially among recent immigrants. During the
1950s and 1960s, the branch gave particularly creative leadership in the field
of citizenship education, with much of it carried out in co-operation with
voluntary organizations (Selman, 1991). The Canadian Citizenship Council
and the Canadian Association for Adult Education worked closely with the
federal department as well as carrying out many projects in this field on their
own. Organizations representing many of the ethnic groups in Canadian society also have an active record in this field.

In the mid-1970s, I attempted to determine which projects in Canadian
adult education were seen by experienced adult educators in this country to
have made the most noteworthy and original contributions to the field as a

whole. I found (Selman, 1975) that the top four projects (five, if one separates National Farm Radio Forum from Citizens' Forum) and eight of the top ten were in the field of citizenship education. The four programs heading the list were the Antigonish Movement, Farm and Citizens' Forum, Frontier College and the National Film Board's Film Circuits. Other citizenship education projects accorded positions in the list of the top ten were: the NFB's Challenge for Change; the Joint Planning Commission (a project of the CAAE which involved frequent meetings between representatives of national organizations involved in adult education and social development); social animation in Quebec (a variety of projects for social development, many of which began in the days of the "Quiet Revolution" of the 1960s); and the Couchiching Conferences (a series of conferences on public affairs issues co-sponsored by the Canadian Broadcasting Corporation and citizens' groups). Overall, it was clear that among the Canadian adult educators consulted, it has been in what might generally be termed citizenship education that Canada has provided most of its innovative and outstanding contributions to adult education.

After reviewing the foregoing account of some aspects of adult education for citizenship in the Canadian experience, one cannot help but notice that most of the projects described here took place some years ago, and in most cases no longer exist. Canadian adult educators currently would be hard pressed to identify Canadian projects in citizenship education of international significance in terms of their innovative nature and contributions to the field of practice. By way of conclusion to this account, it is perhaps appropriate to examine some of the reasons why this may be so.

In analyzing the dearth of outstanding Canadian projects in citizenship education, several somewhat interrelated factors should be examined. The first has to do with the consequences of the increasing professionalization of the field of adult education. It is generally agreed that adult education as a field of practice has in recent decades been transforming itself from a social movement to a more professionalized field. That is to say, whereas at one time adult education was inspired and to a large degree led by people who saw the field as a means of bringing about social change, with professionalization it has largely relinquished such goals and has concentrated instead on providing services to individuals on demand. Thus the field has gone from having an agenda of its own (social change or improvement) to what is more typical of the current period: leaving to the learner decisions about the use to which learning will be put. In the 1930s and 1940s, adult educators, through their organizations, would periodically issue "manifestos" or "declarations" in which they stated goals for the movement, ones which typically spoke of a better society towards which they saw adult education working (see Kidd, 1963, p. 108-110). Declarations by professional groups these days tend to deal with technical competence or the welfare of adult education in its institutional settings. (The exception to this is groups of adult educators who are working on behalf of particular disadvantaged interest groups.) The professionalization of the field seems to have shifted its vision from the improvement of society to providing services to individuals. Thus the field pays less attention to the relationship between the person and his or her society and instead thinks no further than meeting the declared or overt "needs" of the individual.

The foregoing trend, which has been described above in terms of the dynamics within the adult education enterprise itself, has also been reinforced from without. The neo-conservative social and political philosophy which has come to the fore since approximately 1980 has created a social and institutional setting that has not generally encouraged institution-based adult educators to be animators of an examination of controversial questions. There has been a more conservative approach to institutional roles and it has appeared to be safer to "stay out of trouble" by leaving the treatment of controversial current questions to others.

Institutional policies have brought about another change. Institutions have been requiring their adult or continuing education units to become more (or entirely) self-supporting financially. In fact, in many cases these units must now return a net profit to their parent institutions. Such a policy works against programs that require a substantial "investment" of staff time that may bring no financial return, and favours types of activity that bring a prompt return from student fees. Such a policy makes it possible to offer credit courses, continuing professional education and courses about computers or other felt personal needs, but generally does not support programs about citizenship, family life or other socially relevant areas. This trend has caused adult educators of necessity to focus their programming on those areas from which the highest financial return can be gained.

The foregoing is, of course, a generalization, and applies in particular to institution-based adult educators. Social movements and many other non-governmental and voluntary organizations are very much engaged in citizenship education. There is an increasing awareness on the part of those interested and involved in such matters that the voluntary sector must come to the fore and take up this and other tasks in which the public sector at one time played a prominent role. One response has been the establishment of a "popular education" movement in Canada (Selman, 1991). It may mean that adult educators who wish to give their talent and energies to citizenship education increasingly will have to look for employment in the non-governmental, non-public sector or carry out such work in a voluntary capacity. It is to be hoped that a field of practice in Canada that once provided such outstanding and creative leadership will once more contribute creatively to the task. Canada needs us.

2

The Struggle of Memory against Forgetting

Michael R. Welton

In the winter of 1996, I wrote a ten-module course entitled "Historical Perspectives on Adult Education: The English-Canadian Canadian Legacy." Designing the course gave me a good opportunity to do a couple of things: sketch an outline of the history of Canadian adult education, and demonstrate that no practitioner of adult education ought to be without a good understanding of our traditions. What kind of people are we? What kind of adult education streams flow through our historical landscape? For years, I have been arguing that historical understanding is essential to contemporary practice and that forgetting our traditions would be disastrous for the future of Canadian adult education.

The first section of this chapter leads the reader through the pedagogical and thought processes involved in designing a historical course for practitioners. It begins by discussing historiographic issues—What is the role of history in our turbulent world? What are we studying when we study "adult education" history?—and, specifically, what is the role of history in the training of adult educators. The second part of this chapter focuses on the different dimensions of constructing the curriculum.

Historiographic Issues and Dilemmas

The challenge for me as a teacher of adult educational history is to construct a curriculum that is faithful to our "great tradition," from the Mechanics' Institutes of the early nineteenth century to the Antigonish Movement of the 1930s, to the popular education traditions of the 1990s. The folk wisdom of practitioners carries memories of select events and people. Indeed, it is hard to think of our history excluding Frontier College, university extension, Fathers Tompkins and Coady, Citizens' and Farm Forums, or Roby Kidd and Violet McNaughton. Yet new readings of the past are always possible, and many new actors must become integral parts of the ongoing narrative of the history of Canada as a learning society. The history is not definitive; it is the beginning of an open-ended conversation.

I argue that we should think of adult learning broadly and imaginatively. What were the most important learning sites for adults in different times and places? Where did adults acquire knowledge and skills about how to earn a living and live a life? Where did adults learn about why some people suffered or were exploited by others? Who were the teachers of adults in times past? What were their intentions? In Defense of the Lifeworld (1995), I called this broad outlook the *social learning paradigm*: this paradigm would construct the boundary of the field as wide as society itself and would work within a *system* and *lifeworld* framework to comprehend social learning processes. This approach to adult learning makes the historian's task more complex, but the gains outweigh the potential losses. For example, once one realizes that social movements can be thought of as learning sites playing themselves out on the terrain of civil society, women's learning comes into sharp focus. In the early twentieth century, women's learning does not fit easily into conventional adult education categories (as do Frontier College or the Workers Educational Association). But there was an explosion of learning among early twentieth century women. They taught themselves and the public in the richness of their association and movement life. Students learn about women's institutes in British Columbia, prairie women's many association sites, the Halifax Local Council of Women and women in the extension movement. Without this social learning focus, we would pass over women's learning. What is there depends, in part, on what lens we are peering through.

I believe that the past is *usable* in at least four ways. First, it provides a critical vantage-point from which to view the present. History helps us determine what is new, helps us filter peripheral from perennial issues; it adds important voices to contemporary discourse. Without historical understanding, we are unable to penetrate to the heart of our society's central problems and concerns. Second, we can study the past in order to discover its "liberatory moments," and those moments that may illuminate our darkness or troubles. The retrieval of liberatory moments—an "affirming flame," to quote W.H. Auden—from our past may fill us with hope. If adult educators in times past could dream such dreams—we can become "masters of our own destiny"—so can we. If they could launch such bold and courageous projects as the Antigonish Movement or the Challenge for Change film initiative in Newfoundland in the midst of vast poverty and apathy, so can we. What are we forgetting that our forebears remembered? What are we confronting that they did not? Third, historical studies may be a useful way of generating theorems about the many themes and issues having to do with how and where and why adults learn. Historical studies are a good way to test hypotheses about the situated nature of all adult learning. Fourth, historical understanding can play a role in shaping our identity as adult educators. Students can be challenged to "keep faith" with our public-oriented tradition of using adult education as a vehicle for mobilizing citizen action to create a more democratic society.

Constructing the Curriculum

The first of the course's three parts is "Reclaiming our Past: Memory, Tradition and Kindling Hope." In Module one, we think together about the place of memory and tradition in our lives and work as educators and consider the role of history in the training of adult educators. In each module, students are required to prepare an assignment of a few pages. For the first assignment of the course, students write a letter to a hypothetical friend who has been questioning the requirement to take a history course in a master's program. In the second module of Part I, "Early Movements in Adult Education," two important nineteenth-century adult education forums are highlighted, the Danish folkschools and the Mechanics' Institute. At this point we begin to teach students how to think *contextually* about adult learning. What social conditions call forth new forms of adult education? What is the animating vision of those who are educating adults? What projects are developed out of the vision? What methods are chosen to realize the project? Students are asked to think about why the Mechanics' Institutes appeared in the 1830s and not, say, in 1780 or 1870, and whether they see a slight shift away from elitist forms of understanding of who should be educated towards a more populist vision.

Part II, "Adult Education in the Age of the Great Transformation, 1896–1929," includes three modules. This is an exciting and tumultuous time in Canada's history and a time when adult education explodes everywhere. Module three focuses on the education of the workers, Module four on women's organizations as learning sites and Module five is entitled "Pioneers and Pedagogues: Carrying the University to the People" (which explores the origins of the university extension movement at the universities of Alberta, Saskatchewan and St. Francis Xavier).

I use this period as a way of exploring the idea of *historical learning challenges*. Canadians faced at least three marked learning challenges in the late nineteenth century and the first few decades of the twentieth century, as follows.

1. The massive influx of immigrants into Canada in the first two decades of the twentieth century presented Canadians—particularly those of Anglo-Celtic origin—with a challenge: what kind of nation would we become? One leading social thinker of the early twentieth century, J.S. Woodsworth, who wrote *Strangers Within Our Gates* (1909), exhibited a clear preference for "northern races." Life for immigrants was not easy in the early years. Anglo-conformists did not like the sound of "foreign tongues;" they did not like German Mennonites' desire for their own schools; they were uneasy about the

new religious expressions appearing on the prairie landscape. Sometimes, too, men and women from different ethnic groups opted for radical politics. This fuelled Anglo-hostility, and some leaders of the day perceived immigrant workers as dangerous foreigners.

2. Canadians also had to confront the *learning challenge* of the altered balance between city and rural dwellers. During the late nineteenth and early twentieth centuries, Canada was undergoing rapid urbanization. Between 1881 and 1911, the combined population of Halifax, Montreal, Toronto and Winnipeg tripled. In Nova Scotia, between 1901 and 1911, outward migration was continuous, with an estimated loss of 24,000 inhabitants. Men and women left the rural areas, pulled inexorably into burgeoning coal mining towns such as Springhill, Inverness and Glace Bay (which grew from 6,945 to 16,562 between 1901 and 1911), or out to the booming west.

As Module three, "The Education of the Workingman," illustrates, the industrial working classes crowding into urban slums and working in the factories and mines faced no less daunting challenges. Here we need only remind ourselves of the bitter troubles in the Cape Breton coal and steel industries; company stores, feudal management, bitter and violent strikes in the beginning years of the First World War. One objective in this module is to help students understand that the workplace (the "school of labour") is one of the primary learning domains of adults. Students learn about the ambiguous origins of Frontier College and the Workers Educational Association and the forms of learning that emerged within the networks of socialist workers clustered around Winnipeg in the decade preceding the Winnipeg General Strike. Stepping back into the past world of industrial worksites, strikes and rancorous debate between liberals, conservatives and radicals forces us to think afresh about the issues of propaganda, indoctrination and education.

3. During this period of intense immigration, urbanization and industrialization, Canadians struggled with the learning demands of an unfamiliar and often exploitative kind of society. They were, one could say, becoming enlightened about the causes of their suffering and were becoming empowered to change their life situations. On the Prairies, we see the birth of agrarian protest movements. The rhetoric and literature of farm organizations such as the United Farmers of Alberta (UFA) and the Saskatchewan Grain Growers Association (SGGA) contained statements stressing the importance of adult education in the farm movement. In Module five, "Pioneers and Pedagogues," students learn how the University of Saskatchewan's extension work can be located within the democratic impulses present in the agrarian sector and that extension's purpose was to carry useful knowledge to the farm population as they grappled with the many problems of farming a new land.

Women's associations and movements were important oppositional learning sites in Canada's time of "great transformation." Why have references to

Women's Institutes, the YWCA, the Women's League for Peace and Freedom, the Home and School associations been so marginal in Canadian adult education history? Why do we not know about Violet McNaughton, Ella Maud Murray, Laura Jamieson, Sophia Dixon, Beatrice Brigden or Lotti Austin? In Module four, students are introduced to some of the women's organizations and female adult educators who learned, taught and struggled in the opening decades of this century. What stands out for me is just how central the voluntary association was as a learning site for women. These sites enabled women to school themselves for active citizenship. It was in these lifeworld institutions that women entered public debate and began to transform Canadian society. Listen to the stirring words of Mrs. A.V. Thomas in her 1916 address to the Saskatchewan Homemakers' Clubs: "Someone has said since I came here 'Mrs. Thomas', I don't believe in mixing politics with the Homemakers.' We women have not gone out to politics; they have come in, and touched our children, and our homes, and we cannot get away from politics ... [W]e cannot turn to the men and say 'This is your problem ...'" In today's language, women were forging a "citizen politics" that fostered their capacities to exercise responsible leadership for the common good.

Part III, "Adult Education and the Crisis of Democracy, 1929-1960," completes the course. The 1930s were bleak and grim years for many ordinary Canadians. That the world would enter into its "golden era" from 1945 to 1973 could not have been evident to Canadians at the outbreak of the Depression in 1929. Images of blank-faced men and women with a row of children, lined up beside an old beat-up truck piled high with a few pieces of furniture, somewhere on the Prairies, still haunt our Canadian memories. Breadlines, riding the rods, strikes, Bennet-buggies, unemployed men in work camps; these are only a few bitter reminders of the "Dirty Thirties."

I think of this period as a time when adult education in Canada was in its "golden era." Canadian adult educators seemed exceptionally alive and alert to the learning challenges of their era. From the mid-1930s to the end of the war (and extending into the 1950s), Canadian adult education crystallizes around a central purpose: to foster participatory citizenship. I am convinced that the secret of the Canadian tradition of adult education lies in its civil societarian focus. Our pioneers were committed to citizen politics and deliberative democracy. They fought to create the conditions whereby citizens themselves could deliberate about public problems through reasoned reflection. They believed in dialogic approaches to public decision making where citizens could reframe their interests and perspectives in the light of a common quest for the common good.

In his 1943 article "Films for Farmers," Alex Sim argued that "education must be for all the people all the time. The end goal of any program must be to give the people a voice, to develop skills in tackling their own problems, to foster an understanding of the world (social, economic, and scientific) in which they live, and to train them that they may increase their control over this environment." Sim went on to insist that a "group program is important because it provides activity and develops the social sense of the people. It also reaches more people, and it lays the foundation for action." He also thought that "listening-group broadcasts and films" were "important because they can provide a modus operandi for a group and because they represent an effective and direct form of communication."

At the end of World War II, however, this unifying vision began to unravel. The reform wing of Canadian adult education came under increasing attack from right-wing interests (we need to remind ourselves that some of our best adult educators were accused of being communists and were run out of the movement—Watson Thomson, John Grierson, Drummond Wren, Stanley Rands, to name a few). The period from 1945 to 1960 was a deeply conflictual one for Canadian adult education. Its Depression and war years' vision and commitment met with hostility in a changed culture and political world. Some think that the Canadian Association for Adult Education (CAAE) was derailed from its fundamental purposes in the 1950s. Others believe that all a cagey leader like Roby Kidd could do was steer a kind of safe course through the dangerous waters. No more manifestos in the 1950s!

In Module six, "On the Eve of a Great, Mass Movement," students learn to understand the origins of the CAAE in 1935 in the context of economic distress, spiritual dislocation and emergent social movements. They also analyze the promise and perils of the early community development initiatives in The Pas, Manitoba, and in Barrie, Ontario (they are introduced to several of our great pioneer male-female adult education teams, including the Avisons (Harry and Mary) and the Smiths (David and Edith). This module contends that the CAAE eschewed the clearing-house approach of its American counterpart, the American Association of Adult Education, by moving in an activist direction and responding particularly to the plight of rural society. Adult education, for its 1930s pioneers, was clearly perceived as a tool to solve societal problems; it was not merely for individual betterment.

Modules seven and eight, not unexpectedly, focus on the Antigonish Movement. In module seven, "Real Adult Education Springs from the Heart and Pains of the People: The Origins of the Antigonish Movement," students are challenged to develop sophisticated analyses of the movement. One cannot understand the emergence of St. Francis Xavier's extension department apart from grasping the profoundly Catholic nature of the movement. Roman Catholicism was responding to the modern world and the particularities of life in the Diocese of Antigonish in the early twentieth century. Caught in a swirl of pressures from within and without, the Roman Catholic Church developed into a forum for the debate of its relevance to a modernizing and industrializing world. Spearheaded by Father Jimmy Tompkins, a cadre of reform-minded priests began to shape a new "social Catholicism" in response both to the plight of the poor and the plight of the church itself. For the Antigonish reformers, recovering the church's lost influence was intimately linked to their educative and political struggles to emancipate the oppressed peoples labouring in the mines, at sea, on the farms and in households. Tompkins and Coady were *Christian* thinkers of a particular sort. Spiritual convictions fuelled their passions, kept them going through many dark nights and shaped their dream of the "good and abundant life."

Students learn that all of Nova Scotia's economic sub-groups were experiencing severe difficulties: industrial workers, subsistence farmers and fishermen, scattered in villages along the torturous Nova Scotian coastline. But these circumstances, by themselves, cannot make a movement. The people must have the capacity to react: this capacity to react is fundamental to understanding the potentiality of any movement. And I would argue that this capacity to react is anchored, fundamentally, in three components of the lifeworld: meaning, solidarity and self-reliant personality. Dodaro and Pluta (1995) rightly identify the "high degree of regional cohesion and identity as well as stable community structures" present in eastern Nova Scotia. Both at the regional and local level, the church and the cultural heritage of people (Scottish and Acadian particularly) "exerted a powerful integrating function." Without this integrating function, or strong solidarity, people would be isolated and individualized, and would not be able to organize collectively. The church provided a meaningful, if contested, orientation to life (people were not nihilistic and completely bereft of hope), forms of solidarity in communities were strong and people still had qualities (or memory of) self-reliance. From this position of strength, they confronted a piratical economy and *laissez-faire* state. These conditions, however, required human leaders to activate the people. And these leaders came predominantly from the clergy who had a ready-made communication network (priests as nodes on the circuit) in place. If eastern Nova Scotia had been less ethnically and religiously cohesive, and the leadership confused, bewildered or tired, it really is hard to imagine the movement getting off the ground.

The critical dialogic methodology encourages students to ask tough questions of received interpretations and of the pertinence of the past to present problems. In Module eight, "The Antigonish Movement: Critical Reflections, Future Possibilities," students focus some attention on the role of women in the Antigonish Movement. They read two chapters on women—excerpts from Ida Delaney's book, *By Their Own Hands: A Fieldworkers' Account of the Antigonish Movement* (1985). She was a fieldworker, and her account is that of an insider. Ida Delaney challenges us to consider the lives of the women of the Thirties as "heroines of a desperately hard age." Students then read Dan

MacInnes' and Judith MacLean's paper, "What Can Women Do? The Antigonish Movement and its Programs for Women, 1918-1945" (1992). Based on extensive empirical research, they argue that the "dual focus on women as homemakers and co-operators lent a certain ambiguity to the extension department's programs for women." Some feminists might argue that the movement did not challenge the sexual division of labour; rather, it reinforced it. Is this a fair criticism? One can see that a new discourse (women's place is not only in the home) similar to that present in the Saskatchewan Homemakers Clubs begin to percolate through the study clubs and women's consciousness in eastern Nova Scotia. However, MacInnes and MacLean observe that, by 1950, female co-operators were increasingly convinced that "men have dominated all phases of the movement, and the women have been on the outside looking in, with no invitation or very little incentive to enter" (1992).

Module nine, "The Great, New Instruments of Adult Education," invites students to understand the creative ways Canadian adult educators in the 1930s and 1940s used radio and film. I want them to appreciate three of our most renowned educational inventions: the Farm Radio Forum, the Citizens' Forum and the National Film Board's rural-industrial circuits. By the early 1940s, the idea that adult education had to be conceived in terms of reaching the masses had taken firm root among the adult education leadership. Adult educators like Father Coady, Watson Thomson, Isabel Wilson and Alex Sim knew well the power of study groups as the nuclei for general community education and reform, but they also knew that these efforts were not reaching enough people. So they adapted the tried-and-true study group to the radio communications technology, and the listening-study-action model of learning was born. The National Farm Radio Forum was launched in 1941. As Sim tells it in his 1954 article, "Canada's Farm Radio Forum," the "great unalterables of Canadian life-space, snow and a powerful neighbour to the South, were determining factors in the growth of the National Farm Radio Forum. So were depression, the war, and the experience of the BBC with radio listening groups." Sim makes a powerful argument for the way the new technology of radio was contributing to the development of new forms of community. Radio, he exclaimed, was the "magic wand, which has melted down these barriers and moulded the farm population into one community each Monday night each winter since 1941." This is a fascinating observation in light of the way the World Wide Web has been heralded as creating undreamed-of possibilities for new forms of communicative action.

One can imagine members of the farm community travelling down the old dirt roads to gather at a friend's house. One can see the large radio, with its dark wood paneling, conspicuously present in the corner of the living room. If these farmers had gathered on the Monday night of October 29, 1945, they would have listened to the topic, "How important is agriculture to Canada?"

On November 12, they would have discussed, "Can we do without the small farm?" There were, of course, endless organizational and curricular kinds of problems connected with the Farm Radio Forum. For instance, in 1945, Charlie Douglas, agricultural representative for Hants County in Nova Scotia, complained to Ralph Staples, a prominent farm leader, that the January series had been too elementary for his groups scattered around Windsor, Nova Scotia.

An educational form such as the Citizens' Forum makes sense once we understand that Canadian adult educators were attempting to develop an adequate practice of participatory democracy. They valued the maximizing of dialogue opportunities and enhancement of citizen self-understanding and political competence. They thought that the Citizens' Forum institutionalized possibilities for social and political learning. They believed that men and women had to be schooled, through discussion and persuasion, into adopting socially responsible attitudes.

In the early 1940s, Canadian adult educators invented yet another type of adult educator: the projectionist-animateur. From the stories some of them (such as George LeBeau, a friend of Watson Thomson) have told me, they plunged into their task enthusiastically. Often arriving in small prairie towns in the early hours of the morning, they would take their heavy equipment to the nearest hotel. Then it was up in the morning for a showing at the local school, followed by afternoon and evening showings. They were educational circuit-riders. Adult educators who were experimenting with the use of film for educational purposes also grappled with the pedagogical problems associated with this great, new instrument. Some were worried that using films to mobilize "men's minds to right ends" (Grierson) could end up being a kind of propaganda. But grassroots educators, sensitive to this problem, created innovations like the film forum to create dialogical contexts for learning.

The course on "Historical Perspectives" concludes with Module ten: "Adult Education in the Post-World II World: Educating in a Chilly Climate." We usually think of the 1950s as a rather benign time, but the closer one looks at this decade, the less complacent we should be. Gordon Selman says that it was an "exciting time to be a Canadian" (1982). But from the vantage point of adult educators, the 1950s were times of trouble and conflict. Many of our leading adult educators—prominent in national life in the 1930s and 1940s—came under fire for their alleged communist leanings. The cultural climate turned chilly for their experiments in participatory democracy. The Canadian state and their business allies began to attack the small study group as subversive and unCanadian.

Indeed, the world of the "Manifesto" of 1943—"The CAAE believes that in this day of total war and total challenge, academic aloofness and neutrality are not enough and that it is obliged to declare itself categorically upon those basic issues of human principle which underlie the social and economic, and spiritual problems of our time"—was shunted aside and replaced with language such as this: "If ever there was a time when citizens are needed to rally round in support of our Canadian Way of Life, this is the time. Doctrines subversive of democracy thrive in an atmosphere of ignorance ... Adult Education is needed, to keep us all up-to-date" (Muir, 1950). In this module, students learn about the way the purpose and function of adult education in the post-World War II era would get shaped in the context of the emergent welfare state and Cold War. The social reform consensus, forged in the great meetings and actions of the mid-1940s (like the Education for Reconstruction conference of 1943), begins to unravel.

As we enter the post-World War II era, the "professionalizing" tendency emerges and co-exists uneasily with the "education for social action" tradition of the earlier decades. The discussion is focused by analyzing, first, the adult education initiatives of Guy Henson of Nova Scotia ("Volunteerism as the Seedbed of Democracy: Guy Henson's Educational Thought and Practice"), and, second, the trials and tribulations of Roby Kidd, who took over the CAAE's directorship from E.A. Corbett in 1951.

In 1950, the CAAE came under fire from what Moses Coady would have called the "vested interests." Spokespeople for business interests began to attack the Citizens' and Farm Forums as undemocratic. These attacks were such that, in his first director's report in 1952, Kidd told his readers:

> An organization like ours has bounds and limitations which we must recognize. It is not and by its nature cannot be the radical agency of social action which some of you might prefer. Nor can it be a research agency only—simply observing and reporting facts. Our work cannot be done in splendid isolation; we must stay close to where groups are living and working. The CAAE is concerned about the welfare of, but cannot be mouthpiece of, the farmer, the union member, the housewife, the business man.

To puzzle through just what Kidd was up to, several documents are provided (mainly correspondence) which relate to the Citizens' and Farm Forum controversies. Students also read Jean Ogilivie's essay, "The National Film Board and the Cold War: A Learning Tradition is Lost" (1990). She throws new light on the chilly climate for adult education in post-war Canada by taking us into the world of the Kellock-Taschereau Hearings (1946). John Grierson, National Film Board director, and friend of many grassroots adult educators, was dragged into these hearings and accused of "subversion." We need more serious research on these matters. What role did adult educators play in defending civil rights? It does seem clear that adult education—its purposes and projects—is intimately tied to the kind of democracy with which we end up.

The direction of the CAAE in the early 1950s is counterpointed by closely examining Guy Henson's largely unsung work in Nova Scotia. Henson presided over the creation of the Division of Adult Education in 1945. He saw his work as creating the kind of community infrastructure that would lay the basis for developing sustainable, community-based forms of economic and social development. In the 1950s, then, it would be not quite accurate to argue that the story of Canadian adult education is the narrative of a field that is gradually shedding its amateurism. The commitment to deliberative democracy runs deep in the Canadian tradition, and we remain uneasy to this day with a narrow professional identity as "learning experts."

3

Critical Returns: From Andragogy to Lifelong Education

Michael Collins

> *Is this not the time to call for something quite different in education systems? Learning to live, learning to learn, so as to be able to absorb new knowledge all through life, learning to think freely and critically; learning to love the world and make it more human; learning to develop in and through creative work.*
> — Fauré et al., 1972, p. 69.

To a very large extent the discourse on modern adult education practice within the academy and in field-based programs is reflective of developments in the United States. Yet adult educators in Canada have made significant contributions to this discourse. For example, the connections between the emergence in American adult education literature of andragogy and the earlier work of Canadian Allen Tough (1966) are clearly discernible. And others among us—as Canadian-based academics, graduate students and practitioners—have given presentations, taught, published and held office in American adult education forums. By the same token, many adult educators from across the border work, or have worked, in Canada. Several are cited in this chapter. And for some of them, immigrants like myself, Canada is home.

In any event, as adult educators working in Canada we are very much at the centre of an emergent, though increasingly confined, discourse on the modern practice of adult education which, like so many other conventional discourses on professional and academic practice, gains its momentum in the United States.

Despite this understandable intermingling of our work within a discourse on modern adult education practice, there is still a distinctive and significant Canadian dimension that does not constitute a mere add-on. I recall being invited to co-author with an adult educator from the United States a chapter entitled "Federal and Provincial Adult Education Agencies in the United States and Canada" (Collins & Long, 1989) for the *1990 Handbook of Adult and Continuing Education*. Although it was somewhat of a deviation from the original approach identified by the editors, I felt compelled to include reference to exemplary and distinctive Canadian adult education initiatives, such as Frontier College, the Antigonish Movement, the Farm Forum, the Women's Institutes and the Wheat Pool. Fortunately, my American colleagues were happy to accept the deviation in order to bring emphasis to the distinctly Canadian dimension of adult education.

For a quickly appreciated awareness of distinctive Canadian contributions to adult education practice that counter the homogenizing effects of the andragogical model, I refer students here in Canada and colleagues from other countries to texts such as *Knowledge for the People* (Welton, 1987) and *We Have with Us Tonight* (Corbett, 1957). No doubt there are other short texts just as readable and accessible (and somewhat less "male-stream," "anglo-oriented," or "Eurocentric," some may decide) that will serve the same purpose.

In our academic forums, which tend to have much in common with academic forums everywhere, there is still a discernible distinction between the annual proceedings of the Canadian Association for the Study of Adult Education (CASAE) and those of the largely American-based equivalent, the Adult Education Research Conference (AERC). Apart from incorporating francophone interests as a matter of course, CASAE is somewhat less formalized and more accessible to practitioners. Nevertheless, CASAE, in common with AERC (to which many Canadian-based academic adult educators are closely affiliated), can be regarded as a forum for the generation of a largely North American discourse (the United States and Canada in this context) around modern adult education practice. So it is not surprising to find Canadian Allan Quigley reporting on the Town Forum he moderated at the American Association for Adult and Continuing Education (AAACE). In his report, "Trials, Traditions, and the Twenty-First Century" (Quigley, 1991), he refers to the "two great traditions" of adult education. Though he does not make this connection, it is from within the "professional tradition" rather than the "social reformist tradition" that adult educators in Canada have been most influenced by initiatives originating in the United States.

There is another tradition of adult education, variously designated as "critical" or "transformative" (rather than merely reformist) adult education. The emancipatory pedagogy entailed prefigures a learning society that admittedly cannot be fully realized under prevailing conditions of advanced capitalism. It is from within this tradition, and with the learning society Edgar Fauré (opening quotation) had in mind, that this chapter is written.

In case my introduction should be mistaken as a special pleading for Canadian content instead of a relevant concern for an internationalist perspective from a Canadian context, I would invoke the work of Roby Kidd and, in particular, his role in the founding of the International Council on Adult Education (ICAE). The internationalist aspirations Kidd held for a just, life-long learning society, like those of Edgar Fauré, have been temporarily de-railed during the high tide of neo-conservatism. What prospect is there now for a reconstructed modern adult education that can lever these aspirations back on track?

There is no doubt that the neo-conservative agenda has been largely successful during the past two decades in devaluing liberal ideals and undermining social democratic institutions. The neo-conservative success story, connected in the public mind with the political leadership of Margaret Thatcher and Ronald Reagan, is manifested in a popular discourse on the merits of competitive individualism and the enthronement of market-place values at the expense of community values and collective experience. These ideological tendencies have been accompanied by relentless cut-backs in publicly funded services such as education, health, social assistance, aid to developing countries and in the negotiation power of trade unions.

The Modern Practice of Adult Education

Much of my academic work in recent years constitutes a critique on the modern practice of adult education.[1] My critical concern has focused largely on the overall positivistic tendency and technical rationality (the enthronement of pedagogical technique) that pervade, shape and steer the conventional discourse on adult education practice and theory. Further, as part of an emerging critical counter-discourse, I have attempted to substantiate an understanding that the liberal-humanistic discourse on the modern practice of adult education mediates more in favour of government, bureaucratic and business interests than those of ordinary men and women. (See, for example, Collins 1991 and 1995).

More recently, my concern has been with the relativizing effects of post-modernist (dis)orientations within critical pedagogy on the one hand and, on the other, a not unrelated tendency for erstwhile positivists to package critical perspectives as just another paradigm to be taken aboard the good ship Adult Education, Inc. In a postmodern view, this neo-positivism is recognizable as just another discursive practice that diminishes the prospects for an emancipatory pedagogy.

The modern practice of adult education from a critical standpoint serves, most often unwittingly, to de-skill teachers of adults and fosters a notion of permanent inadequacy around the experience of adults as learners (Ohliger, 1974). Hence, the agency of teachers is undermined by an obsession with

pedagogical technique while, at the same time, vital capacities for autonomous learning are being encroached upon by a discernible trend towards
lifelong schooling.

In this chapter, I intend to enlarge on these somewhat compressed introductory remarks about critical perspectives on the modern practice of adult education. In the process, I hope to show how this critique contributes
significantly to an academic discourse on critical adult education (informed
by critical theory, feminist studies, and postmodernist thought) that is now
emerging, particularly in North America.

After describing andragogy as a central tenet of the modern practice of
adult education and addressing the critical discourse that makes this practice
problematic, I explore prospects for a reconstruction of modern adult education as a significant moral and political emancipatory force within a system of
lifelong education. Unlike the explicit deconstructionist and anti-rationalist
intent of postmodernist thought, a discourse on modern practice still holds out
possibilities for identifying *reasonably constituted grounds* from which human action can be enacted and assessed.

To talk in terms of a modern practice of adult education is to emphasize the
relevance of *agency* (that is, the role of the adult educator) and the conviction
that human history—the transformative potential of human experience and
human capacities to learn—are still in the making. Thus, a critically informed
modern practice of adult education that eschews postmodern notions about
"the end of history" refers us once again to a pedagogy of hope. From this
hopeful vantage point, men and women are viewed as having the capacity to
envision and possibly to realize a rational (humane) global society as an
alternative to a state of barbarism that is also conceivable.

Andragogy

An article entitled "Androgogy, Not Pedagogy!" (Knowles, 1968)[2] published in the April 1968 edition of *Adult Leadership* proclaimed "a new label and
a new approach for adult education." The article was particularly auspicious
because in addition to making a clear-cut distinction between adult education
and conventional schooling, it confirmed the direction in which organized
adult education practice in the United States had been developing for more
than a decade. A major feature of that development was an aspiration to
professionalize the practice of adult education and, at the same time, gain
recognition for it as a conventional academic discipline (see, for example,
Houle, 1956; Verner, 1964).

The term describing "a new label and a new approach" for adult education
registers a slight change in spelling—from *androgogy* to *andragogy*—with
the first edition of *The Modern Practice of Adult Education: Andragogy Versus Pedagogy* (Knowles, 1970), which quickly became the sterling text for

andragogy as a conventional discipline and profession. Andragogy became a legitimizing touchstone for those who anticipated advantages to be gained by distinguishing adult education as a clear-cut field of professionalized practice. From this tendency emerged a professionalizing discourse around the concept of self-directed learning, which is regarded as a central tenet of andragogy.

The notion of self-directed learning was further thematized by Knowles in his book *Self-Directed Learning* (1975). In Knowles' scheme the adult educator is characterized as a guide and facilitator. Self-directed learners are viewed as being proactive inquirers who, in mature fashion, seek to learn as much as possible on their own terms. The significant insight for enthroning self-directed learning as the foremost method of andragogy appears in an earlier text by Knowles, *The Adult Learner: A Neglected Species*: "As a person grows and matures his self-concept moves from one of total dependency (as in the reality of the infant) to one of increasing self-directedness" (Knowles, 1973, p. 45).

Knowles drew from a discourse that was already underway in the academy of adult education. In reporting about a study first published in 1966, *Learning Without a Teacher: A Study of Tasks and Assistance During Adult Self-Teaching*, Canadian adult educator Allen Tough acknowledged his debt to a leading professor of adult education in the United States: "It was Professor C.O. Houle of the University of Chicago who first focused attention on men and women conspicuously engaged in learning. The inquiry was then taken up and developed in a variety of studies by younger colleagues" (Tough, 1981, p. iv).

Thus self-directed learning, subsequently under the rubric of andragogy, has spawned a substantial body of academic and practitioner-oriented literature on adult education. Here is what William Draves, author of *The Free University: A Model for Lifelong Learning* (1980) has to say about self-directed learning: "Self-directed learning begins with the learner. It sees the learner as the primary impetus for and the initiator of the learning process. Teachers, classes, and other educational features are then put in a secondary light, as aids to the learning process rather than its central elements" (p. 191).

Prominent among the many techniques and strategies associated with self-directed learning is the individual learning contract in which what is to be accomplished is formally negotiated between educator and learner, and then recorded. The purpose of this approach is to enable the individualized learner to identify his or her perceived needs and to specify learning objectives, learning resources and strategies, evidence of accomplishment and criteria for evaluation. The teacher assumes a *facilitator* role, and the learner that of a *client*.

Clearly, it is a good idea (whether as adult educators or school teachers) to continually remind ourselves of how important it is to involve the learner in the learning process. And in elevating its concern for the individualized learner above a focus on the implied authoritarian role of teacher, the discourse around self-directed learning and the andragogical model has endeavoured to distinguish a modern practice of adult education from that of conventional schooling. This tendency provides support for those who are committed to the construction of adult education as a regulated field of practice and an orthodox academic discipline.

It is evident from published texts, journals and conference proceedings that the andragogical model and the ideology of self-directed learning have become very pervasive within academic and practitioner-oriented contexts during the past two decades. In recent years, the overall discourse, representing a modern practice of adult education, has assumed international proportions. A preoccupation with andragogy is not confined to adult education practice and theory in English-speaking countries.

The November 1994 edition of *The Canadian Journal for the Study of Adult Education (CJSAE)* largely reflects the critical turn in Canadian academic adult education, with articles by Peter Mayo on Gramsci and Freire, Edith Smith and Valerie Norlen on feminist pedagogy, and Bruce Spencer on labour education. But this issue (8, no. 2) features a book review on andragogy as a profession and field of study. *L'andragogie: champs d'études et profession, une histoire à suivre* (Blais et al., 1994) describes how andragogy has been introduced as a guiding force within the graduate program in adult education at the University of Montreal. We are reminded here that andragogy is still pervasive in Canada as elsewhere.

The Lifelong Concept

Even more widespread than the discourse on andragogy and self-directed learning in the modern practice of adult education are the notions of lifelong learning and lifelong education (often used interchangeably), which refer to an expansive vision of learning and education. While conveying a sense of optimism about the future, however, the frequency with which reference to lifelong learning and lifelong education is made has virtually rendered the lifelong concept a catch-phrase. Yet it is still a useful catch-phrase for our times, where it evokes the kind of vision expressed by Edgar Fauré as quoted at the beginning of this chapter.

Frequent reference to the lifelong concept is indicative of a growing realization that education is not confined to schools, colleges and universities. However, though the *idea* that education and significant learning go on beyond the school walls and throughout life is generally acceptable, our schools and colleges still promote an obsession with finishing. John Niemi, a leading professor of adult education, described this tendency in the following terms: "Our emphasis in education from school through university and beyond is always on *finishing* our learning, not on continuing to learn throughout the life-span. We talk of *finishing* elementary school, *finishing* college, and *finishing* our doctorates" (Niemi, 1977-78, p. 5). Hence the significance of the lifelong concept as a reminder to those not already imbued with an understanding of the merits of adult education and continuing education that relevant education takes place outside the restrictions on time and space designated by conventional schooling.

In his article "The Meaning of Lifelong Learning," Niemi cites several works that have been incorporated into modern adult education discourse in North America and elsewhere. In addition to *Learning to Be: The World of Education Today and Tomorrow* (Fauré et al., 1972), these works include a monograph by Paul McGhee (1959), entitled *The Learning Society.* The International Commission on the Development of Education, which was responsible for producing *Learning to Be,* proclaimed lifelong education and the learning society as two fundamental aspirations for today's global society. McGhee's monograph, predating *Learning to Be* by thirteen years, declared with equal enthusiasm for education from "cradle to grave." Subsequently, there has been a virtual torrent of publications on lifelong learning and lifelong education.

In a general sense, it is useful to think of lifelong learning as referring to the actual experience of the individual or of groups of learners. The focus, then, is on how psychological factors, social contexts, teaching practices, curriculum formation and educational management techniques come to bear on the shaping of learning experiences in their immediacy. Lifelong education, on the other hand, draws attention to the nature of the commitment, policies and forms of restructuring needed to ensure that educational services become readily accessible to us throughout the entire span of our lives. In this broader sense, lifelong learning now becomes the central feature of a global learning society.

Other terms that stem from the lifelong learning concept and appear in the literature of modern adult education practice include *continuous learning, continual education, continuing education, recurrent education,* and *education permanente,* There is, however, a distinction to be made between the largely British notion of *further education* and lifelong education. In Britain, the former term designates a separation of vocational training (including instruction in "functional literacy") from a currently declining legacy of adult education that was associated either with liberal studies or with the promotion of progressive social change on behalf of working-class people. In the realm of state-initiated educational policy development, lifelong education has taken on many of the defining features of further education.

Critical Cross-Currents in Mainstream Adult Education

Adult education might well be viewed as a multi-faceted activity reflecting the numerous commitments, preoccupations and ideological perspectives of everyday life. Yet we are inclined to describe adult education, to make sense of it, in a systematic way that is indicative of its relevance to any serious consideration of human experience and historical development. Generally speaking, we refer to adult education in terms of deliberately organized activities, although it is not difficult to appreciate the significance of its non-formal, spontaneous manifestations in our everyday experience.

For Raymond Williams (1990), adult education takes on two distinct forms. Adult education as "the bottle with a message in it bubbling along in the mainstream of history" aptly describes the form taken on by modern adult education practice via the andragogical model and its scarcely original methodological strategies (look for their equivalent in many a creative elementary-school classroom), such as self-directed learning. In its other form, according to Williams, adult education endeavours to become part of history itself, as a driving force within the process of social change. This socially dynamic form of adult education is highlighted in Patricia Hughes-Fuller's paper for *The Proceedings of the Canadian Association for the Study of Adult Education* (1994), in which she demonstrated how Williams' views on the role of adult education in building a genuinely democratic culture remain relevant for us today. These views find their pedagogical expression nowadays in the work of Paulo Freire that gained international acclaim after the publication of his best-known text, *Pedagogy of the Oppressed* (1970).

Williams' portrayal of two forms of adult education is useful even if somewhat simplistic. Undoubtedly, the way the two forms impinge upon one another and the continuing efforts to effect a rapprochement between them merit further investigation. However, though reference to the Freirean approach is often made in mainstream adult education literature, the discourse on "pedagogy of the oppressed" is nicely homogenized, posing little challenge to status quo interests. By the same token, it is questionable whether the social change aspect of Freire's pedagogy on behalf of ordinary men and women manages to retain its revolutionary intent, even in developing countries, bearing in mind how "Modern Adult Education, Inc." as human resource development has been so widely embraced.

In recent years the critical tendency emerging within the academic discourse on adult theory and practice has posed a direct challenge to the andragogical model. This critique tends to illuminate the ways modern adult education practice, steered by technical rationality, is narrowly preoccupied with methodology (pre-packaged standardized learning modules and formulaic approaches to program planning and evaluation), takes on a corporate agenda (human resource development) and plays a role in reproducing patriarchal (andragogy versus androgyny), repressive structures of a (post?) modern global society.

In the North American context, critical cross-currents within mainstream adult education began with a concern about the dominant position of psychology, more especially behavioural psychology, as the guiding discipline for research and practice. A dissatisfaction with the artificiality of positivist and heavily reductionist approaches (aping the tendencies of behavioural psychology) to program planning, evaluation and research was expressed in alternative perspectives informed by phenomenology and hermeneutics (Collins, 1987; Stanage, 1987). Thus, a philosophical basis and the theoretical groundwork were available for so-called "qualitative" research that successfully challenged the virtual hegemony of statistical ("quantitative" research) methods in conventional adult education research forums. In this context, *CJSAE* published a very readable and illuminating article by Virginia Griffin (1988), "Learning to Name Our Learning Processes," which exemplified a phenomenologically informed approach to qualitative investigations in adult education practice. Examples of more recent qualitative studies on adult learning that run counter to linear, reductionistic approaches can be found in studies by Jack Mezirow (1991), Alan Thomas (1994), and Sue Scott and M. Schmitt-Boshnick (1994). These later perspectives on adult learning evince a greater critical concern for the relevance of social context in addition to psychological factors.

A greater tolerance for more adventurous approaches such as participatory research, which had been largely excluded from academic forums (Hall, 1979), and an increased acceptance of philosophical and historical studies were realized with the decline of psychologism's dominant role. Hence, the restricting effects incurred by an overdetermined positivistic orientation to research and practice in adult education were loosened in a quest for meaning, contextual relevance and—in contrast to andragogy's unremitting focus on individualized experience—for inter-subjective communication.

With the shift away from reliance on an overall positivistic orientation and on individualizing pedagogical strategies that had constituted the psychologistic standpoint, questions have arisen about the prevailing socio-political norms and structures that impede our collective capacities to understand fully, to communicate adequately and to effect the kind of personal and social transformations in our everyday world that could increase the quality of life for the majority of ordinary men and women. What aspects of modern society shape social learning processes in ways that still reproduce status quo arrangements in the interests of a privileged minority? How is the realization of *communicative competence*—inter-subjective understanding—curtailed, thwarting prospects for the achievement of genuine participatory democracy and, ultimately, a rational society?

The critical issues these admittedly broad-sweeping questions pose were largely neglected in the development of approaches to adult education practice and research preoccupied with the advancement of professional status and a narrowly conceived positivistic research agenda. However, the entry into the adult education research arena of the Frankfurt School of Critical Theory, especially that of its leading exponent Jurgen Habermas, provided a foundational discourse for those who sought to reclaim prospects for adult education as an emancipatory project towards a genuinely democratic society. The critical social theory of Habermas, culminating in his two-volume *Theory of Communicative Action* (1984, 1987), refers to the notion of a collective communicative competence that is potentially realizable through learning processes and a practice of adult education that is not steered by technical rationality (Collins, 1991; Welton, 1995).

In developing his theory of communicative action, Habermas draws on Alfred Schutz's concept of the lifeworld (Schutz himself acknowledged his indebtedness to the philosophy of Edmund Husserl). The lifeworld is central to Schutz's phenomenological studies on social relations, and so he describes its constituents at great length. He also provides a succinct definition:

> Life-world; also: World of everyday life: The total sphere of experiences of an individual which is circumscribed by the objects, persons, and events encountered in the pursuit of the pragmatic objectives of living. It is a "world" in which a person is "wide-awake," and which asserts itself as the "paramount reality" of his life (Schutz, 1975, p. 30).

However, for Schutz and subsequently for Habermas, the everyday lifeworld is far more comprehensive than even this psychologically oriented quotation implies. The concept also accounts for how in social relations we blend our individual experiences with the lifeworld of others. Thus, the lifeworld incorporates community-forming processes that actively and passively shape it into a social world. As Schutz puts it, "I know that this life-world is not my private world but from the beginning an intersubjective one common to us all" (1973, p. 167).

Schutz's initiatives in developing a theory of the lifeworld have significantly influenced the field of sociology, particularly ethnographic studies and non-ideological research around the social construction of reality. His lifeworld investigations also provide the philosophical foundations and offer much potential for non-positivistic "qualitative" research on adult education practice and adult learning (Collins, 1987).

In his critique of technical rationality (or "functionalist reason"), Habermas is more preoccupied with ideological factors than is Schutz and is concerned with how the lifeworld is colonized by system-world imperatives. He describes the incursions of the system-world into the lifeworld as "the bureaucratization and legal regulation of private and informal spheres of action"

(Habermas, 1984a, p. 19). Our everyday lives are being shaped increasingly by the systematic demands of an overly managed society.

The distinction Habermas makes between a communicatively structured, everyday lifeworld and the system-world, and his account of the emancipatory interests that still reside in the former, provide critical insights into what locations (for example, schools, families, adult education sites) and practices are feasible for the kind of pedagogy envisaged in the work of Paulo Freire and in Raymond Williams' second form of adult education. By the same token, and in our Canadian context, it makes sense to revisit E.A. Corbett's (1957) personal account of his work as an adult educator and the initiatives described in *Knowledge for the People* (Welton, 1987).

While Habermas follows the neo-Marxist Frankfurt School line in not attributing an inevitable revolutionary role to the working class, his critical social theory is very much concerned with the potential of human agency in the quest for social transformation. He builds his position from a careful ontological account of the human capacity for language development. This innate capacity signifies a fundamental drive of human beings both to understand and to make ourselves understood (that is, to acquire communicative competence). From this foundational insight, the Habermasian project affords us *reasonable* prospects for the discovery of a rational basis on which to reconstruct an emancipatory pedagogy. Our attention is drawn via an engagement with critical theory to the significance of social learning processes—to their effects on the quality of communication and the nature of decision making—and, in particular, to the agency of the educator. At the very least, encounters with critical theory suggest that modern adult education practice, rather than fostering communicative competence and its possibilities for advancing the emancipatory interests of ordinary people, has become effectively commodified and given over largely to the ethos of bureaucratic control and corporate enterprise. From this critical perspective, The Modern Practice of Adult Education, Inc. is viewed as serving the interests of a privileged minority.

The scope of the critical discourse within modern adult education has been broadened and enlivened through the influence of postmodernist thought and feminist studies. Michel Foucault's work, most notably *Discipline and Punish* (1979) and *Power/Knowledge* (1980), are drawn on effectively in the disclosure of restrictive practices and hidden agendas that lie at the heart of modern adult education practice. Its complicity in the maintenance of prevailing inequalities in the distribution of power and knowledge (knowledge as power) is also a key concern for postmodernist analysis. An understanding of the connection between relationships of power and the distribution of knowledge is seen as crucial for the planning of strategies towards political and social equality and, hence, for a critical practice of adult education.

The postmodern tendency to deconstruct all authoritative claims about how we should understand, and act in, the world raises questions about any initiatives to professionalize adult education or even to establish foundations of practice. In this regard, a critical theory that aspires to construct a foundational practice from a rational discourse on practical (rather than technical) and emancipatory interests is also relativized by postmodernist critique as just one more discursive practice. Hence, deconstruction as the method against method (exponents of postmodernist discourse delight in irony and word-play) *represents* a systematic challenge, along with critical theory, to the instrumental rationality (obsession with technique) pervading modern adult education practice. By the same token (of deconstruction), however, postmodern sensibilities have no patience with theoretical projects to provide rational grounds from which to reconstruct a modern practice of adult education.

Within the mainstream of academic adult education, postmodern insights have been effectively incorporated into an influential feminist discourse that reveals how the field of practice is shaped to serve a patriarchal worldview. This insight sustains a high level of moral outrage and an ongoing struggle to have other (marginalized) voices heard within the conventional discourse(s) in adult education. A recently published article by Kathleen Rockhill (1995), "Challenging the Exclusionary Effects of the Inclusive Mask of Adult Education," is a strong example of this insistence on the need for greater, more just, representation from minority and otherwise disempowered groups in conventional adult education discourse. Rockhill's article is a ringing endorsement of a paper entitled "Working Across Our Differences—Perspectives on Oppression" (Brooks et al., 1993), published in *Convergence*. The authors, from widely different backgrounds but studying adult education together in a Canadian university, reflect on their personal experiences of difference and marginality: "We speak from our difference in descriptive narratives on the embodied struggle, the process of moving outside of relations of dominance, and reflect as a group on the process of working together across our differences of race, gender and sexuality" (p. 20).

Postmodernist thought has also been incorporated into the adult education arena as an instructive addition to critical theory's analysis of mass culture and the compelling tendency towards the commodification of everyday life (Briton & Plumb, 1993). A first-rate example of analysis informed by postmodern insights is provided in *The University as Text: Women and the University Context* by Canadian adult educator Carol Schick (1994), who outlines how male-centric approaches and methods dominate university life.

Apart from texts informed by critical theory, postmodernist thought and feminist studies that together constitute critical adult education, there is a small but long-standing liberal-humanist (some would say "radical") legacy that has consistently opposed the professionalizing tendency of modern adult education practice. From the North American context, John Ohliger writes in this vein with unflagging conviction about the value of informal voluntary adult education free from the mediation of experts. His outstanding polemics, influenced to a large extent by Ivan Illich (1970), have sustained an ethical concern within modern adult education practice about the de-humanizing effects of mandatory continuing education that prefigures a translation of life-long education into lifelong schooling from cradle to grave (Ohliger, 1974).

Endnotes

[1] The conventional discourse on adult education in the English-speaking world, and increasingly elsewhere, is largely influenced by the work of Malcolm Knowles, most notably, *The Modern Practice of Adult Education: From Pedagogy to Andragogy* (1970).

[2] The article is the script of an address given by Malcolm Knowles at an annual banquet to commemorate Delbert Clark. (Clark had been vice-president of the Fund for Adult Education provided by the Ford Foundation). Knowles: "Adult education is, I believe, on the threshold of a technological breakthrough ... and ... adult education is now big business" (p. 350).

4

Paradigm Shifts

Marie-Thérèse Morin

In 1983, Naisbitt wrote that we are living in a "parenthesis epoch, ... [a] hiatus between two eras" (Naisbitt, 1983, p. 341). Fifteen years later, his declaration has become a reality. This chapter explores some aspects of the profound changes occurring in our time. These changes should be examined on at least two levels. First, there has been a shift in our worldview, a shift in a "meta-paradigm," to use Tarnas's expression (1996), which is occurring in all aspects of society. Second, there has been a capitalist restructuring of the global economic system that has dramatically impinged on society, including the work of adult educators. I limit my thoughts to the paradigm shift, but I will point out at times any major impact that restructuring has had on education—and there are many—and on our professional work.

The "parenthesis epoch" is still in full swing in the 1990s; it is a time of deep crisis in which social actions, leaders and institutions are being questioned. Simultaneously, new trends are emerging or have already emerged, although it is difficult to predict what will be a long-term orientation and what is a passing fad. In this transition period, the dominant capitalist elite is working intensely through all media to imprint its viewpoint.

Why Should Adult Educators Care?

Why should adult educators pay attention to a paradigm shift or even to a capitalist restructuring, since change has always been a constant, and we are used to living in a society that changes? It takes so much effort and energy just to keep up with our work, our students' needs and other tasks; why do we need also to strive for a deeper understanding of the nature of change and to identify what is at stake?

Adult learners come from different educational settings. Some of them have traditional values—one might say they belong to the dominant paradigm—while others have more affinity with the values and paradigms currently emerging. On what basis are the pedagogical decisions of adult education made if adult educators do not understand the worldviews and values of adult learners? If a group of adult learners have values that adult educators consider conservative, outdated and highly questionable, do the educators have a responsibility to the learners and to the community to attempt to bring about changes in attitude? We must understand the nature of change and to envision at least partially which direction current developments are leading us. We cannot afford not to, given the status of adult education in society today.

It is a privilege to teach adults, to see them opening up to new ideas, new possibilities, fighting to gain more autonomy in their lives, acquiring a better understanding of what is at stake within their families, workplaces and communities. If adult educators are not interested in the current economic and social evolution, they will slow down the learning processes of adults.

Such an understanding is imperative for adult educators. Our role and responsibilities have been questioned and critiqued for many years. Boshier and others in the 1960s applied a psychoanalytic model to adult education. This model asserted that people should aspire to establish or maintain the state of "homeostasis," or inner balance. Since social changes often upset adult learners, educators, according to this view, must work with them to gain a better understanding of, if not an adaptation to, the new situation. It was assumed that the adults' needs originated in a state of disequilibrium or lack of self-confidence or of specific tools. Responding to whatever these needs were re-established the state of harmony, resulting in a regained sense of well-being. The adult's motivation was believed to have its source in a deficit state.

According to Boshier, this focus on the learner had its foundations in the work of Carl Rogers (1972) and Malcolm Knowles (1980, 1984), based on the work of Dewey, who described the necessity of taking into account learners' needs and interests. Boshier calls these needs, which refer to the inner thrust one feels to overcome obstacles and to face challenges for the sake of the pleasure and growth it brings, "heterostatic" needs. However, this approach that focuses solely on the personal growth of the learner might have been appropriate in the 1960s but is counter-productive today, when social and planetary needs demand our attention as well.

Leirman (1987) writes of the difficulty adult educators currently face, as we are challenged in both theory and practice. The economic and social crises of the 1980s and 1990s calls for a new paradigm. His proposed social communicative paradigm demands constant ecological and social analysis on a micro/individual and macro/collective or societal level. Work must be done to find new approaches and strategies for meeting the requirements for an ecological education. The new context calls for educator consciousness and courage.[1]

Criticism of adult education is stronger and harsher today than ever. Briton and Plumb (1993) charge that it has been commodified—used by the dominant elite as a commodity, an easy means to have workers accept the new economic evolution as irrevocable. Commodification is a capitalist restructuring strategy that uses education for its own interests, disregarding the needs of the individual and the community.

We have an ethical obligation to help adults make sense of this capitalist restructuring strategy. Workers or communities that become aware of what is really at stake must make their own choice: to accept or to resist the status quo. As professionals who work with the educational aspect of adults' lives, we cannot be indifferent, for having no commitment is a clear choice for the status quo, and is that what we really want? Scholars and adult educators who refuse to acknowledge the current shift are bound to reproduce the traditional way of seeing reality as well as concepts and educational methodology that have become obsolete.

Tarnas (1996) suggests that if we are to understand this moment in our history and where we are heading, we need to know what brought us to this point. Thus, to understand the current condition of adult education, we must know its foundations. Paradigm, according to Di Carlo (1996), is a set of values, concepts and assumptions about humanity and nature that directs each culture's way of being and acting. And, as Kuhn (1962) stated, paradigm is part of the foundation of every discipline.

The Dominant Paradigm

Tarnas (1996) points out that all the necessary conditions are in place for a paradigm shift, that in fact we are in the midst of one, whether we are aware of it or not. What follows is an examination of the dominant paradigm under whose rules and values we have lived for most of our lives.

The Concept of Paradigm

Paradigm as a concept has made an appearance in literature only relatively recently. The term's connotation varies in the many articles and books written on the subject. The first use can be traced to Kuhn's 1962 book *The Structure of Scientific Revolution*. Kuhn stated that a paradigm is related to the foundation of a discipline or a field of research; he explained the way a paradigm becomes outdated and the mechanisms by which a new one emerges to replace it. There are many levels within a field or a science, each having its own paradigm. For example, Tarnas states that there are currently eight different paradigms of reality in quantum physics. That example gives us an idea of how complex reality is. A scientific paradigm is a give-and-take relationship within a cultural worldview, each influencing the other.

DiCarlo (1996) equates paradigm with worldview, suggesting that a world-view is a global paradigm. In the context of this chapter, the term paradigm is used according to the definition drawn from Tarnas's work, which is the most complete definition. Tarnas (1996) states that a worldview is

> a set of values, of conceptual structures, of implicit assumptions or presupposi-tions about the nature of reality—about human beings, about the nature of the relationship between human beings and nature, about history, the divine, the cosmos—which constellate an entire culture's way of being and acting (p. 21).

At any given time in a culture, Tarnas contends, there is an "overarching meta-paradigm" that underlines and affects everything else and is in a recipro-cal or synchronous relationship to all the "sub-paradigms" found in domains such as psychology, religion and philosophy. This overarching meta-paradigm is changing right now along with many paradigms in many fields.

Under what conditions does a shift in worldview or paradigm take place? Many factors come into play, such as scientific discoveries that call into question old assumptions and archaic ideas; or new technologies that render certain methods of working obsolete. New ideas are infiltrating large sections of a slowly evolving culture. The death of thinkers who represented the old paradigm, according to Tarnas, brings flexibility and more freedom of expres-sion to younger scientists with different viewpoints. A shift has also occurred in the "archetypal configuration of the collective psyche" (Tarnas, 1996, p. 22), a basic image that a collectivity clings to, such as how a society sees itself or what constitutes femininity or masculinity.

A shift in one's worldview is a profound experience, and an individual or a collectivity must reach a state of readiness in order to accept such a shift. Kuhn wrote that such a move was comparable to a "conversion experience." Tarnas uses the analogy of a perinatal process where one has been kept for a specific period of time within a conceptual womb, a "matrix of thought"; but one day, this "habitat" becomes too confining for a developing mind and then a crisis erupts. Following a "very critical" period of transition in which ten-sions are high and a feeling of disorientation exists, a deconstruction takes place and a sudden new birth occurs, bringing a "sudden revelation of a new universe"; a new birth on an intellectual level. For Tarnas, it involves a "very deep archetypal death and rebirth process" (Tarnas, 1996, p. 24). Such strong experiences are found in history in events such as the dissolution of the communist empire in Eastern Europe and the sudden, euphoric renewal after the fall of the Berlin wall.

Most people tend to gather evidence to support their worldviews; con-sciousness is the means by which we realize the assumptions and principles that underlie our views of reality. In creating our realities, we are also trans-formed by them. This subject-object relationship appears to be becoming more interactive than before, and the mutuality calls for a greater awareness of our principles of interpretation. Reality is not, these days, an absolute, a kind of fate or God's will over which people have no control. Reality itself is shifting, the biblical creation was not over after the seventh day, contrary to what every Occidental religion has held as true. Today we are living in a deconstructionist period. Many long-cherished principles have been swept away, leading to a radical transformation of all aspects of our culture. According to Tarnas, we now seem to be reaching a new moment, a cyclical acceleration in this transformation and perhaps a culmination to it (p. 27).

Paradigm Description

> The universe is not to be narrowed down to the limits of our own understanding, which has been the practice up to now, but our understanding must be stretched and enlarged to take the image of the universe as it is discovered (DiCarlo, 1996, p. 35).

When a society is experiencing a paradigm shift, the rules of the dominant paradigm are still followed in daily life while the new paradigm emerges. According to Capra (1983), until now the vision of the universe held by scientists was also used as a basis for political and social organization. In order to facilitate the understanding of a great deal of information in describing the dominant paradigm, categorization here begins with the universe's characteristics, followed by social and educational components. The underlying worldview will emerge as the descriptive details accumulate. Major elements of the paradigm are highlighted in a table at the end of this chapter.

The Dominant Paradigm: The Universe's Characteristics

The scientists living at the time the dominant paradigm was forming—Copernicus, Kepler, Galileo and Newton—conceptualized a mechanical view of nature and the world. Capra (1983) described Newton's vision of the universe as a "huge mechanical system which relies upon precise mathematical laws" (p. 56). This universe was viewed as stable; it had a static nature and was composed of solid matter. In explaining the organization of the universe, Newton used the metaphor of a clock, with God as the powerful "clock maker." In his age, a strong belief in determinism and prediction was very much alive. The laws of the universe were simple, easy to explain and understand. The causality was linear; one cause produced one effect. Explanations were possible by going backwards to successive causes, with God as the ultimate, supreme cause. The paradigm called for faith—God's order could not be questioned, as the Catholic Church's history clearly shows.

The Dominant Paradigm: Social Characteristics

The "divine" order described in the above section was applied to society, and thus legitimized the existence of social classes where the rich had power and wealth and the poor were deprived of such possibilities. Following God's model, humanity created machines to do its work, which led to the Industrial Revolution (Ackoff & Gharajedaghi, 1985). The Industrial Revolution led to greater autonomy and freedom and the development of a critical intelligence at least among the elite, which resulted in their exercising some control over nature and the world. People explored new horizons and overcame past limitations. A strong desire for the control of nature pushed aside humanity's responsibility to it, resulting in pollution and the disappearance of many animal and vegetable species, and endangering human life itself. In social organization, institutions were hierarchical, rigid and offered intense resistance to changes that did not promote their own interests. Management was characterized by authoritarianism and paternalism; authority was closely linked to social rank regardless of one's competency.

The main value in this paradigm is individualism, which leads to strong competition among individuals and, on a collective level, confrontations such as international wars. There is a powerful tendency towards uniformity as a means to control the population, which results in a relative social homogeneity and comfort for government. Pursuit of material wealth, which brings power, glory and symbolic capital, is considered a worthy goal in life. The individual appears to be an isolated, "mechanical" being who can be manipulated from the outside. Behaviourism brings a "scientific" view of people's behaviour through psychology. Darwin's theory of evolution gives scientific proof of the so-called "natural order," justifying the law of the strongest, which in turn legitimizes aggression and violence. Behaviourism, Darwinism and Christian religions interact to form the ideological basis of this order. Most of these principles are still predominant today.

In this paradigm, rigorous analysis was the main tool in the quest for knowledge and this led, over time, to a way of looking at the world known as reductionism. Reductionism is a process that studies life through dissection in order to find its essence; but the mysteries remain unsolved. In the scientific world, the atom was discovered and thought to be the smallest part of matter; it was believed to be solid and static.

The Dominant Paradigm: Educational Characteristics

In the dominant paradigm, education follows society's general pattern, the industrial model, which has as its objective the production of skilled workers and is not concerned with human development. Schools are organized like factory production lines; everyone, regardless of their capability, passes through the same processes. The teacher is considered an expert who has knowledge, power and authority. People are seen as mechanical beings, into whom knowledge must be poured; learning, therefore, is defined as giving information to students, who memorize it and repeat it in an acceptable form in an examination. Students are socialized to be good workers and good consumers; in short, to be the kind of citizens the elite needs in order to maintain power and flourish.

Adult learners' education mostly follows a common pattern in the dominant paradigm. They have little or no input into the objectives, content and time schedules of the learning activities. Their experiences are generally ignored, and there is an assumption that nothing can be learned from them. In practical terms, at least in my regional adult educational system, it means short-term training centered on profitability and efficiency, with minimal institutional resources invested. Adults' personal needs are not considered; the training is aligned with needs of business without much consideration for the personal development of the learner.

Plumb (1993) contends that mainstream adult education—the academic model—is effectively designed as a production line in order to meet workplace requirements; the Fordist model is dominant, in which students are gathered in a precise location, thus facilitating control. Knowledge is compartmentalized and presented without any context and learning is carefully measured through continuous assessment and controlled by professors and teachers. Such education is believed by its practitioners to be apolitical. The result of such an education is, according to Freire (1994), a "domestication of man's critical faculties ... he is massified" (p. 34). In such a context, individuals are alienated from others, nature and the environment.

The Emergent Paradigm

Einstein once said that

> creating a new theory is not like destroying an old barn and erecting a skyscraper in its place. It is rather like climbing a mountain, gaining new and wider views, discovering unexpected connections between our starting point and its rich environment. But the point from which we started out still exists and can be seen, although it appears smaller and forms a tiny part of our broad view by the mastery of the obstacles on our adventurous way up (Einstein & Infeld, 1938, p. 152).

Shouldn't we also enlarge our own points of view?

As Capra (1983) among others has shown, a "new order" is wearing away the old one. In this section, new elements are identified that reveal orientations that signal the emergence of the new paradigm. Because the paradigm is currently unfolding, no one can predict exactly what it is going to be or where it is going to go, and therefore a precise description is not possible.

The Emergent Paradigm: The Universe's Characteristics

At the beginning of this century, atomic research produced a significant breakthrough in physics, and the discoveries of Einstein, Bohrs and others resulted in a new worldview. For the first time matter was perceived to be energy, dynamic and always in motion. Capra described matter as "energy bundles," and Einstein's quantum theory introduced the concept of wave-particle duality. Depending on one's point of view, it was shown that matter may be perceived as a wave or as a particle. This paradoxical finding came as a shock for the classical physicists and had an impact far beyond the realm of science. It raised the question of objectivity in scientific research, demonstrating that researchers do influence their findings.

Einstein's theory of relativity put aside notions of time and space, revealing how illusory they were. His conclusions contradicted major beliefs held by classical physics on the predictability and reversibility of time. It was seen as well that causality was multi-directional rather than linear and this breakthrough influenced the worldview in the emerging paradigm. Although it seemed to some extent that the laws of the universe no longer applied and that chaos had taken over, at the same time a new order appeared that accommodated a larger complexity. Thom (1980) and other theorists from a variety of fields put forward their holistic, organic, ecological visions of reality. Their theories implied interdependence among people, nature and nations.

Parallel to these developments, in the emerging paradigm a bridge was being built between life's sciences and nature's sciences by the formulation in thermodynamics of the law of entropy, which postulates matter's tendency toward inertias and neugentropy, which is matter's increase in complexity. In the field of biology workers have discovered that all living organisms have the characteristic of "self-organization," an extremely important discovery since it links nature to humans, who also have the basic capabilities of autonomy, self-reliance and self-determination.

Epistemology has undergone important changes too. Since Descartes, analysis has been the major tool used in the quest for knowledge. Since World War II, however, its methodological insufficiencies have been apparent and its intellectual dominance as a method of inquiry strongly questioned. A new approach to epistemology was introduced, called "systems analysis," which took into account the interdependent relationship between elements within a given system. Systems analysis holds that if one element is manipulated, all the others are affected. The method allows researchers to better deal with complexity, which was avoided at all cost by scientists during the Newtonian period.

Nearly every science is breaking away from its history during this unfolding of a new paradigm, and new disciplines are emerging. Previous human limitations are being pushed aside.

The Emergent Paradigm: Social Characteristics

The impact of our changing worldview is evident everywhere in society. In the 1990s, we are in the middle of this transformation and are in a time of deep crisis. It has been said that the capitalist elite is carrying out a hegemonic plan that is restructuring the economy at a global level. Political power resides in the boards of directors, which are committed only to the realization of their own projects; the public figures who represent political power are becoming mere figureheads.

A major feature of the emerging paradigm is that economic production has led to a service economy where administration, research, health and education play major roles. Globalization of the economy has resulted in a major restructuring of the workplace, profoundly modifying workers' tasks. Manual work has in many cases given way to work requiring specific intellectual abilities and to technical and professional jobs requiring higher education. Theoretical knowledge is growing in importance, since it supplies the tools to master innovations and oversee an organization's development. New technologies are bringing some systematization of research methodologies and problem-solving techniques. Information has overtaken natural resources as the raw material of production. Computer technology allows organizations to deal quickly with huge amounts of data, and the information infrastructures are developing quickly; the possibilities are enormous. The "global village" is now a reality and has been followed by the globalization of all situations and issues, such as the degradation of the environment through pollution (air, water, soil), deforestation, damage to the ozone layer and global warming.

Widespread technological developments have produced new opportunities for job creation and further expansion of business. The transformation of communication technologies has presented learners with opportunities to learn independently, without attending an educational institution. Audio-visual technology, such as computers and video games, are commonplace in our homes, modifying our way of life. But this massive technological development and the ensuing restructuring have had huge social costs: high rates of unemployment and increased poverty, suffering and desperation, resulting in greater incidences of illness and suicide. Family violence, homelessness and drug consumption are on the rise. This systemic crisis of late capitalist society, according to Welton (1995), results from the illegitimate intrusion of state and corporate steering mechanisms into the "lifeworld" of people, so that the elite may retain control of the directions of these processes.

On the political level, there is a certain transnational uniformity of neo-conservative ideology regardless of a party's line. Populations have lost confidence in politicians and in public institutions where one finds yesterday's answers often are put forward as today's problems. A large part of the population is politically demobilized. The economic elite manages to control the political agenda, and our politicians are reduced to the role of puppets, selling to the public the ideological rhetoric of the neo-conservative agenda. It is within this context of rupture and mutation, of "dreadful neo-conservative times," to use Welton's expression, that ideas linked to the new paradigm are slowly and subtly pervading society and bringing some hope.

According to Harman (1996), there is a movement towards a more unifying and participatory worldview, one that counteracts the feeling of separation people experience and brings a sense of connection with the whole. There is a resurgence of what could be called the feminine archetype, encompassing healing possibilities associated with women. Perhaps there is a new openness from men about feminine values. A new sensibility is developing with respect to how humans relate to nature. And many people, exploring ways to make their lives more meaningful, have been drawn to alternative ways of understanding spirituality, many of them linked to Eastern mysticism. Such paths lead individuals to psychedelic experiences, eco-feminist spirituality, liberation theology and other forms of inner quests. The transformation process is a complex, multi-level experience, affecting every aspect of one's personality, as Giddens (1991) contends. Many people are now experiencing a paradigm shift at the personal, individual level. (See Candy, 1982; Mezirow, 1991.)

Other values are also emerging in this new paradigm. Globalization has taught people that they live in an interdependent world. The concept of the global village has brought people together in solidarity, exchanging the ethos of competition for that of co-operation. There is a trend to replace authoritarian hierarchy with authority based on competence regardless of age, gender or social class. People want to have a greater part in the decision-making process when the consequences will be felt for years to come. People have become more respectful of differences and are relatively better able to cope with them. A search for equality can be observed on the levels of gender, class, race and age. We can summarize by saying that in the emerging paradigm, human beings organize their world according to their real potentials and needs.

The global situation as we have come to see it is in a state of deep transformation with many economic, social and educational problems. The capitalist restructuring process, using a powerful neo-conservative ideology, is now taking over the interpretation of social reality. Under that hindering influence, educational policy makers' priorities have radically changed.

Impact on Education and Adult Educators

The new way of looking at the world and at ourselves includes a rejection of the traditional educational process. The academic system must become more open. Barchechath (1988) sees the promise of schools "without walls or any boundaries, such as age, linked with communication networks and with networks of large educational resource systems" (p. 13).

A renewed educational philosophy must take into account the learner's interdependent place in the world. Gang (1996) refers to an education that "should be the drawing forth of the innate spirit of each human being—not a set of imposed restrictions that squelch the spirit" (p. 256). Educators must shift their focus from teaching content to responding to the individual's learning process. Emphasis will be placed on participation, responsibility and autonomy, including respect for the learner's pace and preferred ways of learning. Learners, too, must shift their positions from consumers of knowledge to producers of information and knowledge (Lesourne, 1988; Barchechath, 1988; Rose 1996). Self-directed learning might become an important model in adult education, if it is purified of its distorted use (see Collins, 1995; also, see the chapter "Self-Directed Learning: Highlighting the Contradictions" by Chovanec in this volume).

There is a shift in the educator's role. With the evolution of new technology, educators may become guides, facilitators, as Rogers (1972) put it; become learners as well as educators according to Freire (1974). Weil (1986) uses the term *mentor*. A renewed education calls for new strategies, such as experiential learning, discovery learning and co-operative learning, as well as new techniques, formats and approaches. Educational practices are evolving towards a multi-disciplinary approach. In this context, structure must be flexible, and artificial barriers dispensed with.

Two major trends have appeared in adult education: (1) responding to the employer's demands to increase the worker's capabilities and output, and (2) encouraging adults to follow a critical path to understanding what is really at stake at this new juncture and to acquire "tools" for action. As never before, all categories of workers must study on a continuous basis in order to keep up with the rapid evolution of information, technology and knowledge.

An examination of the foundations of adult education brings to the fore other issues that call for re-examination, such as curriculum and programs. Educating future adult educators presents crucial choices. Will they be dedicated to the elite or to the adult learner's personal, community and social learning objectives? Educators must develop their skills in critical thinking, and is that not what real education is all about?

There are many trends and positions to be found within the field of adult education, ranging from accommodation to the economic system's demands to an adult education deeply committed to community and social needs of adult learners. The latter is referred to as the emancipatory perspective where the educator should work "in the defense of the lifeworld," to use Welton's expression, the lifeworld being the "realm of intersubjective interaction" where most adult learning occurs. Welton (1995) suggests that adult education should shift from an individualist, psychological focus to one that is grounded in social and historical contexts, that it become a field centred on social learning rather than one centred on the individual's learning processes. The debate is broad and deep, and it is far from over.

Conclusion

There is more than one way of perceiving issues in adult education at the end of the twentieth century. The field is facing what Giddens calls some "fateful moments," resulting in "problematic events which necessitate decisions with far-reaching consequences" (Giddens, 1991, p. 155). Adult educators are aware that their discipline has changed significantly in the last few decades. In 1989, Apps concluded that adult educators had already "fallen behind and out of step with the main body of the parade." Now, years later, what are our thoughts? How should we react? Can we remain undisturbed when the "language of possibility" has become the "language of despair," according to Giroux (1992)? The precarious status of adult educators and the absence of a public debate about new policies, at least in my area, have left crucial questions unanswered. I agree with Apps that doing nothing and missing the opportunity to influence this re-orientation could be a tragedy.

It is hoped that readers have gained some insight through the lens of a paradigm shift by our examination of how our reality has moved from a Newtonian view of the universe, with static and predetermined situations, to a more Einsteinian, fluid evolution where events occur at a global level, influencing many if not all aspects of community and of individual lives. Tarnas (1996) contends we are at the climax, a culmination point at which directions are being taken that change the way we perceive ourselves and our world and how we live our day-to-day lives at work and at home. The education of adults is, of course, affected deeply by this change.

In this time of crisis, it is best to explore as many angles as we can. We need to develop a "consciousness" of the paradigm. Being conscious might be the only viable choice, since the elite's henchmen have been at work for a long time and they are ahead of us with the most sophisticated technological tools and nearly unlimited financial resources. In my most pessimistic moments, I think that there is not much we can do. In my optimistic moments, I am more inclined to believe that heightening people's consciousness is *the* way to go, for we never know the amount of creativity a human spirit holds and what it can do in order to survive. Many heroes appear unexpectedly in a critical moment. I believe we should have faith in human beings.

Endnotes

[1]   One has to remember that a nuclear war was still a possibility at that specific time; today the courage called for might have a different orientation.

5

Trends in Adult Education in the 1990s

Claudie Solar

This chapter explores trends in adult education in the 1990s based on an examination of articles appearing in seven Canadian, American and international academic journals between 1990 and 1994.[1] The approach used here was defined partly by my views and values and partly by my knowledge of today's issues in adult education, by content analysis, and by the periodicals selected. In the first section of this chapter, the articles are reviewed; the second section takes stock of current trends in adult education and future possibilities.

The journals analyzed for this study include:

- *Adult Education Quarterly* (AEQ)
- *Canadian Journal for the Study of Adult Education/Revue canadienne pour l'étude de l'éducation des adultes* (CJSAE)
- *Canadian Journal of University Continuing Education/Revue canadienne de l'éducation permanente universitaire* (CJUCE)
- *Éducation permanente* (EP)
- *International Journal of Lifelong Learning* (IJLE)
- *Perspectives* (PER)
- *Studies in the Education of Adults* (SEA)

Each journal had to meet three criteria for inclusion in the study. First, it had to be academic yet of a general nature, accessible and representative of the Western world or of an international perspective. Second, it had to cover research in French and English, in North America as well as in Europe, with attention paid to the international perspective. Last, each journal had to be readily available in university libraries.

Table 5-1: Journal Titles and Data on Articles

	Journals	Origin	n_	Art	Fre	Eng
1.	Adult Education Quarterly (AEQ)	American	18	79		79
2.	Canadian Journal for the Study of Adult Education/Revue canadienne pour l'étude de l'éducation des adultes (CJSAE)	Canadian	9	40	16	24
3.	Canadian Journal of University Continuing Education (CJUCE)/ Revue canadienne de l'éducation permanente universitaire	Canadian	8	35	2	33
4.	Éducation permanente (EP)	French	16	262	262	
5.	International Journal of Lifelong Learning (IJLE)	International	18	95		95
6.	Perspectives (PER)	International	12	51	51	
7.	Studies in the Education of Adults (SEA)	British	9	61		61
	Total		**90**	**623**	**331**	**292**

The final selection includes one American, one British, two Canadian, one French and two international journals. One of the international publications, *Perspectives*, is distinct in that it only publishes solicited articles and covers the entire field of education. It was decided to include this journal because of its international role, its emphasis on basic education and the view of continuing education that it promotes.

As Table 5-1 indicates, 623 articles published in ninety issues were analyzed, 331 written in French and 292 in English, or 53 percent and 47 percent respectively. The slightly higher French percentage may be explained by the number of articles published in *Éducation permanente*. This publication contributed 42 percent of the total of articles and 79 percent of the total of articles in French. The two bilingual Canadian journals reveal different approaches. The CJSAE maintains a balance between the two official languages; however, the CJUCE published only two articles in French during the selected time period.

Methodology

The methodology applied is a content analysis (Bardin, 1977), with each article assigned to one single theme. The content of each article was analyzed

Table 5-2: Overview of Categories

Categories	Themes	Art	%
Adults	12	99	15.9
Adult Education Sector	8	75	12.0
Adult Educators	2	37	5.9
Content	4	34	5.5
Evaluation	3	55	8.8
Fields of Practice	5	135	21.7
Foundations and Approaches	13	171	27.4
Technology	2	17	2.7
Total	**49**	**623**	**100%**

and the main semantic unit in the title was retained. The methodology used has certain limitations. The analysis is primarily qualitative, and the classification is based on the study of the main theme as it is stated in the article title. Inevitably, the variety of viewpoints is lost, as the titles tend to relate to several themes. This classification system also presents an inherently subjective bias tempered by the fact that the purpose of the research was to tease out current trends in adult education based on frequency of publication per theme.

The tables in the following pages correspond to the categories and the themes generated through coding. What follows directly is an overview of the classification system.

Categories

From the coded articles, eight categories were developed thematically using forty-nine themes: Adults, Adult Education Sector, Adult Educators, Content, Evaluation, Fields of Practice, Foundations and Approaches and Technology. The largest category was Foundations and Approaches, followed closely by Fields of Practice. These last two categories comprise more than 20 percent of the total number of articles.

Adults

The Adults category contains articles concerned with two broad dimensions of adult learning and adults. A dimension that focuses on the adult in a general way contains thirty articles (4.8 percent of the total), with themes such as adult development, adult learning, and adult motivation and needs. Half the articles in this group focus on motivation. The second dimension, which fo-

Table 5-3: Adults

Category	Themes	Art	%
Adults	Managers (EP)[1]	16	2.6
	Motivation	15	2.4
	Workers	13	2.1
	Employees (EP)	11	1.8
	Women	8	1.3
	Specific Clienteles	7	1.1
	Adult Learning	6	1.0
	Immigrants and Refugees	5	0.8
	Needs	5	0.8
	The Less Educated[2] (EP)	5	0.8
	Adult Development	4	0.6
	Seniors	4	0.6
Total		**99**	**15.9**

[1] The initials representing the title of a journal appear in parentheses when all the articles within a theme appeared in that journal.
[2] The "less educated" refers here to adults with little formal schooling.

cuses on specific constituencies of adults with the field of adult education, contains sixty-nine articles (11.1 percent of the total) These articles deal with issues centred on diversity.

Despite an increase in the aging population, articles on senior learners do not represent a large proportion of the total articles. Immigrants, migrants and refugees appear as new themes in recent years. Despite the diversity of learners, a large number of publications deal with people who are employed or will be employed as managers or general workers. For this group, there were forty articles (58 percent of the texts written about learners and 6.4 percent of the total number of texts). Some twenty-seven of these articles appeared in *Éducation permanente*. Workers, both men and women, are the topic of twenty-three articles, or one-third of the texts on clienteles and 3.7 percent of the total number of texts. The less-educated members of the population were studied in connection to training or entering the labour force and could, as a result, be included with the twenty-three articles on workers. Seven articles deal with other specific clienteles. They are listed here in decreasing order as adult learners in prison, in agriculture and in schools.

Table 5-4: Adult Education Sector

Category	Themes	Art	%
Adult Education Sector	Globalization	27	4.3
	Organization	16	2.6
	History	8	1.3
	Policies	6	1.0
	School (PER)	6	1.0
	Higher Education	4	0.6
	Funding	4	0.6
	Future Perspectives	4	0.6
Total		**75**	**12.0**

Adult Education Sector

The adult education sector as a category includes themes on organization, history, funding and policy in adult education. Two themes include a substantial number of articles. The first is globalization (twenty-seven articles), which deals with the situation in Europe and other continents. This theme also compares countries or examines the adult education sector in developing and industrialized countries. The second theme is organization (eight of sixteen articles) and it focuses on how adult education is organized in Canada, particularly given the attrition of continuing education centres and ongoing training units. The number of articles addressing this theme points clearly to the impact of budget cuts on adult education in Canada.

The six policy articles focus on access to adult education and reduction in training policies, a reflection of the economic crisis in Canada and abroad. Last, studies on the future of adult education attempt to anticipate which direction should be taken to ensure the field's well-being in the next century.

Adult Educators

Few articles deal with the diversity of people working in adult education or with the diversity of viewpoints in the field. The eighteen articles describing those active in adult education examine the individual as instructor, educator in correctional services, consultant, historian and poet. Profiles of adult educators are the forte of *Perspectives* (which includes a teacher profile column in each issue) and *Studies in the Education of Adults* (eleven articles).

Table 5-5: Adult Educators

Category	Themes	Art	%
Adult Educators	Personalities	19	3.0
	Adult Educators	18	2.9
Total		**37**	**5.9**

Table 5-6: Content

Category	Themes	Art	%
Content	Writing (EP)	15	2.4
	Languages	11	1.8
	Environment	4	.06
	Curriculum	4	.06
Total		**34**	**5.5**

Table 5-7: Evaluation

Category	Themes	Art	%
Evaluation	Prior Learning Assessment and Competence Inventories	27	4.3
	Orientation (EP)	26	4.2
	Evaluation	2	0.3
Total		**55**	**8.8**

Table 5-8: Fields of Practice

Category	Themes	Art	%
Areas of Intervention	Labour Market	62	10
	Firms (EP)	34	5.5
	Competencies	22	3.5
	Literacy	10	1.6
	Miscellaneous	7	1.1
Total		**135**	**21.7**

Content

With only thirty-four articles, Content is not a large category. A significant percentage of these articles come from *Education permanente*, which published fourteen articles on adults and writing in issue 102 (1990) and thirteen articles on foreign-language training in issue 107 (1991).[2]

The relatively few articles in this category confirms Landry's (1992) conclusion about general adult education research journals: articles on subject content are more likely to be published in specialized journals devoted to the subject of teaching adults in whatever discipline is the focus of the journal. Furthermore, a theme such as foreign language instruction is treated differently in anglophone countries than it is in francophone countries. Because English is becoming the international language, learning foreign languages is barely covered in English-language articles.

Evaluation

There were fifty-five articles on Evaluation, forty-eight of them published in *Éducation permanente*. Articles on prior learning assessment (PLA) and competencies inventories and their orientation to professional, industrial and job training perhaps indicate the value attributed to the adult learner's existent experience and knowledge, as well as the need for people to be adaptive. In fact, the articles on PLA and competencies inventories focus on employment rather than integration into a curriculum.

Fields of Practice

The category Fields of Practice covers topics of major concern for adult educators and researchers. More than 20 percent of the total number of articles in the corpus fell into this category, which includes competencies, labour market and workplaces. Almost all the articles focus on labour and the economy. Some 118 articles deal with one of the three themes listed above, representing 18.9 percent of the total. Literacy lags far behind with ten titles. It does, however, constitute the second greatest concern in the Fields of Practice category. The fact that specialized literacy journals exist, such as *Adult Basic Education*, explains the small number of articles on this topic in the general publications. Interestingly, there was only one article within the literacy theme on scientific literacy. Lastly, the theme "miscellaneous" includes articles on museums, leisure, family life and three other titles that did not fit anywhere in the categorization applied here.

Foundations and Approaches

This category contains the largest number of articles (25 percent). It also contains themes that are weighted in a clearly different fashion. The theme of

Table 5-9: Foundations and Approaches

Category	Themes	Art	%
Foundations and Approaches	Approaches and Models	33	5.3
	Foundations	31	5.0
	Social Practices	20	3.2
	Self-instruction	17	2.7
	Learning	13	2.1
	Feminism	12	1.9
	Multiculturalism	11	1.8
	Work/Study	10	1.6
	Democracy	7	1.1
	Teaching	6	1.0
	Knowledge	5	0.8
	Partnership	4	0.6
	Groups	2	0.3
Total		**171**	**27.4**

Table 5-10: Technology

Category	Themes	Art	%
Instructional Media	Technology	11	1.8
	Distance Education	6	1.0
Total		**17**	**2.7**

groups is treated in only two publications; at the other extreme, the approaches and models theme has thirty-three articles. There are articles on adult learning, learning by experience, non-formal learning, cognitive styles, cognition, and work/study (learning in the context of work). Self-instruction was described primarily from the perspective of self-directed learning.

Approaches and models focuses primarily on comprehension in learning and learning objectives and rarely focuses on teaching. A major proportion of the titles (twenty articles) within this theme relate to critical theory, be it the development of critical thinking or perspective transformation according to the writings of Mezirow (1978a, 1978b, 1985). All texts relate to critical theory and with only one exception are written in English. Seven of the articles are included in a special issue of the CJSAE devoted to this topic (1991, v. 5).

Feminism and multiculturalism account for twelve and eleven articles, respectively, demonstrating the questioning inherent in the increased diversity of viewpoints and the need for inclusion. Here the feminism focus deals primarily with critical epistemology and the development of models integrating women; multiculturalism covers ethno-cultural diversity and inter-cultural education. These two themes are related to the theme of democracy (seven articles) as a desirable goal. All articles on feminism appeared in Canadian or English-language journals. The special issue of CJSAE on this theme had not yet been published when this research was carried out (1994, v. 8).

The theme of foundations deals with the nature, principles and philosophy of adult education. Discussed are the learning society (*cité éducative*), the goals of adult education, the field of adult education and ethics and research in adult education. Social practices includes articles on change, community action, participatory research, praxis and local or regional development.

Technology

Only seventeen articles appear under Technology, making this the smallest category. Distance education contains six articles, a low number that makes it apparent that most articles on this topic are published in specialized journals. The eleven articles on technology cover computers, "intellectual" technology and the effects of the new technologies.

Summary

From a content analysis of the articles, 49 themes emerged. Most important among them were labour market (62 titles); work organizations (34); approaches and models (33); foundations (31); globalization (27); prior learning assessment and competencies inventories (27); orientation (26); competencies (22); and social practices (20). Each of these was the theme of at least twenty articles. Given the way in which themes were regrouped in the analysis, as described in the presentation of the data, the thematic grouping on labour market tops the list. Table 5-11 illustrates this order. This new configuration also highlights as key topics all adult clienteles, learning, adults in the workplace, and democracy and adults.

Discussion and Focus

These results reveal how the current preoccupation with the economy, the job market and labour force training has had a tremendous impact on adult education. In fact, the concentration on these themes is even greater than the

Table 5-11: Themes and Thematic Groupings

	Themes and Thematic Groupings	Art
1	R-Labour Market (Job Market, Competencies, Firms)	118
2	R-All Adult Clienteles	69
3	Labour Market	62
4	R-Learning (Learning, Work/Study, Self-Training)	40
5	R-Adults in Work Place (Managers, Employees, Workers)	40
6	Firms (EP)	34
7	Approaches and Models	33
8	Foundations	31
9	R-Democracy (Democracy, Feminism, Multiculturalism)	30
10	R-Adults (Adult Learning, Needs, Development, Motivation)	30
11	Globalization	27
12	Recognition of Acquired Knowledge and Competencies Inventories	27
13	Orientation (EP)	26
14	Competencies	22
15	Social Practices	20

R = Grouping

figures indicate. If all the articles about the labour market were compiled in a single group, they would total 190 articles, or 30.5 percent of the grand total. Three out of ten articles deal with the labour market, thus translating into the academic world the concern expressed by governments and the media since the recession of 1982.

The focus on employment may also be seen in the thematic groupings all adult clienteles. In this grouping, there were fifty-two articles on adults as workers. In a sense, the individual as a psychological and social being is forgotten. The emphasis on the economy and job market necessarily means less attention is paid to other aspects of life. Indeed, organizations active in adult education and research centres in the field are at the mercy of funding that follows government priorities. The Conseil supérieur de l'éducation du Québec (1992), however, suggested serving not just the so-called "paying" clienteles and remembering the social and cultural aspects of education.

Given the current economic climate, it is surprising that there are not more articles on funding (four articles) and on policy (six articles) for adult educa-tion. The economic crisis essentially is discussed in articles on the organiza-tion of adult education (sixteen articles). These articles express the concerns of departments of continuing education and extension in Canadian educational establishments, with seven of sixteen articles from the *Canadian Journal of University Continuing Education*. Another seven articles (five in the *International Journal of Lifelong Learning* and two in *Studies in the Education of Adults*) come from elsewhere in North America or from England, which has an adult education structure relatively similar to Canada's.

Learning as a thematic grouping is the fourth largest, with forty articles. None of the themes within this grouping has more than nineteen articles (3 percent of the total of articles). The threshold for inclusion in Table 5-11 was twenty articles. Twelve of thirteen articles on learning are written in English. On the topic of work/study, nine of ten articles are in French and appeared in *Éducation permanente*. The notably few articles on work/study in the English-language journals do not seem to reflect the current concern about training adapted to the workplace or with the diversity of approaches in education. For example, no article dealt with teaching and learning in co-operative programs, a possible educational approach to training.

The same grouping reveals an absence of articles on the mental processes involved in learning. Only one text treats cognition as linked to work/study programs; another addresses cognitive styles and learning. This output seems low given that this is the era of "learning to learn." Interestingly, no article in this grouping reflects the increasingly recognized important role of affectivity in learning.

Foundations and Approaches, the largest category, contributes 27 percent of the total number of articles in the study. This strong showing accurately reflects the theoretical concerns in learned journals, and an analysis of the themes gives a picture of the current trends. The theme of approaches and models heads the list of all the themes within this category and places seventh (Table 5-11). Five of thrity-three articles deal with change or transformation, drawing primarily on the work of Mezirow (1978a, 1978b, 1985). The remaining fourteen articles are divided in subject matter between critical thinking (eleven articles) and Freire's approach (three articles). Their combined total of nineteen means that more than half the articles in this theme refer to critical theory or perspective transformation. The focus of these articles shifts away from the humanist approaches or approaches based on Knowles. Perhaps the field of adult education is undergoing a paradigm shift (see the chapter "Paradigm Shifts" by Morin in this volume; Kuhn, 1962), i.e., the humanist and adult learner perspectives have been legitimated and developed, the limits of the models have been seen and the theoretical work on understanding continues (Ferguson, 1981, pp. 20-21). The theoretical perspectives are actually expanded to include aspects not covered in previous models.

This expansion is evident in a similar fashion in the theme of foundations, where three articles specifically mention andragogy in their titles. The other twenty-eight articles adopt various points of view on conceptualizing accessibility, on the learning society, non-formal education, ongoing education, or ethics. Unlike the example of critical or transformation theory in the theme of approaches and models, there is no theoretical convergence here.

The democracy grouping sits within this category (democracy, feminism, multiculturalism), which also opens the way to new paradigms. Over the past three decades, articles related to the theme of democracy have dealt with concepts of universal accessibility and the development of human potential. In texts written in the early 1990s, training for democracy (citizenship education) is treated as an educational goal in adult education. Democracy is also viewed from the standpoints of equity and diversity. Feminism, as a theme, attempts to make knowledge in adult education inclusive. On the other hand, multicul-turalism deals with inter-cultural education and the development of inter-cultural skills. Concern about an all-encompassing form of knowledge is evident within the theme of knowledge, in which five titles refer to democratization, knowledge or democracy in knowledge. The notion of democracy itself under-goes diversification and becomes more complex here, which is in harmony with the conceptualization of adult education and current social changes. The idea of democracy also fits into the view held by people active in adult education who consider their area or field of practice as one based on regional or community development and social change. This point of view, very popu-lar in the 1970s, especially in Freire's notion of praxis (1974), is still present in the twenty articles classified under the theme of social practices. As a result, there is also some continuity in the subjects covered by the publications on adult education. In effect democracy allows for work on diversity which seeks to find the relative stability of systems through successive structural adjustments.

The introduction of issues of diversity and inclusion naturally leads to the globalization theme in the adult education sector. If the thematic groupings are removed, globalization occupies fifth place, with articles that primarily present perspectives of adult education in different countries. The common thread of this subject matter reveals the global nature of information and communication conveyed through journals. However, only articles on Europe demonstrate in their titles how adult education fits into the interdependence of training from one country to the next. Of course, globalization is still in the early stages, and in a few more years a fuller picture of globalization and training will be possible, especially in foreign-language instruction.

The subject of adult as learner or as individual in training appears in Table 5-11, but only within a thematic grouping. The relative unimportance of this theme reflects a shift in thinking about adults as learners. The view of adults as workers is much more widespread, and the lower number of articles on adults as learners points to a change in trends and an acknowledgment of the economy as a decisive influence. Half the articles (fifteen) in this theme deal with motivation, and that is perhaps an indication that the field has integrated the concerns of practitioners who will be in the classroom facing adults with little motivation to learn. Government regulations in professional training and income security in North America will force some adults into training programs. Problems with motivation will thus be added to problems with using pedagogical approaches often ill-suited to adults. Literature on motivation was found primarily in *Adult Education Quarterly* and the *CJSAE* (thirteen of fifteen articles). This new context for adult learners is part of the paradigm shift in the view of the individual in adult education. The concept of the adult as an autonomous participant, learning voluntarily, negotiating the goals, means and content of his or her education is compromised by the directives coming from professional and industrial training and by the structural adjustments taking place in the economy.

Adult education is directly influenced by the current economic situation, as the example of motivation illustrates. However, some important developments do not appear in articles on adult education in the journals analyzed here because they have been published as contributions to books. As well, texts on distance education or literacy possibly published in specialized journals are not included here. However, the few articles on groups, partnerships, teaching, curriculum, technology and future perspectives may well point out a lag or an imbalance between current priorities and research in adult education.

We live in an information society, the complexity and diversity of which demands interdisciplinary work and team efforts (Delors, 1996). Our partners may be individuals, organizations, firms or countries. It is surprising to see only two articles on groups and only four articles on partnerships in the study sample. Interestingly, the World Bank (Adams, Middleton et Ziderman, 1992), the Conference Board of Canada (Lund, 1988; Bloom, 1990, 1991a, 1991b) and UNESCO (Haggis, 1991; Fordham, 1992; Windham, 1992) are all strong proponents of partnership.

Only six articles in the sample address teaching. Perhaps this relatively small number of articles attests to a view of the adult as a responsible and voluntary learner and of the educator's job as facilitating or supporting the education the adult alone determines. However, to know how adults learn is not sufficient to know how to teach them. Changes in perspective and in the economic context would necessitate further research on teaching adults and the evaluation of that teaching. The latter is discussed in only two articles.

Curriculum is also among the less popular themes. As the information age continues, as globalization sends data, competencies and technology across the planet, it would be useful to consider which subjects and what kinds of training would be most appropriate in the near future. Yet future perspectives are discussed in only four articles. Future studies or projections may be considered, together with the environment (four articles), another weak point in the corpus on adult education.

As a theme, technology looks rather like a poor relation, with eleven articles, seven of them focusing on how to use technology. Of the remaining four articles, two deal with people who are using technology or being affected by it, and the other two discuss the impact of technology on skill production or continuing education. There is little in the literature reviewed that takes a reflective approach to the subject of technology, its impact on adult education or on adults' learning about technology.

Conclusion

This attempt to outline the trends in adult education based on academic production in a sample of journals has provided an overview that reflects current concerns with the economy and with workplace training. The adult is portrayed most often as a working being. Popular education, literacy, and adult development have all lost ground. As economic needs are given increasing prominence, consideration for the needs of the adult learners themselves are left behind. Employability is considered of national importance.

A paradigm shift is taking place (see the chapter "Paradigm Shifts" by Morin in this volume). The new paradigm retains the former paradigm's views of autonomy and self-directedness in learning while including critical changes and perspective transformation. Adult education theories are accommodating diversity among adults and reflecting a new complexity in learning and knowing.

The foregoing analysis of sample journals suggests that the field of adult education has become increasingly diversified over the years. This diversification reveals a legitimate field of study that is now better equipped to deal with the complexity of current situations. However, diversification translates into fragmentation within the field, which can no longer be viewed as having a single identity. The cohesiveness of the research and subsequent articles seen during the period of legitimation is no longer needed, particularly in adult learning. The broadening of study topics and theoretical approaches has brought about a quantum leap in knowledge. Adult education is thus adapting to the reality—or realities—of this end of millennium.

Endnotes

[1] This chapter is a translation by Kathy Radford of an abridged and revised version of the article "Nouvelles tendances en éducation des adultes," published in the *Revue des sciences de l'éducation XXI*, no. 3 (1995): 443-472.

[2] The articles published in a thematic issue are not necessarily all classified under the same theme heading. The title determined the classification.

6

Confronting Issues Affecting Adult Educators

Susan May

How Canadian adult educators can prepare themselves to work effectively into the next millennium is a topic of intense interest to many in the field who are observers of the political and social landscape. We are constantly warned that "change is the only constant" in our fast-paced world. Indeed, uncertainty is widespread about what the future heralds, and opinions vary among adult educators about the ideal or desired state we're seeking. Perhaps we need to remind ourselves, like Alice in Wonderland, that "which way you go depends on where you want to get to!"

Historians have observed that only during the 1930s and 1940s did Canadian adult education constitute a social movement with goals and visions of its own (Selman & Dampier, 1991). More typically, the adult education field historically has responded to individual and societal needs and has been adaptive (Rachal, 1989). This accounts in part for adult educators' interest in learning about the changes and developments occurring among us. However, Jarvis (1992) notes that learning both "produces change and occurs as a result of it," and Elias (1995) suggests that periods of change "demand bold and risk-taking activities" (p. 40). Conversely, purely reactive approaches are likely to have negative consequences in the future.

Future visions of the adult education field are conceived and conceptualized by futurists and scholars who focus on philosophical and theoretical considerations, as well as by practitioners, who have a large stake in the adult education field's future. Most of these practitioners are rooted firmly within a specific ideology of practice (Courtney, 1989), and they grapple daily with philosophical and pragmatic issues that have long-term consequences. Therefore, using an issues framework developed by Deshler (1991) and by Gal-

braith and Sisco (1992), this chapter considers the important issues confronting Canadian adult education practitioners as a way of contemplating future
directions. The survival and integrity of the field may well depend on our
response to Heaney's (1993) observation that adult education involves "learning to swim in a sea of issues that otherwise threatens to drown us" (pp.
14-15). We need to understand the issues and to question the implications
these issues have for unifying or diversifying the adult education field.

Survey of Practitioners

In order to arrive at an idea of what the important issues influencing the
field were, I surveyed a group of adult education practitioners as a way of
projecting "a big picture." Such a picture can provide adult educators with the
background needed in order to plan individual and collective actions to guide
us into the future. As noted by Spear and Mocker (1991), a proactive approach
is warranted because the field will be influenced significantly by our positive
actions to direct it or our lack of action.

In April 1993 I mailed a pre-tested questionnaire to 227 graduates of the
Master of Adult Education program at a Canadian university. Of these, 149
questionnaires were completed and returned, representing a 66 percent return
rate. The open-ended questions I posed about issues in adult education were
part of a larger, twenty-two-question survey intended to produce a statistical
profile of program graduates and to document their contributions to the Canadian field of adult education.

Survey Respondents

The survey respondents were diverse with respect to geographic location,
age, primary practice roles and specializations. They were similar, however, in
their identification as adult educators and their Master of Adult Education
credentials. Twenty-two percent of respondents were between twenty-five and
forty-four years of age, 57 percent were between forty-five and fifty-four
years, and 21 percent were fifty-five years or older. Women comprised 66
percent of the sample, and men 34 percent. Respondents resided in every
Canadian province, with 7 percent in other countries. Thirty-nine percent had
graduated from the program within the past three years, whereas 28 percent
had graduated between four and eight years ago, 20 percent between nine and
thirteen years ago and 13 percent between fourteen and twenty-two years ago.
The largest group of respondents were employed by higher education institutions (41 percent); others were self-employed (14 percent), worked for various
levels of government (11.5 percent) or worked in health institutions (7 percent). In addition, the majority of respondents assumed primary practice roles
as administrators and co-ordinators (38 percent) or as instructors/trainers (20

percent); others worked as consultants (15 percent), as facilitators (8 percent) or as academics (5 percent).

Although the findings are not necessarily generalizable across all groups of adult educators, issues raised by those surveyed are similar to ones discussed in recent adult education publications (Deshler, 1991). Because the respondents worked in a variety of contexts, such as health education, human resources development, literacy, international development, extension education and counselling, they represented a broad range of interests and perspectives.

Trends Creating the Context

In order to establish a foundation upon which to describe and discuss issues confronting practitioners, I first questioned them about societal trends that had relevance for their future work. Doing so was consistent with Rachal's (1989) contention that adult education "has a direct and symbiotic relationship within the environment in which it occurs" (p. 3).

The aging population, changing demographics and increased racial diversity within communities were identified by practitioners as important trends. Additionally, dwindling resources, fiscal restraint, unemployment, the changing nature of work and a shrinking job market were cited frequently. The emergence of a highly technical society and environmental damage were common developments noted, as were the women's, First Nations' and consumers' movements. On a global scale, concern was expressed about world poverty and the widening gap between the "haves" and "have-nots."

With these trends serving as the backdrop, respondents identified a broad range of issues confronting them. As one respondent noted, however, it is impossible to compile a comprehensive list of issues because there is no such thing as a "generic educator." Another respondent stated, "I can only speak for myself and speculate for others since the field is so diverse." As Heaney (1993) has observed, "the identification of issues is not a minor task for educators" (p. 19), but rather a complicated and contradictory process because the issues themselves are complex and frequently context specific.

Despite the complexity of issues and the range of options offered, several respondents affirmed the importance of planning and preparing for future realities. For example, one woman noted that "futuristic thinking is important" and another commented that "keeping on top of the changing times is essential." The nature of change itself was of interest to several respondents, and they commented that change needs to be understood as a non-orderly process.

Table 6-1: Issues Confronting Practitioners

Nature of Issues	# of Respondents
Global Problems and Development	28
Accessibility and Learner Diversity	25
Educational Policy and Leadership	25
Learning Theory Advances and Applications	21
Visibility and Credibility of Field	19
Technology	16
Retraining and Career Transition	8

The Issues

Having established a context, respondents next identified a broad range of issues and developments confronting them as practitioners in the adult education field. These issues are categorized in Table 6-1.

Twenty-eight of the respondents described the urgency of global problems and development issues. Many thought that failure to act to alleviate social problems would have catastrophic results. For example, one woman identified "the environmental crisis, cultural diversity and Indigenous rights" as important concerns worldwide. In addition, several respondents suggested that community development activities should address racial, gender and class inequities in particular. In order to accomplish this, suggestions were made, such as "adult education should not confine itself to a narrow field but instead, look at society as a whole and try to develop alternative, sustainable lifestyles." Another suggestion was to internationalize curricula as a way to broaden the adult education field's perspective and to improve its responses to global issues.

Twenty-five respondents suggested that issues of accessibility and learner diversity were important. A couple of people spoke generally of "increasing accessibility of learning opportunities," and others identified specific groups as underrepresented in educational programs, including learners with low literacy skills, people living in poverty in the Third World, First Nations people and people with disabilities. Several respondents noted that educational programs needed to deal "with cultural diversity and cross-cultural relations."

Another important issue, identified by twenty-five respondents, concerned educational policy and leadership. Influencing educational policy to address social problems was advocated by some. One woman, for example, suggested that adult educators have important roles to play in "helping society face social crises such as ecology, unemployment and de-industrialization." Several other respondents proposed that the adult education field should work towards the elimination of poverty and the eradication of illiteracy, and three people specifically suggested that the field should assist women in Third World development initiatives. It was suggested by several respondents that adult educators needed to provide effective educational leadership.

Twenty-one respondents noted the impact of advances in adult learning theory and its applications. It was common for respondents to describe a wide range of new learner populations and to suggest—as Cross does (1989)—that new target groups require educators to change approaches and methods of teaching and learning. In particular, it was noted that adult educators have a responsibility to extend access to underrepresented groups, such as senior citizens, immigrants and displaced workers, and it was common for respondents to identify needs for multicultural, feminist and anti-racist learning opportunities and to advocate for Prior Learning Assessment. The educators surveyed also identified a need "to train trainers and educate educators" in a variety of settings.

Respondents proposed lifelong learning approaches as appropriate responses for assisting learners to cope with continual change in their lives. Some noted that an increased commitment to lifelong learning by employers and governments was a positive development, although they also acknowledged that, so far, lifelong learning had not translated into "seamless" learning systems or opportunities. Instead, they observed that adult learning was becoming increasingly intermittent and part time, and that frequently learners were expected to fit into particular eligibility criteria in order to access educational opportunities.

Concerns were expressed by nineteen respondents about the profession's low profile. Several of them acknowledged that the public lacks understanding about what adult education can contribute to the learning needs of individuals, organizations and communities. For example, one respondent stated, "Our colleges and universities do not know we exist! Many administrators and bureaucrats that I deal with have no idea what adult education is, nor the areas of expertise or specialization within the field." Some respondents observed that adult education programs had been perceived as less important than "regular" education programs and that increasingly practitioners were expected to operate programs on a cost recovery (or profit) basis, once again disadvantaging people of low economic status.

Related to these issues, concern was expressed by several respondents about the credibility and competence of adult educators and, in some cases, their failure to demonstrate accountability and competence. One man noted that "adult educators should lead by example; many do but many don't." In addition, one woman observed that adult educators with master degrees have less credibility among government and business employers than do people with MBA and MSW credentials. The accountability and recognition issues led some respondents to advocate for further professionalization of the field. In particular, some educators suggested that standards of practice and a code of ethics be developed. Consensus was lacking, however, on whether professional standards of practice or codes of ethics would resolve problems.

Technology and technological advances were of concern to sixteen respondents. They noted that the way adult educators communicate with learners and organize delivery systems is changing as a result of technological advances. One woman, for example, suggested that adult educators need to assess "the intrusion and/or support of communication technology and to consider how best to help people communicate with one another either with its help or in spite of it." Several persons suggested that adult educators need to question the use versus availability of information and to consider its power. Many respondents observed that a great number of technological changes had undesirable side effects and further increased the gap between developed and Third World nations.

Respondents were concerned about the worldwide economic recession and changes in the labour market, and they noted the negative impact these changes had on job retraining. Questions were raised about the relationship between the labour market and education and about the kinds of training that should be developed for particular constituencies of learners or workers in various types of employment. Specifically, one respondent suggested that "career transition is a growing area and adult educators can help in this area." Not all were so optimistic about the nature of worker retraining and career transition, however. In particular one man emphasized the importance for people "to find a place in the economy—I work, therefore I am." In some cases educators worried about the kinds and availability of jobs they were training or retraining workers for, and they were skeptical about whether useful and long-term employment would result.

Questions and Controversies

The seven major issues raised appear to exemplify Schon's (1995) description of "indeterminate zones of practice" whereby practice issues involve uncertainty, complexity, uniqueness and conflict. The problems we confront as educators preparing for the future are in many respects "ill-formed, vague and messy" (p. 28). Prior to discussing future directions and ideas for strengthening the field as they have emerged from the issues raised, it is prudent to question where we wish to position ourselves as adult educators along a variety of continua. In particular, I note that questions arise from the issues presented relating to three particular controversies: status quo/social action positions, learning/education locations, and marginalization/mainstream positions in the field.

Social Action/Status Quo

"Historically in Canada and elsewhere adult educators have played important roles in movements for social justice and reform" (Miles, 1989, p. 3). However, although historically one of adult education's purposes has been "to facilitate change in a dynamic society," another purpose has been "to support and maintain the good social order" (Beder, 1989, p. 39). I discerned tension in this regard between positions held by adult educators related to supporting the status quo and promoting social change. One respondent commented that she was "concerned about the split between adult education as skills training for conformity to the status quo and adult education as a broader field of critical thought and reflective practice." Similarly, another respondent wrote, "I'm concerned about the tension between the trend toward effective management of programs and the basic concept of education as a liberative and awareness-building process facilitated by the adult educator." These comments illustrate the conflict inherent in a field whose members identify with different social purposes and worldviews.

The majority of respondents who identified social change as being of great importance advocated for adult educators to assume proactive roles. Sustainable development and social reconstruction based on non-violent lifestyles were suggested as alternatives to current realities. Indeed, these views are consistent with Tough's (1993) observation that "a significant number of adult educators are calling for a renewed sense of social mission" (p. 233) in the field.

One woman suggested that the way to be socially responsible and "to make a difference" is to "apply knowledge to the resolution of social issues." Such application of knowledge requires understanding of the political context of education; Deshler (1991) notes in this regard that "the idea that adult education is political is still controversial in North America" (p. 399). Although recognition that knowledge is not neutral can be a threatening idea to governments and mainstream institutions that promote the status quo, it also can be a powerful tool for change for underrepresented learners such as women, racial minorities and the poor. The movement away from teacher-centred and teacher-controlled knowledge to a democratization of knowledge is necessary, according to Cunningham (1991), in order "to address the inequity in our society" (p. 375). Democratizing knowledge, however, raises some interesting questions, such as "who shall be heard and ... what kind of knowledge shall be considered legitimate?" (Group for Collaborative Inquiry, 1993).

Discussion in the field relating to the degree to which we should support the status quo or engage in social activism should not be oversimplified, nor should it be understood in terms of an either/or dichotomy. Change processes are complex, and incremental changes occur more frequently than do revolutionary changes. Many small-group and community changes at local levels have impacts globally. Furthermore, it is false to assume that all adult educators who are employed by conservative institutions or governments necessarily support the status quo. It is misleading also to assume that adult training programs designed to teach skills development cannot be useful and liberating to participants. Questioning these assumptions leads to a consideration of issues related to educators' varying perspectives on differences between learning and education.

Learning/Education

According to Selman (1989), increased attention to learning as distinct from education was championed by Alan Thomas and Roby Kidd during the 1960s and 1970s (for a fuller discussion on this distinction, see Thomas's chapter "Education of Adults and the Future" in this volume). Around the same time, Illich (1970) was promoting concepts such as deschooling and learner autonomy. To what extent then, should present-day adult educators be focusing on education and delivery systems as opposed to learning and personal matters, given that learning and education are not synonymous? A simplistic distinction frequently made between the two is that education tends to imply formal schooling whereas learning occurs both inside and outside of classrooms. In other words, "learning is something which people do, while education is a social institution which provides learning opportunities for people" (Jarvis, 1995, p. 9). Survey respondents noted that adult educators' understanding of adult learning is changing as a result of several societal and educational trends, including the decentralization of learning, different learner populations, the urgency of social problems globally and changing technologies.

Several respondents recommended that adult education initiatives be "flexible, innovative, individualized and focused on practice." Self-directed learning was promoted, as were inter-cultural and interdisciplinary education initiatives. Suggestions were also made to raise awareness about adult learning principles and to educate other educators and trainers about adult learning principles and their effective application.

However, the collective needs of learners also warrant consideration, as do educational delivery systems. Despite respondents' endorsement of self-directed learning, Kulich's (1991) concerns about it warrant attention (see "Self-Directed Learning: Highlighting the Contradictions" by Chovanec in this volume for critique of self-directed learning). He cautions educators to consider the potential danger that governments may use self-directed learning as an excuse for withdrawing financial support from adult education programs and initiatives. Specifically, he suggests that "this direction will lead to the assignment of lifelong learning as an exclusive individual responsibility and thus it will be relegated to self-help alone" (p. 105). Furthermore, Iphofen (1993) suggests that both self-directed learning and distance education approaches to learning can be misused with a hidden curriculum of passive assimilation. It can lead to private, instead of collective, investment in education and can support an ideology of privatization in which choice, flexibility and availability are only an illusion. Another potentially negative outcome of the misuse of these approaches is further marginalization of the field.

Marginalization/Mainstream

A third controversy can be presented on a continuum in which marginalization of the field is placed at one end, and the field as a mainstream activity at the other. Respondents suggested that further marginalization can be attributed in part to the breadth and diversity of the field. Educators tend to work independently and in isolation from one another, within area specializations such as literacy, human resource development, community development and environmental education, to name only a few. As a result, practitioners often lack shared experiences and a common identity.

Concerns about marginalization of the field are also reflected in the literature. Hull and Coben (1991) note that "adult education has suffered a substantial reduction in funding and has become increasingly marginalized" (p. 11). Similarly, Nyerere (1988) suggests that adult education is the "Cinderella" of government departments. Perhaps some of the marginalization can be attributed to what Edelson (1992) calls the ambiguous status of the field. Some researchers question whether adult education constitutes an independent and professional field, and others note that it is marginal because it has purposely chosen to support non-formal and non-institutionalized educational options.

Not all researchers agree that the adult education field is marginalized, however, and some note that much attention has been devoted to adult education in the 1990s. Thomas (1993), for example, suggests that adult education as a field of practice is no longer a marginal enterprise. He suggests that "the education of adults has moved to centre stage, to the top of the political agendas not only in Canada, but in most of the nations of the world" (p. 5). However, Collins (1992) contends that many such adult education programs spearheaded by governments "have to do with social control" (p. 1) rather than focusing on learning and personal development.

A proliferation of providers and programs has resulted from these identified needs, and many providers (not all of whom call themselves adult educators) are specializing in skills training, workplace learning and health education initiatives. Brockett (1991) cautions, however, that a distinction needs to be made between adult educators and those who "do" adult education within the context of other professions such as nursing and social work (p.

11). More important, perhaps, he differentiates between adult educators who do broad-based, socially significant work and program technicians who teach particular competencies. In this regard, several respondents noted the movement towards increased professionalization of the field as a positive response to ensuring high-quality projects, although an equal number of respondents viewed increased professionalization as negative and exclusionary. Concern was expressed also, about the increasing emphasis placed on *credentialing*, and what Jarvis (1995) refers to as *qualification inflation*.

Some respondents suggested that problems might be resolved if adult educators devoted more attention to practice. One woman acknowledged that "doing it right everyday is still the hard part." Several others observed that many adult educators currently are working under considerable stress, given the fiscal climate and the downsizing of many organizations and programs, and that this circumstance is likely to continue into the future. One woman noted, "I think funding cut-backs will have people justifying their existence. Educators will need skills that produce 'results' and ideas that work on the job." Another educator said that "needing to do more with less requires skills in the broader perspective—we need to focus more on merging specialists to eliminate territorial issues and duplication." This broader perspective can be fostered through action research initiatives and professional development.

Strengthening Practice through Action Research and Professional Development

Having broad-based knowledge of adult education as both a field of study and a field of practice was considered to be of great benefit to practitioners. As noted by Cervero (1991), it is wrong to view the relationship between theory and practice as either simplistic or as a problem to be solved. Instead, the theory/practice relationship is one that needs to be negotiated by real people in real situations. This view was reflected by several respondents. In particular, one man suggested that there "needs to be better linkages between applied and theoretical work." He suggested that some research be focused specifically on practice problems. Additionally, a woman respondent suggested that "we need to research how to measure outcomes of our interventions." However, there is concern about the fragmented research being conducted in Canada, and the inherent tension between basic and applied research (Garrison & Baskett, 1989). Schon (1995) describes this controversy as a research choice confronting many adult educators: "Shall he (the practitioner) remain on the high ground where he can solve relatively unimportant problems according to his standards of rigor, or shall he descend to the swamp of important problems where he cannot be rigorous in any way he knows how to describe?" (p. 28). To engage in this "swamp of inquiry," adult educators must be risk takers, as well as skilled researchers and practitioners.

Practitioner knowledge and skills could be enhanced by professional development. Therefore, respondents were asked to identify professional development needs arising from the issues and developments they noted. Of the 149 responses, 42 people selected critical thinking skills as the most important professional development need of practitioners. One woman commented that "critical thinking skills are central to my practice activities and research. I feel they are at the core of my educational pursuits." Next in order of preference, 41 people selected the application of theory to practice as a professional need. One respondent noted, however, that a distinction should be made between applying theory to practice and developing theory from practice; she believed the latter represented a more accurate and important understanding of the theory/practice relationship.

Foundational knowledge was the choice of twenty-three respondents. For example, one man remarked that "foundational knowledge is an essential base needed for understanding one's practice." In addition, four people spoke about using foundational knowledge as a basis upon which to understand the "big picture," and one woman suggested this knowledge provided "a needed foundation for skill development and decision making." Other professional development needs identified included development of program planning and research skills, critical understanding of current literature and networking. Despite practitioners' commitment to professional development, however, several of them commented that they had little time and opportunity to engage in such activities. One respondent despaired about having become little more than "a money machine" for his continuing education department.

Future Directions

According to Gayle (1990) and Thomas (1993), the field of adult education can play an increasingly important role in fostering learning and positive change on individual, community and societal levels. To do so, however, we need to consider what this future should be by considering not only societal trends and the issues facing us, but also by having a shared vision of the desirable or ideal future we are seeking. As documented in this chapter, the process is already underway, through practitioners' explorations of issues and controversies. These issues, though, can serve to further unify or diversify the field, depending on how they are conceptualized and acted on. Indeed, we can begin by questioning whether adult education is a "patternless mosaic of adult education providers, program and services" (Selman & Dampier, 1991, p. 290) or a discipline founded on shared values and principles that can accommodate interests of academics, researchers and practitioners.

Given the breadth and diversity of the adult education field, we need to question whether, and at what point, diversity becomes dissension. How feasible is it to pursue goals that, potentially at least, may conflict with one another? Is there not a danger that professionalization goals can be exclusionary? Is it not likely that closer ties with government may serve the interests of power and wealth and be detrimental to goals related to social justice and ecological sustainability? In order to direct our future as adult educators, we need to address these questions and to set clear directions for effective praxis and advocacy. Clearly, "cloistered scholarship" is not a desirable choice, nor is a two-dimensional view of the world that fails to acknowledge multiple realities.

An examination of the issues survey respondents identified reveals that many are controversial and interrelated. Practitioners offered a variety of suggestions and strategies for dealing with them. Although there was no consensus, there was a shared commitment to addressing common concerns and urgent issues confronting the field. Respondents proposed ideas and strategies intended to assist practitioners prepare for positive futures that included:

- systems and interdisciplinary approaches,
- a commitment to community-based and participatory approaches to development and research,
- recognition of, and advocacy for, the social mission of the field, and
- a higher profile.

Perhaps we can begin to operationalize these strategies by considering the breadth and diversity of our field as a strength and by envisioning ourselves as a strategic alliance of change agents working within a global learning society.

Underlying the strategies proposed were respondents' concerns about learners and communities, being practice-oriented and making a difference in people's lives. These commitments are shared by Lewis (1991), who notes that "meeting the needs of individuals while simultaneously seeing to it that learners are central in the process will remain a major tenet of adult and continuing education" (p. 626). In this regard, increased emphasis on democratization of knowledge, critical questioning, reflective practice and action research appears warranted.

As suggested by Kerka (1995), educators need to reflect upon their knowledge of the field and to question what is myth and what is reality. Then we can determine to what extent our deliberations will assist us to address "messy" practice issues as a way to confront future challenges and realities. One of the survey respondents observed that "the *new world* has direct impact for adult educators." This impact does not need to be either one-way or top-down; an either/or stance prohibits what the field of adult education has accomplished in the past and undermines what it can become in the future. Instead, as adult educators who are reflective practitioners, we can exert a positive influence on this new world, tomorrow and into the new millennium.

Part 2
Aims of Adult Education

7

Philosophies in Action

Sue M. Scott

Everyone has a worldview, a philosophy through which he or she interprets the world. Mezirow (1991) calls this view a meaning perspective; others have called it a mental model (Senge, 1991). A framework unfolds over time, developing from our experiences as adults, our accumulated knowledge. A philosophical framework is an orientation towards life that guides us in our judgments about what is appropriate and what is not appropriate behaviour, thinking and living. It is a philosophy-in-action; what we believe is played out in our actions. A philosophy of education is a part of the broader framework, encompassing our thoughts about learning, teaching and education in general. As adult educators, we take measures to tap into students' frameworks, onto which we attach various kinds of knowledge about how to teach adults, ways of thinking about adulthood, and social and/or cultural contexts to enhance instruction. A philosophy-in-action is a framework through which we interpret, make meaning, and consequently act or behave in our environment.

People often act according to their philosophical frameworks automatically, without being aware they are being influenced by them. As times change, as the players change (both teachers and learners) and as institutions change, we often are acting without making explicit the assumptions and beliefs embedded in our frameworks (Scott, Chovanec & Young, 1994). Periodically, and particularly as students, we must examine our lives to discover what it is that we value most highly and what knowledge we consider to be most worthwhile. In our current time of great flux, it is a helpful exercise to make explicit those values and beliefs we have kept implicit. By posing and answering questions, we can align what we believe with what we do: Does my teaching have relevance for me and my students? Is the way I am teaching in line with the philosophy of the institution? Can I adapt to what the institution wants? Can I survive in an environment that is fundamentally different than my orientation to teaching and learning?

As students and teachers of adult education we have even more fundamental questions to answer in excavating our philosophies of education. In an expanding and fast-paced society, it is difficult to find time for reflection. The questions to sort out in any educational philosophy are: What is the fundamental purpose of education? What is the view of the learner? What is the role of the teacher? What methods and strategies would best facilitate teaching and learning? How do we evaluate or know that we've learned something?

Most philosophers of education focus on the problems we encounter in education, interpreting and addressing these problems through their particular worldviews. The following descriptions of five philosophies, however, are presented as a system-centred, rather than problem-centred, analysis, showing the inter-relationship of the elements within the different philosophical frameworks. While an educational philosophy may begin eclectically, ultimately its elements must relate logically to one another. In this chapter, these five philosophies are presented for comparison and contrast with students' own philosophies of adult education. It is hoped that students will enter into dialogue with one another, examining together their worldviews and asking themselves questions such as, Am I primarily a progressive or a radical in orientation? For adequate critical analysis of one's philosophical investigation, it is worthwhile to note where the emphases lie culturally at particular times in our history. Therefore, the last part of the chapter looks at dominant philosophical orientations in Canadian history.

The philosophical orientations most often used by adult educators in today's society are:

1. liberal/perennialism
2. progressivism
3. behaviourism
4. humanism
5. radical or critical orientations.

Each of these frameworks attempts to answer the above questions and ultimately form a coherent picture (Darkenwald and Merriam, 1982, provide a similar schema). I contend that a person holds fundamentally one philosophical orientation to teaching and learning. Sometimes it is ill-formed or unreflected on; one simply adopts the best ways one has been taught in the past. This usually means that one has *learned* best using particular learning strategies. Without reflecting on the multiple philosophies learners can hold in a classroom and without being aware of one's own philosophical orientation, one may adopt a technique-oriented approach to instruction, sometimes called the basket approach to teaching: just reach into the basket and pull out a technique that might work at the moment. Also, if we are not aware of our true belief systems about education and instruction, as teachers we may adopt uncritically what our institutions claim is best, or what the current trend is in educational thought.

Philosophies of Education

The five philosophies are discussed according to the following framework:

1. What is the aim of education?
2. How is education defined generally?
3. What is the nature of humans and view of learners?
4. What is the role of the teacher/instructor and the instructional strategies that develop from one's particular philosophy of education?
5. What are the primary ways learning is assessed?

Liberal/perennial. The aim of a liberal/perennial education is to discipline or exercise the mind (a mental disciplinist approach) through the study of absolutes, often articulated in the form of principles. Liberal notions of disciplining the mind (Bigge, 1982) assume the mind is like a muscle that must be exercised to develop appropriately. The Hellenistic conception of "liberal" education, derived from Aristotle and Plato, held that people desire to know, have a natural curiosity to pursue knowledge for its own sake and have the ability to develop rationality as the mind is "trained." By studying the great works of literature, philosophy, history and science, individuals develop their rational faculties and form notions of good and virtuous citizenship. What one learns about the past will prepare a person for the future (Kneller, 1971). In the Greek conception of formal education, knowledge acquired from a liberal curriculum is considered the highest form of knowledge, while "utilitarian considerations of applied knowledge and skill play ... scarcely any significant role" (Lucas, 1976, p. 3). The learner is viewed as deficient cognitively, and the mind is viewed as superior to the body. Thus, the teacher, who is the expert in his or her discipline, must transmit expertise or knowledge to students in the form of highly sophisticated and linguistically superior lectures. Because rationality is the highest human attribute, the teacher's job is to ensure students be "self-discipline[d] ... cultivate reason and control their appetites" (Kneller, 1971, p. 43). U.S. adult educators Mortimer Adler and Robert Maynard Hutchins developed a series of readings and discussion techniques that became the heart of the Great Books series, which are "as contemporary today as when they were first written" (Adler, 1939, as quoted in Lucus, 1971, p. 17). This kind of learning can only be evaluated philosophically, through the construction of well-reasoned and argued essays.

Progressivism. By the turn of this century, progressivists "rebelled against the excessive formalism of traditional education, with its emphasis on strict discipline, passive learning, and pointless detail" (Kneller, 1971, p. 47). The aim of education for progressives is to liberate the learner for improving society by analyzing and reconstructing experiences past and present; i.e., learners interact with their environment and continually interpret the meaning of their experiences (Kolb, 1984) to direct the course for subsequent experience. Education is not a preparation for living but is rather life itself (Lindeman, 1926). Learning is determined not by truth generated by academic knowledge but by the concrete needs of a participatory democratic society, and these concrete needs relate to what is in the interest of the groups and individuals in this society. Once intelligence is "trained" by applying it to what interests the learner, the study of organized and more abstract knowledge is possible.

The teacher's role is to be a partner-helper to the students as they "restructure their life spaces and gain new insights into their contemporaneous situations" (Bigge, 1982, p. 11). Learners are viewed as being in charge of their own learning. Subject content becomes meaningful when it satisfies the needs and interests of the student. Students learn by reflecting on their experiences (Mezirow, 1991) through primarily a social or dialogical process. Thus, learning through problem solving takes precedence over acquisition of subject matter.

Behaviourism. Behaviourism focuses on individuals' adjustments to their physical and social environment and has been linked to structural functionalism. B. F. Skinner is the key proponent of this philosophical orientation. He maintains that it is a fallacy that "free" students will learn. All students are under conditions that control their behaviour, both inside and outside the classroom or institution, and he has stated that the "teacher should improve the control of the student rather than abandon it" (Skinner, 1976, p. 225).

In the behaviourist theory of teaching, it is assumed that the learner has been extensively programmed by the environment and thus has little freedom of thought, and that the teacher should diffuse so-called positive knowledge that assumes to be empirically analytical, universal, objective, and value free. The aim of education is to predict, change and control students' actions and re-establish the teacher as authority in the classroom—in contrast to allowing the students' natural curiosity and interests to guide them—by using available knowledge about the laws of human behaviour. If teachers reinforce desirable behaviour, as defined by these laws, this will lead to a better society. The teacher's role is to manage learning by designing an environment that elicits desired behaviour and extinguishes undesirable behaviours; that is, skills can be taught through an extrinsic reward and punishment system. Competency-based education, mastery learning, self-control and assertiveness training are examples of methods and strategies used in the classroom. Assessment and/or evaluation is based on the demonstration of changed behaviour in accord with predetermined behavioural objectives. Objective, criterion-referenced tests are standard evaluations.

Humanism. In contrast with behaviourism, humanism is deeply concerned with the freedom and integrity of individuals controlling their own lives and learning. People are responsible for themselves (Elias and Merriam, 1995). The aim of education here is to allow the learner to become authentically involved in knowledge construction and meaning making. There is an affirmation that freedom and individual uniqueness must not be compromised. Thus the stifling of individuality by social conformism and the tyranny of the majority over the dissenting minority violates a moral system that advocates the expansion of freedom of choice for all. Human nature is assumed to be intrinsically good, and the notion of the self that has potential for growth and development, for self-actualization, results in individualized learning and learner-centred curriculum, instruction and evaluation. Carl Rogers translated these assumptions into education, and Malcolm Knowles resurrected them for adult education in the 1960s and 1970s as he blended behaviourism and humanism in his work on self-directed learning, andragogy and groups.

Concern for individual growth is complicated, since we mostly learn in social contexts. Some existentialist humanists believe groups actually endanger individuality by engulfing a person in the anonymous mask of the group. However, the aim in the end–means continuum of group life, most agree, is the education of the individual who must become authentically involved with life. Subject matter is not the end but the means for the cultivation of the self, where knowledge of self furthers growth toward self-actualization.

The teacher, passionately involved in the curriculum and in life, must expose those tendencies in society that act to dehumanize individuals by undermining their freedom. Knowledge, therefore, must not be detached and "out there" but must engage the feelings of the knower, who must be able to relate to it personally. According to Martin Buber,

> teaching could not be a true dialogue if the teacher were construed as an instructor, one who simply mediates between the pupil and the subject matter ... How then is knowledge to be transmitted? It is not to be transmitted at all but 'offered.' The teacher, said Buber, must familiarize himself fully with the subject he teaches, and take it into himself ... When the teacher has made the subject he teaches a part of his inner experience, he can present it to the pupil as something issuing from himself (Kneller, 1971, p. 80-81).

Evaluation, then, becomes not a "test" of the subject matter under review but an examination of the extent to which people learn anything about themselves in relationship to the subject matter. Consequently, individuation and affective development is difficult to measure objectively and often causes instructors conflict, as they must assign grades based on objective criteria about the content. In this framework, any change of society is achieved through the development of the individual. Thus a humanist teacher becomes a mediator who enables as much freedom of choice as possible within a variety of learning strategies to accommodate the unique personalities in any one learning group.

Radical orientation. For the radical orientation to education, true humanization takes place in the world only when people become conscious of the social forces influencing them, reflect on these forces and become capable of acting to change those forces that hinder our liberation (see Collins' chapter "Critical Returns: From Andragogy to Lifelong Education" in this volume for a fuller discussion of the radical/critical orientation to adult education). The aim of education is to transform society through political action by educating its members to a new vision founded on a "genuine democracy whose major institutions and resources are controlled by the people themselves" (Kneller, 1971, p. 63). Unlike the progressives who see democracy as basically good and assert that change can be brought about by reforming the system, radicals view capitalism and democracy as fundamentally flawed. Adult educators Paulo Freire and Ivan Illich are considered "radical in the political sense of utilizing education to bring about social, political, and economic changes in society" (Elias & Merriam, 1995, p. 139). Central to a radical education is the study of power and empowerment, "which are intricately intertwined. Student empowerment, therefore, will depend upon negotiating, not avoiding, the power dynamics" (Briskin & Coulter, 1992, p. 259). The essential strategy of a critical teaching practice, therefore, is critique. "Critique calls for a special and suspicious interpretation of those ideologies and institutions which support and maintain ruling power structures" (Gallagher, 1992, p. 240). As one critically reflects in dialogue with others and acts on that reflection, both personal and social transformation occurs.

Similar to critical theorists' social critique, feminist theory is "premised on the recognition that gender is a phenomenon that helps to shape our society. Feminists believe that women are located unequally in social formation and are often devalued, exploited and oppressed" (Kenway & Modra, 1992, p. 139). While there are an array of variations within feminist theory, race and class are commonly integral to a feminist analysis. Thus, feminism is a worldview, a lens through which all human interaction and social structures are interpreted. For feminist pedagogues, the relationship between teaching and learning requires not only a discourse about practice (what one does in the classroom) but also the social visions they support as they teach. Because of a commitment to end social arrangements that lead women to be less than, put down and put upon (Briskin & Coulter, 1992), feminist pedagogy involves a personal political practice.

An analysis of one's own philosophical orientation could be endangered by reading and thinking about the frameworks above, as they could influence the beliefs one holds if what sounds good is not examined critically and through dialogue. However, offering these frameworks for thinking about one's philosophy of adult education perhaps will help students compare and contrast their own philosophy with one or two of the above. This method of examination is preferable to the objective tests or inventories referred to in Merriam and Brockett (1997), which quantify very complex issues into a set of questions that overlook the nuances and debates that have come to shape the pattern clusters in the philosophies. It is important to be aware of some of those debates, and therefore this book includes an extensive reference list for those interested in differentiating their teaching and learning as they strive to become good adult educators.

Philosophical Patterns in the History of Canada

Canadian history can be viewed as evolving through particular philosophical orientations at certain times. Adult education in Canada has its roots in the settling of this country by immigrants and is most obvious in the Antigonish Movement, as discussed elsewhere (see the chapter "Spiritual Lessons from the Antigonish Movement" by Mary A. Gillen in this volume). Kitchen meetings instigated by Father Moses Coady and his staff provided dialogue premised on questions such as, Do you want to live like this? What is keeping you from organizing to think and act collectively to get out of this mess? The assumption was that people regardless of class, race or gender could improve their lot by critically analyzing their concrete situations, becoming aware of how the situation came to be, determining who holds the power and deciding what to do to improve their situation. The pioneers who settled in Canada learned by doing, with little previous knowledge of how to build houses, towns or roads. They asked questions, banded together and collectively decided what was best for the common good. This communitarian concern is waning today.

After World War II, our society enjoyed a period of abundance. In the 1950s, 1960s and 1970s, an orientation of liberal democracy prevailed and an ideology of lifelong learning took hold as more and more adults clamoured for learning and knowledge. In Britain, liberal adult education as a political force continued during this period to mean social action, community education and social purpose education (Taylor, Rockhill & Fieldhouse, 1985).

The progressives established the social safety net to assure a high quality of life for all citizens regardless of their physical or mental capacities. Socialized health care provided sophisticated and advanced medical services. A vision of progressive reform was both promoted and acted upon. Humanist concerns evolved during this time, as freedom from material constraints made room for self-actualization and individuality of expression (not individualism) emerged as a social phenomenon.

However, economic recession and the advent of fundamentalist neo-conservatism in the 1980s and 1990s has dampened the progressive/radical spirits of our forebearers. Adult educators with a communitarian orientation to life in which dialogue and progress imply more humane policies and structures are forced to retreat as technology threatens to isolate and objectify us. The social milieu promotes the seduction of the computer, in front of which people often spend inordinate amounts of time. Individualism, an orientation of self-interest, becomes prevalent as we isolate ourselves and forget how to create communities for dialogue and analysis. As we enter the twenty-first century, it is important to know who we are, theoretically and practically. Without honest reflection on the premises that guide our action as instructors inside and outside the classroom, we become co-opted into dominant forces around us. It is my experience in teaching the foundations of adult education that most students in adult education seem to adopt a progressive, humanist, or radical stance in their educational philosophy. The jury is still out on the role that technology will play in the future. If we choose to stay focused on our original communitarian ideals for practicing adult education, technology will remain a tool. Technology should not replace the need for face-to-face dialogue, or for groups committed to helping their members or others groups questing for deeper understandings of who we are and what we are to do.

The issues that emerge in a discussion of one's philosophy of adult education centre on beliefs about the capacities of humans in general and students in particular. Are we basically good, capable of growth and development? Or are we bad and need to be controlled and manipulated by social forces that would enable society to move forward as it has in the past? Do we not, as adult educators, want people to be critical, reflective, choosing change agents who are conscious of those social forces around them? As a society based on freedom from that which constrains our individual and collective rights, we are concerned about preserving what promotes human compassion and changing what is not life-giving. What is the role of teachers in all of this? Should they facilitate a process that essentially pulls from students what they already know, or do teachers have an obligation to present information to students? If the latter, then how might that "silence" students into adopting the voice of the teacher as their own rather than encouraging them to develop their own belief systems? If we want to increase the cognitive complexity of students, how do we present the issues, the alternatives and many different points of view that will engage learners in broadening their scope of awareness? If we want our students to grow and change into more responsible adults, capable of influencing social progress, to what extent are we obligated to challenge the premises or assumptions on which they base their lives? Do we not need to do that first ourselves, as educators, if we are to ask our students to clarify their own premises about education?

The distinctions between the five philosophical orientations are drawn fairly sharply in this essay. While the categorization provides an introductory grasp of the various assumptions, "there is danger of fencing off schools of philosophy without adequate recognition of the contrast inside, and the fluidity between, the fences" (Pearson & Podeschi, 1997). The reader is encouraged to inquire widely and in more depth into the philosophical orientation that captures his or her imagination. A comparison to other, similar philosophies also would help clarify the foundational assumptions that ground one in adult education. As adult educators we must be aware of the vast array of orientations that professional and action labourers hold as they enter into decision making, policy making and education making. The ability to articulate one's cognitive framework or philosophy-in-action in regard to adult education is essential; otherwise we become vulnerable as we attempt to make change.

8

Lifelong Education as Emancipatory Pedagogy

Michael Collins

When we do think and feel things privately and in secret, even when
thousands of people are doing, thinking, whispering these things privately
and in secret, there is still no general collective understanding from which
to move. Each takes her or his risks in isolation.
— Adrienne Rich, 1993, p. 57.

The concept of "lifelong education" has been neatly hijacked for state-initiated educational policy formation, school curriculum development and an ideological distortion of lifelong learning to mean schooling from cradle to grave. The position taken in this chapter is that a critically informed perspective on lifelong education can still hold out prospects for the reconstruction of education as a reasoned emancipatory project in line with the global vision of Edgar Fauré (1972), the pedagogy of Freire (1974) and the critical social theory of Jurgen Habermas (1984; 1987).

Re-Enlarging the Vision

The connection between modern adult education practice and lifelong education as lifelong schooling—a "guarantee of permanent inadequacy" (Ohliger, 1974)—reminds us that andragogy, for all its preoccupation with self-directedness, does not pave the way for an emancipatory pedagogy. Moreover, the andragogical model has not even met the aspirations of adult educators who yearn for the privileges of professionalized status and the validation of a conventional academic discipline. Leaving aside the effects of a critical discourse in adult education, andragogy is effectively deconstructed in light of its own initial claim to establish a new method marking out adult education as a distinctive field of practice. The numerous and varied initiatives emerging under the rubric of lifelong education (lifelong learning) simply cannot be contained within the confines of a professionalized discourse or the boundaries of a single conventionally organized academic discipline. Andragogy was an unfortunately conceived and misleading concept from the outset.

The thought-provoking article "Vivisecting the Nightingale: Reflections on Adult Education as Object of Study," written a decade ago by Canadian adult educator Michael Welton (1987) for the British journal *Studies in the Education of Adults,* highlights the folly of attempts to pin adult education to the andragogical model. Andragogy is seriously flawed because it "neglects the social, cultural, and political dimensions of adult education" (p. 54). In its narrow preoccupation with technique ("pure instrumentality" according to Welton), andragogy has held in check broader aspirations for an emancipatory pedagogy.

This assessment of andragogy is not intended to imply that the legacy of adult education, in theory and practice, does not have a critical role to play in a reconstructed discourse on lifelong education. On the contrary, that other form of adult education, viewed by Raymond Williams (1990) as a driving force within the making of history itself, is relevantly linked to Fauré's larger conception of lifelong education: "Learning to love the world and make it more human; learning to develop in and through creative work" (1972, p. 69).

A direct concern for human development and the quality of creative work can be sustained through a reconstructed modern practice of adult education shorn of narrow preoccupations with a professionalizing ethos, conventional management-oriented perspectives on workplace education and training (human resource development) and positivistic, standardized approaches to program planning and curriculum design.

No doubt, it is all too easy to overstate the case for emancipatory pedagogy, identifying political strategies, forms of protest and immediate prospects that are not sensibly within reach. In these times the pedagogical task of sustaining even a modest level of critical discourse is difficult enough, especially in view of the ease with which earnest advocacy (however carefully reasoned) on behalf of social justice can be derisively dismissed as moralistic whining by the "politically correct."

In these times, strategies of emancipatory pedagogy, i.e., educational practices that go against the grain of status quo relationships of power, must be played out in a far-reaching political context largely created during the neoconservative ascendancy. In this ideological context, antithetical to socially egalitarian and good-quality publicly funded education, liberal values of social justice are severely constrained, while what is left of the left seems to opt for silence, self-deprecating mockery or ineffectual sectarianism.

Even so, there are many issues from which an emancipatory pedagogy, embracing rather than shrinking from an aspiration to be politically (and theoretically) correct, can select as immediately relevant to its commitments.

The struggle to ensure that educational programs and curriculum designs engage to some extent with critical concerns such as sexism, racism and class analysis remains feasible and worthwhile. And, within the larger public arena, it is vitally important to foster an ongoing climate of opposition to ideologically motivated cut-backs in publicly funded education and other valuable public services. In this regard, a more proactive role can be adopted sensibly by teachers, academic educationalists and their associations. Neo-conservative ideology, for all its pervasiveness (even within liberal and social democratic political arenas) is not monolithic.

In its capacity to establish connections among various social constituencies and across different age groups, adult education is itself integral to any notion of lifelong education. In particular, adult education can be rightly viewed as a vital process in the mediation of community, school and workplace interests. The point to be emphasized here is that adult education as vocation—conscious of its moral and political role in today's society—is well positioned to forge the kind of alliances needed in furthering the prospects of lifelong education as emancipatory pedagogy.

The University Context

Within a university-based setting, adult education is represented as the means through which knowledge production can be disseminated beyond the campus while informing the academy of wider community needs for such knowledge. At the same time, as a university-based area of study in the education of adult educators, adult education in the academy becomes a meeting place for the conventional disciplines. Typically, well-qualified graduates from any one of a number of the conventional academic disciplines are attracted to studies in adult education following a period of practical experience as adult educators. Adult education, then, especially since the deconstruction of andragogy as a central discourse, can be viewed in part as a relevant academic location for interdisciplinary research and practice. Further, providing that the vocational commitment and political will can be mustered to make the case for its continuing relevance within the academy, university-based adult education has a key role to play in the development of lifelong education as emancipatory pedagogy that draws its insights pragmatically from *across the traditional disciplines.*

At this critical juncture, several commitments must be made in order for university-based adult education, whether or not it manages to retain a clear-cut academic location, to position itself for a key role within an emancipatory practice.[1]

1. A willingness to work with and learn from off-campus groups for whom the achievement of social justice in a genuinely democratic society is a central aspiration.

2. A determination to legitimize and enlarge upon the political dimension of adult education in the academy and in off-campus settings.

3. A recognition of how adult education should assume a key role in teacher preparation and in the contemporary discourse on schooling practices.

4. An understanding that adult education must engage in a critical discourse around work and education as an alternative to the ideology of management-oriented Human Resources Development.

5. A conviction that the modern practice of adult education should be in a position to embrace forms of learning, curriculum design and development and research in which pressing global concerns about social justice are given the highest priority.

These guidelines for strategic action within the academy of adult education represent a slight variation of those advanced as a basis for critical assessment in *The Canmore Proceedings* (Collins, 1995). I am writing here about the politicization of adult education emerging in large measure from initiatives in the academy. Am I asking too much?

Political Re-Engagements

Objections likely will arise about placing so much emphasis on politics under the rubric of lifelong education. In response to such objections, it is useful to invoke a key insight that guides the pedagogy of Paulo Freire (1974): the very act of teaching, and educational practice in general, has political consequences. Even when teachers claim, and genuinely contrive, to be "neutral," their alleged neutrality unwittingly supports status quo interests in consequence of their predisposition to take these interests for granted. At the very least, a purposeful focus on the political dimension of adult education will pose a challenge to this naïveté and to prevailing conditions that sustain an unequal distribution of knowledge.

In any event, a move towards the politicization of lifelong education via a critical practice of adult education concerned with social justice does not preclude a focus on other areas of educational interest and on careful teaching in many subject areas. A purposively politicized practice of adult education is more likely to further substantiate the notion of lifelong education by drawing attention to the need for wider accessibility to good quality teaching.

Prospects for a genuine participatory democracy cannot be realized in the absence of informed political engagement by the majority of ordinary men and women. In these times of deepening cynicism about politics and the morality of career politicians, there is all the more reason to engender within the context of lifelong education a political pedagogy that can still envision a civil society that attends to the needs of the majority rather than the interests of a privileged minority.

In adopting a more politicized agenda that entails a commitment to a robust *realpolitik* (that is, one that eschews the debilitating petty personal politics that seem to thrive in the academy) as well as a concern for critical thought, the critical discourse in adult education needs to clarify its own politics. In this regard, it is time to make a distinction between the project of critical theory and the deconstructionist endeavours of postmodern critique.

Against Postmodernism

While one has found postmodern insights instructive, most notably those attributable to Michel Foucault (Collins, 1988), such insights are also accessible from the larger legacy of critical social theory, which still holds out *reasonable* prospects for the discovery of a rational basis on which to (re)construct an emancipatory pedagogy. Since postmodernism spurns any such quest to identify rational grounds from which a process of social change can be instigated, attempts to effect a rapprochement between critical theory and postmodernist thought within the discourse on critical pedagogy would seem to be fundamentally misguided. This is the confused tack taken by much of critically informed academic writing on conventional schooling.

We can look to Jean Braudillard (1991), a leading figure on the European postmodern scene, for an example of analysis revelling in the cult of the irrational. Immediately prior to the Gulf War, Braudillard confidently predicted that the war could not happen. When it did happen, bringing with it real deaths and real suffering on a wide scale, Braudillard insisted that the Gulf War was not really a war. For postmodern Braudillard, the Gulf War *signified* a non-event. It was mere *representation*.

For Alex Callinicos (1990), a British professor of political science, "the upshot of Braudillard's analyses is to license a kind of intellectual dandyism" (p. 147). Even before Braudillard's remarkable proclamation that the Gulf War was not a war, Callinicos had tagged this leading exponent of postmodern discourse in the following terms: "Braudillard is caught on the horns of one of the characteristic dilemmas of Nietzschean thought—how can he substantiate his claim that we have moved beyond a world to which theoretical enquiry is appropriate without relying on the assumptions and procedures of such enquiry?" (p. 148). It is unfortunate that so few educators attracted to postmodernist analyses manage to make even a relevant connection with the work of Nietzsche.

In Braudillard we can discern the *serious* problem with the artful postmodern deconstructionist play around signification and representation. It *plays* right into the hands of a neo-conservative ideology proclaiming "the end-of-history" and "the new world order." Though the end of history discourse and former President Bush's new world order are already history, the political ideology from which these tenets emerged is still thriving. This ideology is rolling back the progressive gains made for public education in past decades. There is a significant connection between the neo-conservative politics of our times and the attractions of decentred postmodernist thought. Unhappily, too many progressive intellectuals (including social activist educators) have been unwittingly caught up in these fatal attractions. Here is how Callinicos views the situation:

> The discourse of postmodernism is best seen as the product of a socially mobile intelligentsia in a climate dominated by the retreat of the Western labour movement and the "over-consumptionist" dynamic of capitalism in the Reagan-Thatcher era. From this perspective the term "postmodern" would seem to be a floating signifier by means of which this intelligentsia has sought to articulate its political disillusionment and its aspiration to a consumption-oriented lifestyle (p. 170).

In view of postmodernism's relativizing and fracturing effects and the fact that its otherwise brilliant critical insights (into gender, class and race) can, in any case, be *reasonably* derived from critical theory as commentaries on our times, it is no longer premature to speak out against postmodern sensibilities within a critical discourse on adult education. Otherwise, there is little sense in talking about a foundational practice or a reconstuction of adult education. A shift from the "pure instrumentality" of andragogy to the relativizing deconstructions of postmodern discourse in education does not advance the prospects for lifelong education as emancipatory pedagogy.

Internationalist Perspectives and Guiding Principles

The original article that introduced andragogy as a new approach and a new method (Knowles, 1968) was devoid of any reference to internationally significant social and political upheavals taking place at the time of its publication. It was as though the momentous events leading to the 1968 uprising in Paris and the Prague Spring revolt had no consequence for the newly emerging modern practice of adult education. In contrast, perspectives on adult education informed by critical theory for an emancipatory practice of lifelong education are motivated by a sense of connectedness to international events. The politics of critical theory and a critically informed practice of adult education are decidedly internationalist.

I propose that an emancipatory practice of lifelong education, drawing from critical perspectives in adult education, should constitute an internationalist pedagogy that articulates *reasons* for why education must be linked to a quest for social justice (freedom from oppression) and, hence, human emancipation. In this quest it still makes sense to invoke universal central values about caring relationships and aspirations for a just society. Ironically, it is a *reasoned* rather than a *deconstructionist* critical discourse that must raise a defiant voice against the fracturing defeatism of postmodernist sensibilities. For in our hearts and minds, we know that *the centre must hold* even in our struggle to define it. Otherwise, "we leave out of our account the possibility of a global social transformation which could impose a new set of priorities, based upon the collective and democratic control of the resources of the planet" (Callinicos, p. 174).

Thus, a call for the construction of a carefully reasoned emancipatory pedagogy is not merely a defiant gesture in the face of current neo-conservative politics and postmodern sensibilities. Rather, we are invoking once again the morally and politically committed pedagogy that was envisaged by adult educator Thomas Hodgskin, co-founder in 1823 of the Mechanics' Institutes Movement:

> Men had better be without education than be educated by their rulers. For then education is but the mere breaking in of the steer to the yoke. The education of a free people will always be directed more beneficially for them when it is in their own hands (Halevy, 1956, p. 86).

Herein lies the guiding principle for an emancipatory practice of lifelong education. The pedagogical task implied is to help us find within ourselves that "general collective understanding from which to move" (Rich, 1993).

For all of the earnest endeavours needed to sustain prospects for an emancipatory practice of lifelong education, the aesthetic and spiritual dimensions of adult education must still be attended to. An emancipatory pedagogy that prefigures "the education of a free people" should not be disassociated from the creative urge to celebrate, to enlarge on and enjoy life as it is immediately experienced There is a romantic tendency within the legacy of adult education—of "friends educating friends"—that is ready for rekindling. Poetry, passion and making music together add meaning to the politics and theory of an emancipatory practice of lifelong education.

Currently, modern adult education, as a university-based discipline and expressed in terms of andragogy, is simply not party to the most significant developments taking place under the rubric of lifelong education, developments that are bypassing the academy of adult education. Yet, for those still wedded to the view of adult education as a driving force within the making of history itself, the large terrain staked out by lifelong education offers increasing opportunities for critical engagement and vocational practice. And there is still a space here, at the centre of the action, for university-based adult education.

Endnote

[1] Here I draw from past experience in business and in teaching business and other subjects in schools and post-secondary institutions, and from field-based work with various off-campus groups while holding an academic position in adult and continuing education.

9

Parameters, Pedagogy and Possibilities in Changing Times

André P. Grace

We live, learn and work amid the instability and insecurity generated by federal and provincial governments and other institutions concerned with survival in a global economy. The common disaster is the undermining of the social as it melds with the economic, an undermining that fosters social inequities and constructs enemies within national borders with names such as single mothers, unemployed young adults and ethnic minorities. We are failing to address the employment and living interests of Canadians in respectful and meaningful ways. The plight of workers and learners is compounded by factors that include the normalization of a *knowledge-for-now* training treadmill that provides skills with short-lived usefulness. The sorry result of this learning process is the maintenance of an alienated contingent of functionally unemployable persons in this country. This state of affairs is an erosion of the social that seems intensified by the times we live in, when hope and possibility are themselves in malaise:

> The future promises on-going fiscal restraint and federal-provincial uncertainty. These, combined with a labour market characterized by high unemployment and polarization of earnings, changes in family structure that have increased vulnerability and a growing impatience and skepticism about governments' ability to solve problems, imply that the commitment to social equity will be strongly tested (Human Resources Development Canada, 1994, p. 7).

The Contemporary Culture of Crisis and Challenge

There are many challenges confronting Canadian adult education in the midst of its own instability. As a social enterprise existing in this culture of crisis and challenge, adult education is in a state of flux. Critical adult education as a way of knowing steeped in a history of concern with social education has an important role to play here. It can assist the larger enterprise, of which it has traditionally been a marginal part, by informing practice through building a critical postmodern Theory of Adult Learning Community (TALC and pronounced *talk*). TALC is a theory that values, respects and fosters the knowledges and experiences of educators *and* learners. Before outlining such a theoretical scaffolding, it is worthwhile to briefly reflect on the emergence of the modern practice of adult education since World War II. The following social-historical overview provides a gauge to set the parameters of critical adult education. A consideration of themes to guide the development of TALC follows, and the chapter concludes with a look at possible paths critical adult education may take in the future.

Critical Perspectives on the Emergence of the Modern Practice of Adult Education since World War II

Alain Locke, who became the first African-American president of the American Association for Adult Education (AAAE) in 1945-46 (Stubblefield & Keane, 1994), reflects in the foreword to the 1948 AAAE *Handbook*: "We in America have tended to forget the social aim of adult education, or to subordinate it to opportunities for individual self-improvement ... The corporate age of adult education confronts us" (Knowles & DuBois, 1970, p. xxi). His words encapsulate a major trend of the new period of modern practice emerging after World War II. Knowles and Klevins (1972) describe this period as a time of enterprise expansion. Mainstream adult education changed in reaction to the pressures of an unfolding post-war North American knowledge and service economy marked by techno-scientific advances and the exponential growth of consumerism. Bell (1967) calls the years from 1945 to 1950 "the birth-years, symbolically, of the post-industrial society" (p. 159) that is characterized by "the rise of the new elite whose status is based on skill ... [and] the simple fact that knowledge and planning ... have become the basic requisites for all organized action" (p. 165). The post-industrial society expanded in the United States during the 1950s in the face of Cold War fears. During this expansion, Thompson and Randall (1994) contend that Canada became an important part of a new American Empire. They relate that Canada was a target of U.S. imperialism because the U.S. coveted the rich resources to the north that could feed its growing Sovietphobic military-industrial complex. Canada was also increasingly subjected to U.S. social and cultural influences in this period as rapid scientific and technological changes (including the influence of television) blurred national borders. In many ways Canadian society mirrored the post-industrial society emerging in the United States. As part of the U.S. social and cultural invasion northward, an increasingly instrumentalized form of American adult education was taken up by many Canadian adult educators concerned with professionalizing the field. In the drive toward a *scientized and technicized* modern practice, Canadian mainstream adult education seemed to forget a rich national history of social education that defied the narrow utilitarianism of the technicist approach.

The metamorphosis of North American adult education following World War II was affected by a growing identity crisis, as visions of a professionalized practice brought change and conflict to a historically social enterprise. Selman (1984) relates, "This was a period, especially in the 1950s, in which a sense of professionalism was emerging in adult education" (p. 13). What is adult education? became a much debated question—is it a discipline, a profession, a field or a movement? As the debate continued, adult education's historical role in social education seemed increasingly at odds with its desired role within a scientized and technicized practice. Some adult educators, fearing the enterprise was shirking its social responsibility, raised concerns that mainstream adult education was engaged in an endeavour primarily valued for its utility in contributing to the techno-economic advancement of the dominant culture. These critically concerned educators challenged status seekers whose myopic professional gaze focused on an instrumentalized practice, one that would be supported by universities giving increasing prominence to science and technology. They critiqued an emerging modern practice that mirrored the values of the post-industrial society and moved away from adult education's traditional social focus and pluralistic and voluntary nature. They investigated the *Ization Syndrome*—scientization, individualization, professionalization, and institutionalization—that was shaping adult education's post-war development as an ordered and orderly enterprise caught up in the emerging knowledge economy. The Ization Syndrome was setting the parameters of a professionalized enterprise. For adult educators like Roby Kidd (1966) and Alan Thomas (1961), this was problematic because professionalization switched the focus from continuous learning, the traditional emphasis of Canadian adult education, to education in its more formal and institutional delineation.

For many adult educators, the modern practice of adult education in the post-war era has become increasingly sanitized, neutralized and process oriented. Mezirow (1991) concludes that, in our field, "education designed to facilitate instrumental learning is the most familiar kind, a fact that reflects [North] American convictions concerning the power of the methods of problem solving codified by the natural sciences" (p. 213). Collins (1991) adds that in embracing modern practice with its ideology of technique "we *educate to alleviate* concerns rather than to raise questions about their validity" (p. 101, his emphasis). Our preoccupation with elements of the Ization Syndrome has seemingly outweighed concerns with social activism and cultural advancement. A slight critical turn in adult education has been noticeable since the 1980s, but today the social and cultural purposes of adult education are too frequently supplanted by instrumental designs that keep the enterprise in a shallow survival mode in response to the melding of the social and the economic.

Critical Adult Education and Modern Practice

Critical adult education, as a way to think about collective human interests, has been concerned predominantly with advancing social and cultural forms of education. It critiques instrumentalized forms as generally demonstrative of the commodification and tendency towards reductionism shaping contemporary practice. In its deliberations over the form and function of adult educational practice, critical adult education takes up ethical issues and emphasizes the political ideals of modernity: democracy, freedom and social justice. It fosters an interdisciplinary approach in theory building and practice, valuing perspectives drawn from disciplines such as sociology, philosophy and cultural studies. Critical adult education examines institutional structures and practices in its exploration of the politics of domination of workers and learners. It explores the beliefs citizens have about themselves and their learning places, workplaces and communities. Critical adult education takes up social, cultural, historical, economic and political considerations as it radically questions the status quo, corporate capitalism and threats to social democracy. In exploring all these issues, it asserts that knowledge is socially and historically constructed. It emphasizes collective action and reflection in learning processes and community building. It asserts the necessity for dialogue, communication, conflict and change.

Critical adult educators have offered important critiques of increasingly technicized and professionalized forms of adult education. Kulich (1991) captures a key point in this critique when he protests the permeation of technicism through the contemporary field, observing that "adult education in North America is predominantly institutionalized and professionalized, oriented more toward individual rather than social and societal needs, and marked by competition rather than co-operation among its providers" (p. 94). Briton and Plumb (1993) add that the post-war shaping of mainstream adult education in a milieu valuing individualism and psychologistic theories of learning led to "a discursive field that drew on the science of behaviourism, argued for the distinctive nature of the adult learner, posited concepts like 'self-directed' and 'goal-oriented' learning, and promoted 'contractual' learning processes and 'facilitated' learning practices" (p. 56).

This "narrow utilitarian approach" (Legge, 1989, p. 303) is amply critiqued. Little (1991) claims that "adult education as it is practiced in Western industrialized countries supports individual learning to enhance the maintenance of society, at the expense of the actualization of human potential to foster the advancement of society" (p. 3). Brookfield (1985) addresses the reductionistic tendency of technicism and acknowledges ineffectiveness in our modern practice. Grace (1996) argues that andragogy is a *disgenuine* theory of adult learning that limits possibilities for advancing contemporary practice. This argument purports that andragogy has detracted from learning-theory building by restricting the facilitation of learning to a distorted view of individual freedom and by insufficiently attending to relations of power, contexts and the foundations of adult education.

In the view of many adult educators, post-war modern practice is predominantly shaped by economic forces and heavily influenced by technological orientations. Jansen and Van Der Veen (1992) warn that adult education must stop "fulfilling functions that are merely instrumental to the dominant institutions and values of industrial society" (p. 281). Finger (1989), concerned with how we might learn our way out in the face of today's rapid social transformations and threats to security and survival, contends that we need to achieve a new "relationship with modernization, in particular with its core components of rationality, science, technology, and [state] politics" (p. 17). In contemporary times this relationship should take place in the intersection of the social, the cultural *and* the instrumental in an expanded enterprise (Grace, 1997). We must move beyond "a present situation in which the 'fault line' of individualism and social reform is ever-deepening and ever-widening, while both parties to the fault are increasingly inundated by the fragmentizing (and more heavily funded) demands of external sources articulating the reductionistic nuts and bolts programs generated too often by technical rationality" (Stanage, 1994, p. 349). As Legge (1989) concludes, "the education of adults in all its diversity is vital to the well-being of both individuals and the whole community" (p. 306).

Critical adult education has been criticized for its past inadequate attempts to address knowledge-power issues affecting the everyday lives, learning and work of people. An expanded critical approach to adult education demands that we focus on the "big picture," which must include a focus on relations of power that have impact on individual dislocation and worker obsolescence as well as possibilities for future work placement. In addressing this issue it is useful to refer to theory, using an eclectic approach. Dialogue and debate in critical education are expanded and enriched by drawing on feminist, postmodern/poststructural, Black insurgent and other theoretical scaffoldings that take up issues of power. Collins (1991) fosters such eclecticism and raises the value of theory in his call for academic adult educators to move beyond timid armchair intellectualism to develop a theory of action guiding practice. Recognizing that theory and practice are mutually informative, he concludes, "It is not so much a matter of trying to put theory into practice as of critically engaging with it while we try to put ourselves into practice" (p. 109).

Building TALC to Shape a Pedagogy of Community

How might critical adult education contribute to an enhanced enterprise aimed at meeting people's needs in their lives, their work and their learning? In the spirit of the Antigonish Movement's pedagogy of the people, we might begin by building a critical postmodern theory of adult learning community. TALC gives space (a recognized position) and place (a respected and valued presence) to both educators and learners. Drawing on ideas historically important to critical adult education, five themes that may contribute to the development of this theoretical scaffolding are explored below.

First, TALC emphasizes community by taking adult educators and learners beyond reductionistic roles such as facilitator and self-directed learner to foster new relationships where they may engage and challenge one another. Second, the theory focuses on knowledge production rather than knowledge consumption and values knowledge informed by experience and disposition. Third, it addresses issues of language and form in theory development and considers how theory and practice can inform one another. Fourth, TALC draws on the foundations of adult education and emphasizes the importance of a philosophical rationale and the historical context in shaping an interdisciplinary enterprise. Fifth, it asks critical educators to use these ideas to invigorate forms of adult education that address the instrumental, social and cultural concerns of people living in a contemporary culture of crisis and challenge.

Theme 1. TALC Encourages Educators and Learners to Share Leading Roles and Inform and Challenge One Another

Community has historically been important to Canadian adult education as an organizing social construct shaping the adult learning milieu. The pedagogy of the people embodied in the Antigonish Movement, for example, accents the value of continuing to foster community-based adult education, and is an example of the kind of collective action central to TALC. Tierney tells us that "a critical theory of community reconfigures centrality, margins, borders, and the landscapes of knowledge" (1992, p. 143) so that "community is in constant negotiation, dialogue, and reformulation" (1993, p. 140). In his critical theory of community it is important to account for relations of power and "create conditions by which we honour difference" (p. 140). In this light, community is a political place where empowerment and action demand a collective engagement with educator *and* learner cultures, situations, dispositions, experiences and histories. Contexts and relations of gender, race, ethnicity, class, sexual orientation, age and ability affect the degree to which educators and learners become informed and transformed individuals in the learning community.

TALC invigorates classroom practice by recognizing and fostering teaching and learning as dynamically interactive political acts. It requires adult educators to reflect on the value of their own knowledges and how they are produced. This theory moves beyond supposedly neutral andragogical notions to recognize the "political power of teaching" (hooks, 1988, p. 50). Adult educators and learners take on roles as investigators, challengers, communicators, knowledge producers and enablers in the teaching-learning process. Collins (1991) and Brookfield (1995), advancing a proactive role beyond facilitation, argue that adult educators must address concerns with methodology, technique, and performance within a broader framework that raises questions of purpose, interests, contexts, and assumptions underlying utility. In this scenario, the role of the adult educator is to be respected and valued within a learning community where transformation and information are both concerns in the learning process. This changing role of the adult educator need not undermine the role of the adult learner. In fact, increased educator visibility in the learning process can enhance possibilities for learners to become informed, transformed individuals. Mezirow (1991) contends that while the visible "educator must accept the learner's initial learning priorities ... the educator is not ethically bound to confine the learner to the learner's initial limitations or constraints in perspective" (p. 202). Operating in a critical mode, the educator is willing to challenge learners' voices as part of holistic learning process. Simultaneously, the visible educator recognizes that her voice is one voice in the learning community and provides opportunities for her own voice to be challenged. Educators aim to move the learner beyond the boundaries defined by the learner's present way of knowing. They want the learner to engage with or develop new learning paradigms emphasizing action and reflection and enhancing life, learning and work possibilities.

Theme 2. TALC Emphasizes Knowledge Production and Values Knowledge Informed by Experience and Disposition

TALC challenges the institutionalization of knowledge production, exchange and distribution in contemporary times. These knowledge dynamics are intimately connected to questions of voice and value in adult education. They have as much to do with experience and disposition as they do with facts and techniques. TALC gives space and place to dispositional knowledge and it views knowledge as a changing construction. A key objective is how adult educators and learners might produce knowledge that reflects an enterprise where individual contexts are recognized, respected and fostered.

In contemporary times, *knowledge is for now*. It is a trend that results in many learners coming to adult education classrooms with inferiority complexes perpetuated by continuously facing their ignorance of new skills and trying to keep pace on the instrumental-learning treadmill. Too often, learners acquire only a fleeting knowledge whose facts and *how-to* descriptions are carefully controlled. The resulting learning experience is reduced to episodic skill acquisition (Bauman, 1992), a partial and transitional encounter in a cycle of learning for the moment.

This scenario is normalized by the contemporary melding of the social and the economic and by "the increasing importance of the knowledge economy and its associated productivity-increasing technologies in the areas of electronics, computers, communications and robotics" (HRDC, 1994, p. 12). In the face of world demand for these "knowledge-intensive products and services" (p. 13), adult educators must be wary lest learners fall prey to educational forms serving agendas that devalue people. They must infuse contemporary practice with sociological critiques of science and expert knowledge (e.g., Bauman, 1992; Beck, 1992) and reject non-contextual, non-relational instrumental forms of education that provide solutions for today and problems for tomorrow. This does not mean that TALC ignores what Nietzsche (1964) called "instruction in bread-winning" (p. ix). Rather, it means that critical adult educators draw on other disciplines to frame and incorporate instrumental concerns within a broader, reflexive practice.

Theme 3. TALC Considers Language and Form in Theory Development and Emphasizes That Theory and Practice Inform One Another

Since World War II, the emergence of modern practice has been encumbered by the ambiguity between adult education as a field of study and adult education as a field of practice (Schroeder, 1970). This ambiguity limits possibilities for theory and practice to significantly inform one another. TALC seeks to build on the theory-practice connections made by critical educators in recent decades. It sees theory "as a borderland where conversations begin, differences confront each other, hopes are initiated, and social struggles are waged" (Giroux in Tierney, 1993, p. x). It holds the reflexive view that practice is theory lived out in the everyday. Theorists and practitioners operate interdependently to contribute to a transformative practice of adult education. Each is a support and a resource for the other.

TALC takes on language and meaning issues, focuses on presences and absences in theoretical discourses and brings theory to bear on identity differences shaped by relations of power. It focuses on theorizing as an active process informing practices aimed at meeting learner needs, addressing access concerns, achieving equity and fostering human diversity. It values theoretical eclecticism, drawing on critical theory's concern with collective change, postmodernism/poststructuralism's considerations of identity, difference, language, and meaning, feminism's focus on politicization, post-colonialism's emphases on privilege and exclusion and Black insurgency's engagement with culture and power. It asserts that each discourse is contributory to theory-practice deliberations in contemporary adult education.

Theme 4. TALC Values the Foundations of Adult Education in Shaping a Critically Reflexive and Interdisciplinary Practice

Post-war modern practice has been criticized for its inattention to its sociological, philosophical and historical foundations. Since the 1980s, however, a valuing of the foundations of adult education is increasingly discernible in adult education. Collins (1991) suggests there has been more emphasis on critical social-historical research, coupled with a move to draw on other disciplines to inform critical reflection, qualitative forms of research and contextual analyses in North American adult education. He believes that these trends can be positively viewed as contributing to the retrieval of the foundations for an emancipatory practice of adult education and is optimistic that the technicism shaping much of modern practice can be problematized and resisted in this practice. TALC emphasizes the importance of this retrieval, supporting an interdisciplinary approach to theory-practice in the creation of pedagogical possibilities for moving classroom practice into the intersection where the technical and the transformative are both considerations.

As part of valuing foundations, the importance of the social history of modern practice to the development of TALC cannot be overemphasized. This history helps us to understand our present place and difference by giving us a sense of the factors that have shaped contemporary adult education. It provides perspectives on what is possible in an enterprise where the learning culture shaped by the Ization Syndrome values individualism to the detriment of collectivism. This history also reveals the tensions between elements of the enterprise that maintain the status quo and other elements that seek to change it. Welton (1991) accentuates the importance of historical work, contending that the social historian, operating from critical perspectives, is "searching intensely for *a usable history* [emphasis added]: retrieving a past that contests the professionalization of the field of study and practice and speaks to the current debates about how the study of adult education ought to be constructed" (p. 286).

Theme 5. TALC Gives Space and Place to Instrumental, Social and Cultural Forms of Adult Education

In the contemporary culture of crisis and challenge it is defeating to maintain the gulf that has existed between instrumental versus social and cultural forms of adult education (Grace, 1997). Social and cultural educators can never be fully insulated from technicists who also carry out front-line work in our enterprise. This is true despite their efforts to reciprocally isolate one another. Since the genesis of the modern practice of adult education in 1919 (Knowles & Klevins, 1972), instrumental, social and cultural forms of education have *all* been variously explored and valued. Adult education has built on instrumental understandings of practice that includes Knowles's (1970) notion of andragogy and Verner's (1961) concern for precision as demonstrated in his work on adult educational method, device and technique. It has explored Lindeman's ideas on adult education as social education (Lindeman 1926; 1961) and has considered adult education as cultural education that Echeverría (1983) suggests can.enable "the transformation of the world for an authentic development" (p. 37). Echeverria contends that we must "re-think, re-define, and characterize with precision the new role adult education can play in order to contribute effectively to the quest for new ways, truly different alternatives" (p. 37) to assist this development. TALC holds that, in the face of contemporary technological change and socio-economic ebb tides, it is more important than ever for adult educators of all persuasions to work together. It is also advantageous for adult education to bring instrumental, social and cultural forms of education into a learning intersection where they can inform and transform one another. TALC purports that the sum of these forms increases adult education's value to learners and workers.

While, as Finger (1991) suggests, we must "conceive of adult education practice in a broader perspective than one of technical training" (p. 134), TALC realizes that bread-and-butter issues cannot be ignored in transformative learning processes. The homeostasis of the learning community demands contributions by all three forms of education. This theory contends that adult education's impact on humankind is as a social and cultural movement *and* as an enterprise responsibly executing instrumental functions within a broader, more reflexive practice. A critical practice for contemporary times must "[re]integrate the teaching and learning of practical skills and knowledge that people need for daily living with the stimulation of questions and public debate about the future of society and the possible designs of individual and social life" (Jansen & Van Der Veen, 1992, p. 281).

Possible Roads: The Future of Critical Adult Education

In its 1994 presentation of research themes for HRD policy research and experimentation, Human Resources Development Canada addressed three broad life areas: security, work and learning. It predicted that policy development in the anticipated future will be based on the assumption that economic and social policy would continue to be brought closer together. This fusion demands that Canadian adult educators rethink and revise their umbrella form and functions. As suggested, an expanded role and purpose for critical adult education could be embodied in a critical postmodern theory of the adult learning community. This theory advances notions of collective learning and problem solving and advocates inclusionary educational practices. It contributes to a transformative pedagogy sensitive to human diversity and sensible about the need to incorporate instrumental, social and cultural learning in holistic learning processes. Collins (1991) cautions that a commitment to transformative pedagogy involves some risk around knowledge-power issues. He suggests this starting point: "An entrée to such a commitment can be made, virtually from a negative standpoint, by rejecting the implicit message of contemporary adult education practice: Learn to cope; be happy; don't question" (p. 103).

So we begin by questioning: In the face of the contemporary melding of the social and the economic, how can adult educators move beyond the survivalist strategies and reactive stances marking our contemporary learning culture? In times when lifelong learning is codified as HRD, how do we develop policies and programs that respect and honour learner identity differences? How can critical adult educators form linkages with educators in HRD so they can work together to build an encompassing, reflexive practice of adult education? How should academic adult educators revise graduate education in light of program erosion or eradication? What kinds of research should they be doing in these times of crisis and challenge? The future of adult education depends on how educators and learners answer such questions. It requires the Canadian adult education community to take on these questions as a starting point for an agenda of renewal and revitalization.

SECTION 2
PURPOSES

British Canadian Co-op Society Ltd., Sydney Mines, Nova Scotia.
Courtesy of St. Francis Xavier University Archives.

Part 1
Education for Economy

10

Training and Work: Myths about Human Capital

Paul Bouchard

The planning system relies on the state for its large needs in qualified and educated manpower. This, as we shall presently see, is a matter of considerable social portent. The state not only educates those who accept and defend the values of the planning system. It also nurtures its critics— for there is no practical way of doing the one without the other.
—John Kenneth Galbraith, 1973, p. 156.

Ongoing changes in global economic structures and the much-talked-about information revolution have produced an environment where knowledge and skills, and by extension education and training, are considered increasingly valued commodities in the workplace. This trend is not only reflected in changes in today's employment requirements, where more years of schooling are expected of entry-level employees; it is also the basis of a perceived need to increase efforts at maintaining and upgrading work-related knowledge and skills. This has direct implications for the education of adults. In recent years, adults over twenty-five years of age have come to represent 83 percent of the Canadian population. Unless we witness a colossal baby boom in the next few years, a sizeable portion of the workforce twenty-five years from now will consist of people who are currently employed. If the current situation is maintained (and there is no reason to believe that it will not), the importance of adult education resources is likely to increase rather than decline in the future.

Underlying the growing interest in educational resources is the widespread idea that the nation's economic performance is somehow linked to education and training. That notion is embodied in the theory of Human Capital, according to which the knowledge and skills found in the workforce represent valuable resources for the market. Perhaps the most well-known proponent of the Human Capital Theory is the Nobel prize-winning economist T. W. Schultz (1961, 1981). In the 1960s, dissenting with then-popular Doomsday scenarios proposed by scientific groups such as the Club of Rome, Schultz heralded the advent of a new age in economics. He objected to the Malthusian view of ever-diminishing resources and of a world doomed for lack of unlimited natural capital. He did not subscribe to the entropic view of human economics, where human survival was linked to the direct exploitation of the finite resources of the natural world. Instead, Schultz (1981) proposed that the key to economic growth lay in the "quality of the population" that comprised the economic unit. In Schultz's view, human beings themselves represent the greatest potential for economic prosperity:

> ... Increases in the acquired abilities of people throughout the world and advances in useful knowledge hold the key to future economic productivity and to its contributions to human well-being ... Investment in population quality and in knowledge in large part determines the future prospects of mankind (Schultz, 1981, p. 31).

Human capital is different from the other two forms of capital, often called "natural" and "machine" capital (for example, the forests, and the machines used for cutting them down). Human capital, according to Schultz (1981), represents "those *abilities* and *information* that have economic value" (p. 61, italics mine). The intangible inner resources of human beings thus replace material assets as the defining dimension of wealth. Furthermore, human capital is a renewable resource and, unlike other forms of capital, there is no theoretical limit to its supply!

Schultz also contended that education influences favourably "the ability to deal with disequilibria associated with economic modernization." With the recent explosion in technology and global competition, Canada's economic prospects seem linked more directly than ever to the development of a knowledgeable and well-trained workforce and hence to human capital. Canadian economic policy has mirrored that assumption in no uncertain terms. In 1992, the Economic Council of Canada stated that professional training was the key to future competitiveness of Canada's industries. The Conference Board of Canada declared that educated Canadians were essential to the economic well-being of the nation. In 1993, a Department of Finance report estimated that half the new jobs created in the 1990s would require at least sixteen years of schooling.

There is some debate, however, regarding the actual or "absolute" value of education in our changing economy. In order to derive some real measure of the relation between educational attainment and economic benefit, we would have to consider not only the levels of education found in today's workforce, but also other factors affecting employment and economic activity. For example, while it can be shown that individuals' educational level is linked to their employability (university graduates are three times more likely to find employment than non-graduates), it has not been shown that the levels of skills required to perform specific jobs has undergone a corresponding increase or even an increase in a direction that matches the training received.

There is a need to review some of the basic assumptions of Human Capital Theory. Government policy is being shaped in Canada by a generally uncritical acceptance of some of these assumptions, without regard to their accuracy or relevant context. What follows is a discussion of some of the underlying postulates of Human Capital Theory and their relation to adult education and training-related policy.

Seven Assumptions of Human Capital Theory

1. Human capital is an investment for the future. One of the basic tenets of Schultz's Human Capital Theory is that training is a response to future needs and that it represents a safeguard against the ever-present threat of economic obsolescence. According to this view, today's training programs should prepare us for tomorrow's reality and the economic challenges to come. However, forecasting labour requirements is not an exact science; there is considerable doubt as to the feasibility and accuracy of such predictions. The methods currently employed for estimating medium and long-term training needs fall admittedly short of empirical certainty and offer at best a marginally credible appraisal. For example, the following three widely used forecasting methods suffer from important shortcomings (Bezdek, 1974).

- *Forecasting by surveying employer estimates.* This method is considered relatively undependable because, in their forecasts, employers are more typically concerned with short-term results than long-term projections. In their everyday activities, entrepreneurs are more likely to react to environmental changes rather than to plan ahead for them.

- *Forecasting by using a "combined indicator approach."* This approach, which groups a large number of indicators by economic sector and identifies trends, is questionable in today's economy because it assumes that past trends will continue in the future. Because of the nature of change that affects all economic sectors, it becomes less reasonable each day to hold such an assumption as true.

- *Forecasting by stating economic goals and inferring future labour needs.* This method is problematic because it does not take into account the *current* educational needs and capacities of the workforce. Thus, it fails to recognize that certain goals are better matched than others to the actual capacity of the workforce—and the education system—to respond to them. There is little support for the idea that a more capable or knowledgeable workforce will necessarily emerge from this kind of economic wishful thinking.

2. More training leads to better work skills. In recent years, we have been moving from task-specific definitions of training needs to more inclusive, or generic, views of employee qualifications. Since it has become increasingly difficult to predict the direction of future shifts in technology and the economy, it seems more advantageous to target competencies that can be transferred across a wide range of tasks rather than those that can only be applied to specific work environments. The question is, *which* competencies?

The notion of generic skills is not a novel idea but has evolved over the past two centuries. During the Industrial Revolution, workers were required to perform low-skill job-related tasks, such as operating a machine or otherwise assist in machine-based industrial processes. The need for formal education was low, and the most sought-after generic competencies were *experience based*. For example, being handy with tools or mechanically inclined were valued employee attributes.

Later, with accelerating industrialization, there was a need for higher-level abilities among employees. A corresponding increase in educational requirements ensued, and schooling took on new importance and meaning. Education was expected to develop individuals' cognitive and problem-solving abilities, through mastery of disciplines previously reserved for elite scholars of the liberal arts, such as mathematics, philosophy and semantics. During this period, generic competencies were *cognitive based*. Valued employee traits included "being bright" and problem-solving abilities.

Today, government and employers claim that even with unprecedented levels of education,[1] employees are lacking fundamental competencies necessary to maintain a competitive edge in the new economy. Employees are expected to be responsive to technological changes, to be interested in seeking out flexible organizational alternatives and to share with their employers a sense of autonomy and responsibility for the job. It is no longer satisfactory for employees to perform well, they must now also *want to*. They are expected to be proactive and to display an eager willingness to confront change with innovative ideas. The generic skills have moved from an experiential to a cognitive dimension, to a *cultural/affective* dimension (Schutze, 1992).

The development of "desirable" employee attitudes may be the next challenge of the postmodern organization, but it would be hazardous to consider such an objective as a replacement for training that actually produces useful skills, rather than the socialization of workers to organizational imperatives.

3. Educational institutions play a central role in the development of human capital. Recent developments in the workplace have virtually redefined the nature of work and the nature of learning, both on the job and in academic institutions. The traditional approaches to training and education may no longer fit the demands of the situation.

- *Learning on the job.* Many job specifications change so quickly that by the time instructional programs are put together, their content may have become obsolete. Furthermore, as workstations become more specialized, there is more need for individuals to update their knowledge independently of their co-workers' equally specialized—but often divergent—learning needs. There is a growing consensus that in order to keep up, organizations must reduce their dependency on employer-initiated programs and turn to a culture of self-directed, autonomous learning (Foucher and Tremblay, 1992).

- *Institutional learning.* Traditional approaches to teaching and learning have been characterized as ill suited for the purposes of the emerging "learning society" (Drucker, 1994). Educational approaches that have been passed down through the last several centuries are becoming less than viable. While the nature of educational goals is shifting towards a broader base of skills acquisition, it is becoming more difficult to prescribe universally relevant program contents. Not only are the requirements of the job market constantly shifting, the nature of knowledge itself is being redefined, at least in terms of its relevance to specific needs and situations. In short, schools, colleges and universities must change their role from being dispensers of knowledge to become places where people learn how to negotiate the paths of fluidly changing information and meaning.

4. Employees need to improve their skills. The technological revolution is often cited as the most pressing reason why education and knowledge are becoming valuable economic commodities. However, in the context of computerization, robotization, and mechanization, the development of new technologies often has produced an opposite effect. For example, just a few years ago it was believed that computer programming would be a universally required skill in the ominously computer-ridden future. Consequently, computer language programming was taught to school children, as it was generally accepted that learning Fortran or other basic programming languages was a prerequisite for accessing tomorrow's technology.

This example again underscores the difficulty of making accurate predictions about future knowledge needs. Today, computer technology does not require users to have high-tech programming skills any more than driving a modern car requires the driver to possess extensive knowledge in mechanical engineering. In fact, computers are becoming easier to use every day. Furthermore, although information technology is an area of economic growth, it does not create a large number of jobs, certainly not enough to justify massive educational investments in that particular area.

Another problem associated with the "improved skills" theory is that no matter how much training a person receives, the possibility of applying that knowledge is directly dependent on the opportunities found in the job market. In the words of Berg and Gorelick (1971), "there can be problems in countries that educate a stratum of the population whose occupational expectations are well beyond the opportunities the economy may provide in the short or even the long run" (p. 24).

5. *Training enhances employability.* It is widely assumed that higher levels of education create a more competent workforce (Canada, 1986a; 1995; 1996). Employers, ostensibly subscribing to that logic, tend to use educational attainment as a criterion for selecting employees. In the recent context of diminishing job opportunities, this has translated into a frenzy towards educational attainment in the job-seeking population.

Nevertheless, Canada is still struggling with rampant unemployment and that new scourge of the 1990s, underemployment. Strangely enough, this situation has not brought about a crisis of confidence in the claims of the educational system. It would appear that there is no perceived contradiction between the need for increasing levels of education and the lack of effect higher educational levels have had on unemployment rates. Since the workplace demands higher skill levels, it seems logical that more education is needed just to keep up with the changes. High-tech jobs require new technical skills, while repetitive jobs have been taken over by machinery. However, increases in skill-level requirements are not as widespread as is generally believed. Automatization and computerization as a rule have tended to make tasks *easier*, not more difficult. This is the phenomenon that Rubenson (1992) has described as the simultaneous "upskilling" of a small part of work tasks with the simultaneous "deskilling" of the larger portion.

Another reason to doubt the assumption that education and training enhance employability is that most new jobs are created in sectors that have *not* been affected by labour-saving technological advances. According to recent surveys (Canada, 1995), the largest growth in job opportunities has been in the service sector, in areas such as food preparation and retail sales. Also, most new jobs are created by small and medium enterprises where employer-based training is the exception rather than the norm (Canada, 1995). It appears that the job market is growing in precisely those areas offering few prospects for and requiring the least training or educational attainment.

6. *Training can compensate for skill shortages.* The fact that many job vacancies are not readily filled, even in times of relatively high unemployment, has been attributed to a corresponding shortage of skills in the workforce (Sørensen & Kalleberg, 1994). According to this view, the problem is not the scarcity of potential employees but the fact that those employees do not possess

the skills the market requires. Training is seen as a way to bridge the gap between offer and demand by providing the needed human capital. However, the problem of matching jobs to individuals is not solely based on the non-availability of specific skills; it can also be attributed to the difficulties encountered in matching those individual skills with the expectations of their potential employers (Haughton, 1993). The problem is presented as one of skills "mismatch" rather than skill "shortage." Typical barriers to matching fall into three categories: (1) labour market dynamics, (2) structural discrimination, and (3) employee self-selection.

First, the relationships that define labour market dynamics have been shifting considerably. Entire populations that until recently were excluded from the paid workforce are coming forth with their own demands and expectations. For example, childcare and transportation were cited as the most significant barriers to employment in a recent labour survey in Britain (Haughton, 1993). Another factor is the decline in the numbers of youth entering the labour market for the first time. This demographic occurrence deprives the market of a traditionally cheap source of labour, thus exercising an upward pressure on wages. In this instance, to attribute labour shortages to "low skills" may be in fact a way of transferring low-wage expectations to other (i.e., older, more experienced) segments of the workforce.

Structural discrimination is another phenomenon that accounts for a portion of skills mismatch in the job market. When selecting employees, many employers admittedly apply criteria linked to cultural norms, such as physical appearance, language, even family background and address of residence (Until recently, hiring practices of inner-city firms tended to favour suburban commuters; the trend now is to move plants to suburbia, where most employees live.) (Haughton, 1993). Employers also consider job stability as a positive factor when hiring workers. This effectively discriminates against several groups, namely youth, women and those who work in particularly volatile sectors of the economy, such as the manufacturing sector, where high turnover is a fact of life.

Third, employee self-selection can be described as the limitations that social-economic groups impose upon themselves for various reasons. For example, social conditioning may be responsible for some women's reduced or stereotyped job expectations. Similarly, working-class youth tend to "emulate their peers, leave school, and end up in similar jobs, in the same locality" (Haughton, 1993). In these instances, no matter how difficult it may appear to devise effective remedial tools, it is clear that they will have little to do with a quantitative increase in technical job training.

7. Employment and unemployment are economic concepts. In light of what precedes, it should be apparent that the relations between education/training and the fluctuations in national economic prospects are more complex than

Schultz would contend in his theory of Human Capital. How, then, are we to understand the sweeping changes affecting the development of the "new" economy, and the changes in defining the need for and the distribution of education and training in the population? The answer of course may be that the systemic processes that define those relations will forever continue to elude economic analysis because of their unmanageable complexity. However, an interesting corollary to that observation is that any attempt at analysis would necessarily take into consideration those factors that lie outside the field of economics.

In economic theory, the discrepancy between market demand and the failure of the environment to fill that demand is attributed to imperfections of the market. If markets were perfect, the theory goes, jobs and job expertise would be distributed evenly across all occupations. There is a fundamental error in considering the labour market as a market just like any other, with offer and demand as the principal balancing factor. The dynamics of employment and unemployment also include the mediating *social* factors that account for their fluctuations. Rather than simply juxtaposing the notions of labour market and labour policy as the two contributory forces shaping the employment landscape, we should consider social issues, such as demographics; culture; diversity; segmentation along race, gender and class lines; trends in employment status; and perhaps most important, the "new values" affecting the distribution of wealth in society in order to derive a real understanding of the forces that shape and are shaped by employment and unemployment in Canada.

The Need for Critical Analysis

What do we mean by the word *employment*? Defining that term has been problematic for many writers, over several decades (see Pigou, 1933:1968; Maruani & Reynaud, 1990). The notion of "work," in itself, does not provide an adequate basis for defining employment. While work can be defined as the production of goods and services, employment refers to the modes of access to labour markets and the resulting status that access confers to those who possess it (Maruani & Reynaud, 1990). Today, we are witnessing some major shifts in the levels of access to employment for specific social groups. The massive influx of women in salaried occupations and the shrinking age pyramid at both ends of the population's lifespan are major factors that have modified the balance of inclusion and/or exclusion between specific groups in society. For example, women have always worked, but only recently have they begun to demand inclusion in the employment (i.e., the salaried labour) sphere. Similarly, the bulge in size of the forty-to-fifty-year-old age group has pushed back the time of full entry into the workforce for youth and moved forward the age of retirement for middle-aged workers. Here, the interplay of demographics and culture, rather than economic principles, performs a central role in determining the fluctuations in employment among the social groups.

While it cannot be said that the often-stated need for more training is based on false assumptions, these assumptions would benefit from a more critical analysis. In Canada, employers have been reticent to invest their own funds in training, perhaps because training is considered a high-risk investment in an economy that is characterized by, among other things, high employee turn-over. Also, retraining of current employees may not seem profitable when it is cheaper to hire new trainees who have graduated from programs, many of them government funded. This could be the real incentive behind employers' sudden interest in the virtues of school-based or government-based certification. In this view, needed skills perhaps are not hard to come by, but they do not come as easily or as cheaply as employers would find advantageous. In absolute terms, this does not necessarily indicate a shortage in the availability of job-related skills, but it does point to a breakdown in cohesion between the economic agents concerned, namely business, government and educational institutions. Above all, it is symptomatic of a tension between the imperatives of productivity, as defined by employers, and those of social equity in terms of who should pay the bill for work-related training.

Education and training have long been considered the "great equalizers" in an otherwise unequal society. This view would lead us to believe that education has the potential of reducing the inequalities in the economic status of individuals by providing all people with the possibility of accumulating educational (i.e., human) capital. But education in itself does not create jobs. High competition for available jobs, combined with the widespread use of educational attainment as a measure of employability, has resulted in a trend towards educational inflation. It seems that the more "educational capital" one acquires, the more one needs!

The strict adherence to the notion of education/training as a subset of human capital no longer satisfactorily describes the roles of adult education and training. There is a very real need for renewed interest in work-related learning: faced with the proliferation of new forms of knowledge and with a widening gap in access to employment, traditional approaches to training are proving to be ineffective. Rather than blindly subscribe to the idea that economic prosperity depends on *more* education and training, perhaps we had better look into the nature of training programs, their modes of organization and their real, rather than their imagined, effects.

The Function of Ideology

For many critics, among them members of the editorial staff of the conservative British publication *The Economist*,[2] the claim that training is the key to economic prosperity and that it is one of the best ways to get people "off the dole," is simply not supported by observation or analysis. In short, the argument for increased investment in human capital does not seem to serve any particular social or economic purpose. Why, then, all the hype?

Perhaps the answer to that question can be found by looking at the "big picture." One of the major trends in world economic policy over the past decades has been a movement towards a redistribution of wealth that allows greater capital accumulation among the rich, at the expense of the poor and the working class. This trend has been accompanied by the erosion of the welfare state, and the globalization of capital markets in favour of more competitive relocations of units of production. This has had a deleterious effect on social programs, on the number of middle-income jobs in Canada, and indeed on the availability of any job for a great number of Canadians. In other words, the new so-called "global economy" serves the few at the expense of the many. Not exactly a popular or welcome change for the citizenry at large.

This situation prompts a disturbing question: If the relations between economic agents is so severely skewed in favour of one group at the detriment of all others, how then does the dominant group get away with it? How can an unbalanced and unfair economic agenda go unchallenged by so many of those who are directly affected by it?

I would argue that the only way to pursue such an agenda without provoking a generalized crisis of confidence in government and business is to couch the program in a carefully constructed *ideology*. Ideology has been the focus of much of the recent efforts at "hard selling" investment in training. According to Thompson (1990), ideology is a set of unexamined assumptions that are so deeply rooted and "generally accepted as normal," as to be virtually invisible. Two of the distinctive functions of ideology are *reification* and *legitimization*.

Our government's eagerness to subscribe to the idea of "training-as-panacea" can be seen as an attempt to reify ("to present as concrete") its abstract view of the economic order. If we can be made to believe that the prevailing climate of economic hardship can be remedied through job-related training, then we are only a step away from believing that a new prosperity is within reach, *providing we acquire appropriate educational capital*. The implication here, of course, is that the only reason why this "new prosperity" remains elusive is that we have failed to take appropriate steps to attain the required levels of training.

The ideology of training can also be seen as serving a function of legitimization. The traditional view of education as a necessary requisite for affluence, freedom and democracy has been criticized by sociologists such as Pierre Bourdieu (1968) and Bowles & Gintis (1977). According to their view, education serves primarily to reproduce the existing social order, and to *legiti-*

mize its power structure. The mechanics of this process are quite evident in the rhetoric surrounding the training issue. As we have seen, people become unemployed only when they *desire* to work, thereby confirming that wage labour is, in that person's view, a legitimate form of economic organization. In the same way, people become "employable" by seeking further training, thereby subscribing to the logic of more-training-for-more-jobs. Unfortunately, training is a scarce commodity—much like the jobs it is supposed to give access to! Thus, the focus shifts from the lack of jobs to the lack of training. In other words, using that logic, it is quite *legitimate* for employment to be unavailable for people who do not have the requisite amount—or the right kind—of training.

The Roles of Adult Educators

As adult educators, we are faced with a strange dilemma. After acknowledging the limitations of education and training as cure-all solutions to economic and social inequality, should we abandon our current activities and take on more direct forms of social activism that are more in line with our social ideals? Or should we concentrate on what we do best, which is to provide educational services to those who require them, regardless of the fact that in doing so we may knowingly contribute to the perpetuation of an oppressive cycle?

Because of their particular functions in society, adult educators exercise a significant influence on the human and organizational forces that shape the social landscape. Malcolm Knowles (1980), with his usual keen insight, believed that adult educators functioned within three distinct professional spheres of influence and responsibility. It is appropriate to review these roles and obligations in light of our perplexing quandary.

First, the responsibility of adult educators is to individual learners, in helping relationships aimed at facilitating self-actualization. This is in line with the humanistic roots of adult education, put forward by proponents of lifelong learning such as John Dewey and Eduard Lindeman. From that perspective, learning is an empowering process through which individual learners gain access to the instruments of their own advancement. In the context of generalized economic double-speak, it seems particularly important for adult educators to be watchful of corrupt rhetoric, and to direct their practice towards the emancipation of learners rather than their renewed servitude. This can be achieved through the critical analysis of the educational situations one is involved in and by keeping a vigilant eye on interests that are in opposition to those of the learners.

Second, adult educators play a central role in the workplace. Here, the scope of their responsibility expands with the awareness of the task at hand. In order to reconcile the divergent needs of the individuals and the organizations that employ them, adult educators should avoid viewing themselves as simple executants in the corporate agenda. Rather, they are in position to act as consultants both to the learners entrusted to their care and to the employer-organizations that pay for their services. In this sense, adult educators can directly and effectively become agents of change. For example, employees are not infrequently kept out of the decision loop when it comes to assessing training needs and devising training agendas. This leads to poorly designed learning environments, reticent and unmotivated groups of learners, and armies of dispirited trainers. Corporate trainers can avoid such a situation by acting as intermediary and advocating the importance of cohesive action. After all, they are well placed to observe how top-down decision making and training policies aimed at sub-minimal skills produce sub-minimal results.

Third, adult educators have a social responsibility that entails a commitment to certain basic values, such as equity, tolerance, co-operation and recognition of the diversity of human experience. Adult education is a powerful tool for shaping people's worldview and as such requires an acute sense of social propriety from those who plan, design, implement and dispense training activities of any kind. It is perhaps in this context that the roles of adult educators can best be understood. Without an overarching vision that is truly conducive to the promotion of worthy societal values, a self-proclaimed propagator of knowledge is indeed something to be wary of.

Adult education and training are notions that have been used for proclaiming the intrinsic value of human capital. We have seen that this contention rests on a series of assumptions that, when viewed in their proper context, are less than convincing. We have also argued that beyond the interplay of business and government interests, the ideology of human capital performs a function of reification and legitimization for the new economic order. By looking at their three fundamental roles, we are reminded that adult educators are dynamic actors in the relationship between learners, production organizations and the larger needs of a democratic society.

Endnotes

[1] Between 1961 and 1986, the number of Canadian university graduates rose 432 percent. The number of university degree holders in the workforce has been increasing at a rate of nearly 10 percent a decade since 1979. The proportion of workers who have had at least some post-secondary education has doubled since 1979. And this upward trend in educational attainment is likely to continue, as older people who have less education leave the labor force and are replaced by more educated cohorts (Statistics Canada, 1995).

[2] See *The Economist* 339, no. 7960 (April 1996).

11

Questioning the Concept of the Learning Organization

Tara Fenwick

Hit the ground running or you won't keep up!, shouts Nuala Beck (1995), a Toronto economist and popular speaker-consultant in Canadian human resources circles. Beck warns that only workers who learn and change continuously to accommodate the demands of the marketplace will survive in the new economy. Educators and human resource developers have adopted this rhetoric of urgency, declaring that "learning is the necessary response to change" (Dixon, 1993, p. 18). The concept of the "learning organization" is gaining momentum in both private and public sectors as the new panacea for coping with the most perplexing and frightening changes swirling about the labour market. An ideology of values, structure and prescriptive strategies, the learning organization concept offers a cuddly vision,of "community" and collegiality, a workplace where trust, sharing, reflective practice and empowerment flourish. Common principles reiterated among learning organization theorists direct organizations to reinvent themselves so that they might: (1) create continuous learning opportunities, (2) promote inquiry and dialogue, (3) encourage collaboration and team learning, (4) establish systems to capture and share learning, (5) empower people toward collective vision, and (6) connect organizations to their environments (Watkins and Marsick, 1993).

Certainly such principles hold promise for creating a more humanitarian, egalitarian, growth-oriented workplace. But amid the enthusiasm attending flurried efforts to implement these principles, important questions remain unasked in the dominant literature on the subject, questions about what is meant by a learning organization, what it values, its assumptions about learning and the nature of knowledge and how its discourse structures the relations and practices of the workplace. As organizations come to recognize their position in the continual flux of an unpredictable global economy, the place of the worker in a learning organization has become relegated to one of eternal, slippery deficiency: workers must learn continuously and embrace instability as the normal order of things. That the workplace appoints itself as the individual's educator, personal development counsellor and even spiritual mentor is rarely questioned.

This chapter critically examines the ideology and discourse of the learning organization in two sections. The historical context, principles and people involved in developing the learning organization concept will be outlined briefly in the following section. The second section challenges assumptions embedded in learning organization ideology.

Historical Contexts and Principles of the Learning Organization

The "learning organization" arose from the convergence of three important currents: (1) the tradition of organizational development (OD) and particularly concepts of organizational learning; (2) economic shifts to globalization, deregulation and information-based industry; and (3) Total Quality Management (TQM).

Organizational learning is not a new concept. Finger and Woolis (1994) argue that five schools of thought about organizational learning led to the appearance of Senge's (1991) learning organization concept. The earliest notions of organizational learning centred on organizational continuity and assumed the essential stability and coherence of the organization. Learning was viewed conservatively as a process to "encode, store and retrieve the lessons of history despite the turnover of personnel and the passage of time" (Levitt & March, 1988, p. 319) or to continually improve existing procedures for adaptation. Later approaches viewed organizational learning as a transformative process.

Organizational development—a process that actively implements planned change to help organizations examine and change their routines and cultural norms—was well established in the work of Argyris and Schon (1978). The OD goal was to develop the organization's ability to maintain a pattern of homeostasis despite fluctuations in the external environment through an *action science* approach. Because the organization was encouraged to incorporate critical thinking into a continuous evaluation of its routines and norms—what Argyris called "double loop learning"—the change process was dynamic and even subversive, although fundamentally conservative.

Finger and Woolis (1994) argue that a third group writing in the 1980s took a more sophisticated view of learning (i.e., Fiol & Lyles, 1985), clarifying important distinctions between organizational change on the one hand and learning on the other. They described different levels of learning and different

learning systems and acknowledged the complex dynamics of the organization interacting with the various communities and forces comprising its environment. Thus, the concept of learning organization was incubated during
growing interest in the nature of collective learning and the notion of an
organization as a continuously adaptive and proactive agent.

The economic shifts of the 1980s was the second trajectory associated with
the emergence of the learning organization concept. These shifts raised considerable alarm: business viewed itself in constant jeopardy in a new competitive climate that moved at fiber-optic speed, embraced global dimensions of
cultural and market influences and communicated through constantly changing technologies. Businesses envisioned themselves as caught in a "paradigm
shift" and looked for new organizational structures and leadership approaches.
Continuous learning offered a survival strategy.

During this period, the third contributing influence to learning organization
notions, the movement toward Total Quality Management (TQM), transformed business and government. Under TQM dictates, organizations were
restructured to become flatter and more fluid, action-oriented, accountable for
outcomes focusing on quality, mission and culture. People were grouped in
multi-skilled teams that ideally defined and regulated their own work. These
changes prepared the ground for the germination of the learning organization
ideology.

Senge (1991), whose book *The Fifth Discipline: The Art and Practice of
the Learning Organization* is often credited with popularizing the concept,
defines learning organization as "a place where people continually expand
their capacity to create the results they truly desire, where new and expansive
patterns of thinking are nurtured, where collective aspiration is set free, and
where people are continually learning how to act together" (p. 3). The learning organization concept presumes continuous change to drive the centre of
the organization's activity and stresses continuous innovation as the key to
productivity in an environment of constant change (Watkins & Marsick,
1993). For Senge and his associates (1994), there are five interwoven forces
or "disciplines" to cultivate when "building" a learning organization: (1) personal mastery, or making personal capacities and dreams explicit; (2) mental
models, or examining and overturning deep personal beliefs; (3) team learning, or collaborating to develop and share knowledge effectively in small
groups; (4) shared vision, or building a collective dream to guide future action; and (5) systems thinking, or coming to view one's own actions and
agendas from a big-picture perspective that accepts one's fundamental inter-
connectivity with everyone else. Central to these disciplines is the assumption
that employees need to engage in critical reflection and open dialogue, expos-
ing their own belief systems and critically challenging others' belief systems,
to break free of thinking patterns which perpetuate dysfunction and prevent

innovation. A flexible, self-reflexive, but vividly clear vision is supposedly essential to carry the organization through the rapids of tumultuous change.

The Fifth Discipline was treated like a manifesto, cited so often in board-rooms and journals of the early 1990s (e.g., see Gavin, 1993; Shaw & Perkins, 1991; Wick, 1993; Ulrich, Jick, & von Glinow, 1994; Redding & Catalanello, 1994) that it began exercising wide influence on organizational reform and restructuring efforts. Canadian federal task force reports and policy back-ground papers in 1992-94 (e.g., CCMD, 1994) demanded that public institu-tions restructure to integrate continuous learning principles. Large corporations such as Canadian banks (Flood, 1993,) and NOVA (Sass, 1996) announced commitment to transform themselves into learning organizations. A consortium for organizational learning launched in early 1995 by the Cen-ter for Public Management invited private and public organizations to collabo-rate as they worked through issues in becoming a learning organization (Prospectus, 1994).

So why question this enthusiastic Canadian plunge into intentions of con-tinuous learning and innovation, trusting communities and caring, collabora-tive teams? Critics from the left dismiss the human capital orientation embedded in learning organization literature, which regards people as "re-sources" that serve the organization's pursuit of profit (see Bouchard's chapter "Training and Work: Myths about Human Capital" in this volume). The power structures of the market-place and the selected knowledge it values remain unexamined, argue Finger and Woollis (1994), and learning is distorted into a tool for competitive advantage. Learning theorists might argue that the learn-ing organization concept largely ignores current knowledge about adult learn-ing and development. The ideals associated with learning organizations of interrelations, unity, co-operation and wholeness have been criticized by Ed-wards and Usher (1996) as rampant moralism subordinated to overarching order, the system's totality. Meanwhile the moralism-by-consensus that con-structs the shared vision supposedly guiding the organization is relativist, "emotive and inherently subjective," argues Campbell (1995, p. 94); such a vision lacks a deep conceptual grounding in objective principles of right and wrong, and the possibilities for variant values are infinite.

Problems with the Learning Organization Concept

What follows is a critical examination of six premises of the learning organization that focus on: (1) the organization as a site and frame for learn-ing, (2) the dominant role of managers and educators, (3) the subordinate role accorded to employees as undifferentiated learners-in-deficit, (4) the emphasis on problem solving and instrumental knowledge, (5) the organization's appro-priation of critical reflection, and (6) the reliance on "open" dialogue for group learning in the workplace.

The Organization As a Site and Framework for Learning

Learning in the workplace is spatially and temporally bounded by the organization's contours. The individual's learning becomes understood as a 9:00 to 5:00 phenomenon that is motivated by the job, developed through the job and measurable only through observable behaviours linked to competencies that benefit the job. Learning is recognized only in knowledge that the organization can access, knowledge which can be spoken, deconstructed and shared (for example, through dialogue), rather than knowledge which might be tacit and embedded in practice, communicative relations, visions, choices and intuition.

One problem here is the conflation of individual and organizational learning. There is a leap from individual learning processes of action and reflection, constructing and transforming meaning perspectives, to applying these concepts somewhat cavalierly to an organization. The organization is thus construed as a unitary, definable, intelligent entity. It is not, nor is it stable and bounded. Consider the multiple sub-groups comprising an organization, each characterized by distinct cultures, each changing according to its dynamic interplay with other groups and shifting shape with the nomadic movement of individual workers. How can this fluctuating combination of sub-groups be totalized as a single, monolithic organism that somehow "learns" and has memory?

From the individual's lifeworld perspective, a single workplace organization is only one part of the individual's purposes, growth curve, dilemmas and preoccupations. People often work part time, hold jobs in different organizations or work at home while loaning themselves to many different organizations to conduct business. People flow among various overlapping organizational communities. When learning is defined in terms of what perspectives and skills one particular organization most values, such as its own shared vision and need for multi-skills, each person's multiple identities (and knowledges) are obscured in the organization's perceptual field, which coheres around itself. The meanings, dilemmas, insights and changes comprising people's daily experience are neither acknowledged nor valued because these various kinds of knowledge do not fit the organization's perception of itself as a unitary, rational container of subjects. Marsick and Watkins (1990) go so far as to describe as "dysfunctional" a person's ongoing "incidental" learning that does not advance the organization's purposes. Too rigid and narrow a formulation of what counts as knowledge in the organization's gaze potentially alienates the individual from his or her own meanings and fails to allow these meanings to flourish and contribute to the community.

Literature about the learning organization tends to be written by and for those most concerned with the overall health and existence of the organization, those whose own identity is most closely aligned to the organization's goals and success. These are the managers of the organization and the educators who serve them. Two issues attending this circumstance deserve attention. First, despite the emphasis placed on dialogue among "multiple perspectives," the production and consumption of the learning organization discourse omits many important perspectives. Among the excluded are workers' agendas and visions, small businesses struggling to compete in the accelerated markets of constant innovation, growing multitudes of independent contractors serving corporations through part-time temporary service, labourers in semi-skilled or de-skilled activities whose work is not knowledge reliant, and those who lack the learning capabilities required for critical reflection, visioning and team learning.

Second, the literature typically approaches the learning project as something that "empowers" others, or "helps" others to learn. The voice of the learning organization sculptors is not self-reflexive. The agenda and vision of the leader or educational agent is bracketed out, obscuring the partiality and positionality of the voices calling for continuous learning and learning organizations. This situation is reminiscent of the emancipatory pedagogue who presumes the privilege to enlighten and speak for the "oppressed." Who is controlling the vision, the goals, the definitions of learning—and for what purposes? The pragmatic issue attending such myopia is the inevitable incongruence between the workers' perspectives and those of the manager or educator.

Employees As Undifferentiated Learners-in-Deficit

If managers and educators are the architects of the learning organization, employees are colonized as its subjects. Constituted as always learning and exhorted to remain balanced on the precipice of risk, these subjects are particularly vulnerable. In a climate of "continuous" innovation the individual theoretically can never be grounded in a sense of expertise or stability. Nor does the individual have control over pronouncing what counts as knowledge, including personally constructed knowledge. From the continuous learning perspective, the individual is supposed to learn more, learn better and learn faster, and is therefore always in deficit. An ideology of "constant improvement" tends to create a competitive track where the racing dogs never reach the mechanical rabbit. The anxiety-inducing press to avoid "being left behind" is common in workplace learning literature. Meanwhile the organization's knowledge—considered the key to success—is linked directly to the employee's demonstrable ability and willingness to learn. The worker becomes responsible for the organization's health without the authority to determine alternative frameworks to "learning" through which this health might be considered and measured.

The focus of the learning organization is on employees whose work is knowledge reliant. Thus the only individuals who are explicitly included in continuous learning initiatives are those whose learning power and stock of learnings are valuable to their employing organization as commodities that can help accelerate the productivity, improve the competitive performance of the business and generate profit. Workers who do not generate knowledge, who, according to Paquette (1995), are increasingly the kinds of employees most hired and required to fill Canada's job openings, are excluded from or outside the borders of the maps being constructed of today's market-place by the continuous learning promoters. Many writers are currently drawing attention to technology's dehumanizing impact in workplaces, diminishing the need for workers who think, create, change and proactively generate new knowledge (Zuboff, 1988). Agendas for continuous learning and growth evidently are oriented most towards the continuing privilege of the technocratic-professional-managerial elite, who are already the likeliest to be most educated and to have most access to learning opportunities.

Learning organization literature makes little attempt to distinguish meaningfully among the unique learning processes of individual worker-learners. Learning is understood to be essentially problem solving; "deeper" learning supposedly transpires through processes of critical reflection (especially through verbal disclosure and deconstruction of belief systems), and a self-directed approach to learning becomes an ideal toward which employees should be encouraged to strive. These assumptions ignore literature showing that self-directed learning is *not* a generalizable approach among adults (see the chapter "Self-Directed Learning: Highlighting the Contradictions" by Chovanec in this volume; Pratt, 1988; Collins, 1991) and that activity and tools more than dialogue affect what and how people learn (Lave & Wenger, 1991). Gender, race and class dimensions, all ignored in the learning organization discourse, create important distinctions among individuals in what holds meaning for them and how they construct these meanings. For example, studies in women's workplace learning (MacKeracher & McFarland, 1994) report complexities in relational learning and the centrality of self that contradict many learning organization assumptions. Individuals' workplace learning has been shown to vary dramatically according to their intentions, the disjunctures they apprehend, their positionality and relations in the workplace community, their values of knowledge and views of themselves as knowers (Fenwick, 1996). The target group for continuous learning in the workplace neglects large groups of people who are implicitly "other" but whose individual work-learning struggles continue to produce knowledge, whether or not these kinds of knowledge are recognized by the learning organization. Meanwhile, learners with special needs, disabilities, low literacy skills or other characteristics which don't fit the learning organization's preferred approaches (self-directed learning, critical reflection, risk and innovation and dialogue) are in danger of being discarded altogether.

Emphasis on Problem Solving and Instrumental Knowledge

The learning organization literature emphasizes two kinds of knowledge: innovative problem solving and "detecting error" (Argyris, 1993). The problem-solving orientation frames learning as continually seeking freedom from difficulty, which is a negative orientation to understanding cognitive construction of meaning (Prawat, 1993). When the understanding of learning becomes driven by a metaphor of problem solving and innovation, learning is limited to instrumentality. Productivity is thus used as the ultimate criterion to evaluate efforts towards personal growth, building relationships in teams and building cultures and close communities. The usefulness of what is being produced is removed from the question. Worse, the unpredictable, fluid, emergent process of learning is linked to the production of goods, which depends on certainty, bounded time periods and concrete products. Strange fruit is produced from the union of learning and production, evident in business literature that discusses "intellectual capital" (Stewart, 1994) as though the ephemerality of meaning making could be packaged, measured, bought and sold.

The purpose of "continuous learning," indeed the very term, promotes an expansionary view of development. The question "Learn what?" is rarely addressed. Employees might discern that the organization will premise future staffing decisions on particular skills or work experiences. The question "Learn how?" is the programmatic focus of most learning organization literature, which provides lots of advice about learning process derived from romanticized humanistic principles of holistic learning and building family-like communities that care and share and notions modeled from action research. Because there is no explicit curriculum (naturally in the ideology of constant change, the learning architects can defer commitment to particular content: content emerges unpredictably), decisions about the "what" of learning presumably are never made. Innovation to "keep up" with constant change is the focus. This not only ties employee learning to the bumper of the overall company direction controlled by management, but also privileges breakthrough thinking and "new" (profitable) knowledge over other kinds of knowledge, such as relational, cultural, procedural and personal. From such a perspective, alternative views of learning are invisible. For example, might include deepening inward rather than expanding outward; enriching existing meaning structures, confirming and extending them, rather than adding to them or transforming them; might be recursive, circling back to concepts and internalizing them into behaviours and beliefs, rather than generating new concepts.

Hart (1992; 1993) offers an elegant critique of the current imperatives driving the workplace and its learning orientation. She raises questions about what is truly important and productive work, and to what extent the expansionary, innovation-oriented perspective fits how individuals view their learning in the workplace. Hart's vision of "sustenance" work, predicated upon communicative dimensions rather than the hyperactive productivity driving the industrial machine, is only one example illustrating the possible alternatives driven to the margins by the domination of continuous learning initiatives for organizational competitive advantage.

The Organization's Use of Critical Reflection

Watkins and Marsick (1993), like Senge et al. (1994) and Argyris (1993), emphasize reflection, especially critical reflection through small-group talk, as a key activity in a learning organization. They assume that learning occurs when understandings become shaped through rational thought and language. This cognitive bias is evident in Bohm's (cited in Senge, 1991) description of the importance of talk to clarify an individual's ambiguous, disordered, contradictory or "inaccurate" meanings. Thus knowledge that is generated and embodied through sensual, kinesthetic, intuitive, relational, spiritual and emotional meaning systems would not count as "learning" until it is made explicit and conscious to the rational mind. Strands of research exploring workplace intuition (Mott, 1994) and the "feeling-sense" developed by professionals through non-rational learnings (Boreham, 1992) refute this dominance of cognitive reflection in learning organization precepts.

Critical reflection in learning organization literature presumes that if people could just detect their dysfunctional and paralysing taken-for-granted assumptions and deep-seated beliefs, they would be free to find new and more creative ways to frame the problems of practice and thus improve their performance in the workplace. In demanding explicit confessional critical reflection of its employees, the organization appropriates for its own purposes the most private aspects of individuals' worlds—their beliefs and values—and conscripts them for the organization's purposes. Good example of this practice are the personal development exercises described in popular learning organization handbooks (e.g., see Senge et al., 1994), leading individuals through intensely private scrutiny.

Assuming that all people can engage in dialectical, critical reflection—a dubious premise in light of cognitive and psycho-social adult development theory (Benack & Basseches, 1989; Belenky et al., 1986; Perry, 1970)—serious questions need to be raised about the goals of critical reflection in the learning organization ideal. The assumption is that individuals' current beliefs and moral structures, which make up their identity and whatever stability they can manage to create in a whirling workworld, are not good enough. Whatever perspectives exist in a person probably need to be critically challenged and changed, but it is incumbent only on the individual employees to critically reflect upon and change their mental models. Thus the Canadian Imperial Bank of Commerce (CIBC) chairman declares, "Learning is now everybody's business," and the organization's job is to "encourage" people to "adopt different mental models that better reflect competitive and workplace realities" (Flood, 1993). The objects for critical focus are carefully delineated to exclude the fundamental structures of capitalism, the CIBC's and other corporate interests, and assumptions like "life serves economic imperatives," and "learning will save business." Employees are supposed to reflect critically on the operational procedures of the corporation, but only its surface. From a radical left perspective (i.e., see Noble, 1990; Cunningham, 1993), employees' minds are expected to remain colonized and loyal to the imperial presence of their employing organization. Critical scrutiny is deflected from the power structures and the learning organization ideology itself and focused on the individual.

The organizational perspective is oriented to the status quo and is self-serving: it cannot conceive of its own death or life after its death. Workers' learning is to be innovative and critically reflective so long as the outcomes ensure the survival, indeed the prosperity, productivity and competitive advantage, of the employing organization. Learning that threatens the existence of the organization, such as liberated workers finding ecological and communicatively nurturing ways to achieve their purposes that begin with dismantling the organization, are not possible from the organization's perspective. Meanwhile the focus is on changing individuals to become the kinds of workers corporations demand. From the organization's perspective the continuously learning individual is in perpetual deficit, harnessed to Beck's (1995) vision of the "powerful engines" of the economy and struggling to "keep up."

The Reliance on "Open" Dialogue for Learning in the Workplace

The most promoted vehicle for reflection in learning organization literature is team dialogue. Extensive strategies are offered to promote a balance between "inquiry" and "advocacy," to create open, trusting climates where honesty is not punishable and personal disclosure is permissible, where communication is clear and authentic, where people are exposed to multiple perspectives and where challenges to one another's assumptions are encouraged. This literature accepts the possibility of an "ideal speech situation" where, according to Habermas (1984), participants communicate accurate but often incomplete information, are free from coercion or deception, are able to weigh evidence and assess arguments objectively, are open to alternative perspectives and are able to reflect critically on their own assumptions. Dixon (1993) recommends the "ideal speech condition" as the best way an organization may help staff turn all experience into learning: presumably they will listen to each others' experiences, find causal relationships and overall consequences, talk about failures and analyze each others' mistakes. Emphasis is on achieving "transparency" through talk.

Thus words are privileged over other means of expression between people, such as kinesthetic, sensual, oral non-verbal, artistic and intuitive. All complexities of meaning are supposedly reducible to the linear stream of language structures. This is an orientation of management and control that raises questions about agenda and about the links among all languages and learning. Is the most valuable workplace learning produced in the dynamic of interchange? Is giving voice to experience necessarily a useful process or a necessary part of learning? Usher and Edwards (1995) argue that a related problem with dialogue is its disciplinary function. To disclose one's opinions, and particularly to disclose for the purpose of critical scrutiny one's belief systems and values, is to surrender the last private space of personal meaning to the public space of workplace control. The demand for such disclosure could be construed as an exercise of surveillance and disciplinary regulation constituting gross violation of an individual's rights.

Simplistic understandings of workplace dialogue also ignore power assymetries as these configure the communication process, especially in the workplace when conversations and relationships are structured according to politics of gender, class, age, job status and other factors. Critics have shown the difficulties of achieving truly democratic "ideal" speech situations when little or no attention is given to the multiple social positions, conscious and unconscious pleasures, tensions, desires and contradictions present in all subjects in all historical contexts (Ellsworth, 1992; Orner, 1992). The reality in the workplace is that all people cannot possibly have equal opportunity to participate, reflect and refute one another in a "team dialogue." Brooks (1995) reports contradictory meanings, conflicting interests and subversion in her studies of workplace teams. Shaw and Perkins (1991) report many barriers that preclude reflective talk in many workplaces: pressure, "competency traps," bias towards activity, people's sense of powerlessness, a focus on measurable performance and strong inter-group boundaries.

The notion of dialogue is grounded in Senge's "fifth discipline" of teaching employees in an organization to view themselves as connected in a web-work of groups that function interdependently and benevolently to achieve a common purpose. Systems thinking essentially equates a social and cultural entity structured by power and composed of complex, constantly shifting human relations with physical phenomena. Thus the organization is conceptualized as a biological system. A short jump allows idealogues to envision a learning system where all system components are equitably and functionally interlinked. Systems thinking is a-structural, a-contextual, a-historical and apolitical. Knowledge is considered to be freely available to all; conflict is viewed as resolvable differences between equally competing individuals; and culture is treated as a set of environmental conditions which can be manipulated through thoughtful leadership. Such assumptions cannot reasonably be validated against organizational reality.

Paradoxes in the Learning Organization

The fundamental problem with the concept of the learning organization is that the popular notion of "empowerment," while prevalent in learning organization literature, is not critically examined. Questions as to whose empowerment and to what ends are not asked. West (1994) concludes in his critical review of this literature that the learning organization meets the learner's needs only if these are not in conflict with the organization's needs. He shows that despite rhetoric representing itself as a worker-centred philosophy, the learning organization concept emphasizes productivity, efficiency and competitive advantage at the expense of the worker. And as Shaw and Perkins (1991) point out, these goals orient the company culture to values and activities which actually inhibit learning.

Another paradox is that learning organization literature is often prescriptive, performing a normalizing and regulatory function while claiming to emancipate workers. Thus the very hierarchies of power and technical knowledge that are supposedly democratized in the learning organization are in fact wielded by the organization to control and subvert worker resistance to corporate downsizing and restructuring. A third paradox is created by context: the warm rhetoric in the literature of connectedness, trust and opportunity is unfurled in a climate darkened by an ethos of anxiety, a darkness that is not acknowledged in the rosy visions of the learning organization. Employees, told to trust in the corporation's benevolent human-growth-centred agenda, are invited to confess and transform their innermost desires and beliefs, to stick out their necks and keep learning and forget that they are in constant danger of being summarily ejected.

In the implementation of concepts of a learning organization there is perhaps another paradox: assumptions of continuous learning, based on a theory of knowledge produced through exploratory experimentation and innovation, collide with organizational norms of productivity, accountability and results-based measurement using predictable outcomes. Rough (1994) shows how traditional assessment measures of organizational performance and training are still prevalent and distort the holistic and dynamic notions of learning in the new paradigm. Moreover, the learning organization concept, based on administrative control of staff dialogue, paradoxically precludes the assumptions of the open, provisional, relational knowledge the technologies of learning organizations are supposed to produce. Multiple perspectives are urged by the learning organization ideology, but the ideology itself is a universal coherent set of simplistic ideals. What perspectives and differing abilities truly would be tolerated?

These paradoxes and the problematic implications of the six focuses of the learning organization become internalized in the workers, creating a problem in the constitution of worker identity and knowledge. Workers struggle to find and/or create an identity, meaning and purpose within their work (Fenwick, 1996). The learning organization discourse presents itself as a romantic ideal encouraging workers' personal growth and imaginative engagement—yet this discourse continues the workplace tradition of dictating which kind of growth counts most, what imaginative endeavours are most valued, what kinds of talk, relationships and identities are allowed and which are out of bounds or even meaningless. Perhaps the situation is rendered even worse by the learning organization's ubiquitous adjuration to workers to be "open and honest" and name the "undiscussables" (Argyris, 1993). The reality of workers' multi-situated and continually shifting identity, as well as the complexities of their workplace learning (Fenwick, 1996), are neither valued nor even acknowledged. The practical outcome may be the precise opposite of what the learning organization ideal hopes to achieve: rather than co-operation, commitment, and community, what may be produced is workers' withdrawal or cynicism, confusion and alienation.

Conclusion

Questions about these issues are posed not to destroy the promise held by learning organization approaches to workplace learning but to clarify its discourse. Until its premises become clear, efforts to implement the learning organization ideal will continually be challenged by real human beings and their needs, which weave together to create an organization. Meanwhile, educators need not discard precepts of continuous learning but should continue to work with others to explore their potential. Educators can provide fresh perspectives towards truly empowering work-learning activities.

12

A Decade on the Training Rollercoaster: A Unionist's View

D'Arcy Martin

Training is not just about jobs. In society, training is conducted by community organizations, unions and others in the voluntary sector to equip people to be active citizens and advocates (see Gordon Selman's chapter "The Imaginative Training for Citizenship" in this volume). Each year, Canada's labour movement provides tens of thousands of members with training so that they might represent their fellow workmates as health and safety monitors, stewards, negotiators and grievance handlers. This kind of adult education—variously called union education, labour education or workers' education—has a long history and a developed infrastructure.[1] It aims to build the skills, knowledge and confidence of people elected by their fellow workers to provide a counterweight to the increasingly arrogant and arbitrary power of employers both in the public and private sectors.

People volunteer to be representatives for their unions while, in most cases, working each day for an employer. Because their past experiences in union education generally have been positive, when they are looking for approaches, methods and structures to develop job-related competence, they naturally turn to their union for guidance. As an educator in the labour movement for the past twenty years, I have been one of those called on to respond. This chapter captures some of the experience of a unionist drawn into the public policy debate around job training. It focuses on one province, Ontario, and on one decade, 1986-96. It reviews the "long climb" toward establishing the Ontario Training and Adjustment Board (OTAB), an innovative approach to training that included participation of social partners beyond the workplace. It recounts my learning of, and reflection on, the viewpoints of others as we rode the training rollercoaster. It also records my unions' disappointments and hopes for the future as one part of the ride came to an end.

Before examining the Ontario experience, it might be helpful for readers if the broad principles of a union approach to training are outlined. Unions favour training that is portable, developmental and equitable. By portable, they mean that skills should not be limited to the current equipment and uses or even to the current workplace, but should be broad enough and sufficiently certified that workers can carry their "educational capital" with them. By developmental, unions mean that training courses should not be a dead end but should increase the capacity and desire to learn, so that workers are encouraged and guided toward further study and practice. And by equitable, they mean that training should be a universal right in the same way that Medicare or basic public schooling are, rather than a favour handed out by employers based on their unilateral definition of the needs of the workplace.

In this context, it makes sense that unions advocate:

- skills-based agreements that link job classifications to skills and train-ing. This helps create pressure to use higher and broader skills. It con-strains employers' attempts to divide training into small segments of job-specific and employer-specific training.
- training based on nationally recognized standards that are transportable from province to province. These standards should specify broader skills and prevent use of narrow task-specific training.
- negotiated agreements on the availability of training and education op-portunities and on the introduction of new technologies and new work practices.
- training for the unemployed that is linked to real employment opportu-nities and not just training for training's sake.

Unions want better and more interesting jobs for their members, they want their members' skills recognized, and they want the above principles en-trenched in freely negotiated collective agreements.

Setting Up the Ride

From the start, it looked bumpy. Most employers considered training to be a management right, with management making decisions in hiring, promotion and workplace reorganization without consulting the collective voice of the employees. Historically, in the early part of the century, the construction trades had addressed job skills by providing training for their members, thus giving workers bargaining power with their employers. But this training, in the form of apprenticeships, was limited to those who could integrate into an old-boy's network—an ironic mirror of today's economic elite—that excluded groups such as young workers and women. It was training that kept wages up but ran against the egalitarian culture of the emerging industrial unions.

With the public-policy door on training swung open for the next wave of unions, industrial unions (such as autoworkers and steel-workers) moved through the door. Still left outside the discussion were service unions such as those in hospitals and restaurants, and workers in the public sector.

The first issue about "co-determined" training, i.e., training policy developed through participation of all stakeholders, is that the employers were there first; and most government officials saw their continuing claim to primacy as legitimate. The second issue is that different parts of the labour movement climbed on board at different times. And the third issue is that the unions themselves had to change in order to accomplish their declared goals:

> Some changes are on the surface
> And others are profound.
> Ways of thinking shift
> Along with everything else in this world.
> Over the years, the climate changes
> Pastures change the herds that they feed.
> Since everything else changes,
> It shouldn't be surprising that I change.
> —Mercedes Sosa

In the dream of economic and social justice that animates union activists lies a deep commitment to democratizing knowledge. Yet, the desire of unionists to have a voice in their work lives requires controlling their job-related skills, both formal and tacit.[2] When they try to influence the fragmented and exclusionary structures in Canadian skills training, issues arise particularly because these structures are, on occasion, mirrored within the unions themselves.

The research and education departments of the major unions did have a practice run in which these tensions were well handled. In the early 1980s, the federal government was seriously considering a national Paid Educational Leave (PEL) initiative. Variously called "skill development leave," a "levy-grant system," and a "training tax," this policy area was open to labour's participation.[3] Led by Daniel Benedict, the Canadian Labour Congress (CLC) nominee on the tripartite task force, labour educators studied the options, polished up their arguments and worked out in caucus their internal differences. Hence, a large and unified labour delegation turned out to a 1983 conference in Hull. From English Canada and Quebec, from building trades and service unions, the labour delegation worked in solidarity.

However, the other three parties in this social negotiation were not willing or able to reach an agreement. The government delegation split along federal-provincial lines; the education providers split among post-secondary, school-board and voluntary-sector educators; and, while the employer delegation held together, it was in order to resist legislation of any kind. The moment passed.

As secretary of the labour delegation, I was frustrated. But when the door opened again at a provincial level, several of us could reach back into our kit bags, pull together the contacts and arguments that had proven solid a few years earlier and return to the debate. In each province it played out differently, but my own involvement was largely in Ontario, and I will restrict myself to that province in the remainder of this article.[4]

Climbing the OTAB Hill

The political culture of Ontario shifted decisively during the 1980s. The Conservative Party's stranglehold on power at Queen's Park, tightened over decades, was loosened by an alliance of Liberals and the New Democratic Party, who shared government on the basis of an accord. When the Liberals won a majority government in the mid-1980s without NDP support, they were sensitive to pressure from the left. One indication of this sensitivity was the decision by then-Premier David Peterson to invite three labour leaders into his main strategy think-tank, the Premier's Council. With Leo Gerard of the Steelworkers, Fred Pomeroy of the Communications Workers and Gord Wilson of the Autoworkers (at the time, president of the Ontario Federation of Labour), Peterson had three capable and articulate union advocates on his hands, rather than in his pocket.

The Council's first major policy document on technology and economic restructuring came out with little labour flavour; however, $5 million was provided by government for labour-led research on the impacts of technological change. The "Technology and Adjustment Research Program" (TARP), became the focal point of labour-positive social research outside the academy until funding was cut off by the resurgent Conservatives in 1995 (Anderson, 1995).

As drafting began for the Council's second major report on the "people side of the issue" (Government of Ontario, 1995) as compared to the technology side, the three labour representatives moved to influence the content. In successive drafts, they pushed to broaden access, to require employer funding and to recognize and support a public rather than privatized delivery structure When John O'Grady and I took the final draft to then-Opposition Leader Bob Rae, he commented that the report recommendations gave labour a stronger voice than an NDP government could. When the NDP, to everyone's surprise, won the election in the fall of 1990, his words proved prophetic.

Parallel to the process in the Premier's Council, the labour movement was building capacity to address training issues. A subcommittee on training was formed at the Ontario Federation of Labour (OFL) to provide a forum for the increasing number of union staff involved in sectoral-training initiatives,[5] in workplace-training agreement, and in labour-provided programs such as the Basic Education and Skills Training (BEST) literacy initiative.[6] By the 1989 convention of the Ontario Federation of Labour, a policy statement on training had been developed with full input from the subcommittee. The statement was strongly endorsed by the leadership of the labour movement and supported by delegates during the floor debate.[7] Training was now officially part of Ontario labour's agenda as a priority item.

Of course, getting training on the agenda as a priority also was the outcome of internal struggles. Increasingly, local unions and affiliates were being presented with "packages" of workplace reorganization in which new technologies, production teams and training plans were combined. In each, there were elements attractive to unionists—less hazardous work, more scope to make decisions on the job, and opportunities to learn. Yet management's version was naturally enough aimed at increasing productivity and overall control. For unionists, it was essential to work through the package piece by piece in order to see which elements could form the basis of a positive and unified proposal for improving the dignity and security of the members.[8]

The OFL training policy document was one step in this process. Yet the labour movement had to sort through the ways of implementing it in practice—in collective bargaining, in sectoral initiatives, at the provincial level where an Ontario Training and Adjustment Board was emerging, and at the federal level with the Canadian Labour Force Development Board.[9] This new set of structures constituted as important an advance organizationally as the OFL policy signified ideologically. From collective bargaining at the local level—the North American tradition—the labour movement was now engaged in "open field bargaining," whose participants and scope varied with the issue being addressed. Open-field bargaining includes participation from social movements, community groups and other interests outside the workplace.

I got an interesting glimpse into this new terrain in the spring of 1993 when I was nominated by the Ontario Federation of Labour as one of two labour participants in a panel organized to hear community views about training and adjustment. Erna Post, of the Canada Employment and Immigration Union (a component of the Public Service Alliance of Canada) and myself heard a thousand formal presentations and many informal comments about the suitable structure, mandate and process by which the users of training might have a voice in the delivery of training at the community level.[10]

The biggest shock for me was the breadth of animosity toward unions. The idea that unions might have a central voice in skill training, equal with that of employers, simply enraged many people. From my perspective, snug inside the union culture, workers co-determining their job skills made perfect sense. But not all the hostile comments came from business representatives. Erna and I were showered with many criticisms of unions from groups we would have expected to support us. Once again, the negative images of "labour bosses" haunted us.[11]

A second unexpected lesson was the intricacy of the interests involved in the issue of training. This was not a straightforward face-off between business and labour, of the sort involved in collective bargaining. The boundaries of collective bargaining are fairly clearly delineated in Canada, and introducing new items such as maternity leave, occupational health or, indeed, training does not alter its basic dynamics. In the public process around the training issue, however, labour faced the employers, largely as antagonists; as well they had to address a bewildering array of explanations for the failure of the current training system and consider proposals for restructuring that system. Frequently, labour representatives were at a loss about whether to support or resist a suggestion; in short, they were obliged to learn.

Throughout the hearings, labour advocated training as a universal social right, like basic formal education and health care. Several labour participants supported the concept that education and training must "develop and enhance" because "a mind is a terrible thing to waste"[12] Training should be more equitable and accessible, of better quality, more relevant, and employers should assume a far greater share of the funding. Some presenters urged that training should include the unemployed as well as the employed and be linked to an industrial strategy. For example, in Cornwall, many of the unemployed had been trained in welding and held welding certificates: "If Mulroney wants to build frigates in Cornwall," Mike Oliver of the Cornwall Labour Council said in his presentation, "we're ready!"[13] Training people for jobs that did not exist was seen as a waste of training resources and was a source of discouragement and cynicism among trainees.

Employers, especially in the private sector, asserted that training should be "needs-driven," rather than perceived as a right of citizenship. Learning that did not directly and expediently lead to employment and increase productivity could not legitimately be called training, and employers were best situated to make this judgment. Business representatives spoke of the need for economic renewal, reduced government regulation and taxes and training that enhanced the competitiveness of Ontario employers. They proposed that the mandate for the Ontario Training and Adjustment Board (OTAB) and local boards be "to increase and enhance the productivity and effectiveness of people by establishing a training culture."[14]

However, labour and business viewpoints were just the beginning of the conversation. Women's representatives forcefully advocated change to their marginalized position in society. Women earned only 65% of men's wages and had the added burden of housework, childcare, sexual harassment, sex discrimination in hiring, promotion, job assignments and performance evaluations. As well they faced the pressures of token status in non-traditional occupations. This opened up discussion of the full range of social relationships around training: "Children form many of their opinions and attitudes about the world of work/education/training from their parents' experiences," presenter Mary Lynch Taylor stated. "If their mothers are excluded from high-paying jobs, are victims of discrimination and harassment, are tired and frustrated from too much work for too little money, are crushed by poverty and lack dreams, hope, vision, they *cannot* form a good view of the world of work ... "[15]

As the discussions proceeded, most participants came to agree that the new training system should be grassroots, bottom-up, inclusive, simple, co-ordinated and integrated. This consensus was very encouraging to labour, linking smoothly to our policy positions. However, the myriad of other concerns raised were rather overwhelming.

By challenging employer-driven training, the union movement was plunging into a set of cross-currents. Among those groups that felt they were not represented by the traditional labour market partners as defined in the proposal were small unaffiliated business, non-profit agencies, the unemployed, the poor, racial minorities, rural areas, youth, unorganized labour and the franco-Ontario communities.[16] These presenters requested that their voices be part of the local board and that their training needs be addressed. Different levels of government, old community rivalries, a range of equity advocates, turf wars among education providers—this was the terrain on which "open-field bargaining" occurred. New information and skills were required to engage in this process. This certainly was more complex than simply presenting grievances to management; yet it was a natural extension of the challenge to arbitrary power the grievance procedure embodies.

The local board hearings acted like a pause button on the community video. They highlighted the differences in communities in the relationships among labour market partners and reaffirmed people's desire to control new processes at a local level as much as possible. For the labour movement, they indicated the scale of the challenge undertaken to actually implement the broad generalities of the OFL policy document on training. And they provided warning that any attempt to meet all these groups' expressed needs by an institutional structure, whether at the community level or provincially, would inevitably bog down. Some hard choices would have to be made in priorities, by labour and by the pro-labour elements in the NDP government, or the delays would mean that this opportunity, too, would pass.

I remember vividly one meeting between the Ontario Federation of Labour and the senior government bureaucrats involved in establishing the Ontario Training and Adjustment Board. I had only one point to make during the meeting: that any delay in moving forward with this process was reactionary. Nevertheless, these and other players stubbornly hung on to their positions, so it took the NDP three years to set up OTAB. The local boards were just being established when the NDP lost power in 1995.

A shared-power model of training had no legs. It was quickly abandoned by business and swept aside in the Conservative storm that followed. While protests sprouted over cuts to health care, formal education, culture and public service jobs, few voices were raised to mourn the passing of this remarkable and innovative public-policy initiative. It had yet to become anchored enough in people's lives that they mourned its passing.

When Unionists Compare Notes

With the gradual undermining and ultimate demolition of OTAB, the unionists engaged in training issues found the rollercoaster hurtling downwards.[17] A broader range of internal interests were also now at play. Some unions, the Food and Commercial Workers, for example, had set up major retraining programs for displaced workers. Some labour-led providers, such as the Metro Labour Education Centre, had expanded their staff to the extent that their education departments were larger than that of the Canadian Labour Congress or any affiliate. The OFL's BEST program was extending its initial definitions of literacy while continuing to reach those members least well-served by established labour educators. The key people in such initiatives— Janet Dassinger, Trish Stovell and Jean Connon Unda—now met continually with labour representatives in joint training councils in sectors such as steel-making and electrical/electronic manufacturing. They worked with Kevin Hayes and Ursule Critoph to clear the way. By then, the three hottest potatoes were shifts in political jurisdiction over training, job losses in public education, and strategy for dealing with the employers.

New jurisdictions. Since the Charlottetown Constitutional Accord, the federal government had been devolving to the provinces at an accelerating rate the financing, planning and delivery of training. Apart from Quebec and British Columbia, most provincial governments were passing the fiscal squeeze along to both providers and trainees. As a result, there was increasingly a patchwork situation, where labour's perspective on training as a right was *de facto* being undermined by employer-driven schemes of training for immediate and narrowly defined job requirements.

In 1995, the federal government moved decisively to transform Unemployment Insurance, creating instead Employment Insurance, and to turn over jurisdiction for training to the provinces. This indeed was a "sea change in approach and practice" (Critoph, 1997), which profoundly altered the pressure points for training politics in Canada.

Job losses. As public-sector budget cuts reached the education sector, a new intensity could be felt in labour-training debates. The community college locals of the Ontario Public Service Employees Union, for example, had rarely participated in labour councils. Now, they entered more fully as OTAB assigned power to the labour councils for naming representatives to local boards that would affect college funding. As changes in Employment Insurance pulled the rug out from under college funding, wholesale closures began. Pubic-sector unionists mobilized to have the CLC include in its definition of privatized training the initiatives so carefully built by private-sector unions to address workplace needs unmet by the colleges. This was no longer a policy discussion in a context of increasing labour influence; it was a survival discussion, with labour overall on the defensive. Predictably, the plenaries in the CLC Training Conference of June 1997 returned to this conflict again and again without a satisfactory conclusion.[18]

Strategy with employers. Traditional business came to the table with the forming of the Canadian Labour Market and Productivity Centre and the Canadian Labour Force Development Board. And, they have stayed at the table as long as government is footing the bill, and neither the Centre nor the Board has any power. The individual representatives at the table are often very progressive and capable, but they can't hide the fact that business isn't willing to share power on the issue of training. As public funds are pulled from sectoral training councils, most employers are backing away. And in some instances, notably the Ontario Training and Adjustment Board, they sow salt in the earth before abandoning the fields.

In the private sector, then, unionists can feel bitter about the shallowness of employer commitment to "training partnerships." But feelings are more mixed with public sector and third sector (voluntary and community-based) employers.

The glacial pace of change among managers in the public-sector training providers in regard to Prior Learning Assessment and Recognition, or PLAR is quite striking. The basically democratic impulse behind PLAR has been to assign credit to people for experiential learning and for learning acquired in other cultures so they can have easier access to the educational capital tied up in colleges and universities (see the chapter "The Tolerable Contraditions of Prior Learning Assessment" by Alan Thomas in this volume). A revealing debate occurred during 1995-1996 at the Canadian Labour Force Development Board. The management of English Canadian post-secondary institutions fought against inclusion of the word "Recognition" in the title. By only calling it "Assessment," the balance of authority in conferring credit would rest squarely in their hands. After some ridicule, based on the fact that their own literature always translated the concept as *Reconnaissance des Acquis,* or recognition of acquired knowledge, they finally agreed to add an R to PLA. Such turf protection by public-training providers and their inertia in connecting to the needs of any but the young, full-tuition, full-time student have been frustrating for all unionists. They have made it difficult to sustain labour's defence of public over private education, our principled opposition to privatization and contracting out of training.

While the attack on the public sector and the ruthlessness of the traditional market sector are being carefully monitored, the third sector continues to pitch up new economic initiatives. Among them are the community-based training providers, with whom unions have had shaky relations at best. Unorthodox, entrepreneurial community organizations are growing rapidly.[19] They are characterized by social vitality, youth, and ethnic diversity—in short, the qualities needed by the labour movement in order to move ahead. But because they are not unionized and, in some cases these organizations compete directly with unionized producers, they are kept at arm's length. Clearly, unions need to negotiate with third-sector, community-based employers in order to strengthen the movement and improve the training available to workers.

After a decade of work with traditional business, public sector employers and the third sector, unions are developing the subtle skills required for open-field bargaining. Even in direct dealings with management, the process is more fluid and diverse than it was a decade ago.

The job training issue has moved to the centre of union policy discussions, just as employment equity did a decade ago and occupational health and safety did the decade before that. For unionists, adult learning is of high value both for remedying injustices in the distribution of educational capital and for building a social movement for struggle. The focus on training and other emerging issues suggests that the Canadian labour movement is alive and kicking, an effective resource for progressive adult education in the years to come.

Endnotes

[1] For more information, see my material in *The Foundations of Adult Education in Canada, Second Edition*, by Gordon Selman, Michael Cooke, Mark Selman and Paul Dampier. Toronto: Thompson Educational Publishing, 1998.

[2] These tensions are comprehensively mapped in Dassinger, 1997.

[3] See Employment and Immigration Canada, 1983.

[4] A concise and clear summary is available for the Quebec experience in Miller, 1997.

[5] Four of these deserve particular mention: in the health care sector, the HSTAP; in steelmaking the CSTEC; in auto parts the APSTC; and in electrical/electronics the SSC. Each of these is a story in itself.

[6] For a provocative analysis of the BEST program, see Connon Unda and Clifford, in M.C. Taylor, Ed., 1997.

[7] The document "Education and Training" is available from the OFL, 15 Gervais Drive, Suite 202, Don Mills, Ontario M3C 1Y8 (phone 416-441-2731). It is also reprinted as Appendix I in the excellent issue "Training for What? Labour Perspectives on Skill Training," in *Our Schools/Our Selves*, November 1992. More widely circulated has

been a brochure summarizing the policy, entitled "Training: A Labour Perspective," available in bulk from the OFL.

[8] This was hotly debated within the labour movement and formed the basis of several projects within the TARP initiative. My own union's perspective is summarized in Groff, 1993, and in Jorge Garcia-Orgales, 1995.

[9] While the CLFDB has only had advisory status at the federal level, it has accomplished much in influencing public debate. See, for example, its "Training Standards" released in September 1995 and its subsequent work in "Prior Learning Assessment and Recognition."

[10] For a summary of the public consultations, see Ontario and Federal governments/CLFDB, 1993.

[11] For a thoughtful summary of public-sector union views in the late 1980s, see Rose, 1991. Some reflections on the "union culture" and its public image can be found in Chapter 3 of my book, Martin, 1995.

[12] Marg Harbert, Local 51 of the Communications and Electrical Workers of Canada (CWC), presentation to the Ottawa hearing, April, 1993.

[13] Mike Oliver, Cornwall Labour Council, presentation to the Cornwall hearing, April, 1993.

[14] Barry Spilchuk, business presentation to the North Bay hearing, May, 1993.

[15] Mary Lynch Taylor, Women's Training, presentation to the Peterborough hearing, April, 1993.

[16] The Franco-Ontarian community made a strong case for guaranteed access to training in their own language. The socio-economic realities of the francophone population (family income ranking 28th of 29 ethno-cultural groups), the illiteracy rate (in the order of 50% in certain areas), the high drop-out rate, and the low sense of self-esteem were underscored. "On n'est même pas dans le jeu ... " (Serge Arpin, Cornwall hearing, April 1993).

[17] This pattern was, of course, much broader. See Beaudet et al., 1997.

[18] An interesting compromise was proposed in 1997.

[19] See Wayne Roberts et al., *Get A Life*.

13

Workers' Education for the Twenty-First Century

Bruce Spencer

Unions represent a significant part of the adult education movement in Canada and are responsible for crucial areas of education not touched by the formal educational enterprise.
— Verner & Dickenson, 1974, p. iv.

This chapter discusses the origins of workers' education and labour education since World War II. It examines the forms of workers' education that are emerging in the context of labour union and corporate restructuring and the increasing globalization of capital. It explores the extent to which accommodation or resistance to these new global forces is bolstered by workers' education and whether or not any new models of workers' education are evolving in Canada or elsewhere that will provide workers with an "independent working-class education" (Simon, 1990, p. 23) for the twenty-first century.

Introduction

The term *union education* describes education and training provided by particular unions and federations for their members with the practical purpose of bolstering union representation and activity. *Labour education* is considered broader in scope, encompassing union education as well as other provision targeted principally at union members and offered by educational institutions; in addition to the practical objectives of union education it strives to create an understanding of the union context. *Workers' education* refers to essentially non-vocational education available to all workers and pre-dates the concepts of union and labour education.

The traditions of workers' education are found in several early initiatives in adult education. Some of these, such as the Mechanics' Institutes and the Workers' Educational Association (WEA), were British transplants. Others, such as Frontier College and the Antigonish Movement, were Canadian. Although the Mechanics' Institutes were initially concerned with technical education and Frontier College with basic education, workers' education, as it is generally understood, is usually associated with the turn-of-the-century provision of non-vocational liberal adult education. This provision was a response to the belief that newly enfranchised workers needed to be educated in the workings of liberal democracy and economics in order to understand the issues of the day (and of course to accept "order" and "parliamentary democracy," i.e., democratic gradual change rather than revolution).[1] The Workers' Educational Association (WEA) was formed in 1903 to make this education more accessible and to bring it more under the control of the students themselves.[2] However, the WEA was viewed suspiciously by some radical workers, and in Britain they responded by establishing the Plebs League and the National Council of Labour Colleges, which was committed to an "independent working-class education" not influenced by bourgeois concerns (Simon, 1990, p. 23). Elsewhere, the emphasis in workers' education was put on independent unions (for example, the International Ladies Garment Workers' Union was particularly active educationally) or political education (for example, the Communist Party).[3] Although much can be made of the splits in workers' education between the more establishment provision and independents, in general the kind of workers' education that emerged from these inter-war rivalries was broad in scope and supportive of workers' organizations such as labour unions, co-operatives and credit unions (McIlroy in Simon, 1990, p. 176).

Some of the post-World War II union education fostered by this workers' education movement was principally aimed at improving labour's organizational effectiveness. Unions in Canada had experienced uneven development in the inter-war period, but union strength grew during World War II and in the immediate post-war period. Unions achieved legal status as bargaining agents, which, together with the expansion of public services such as education and the social safety net, took some of the urgency out of workers' political campaigns. Public education institutions took over some of the broader liberal education and vocational training needs of workers and promised a brighter future for the sons and daughters of working people. But public education was not able to meet the organizational needs of unions. Thus unions took on that task themselves (Verner & Dickenson, 1974) and, to a lesser or greater degree, also retained some of the broader objectives of workers' education.

Union education can be understood as all education offered by unions for their members and is particularly focused on preparing activists for leadership roles in the union (safety representative, steward, or local union president, for example). Because unions have only small full-time staffs, they rely on the voluntary activity of their members to sustain union organization, representation and bargaining: union education is therefore a major contributor to building an effective volunteer force. Unions may also provide vocational training or basic education for members, but this is outside the normal understanding of the term *union education*, which usually refers to the union training or collectivist programs. In the "first major attempt to provide a detailed analysis of union education in Canada" (1974, p. iv), Verner and Dickenson describe it as a

> ... particular kind of workers' education intended specifically for members of labour unions and dealing primarily with matters of special concern to union members rather than adults generally. These matters pertain to the role and function of the union in society and to the organization and operation of labour unions as the instruments to protect and develop the rights of working people (p. 6).

Labour Education

Labour education is union education combined with additional education offered primarily for unions and union members by other educational providers. In some cases in Canada a local college or university, such as Capilano College or Simon Fraser University in Vancouver, will offer union training courses similar to those offered by individual unions. More typically, the few colleges and universities offering programs, such as the University of Saskatchewan, have specially designed labour studies courses neither similar to nor offered by individual unions.[4] Thus labour education, broader in scope than mainstream union provision, can encompass all labour studies courses targeted at union members, and perhaps workers generally, but should be interpreted as excluding labour studies programs targeted at a general student body.[5]

Labour education, thus defined, has three main purposes:

- to prepare and train union lay members (and staff) to play an active role in the union;
- to educate activists and members about union policy, changes in the union environment, such as new management techniques, and changes in labour law;
- to develop union consciousness and support social action, to build common goals and to share organizing and campaign experience.

Labour education also helps to sustain and build a "labour culture"—an alternative perception of events and society.

Three main types of labour education courses seek to achieve the above purposes: *tools*, *issues* and *labour studies*. Most of the courses provided by unions are *tools* training, essentially meeting the first and to a lesser extent the second of the above purposes. The next largest category is issues courses (for example, on sexual harassment or racism), which often seek to link workplace and societal issues. The third category, labour studies for trade unionists, examines the union context or perspective (for example, labour history, economics and politics). While all three categories of courses aim to build union consciousness, it is this third type that most clearly resonates with early images of workers' education, particularly "independent working-class education" and seeks to establish and sustain an alternative labour knowledge and culture, as illustrated by the Canadian Autoworkers (CAW) paid educational leave (PEL) program outlined below. But it must be remembered that there were many strands to inter-war workers' education, both in Canada and abroad, and building workers' organizations was certainly one of them: tools courses are not just a post-war phenomena.

Most union members learn about the union while on the job (i.e., informally or incidentally). They probably learn more, and are most active, during disputes (for example, in strikes, lockouts, grievances or negotiations), but they also learn from union publications and communications, from attending meetings, conferences and conventions, as well as from the union's educational programs. Labour education only caters to a small number of members in any one year, approximately 120,000 or 3 percent of the total union membership (Spencer, 1994). However, it is "social" as opposed to personal education, designed to benefit a larger number of members because the course participants bring the benefits of their learning to the service of other union members. Labour education thus has a social purpose: to promote and develop the union presence and aims, thereby advancing the union collectively.

Unions in Canada

Unions in Canada are not generally a topic of public debate. They only feature as newsworthy when there are major strikes. While they may have some influence with provincial New Democratic Party (NDP) governments, they have not, particularly in recent years, been viewed as a major legitimate interest by Conservative and Liberal federal governments. This uncertain location within Canadian society has had two major consequences:

- a general ignorance about unions and unionism
- "social unionism"—the seeking of social partners by unions in order to help bring about social change.

Labour unions are associations of working people formed to protect their common interests, both socially and economically. On one level, it can be argued that unions exist because employers exist. Labour is employed to work in private and public industry and service in such a way that individuals employed enjoy little control over the terms and conditions of their employment. Working people in the workplace are subject to the nature of this employment contract, which favours employers' rights and interests. As a consequence, workers gather together in order to influence the way they work and the rewards they receive. Generally, the larger the employer, the more impersonal the relationship between the worker and the employer and the more likely it is that workers will join collectively to bargain with the employer. Seen in this way, unions are a result of the social relationships created by the processes of production (including the generation of services).

Divisions in the ownership and control of work create divisions in workplace relationships of employer and employee, boss and worker. These relations of wealth and power extend to society at large, creating social classes of workers and employers. Labour unions, therefore, may not limit their activities to the workplace or to their industry or service. For example, the wealthy will have little need for public and welfare services such as for seniors' pensions, public schools and subsidized medical care, but working people do. Thus unions campaign for improvements in these services—the "social wage"—and try to influence the social and political agenda generally. Unions may try to do this by:

- bargaining within the existing economic, political and social structures;
- organizing workers' power to displace the existing economic and social system.

Union Structures in Canada

Early attempts to organize all workers into one general union such as the "Knights of Labour" or the "Wobblies" with the objective of replacing an unjust economic and social system met with only limited success in recruiting Canadian workers. The Winnipeg General Strike of 1919 and the inter-war, working-class revolutionary political movements also achieved little. Union membership in Canada remained low and had little impact outside of the skilled trades.

International craft unions represented trades in both the United States and Canada throughout the inter-war period, and these American Federation of Labour affiliated unions established what control they could within the sectors where they were organized and recognized for bargaining. Industrial and general workers' unions, however, were slower to establish themselves north of the 49th parallel than below it. The growth of industrial unionism in Canada dates from World War II, when the necessities of war production combined with labour scarcity to create opportunities for organizing. Union density— the unionized proportion of the employed non-agricultural workforce—was just 16 percent in 1936; by the immediate post-war years, it had risen to nearly 30 percent. The conversion of public-sector staff associations to unions in the 1960s, combined with the growth of public-sector employment, pushed union density up (it has averaged approximately 37 percent over the last twenty years). Although there has been some recent decline in the unionized proportion of the employed workforce, actual union membership has remained buoyant in Canada in contrast to major declines in countries with similar union structures, such as the United States, Britain, Australia and New Zealand.[6]

Approximately 30 percent of unionists are members of American-based international unions and 70 percent belong to national unions. The majority of Canadian unions are affiliated to the Canadian Labour Congress (CLC), which represents more than 65 percent of all unionists in Canada. The next largest grouping, with approximately 5 percent is the Confederation des syndicats nationaux (CSN/CNTU), a Quebec union central. Many provincially based professional unions, such as those of nurses and teachers, are not affiliated to any union centrals, nor are some smaller independent unions. Traditionally, unions have been described as "craft" (catering for skilled workers regardless of the industry they work in) or "industrial" (organizing all workers in their particular industry, such as steel or autos). Other labels such as "professional" or "public sector" have also been useful in differentiating between union memberships. However, some industrial unions, such as the Steelworkers or Autoworkers, have been merging with unions outside their sector, while some public-sector unions, following privatization, now have private-sector memberships. Thus, union mergers and economic restructuring have resulted in fewer unions with larger, more diverse memberships. Perhaps this marks the emergence of a new general unionism.

Larger unions are more likely to have educational programs run by designated education officers (Verner & Dickenson, 1974) and are more likely to be affiliated to union centrals whose educational resources are available to them. The more diverse the union, the more important it is to cater to the educational needs of all sections and to use union education to build unity. For this reason, labour education is likely to become more important to the newly emerging "general" unions. Traditionally, craft unions have been most concerned about vocational training for their members and have been major providers, sometimes in collaboration with employers, of job training. Increasingly, however, all unions are making job training a priority, and a "service" for their diverse membership.[7] We can therefore predict that both labour education and union-sponsored vocational education will be strengthened by the growth of larger general unions, and it is possible that a new, blended "workers' education" will emerge from these trends.

In contradiction to the above argument for the emergence of a new general unionism, a more unified labour movement and a more common labour education, it should be noted that:

- union histories are very different and the memberships of unions such as the Teamsters, Public Service Alliance of Canada and the International Brotherhood of Electrical Workers remain largely distinct from one another. Union education within these organizations will continue to re-flect their divergent concerns;

- the Federal funding supporting union education programs that had been available since 1977 ceased in 1995. Some of the money had been used to provide common curriculum materials. Also cut was the funding that supported the Labour College of Canada, an eight-week residential course that brought together members of different unions (Spencer, 1994). These cuts could result in a more fragmented labour education.

Worker Education/Training

In contrast to our broad definition of workers' education, the term *worker education* is often used as a descriptor for worker training, or more recently workplace learning (particularly in North America, where some authors also misleadingly use "workers' education" to describe this vocational and em-ployer-oriented education and/or training). Thus worker education is used to describe what is essentially an education for work, not for workers. Because of this new emphasis, and because there has been a decline in publicly pro-vided workers' education, some unions have become interested in creating a form of workers' education that includes both labour education and labour-sponsored adult education and vocational training, as illustrated below by the UNISON Open College.

Unions have also always been involved in educational initiatives that go beyond the three main purposes of labour education already outlined. Educa-tion courses for the general membership include union-run literacy and nu-meracy courses, vocational training, general health and safety programs and even arts classes and recreational courses. Although these programs may pro-vide a vehicle for union perspectives, their primary purpose is the delivery or sponsorship of broader adult education to workers. This emphasis is particu-larly important if we accept Friesen's (1994) critique of the decline of pub-licly provided adult education for workers and Huot's assertion that Canada's community colleges have "no commitment to educating workers beyond the hands-on skills training" and teaching "the virtues of loyalty, obedience, and conformity to established authority" (1989, p. 35).

Before we go on to evaluate newly emerging forms of workers' education in the context of globalization, we need to recognize that in the methods of unions I have outlined above there is an inherent contradiction. Unions repre-sent both collective worker accommodation (via collective agreements) and collective worker resistance (via workplace and political actions) to the em-ployment relationship. This dichotomy has always been reflected in labour education. The dominant form labour education takes within a particular country or union reflects a number of factors. For example, within North America, some labour education has a greater emphasis on American-style business unionism (negotiation and agreement, acceptance of management rights), while other labour education has an orientation more in line with Canadian social unionism (active outside as well as inside the workplace, links with other social movements, advancing "class" interests). The American style will result in support for a narrower curriculum, a focus on *tools* training courses and workplace problems, with less emphasis on *issues* and *labour studies* courses.

Globalization and Union Responses

The effect on adult education of the globalization of capitalist production and the associated restructuring of economies and companies has been discussed elsewhere in this volume. There are several perspectives from which to view the shift to "learning organizations," "teams," and other global corporate "re-engineering" projects and their implications for workers and labour education. For example, they may be viewed as:

- an opportunity for enhanced worker participation and re-skilling or
- a challenge to unionization and workers' independence that must be resisted.

The first perspective leads to an emphasis on worker education for accommodating and participating in these changes, a perspective consistent with business unionism perhaps. It might also advocate worker job retraining as a priority. An educational response to the second emphasis might include union educational programs aimed at bolstering worker resistance to the corporate and right-wing political agendas. It would support an argument for a renewal of social unionism, including an independent workers' education that can prepare students to resist these changes.

Within Canada the International Steelworkers and the Communication Energy and Paperworkers (CEP) are examples of unions trying to use the new management rhetoric to their advantage. They are arguing for genuine teams and genuine participation. Thus, labour education is being used to encourage unionists to engage in workplace learning, albeit on union terms.

Union attempts to influence vocational training have become central to union strategy in the face of globalization and restructuring. Unions have responded to companies that are operating restrictive, company-specific job training by arguing for broader, sector-based training programs that fit into nationally recognized skills and/or education schemes (see Martin's chapter "A Decade on the Traininng Rollercoaster: A Unionist's View" in this volume). This argument resonates with government desires to improve the overall skills of the workforce and had gained some leverage in Ontario until the change of government heralded a non-interventionist ideology. The move to a national training scheme has made more progress in Britain (where provincial educational restrictions do not apply) and Australia (where in addition there has been a strong tradition of tripartitism, although this may change with the current federal Australian government).

Perhaps the best example of a critical labour education promoting awareness and resistance to the globalizing economic forces is provided by the Paid Educational Leave (PEL) programs for the general memberships of the Canadian Autoworkers (CAW) and Canadian Union of Postal Workers (CUPW). The main features of the CAW program (which at the time of writing is being revamped) include a negotiated, employer-paid levy to a union-controlled trust. The union uses the funds to pay for lost wages and expenses of its members who attend the four-week residential PEL course. The core PEL program consists of four week-long residential courses that can be categorized as labour studies. Each week of the basic PEL program has a separate theme: the present as history, sociology, political economy and social and political change.

The CAW program is not focused narrowly on preparing representatives for collective bargaining but rather on promoting an understanding of the union's social and political goals. The union's purpose is to provide a broad educational experience that challenges its members to question the dominant political hegemony of globalization. This kind of labour education will be most attractive to those unions that wish to foster an independent workers' knowledge leading to greater awareness and resistance.

Even if unions embrace an educational program promoting awareness and resistance, they likely also will pursue some accommodation and retraining strategy, as is evidenced by the Steelworkers. The Steelworkers run an educational program from their Humanity Fund designed to increase members' awareness of the impact of globalization on the Third World (Marshall, 1992), while putting their main educational emphasis on promoting participation in workplace "teams" and workplace reorganization. "Union Judo" is how the CEP refers to its courses on responding to new management techniques, a title which recognizes that while management may have some new momentum and even a grip on the union, that momentum and grip can be used to the union's advantage! Even when unions are accommodating to, and participating in, globalization and new management techniques, they may also be promoting resistance.

UNISON, Britain's largest union, provides an instructive example of how a union may address diverse objectives. It has gone further than any Canadian union in promoting broader educational opportunities for its members and is perhaps a new model of workers' education for the twenty-first century.

UNISON Open College: New Model Workers' Education

When UNISON was formed in 1993, it brought together the vocational, professional education traditions of a white-collar association and the basic education experience of a progressive manual union. This merger provided the opportunity to integrate membership training and education to provide pathways for learning that linked basic education to degree and post-graduate studies. The concept of "UNISON Open College" was born. The college is not a physical institution but a range of provision, with a focus on open and distance learning methods.

The union established a consortium of providers including colleges, universities, the Workers' Educational Association and residential colleges to augment its own provision. The resulting college is based on four phases of provision ranging from basic educational skills to introductory study skills to accreditation for prior learning to degree-level study. Students can opt for accreditation at any stage and can carry credits forward to the next phase. Generally the course materials reflect workers' concerns and advocate collective solutions to social problems.

This provision emphasizes education, not just vocational training, and challenges employers to grant their employees PEL and other support. Members can gain vocational qualifications that are not employer-specific, vocational qualifications that are linked to broader educational opportunities: in this scheme, training and education are complementary. For example, the second phase includes the union-developed, WEA-delivered "Return to Learn" (R2L), which has already proved very successful in promoting individual learning as well as union involvement (Kennedy, 1995). In the R2L course, which runs for nine to ten months, as many as ten students meet together every two to three weeks in a local study group and progress through a series of work-books; as well, each student is allocated a personal tutor. Further along on the spectrum, the level-four studies include a specifically designed, university-delivered, critically aware labour studies program available by distance delivery and offered as a stand-alone certificate or as a component to be integrated into a degree program.

The UNISON college thus encompasses both re-skilling components and the critical education identified as key responses to globalization and combines them with a rebirth of adult education (albeit credentialized).[8] The union has responded to the decline in traditional adult education provision for working people by plugging the gaps itself and shaming providers and employers into supporting its efforts. The result is an education that supports members and the union. The UNISON model is being adapted by the Manufacturing Science and Finance union, which, through a link with Leeds University, is credentializing all its tools courses and developing new distance education university credit courses specifically designed to allow its members to gain a university certificate (equivalent to first-year degree level studies). A limited version of this model was pioneered in Canada by Toronto's Metro Labour

Centre and George Brown College, but it never had the range and breadth of UNISON's Open College.

New Model Labour Education: CUPE's Computer Network

The Internet will be a strand in any new model of workers' education and will provide opportunities for global union responses to the globalization of capital. Computer-mediated communication (CMC) is being explored by several labour unions, as evidenced by their web sites. One of the first unions to provide an electronic mail and conferencing system was the Canadian Union of Public Employees (CUPE), which established the Solidarity Network (SoliNet) in 1987. The network is available to all Canadian labour and links subscribers across Canada and abroad, providing a "resource and meeting place," a virtual workshop for trade unionists. SoliNet conferences are now accessed through the World Wide Web.

SoliNet is important to CUPE as a communications system that can link members across Canada's six time zones, providing a forum for discussing union issues. Conferences may be closed or open, with the former reserved for negotiating teams or members of a particular local who need confidentiality, for example. Open conferences include a "lounge" for general discussion and short "courses" offered to subscribers on topics such as "Workers' Controlling Technology." SoliNet conferencing is also available as an option in the Labour College of Canada/Athabasca University (LCC/AU) distance education "Labour Studies" course. (For a detailed discussion of SoliNet's educational role see Taylor, 1996.)

Distance-delivered labour education, particularly computer-mediated courses (CMC), has great potential but also particular problems and limitations, some of which have been discussed elsewhere in this volume. The discourse available via CMC goes beyond what is possible in traditional distance education and is closer to the collective learning experienced in most face-to-face labour education courses. As Taylor notes, "CMC is interactive, there is a degree of social agency in the medium" not present in other distance courses (Taylor, 1996, p. 286). This interactive element is important because union education is social and has a social purpose requiring "social agency."

Conclusion

Some commentators believe unions have lost their social purpose and have essentially become "service" organizations for their members (Aronowitz, 1990). A service model of unions and union education would predict a labour education focused on workers' individualized learning and advancement rather than collective action. It would also fit with Friesen's (1994) argument that labour education is not providing broader education to workers. However, it would be a mistake to describe Canadian unions as just service organizations, not only because all representative labour education is social and has the potential to teach collectivist values, but because membership educational schemes such as those of the CAW/CUPW PEL and the Steelworkers Humanity Fund program contradict such critique. Further, the UNISON model shows how service unionism can be blended with collective goals, and how unions do not have to accept the available adult educational provision but can mould their own. With its emphasis on open and distance education, UNISON provides a model for workers' education in the age of globalization. If the principles of UNISON's scheme can be melded with the CAW/CUPW's PEL provisions, and with other new developments such as CUPE's electronic delivery (SoliNet) and the CLC/AU Labour Studies course, a new international model of workers' education, drawing on the traditions of "independent working-class education," can prosper into the new century.

Endnotes

[1]   "Training for Citizenship," described by Gordon Selman in Chapter 1 of this volume, reflects some of these concerns as they were experienced in Canada.

[2]   The Canadian WEA was established in Toronto in 1918.

[3]   Ironically the WEA was also accused of being under Communist influence by some union officials, and in 1950 they lost their provincial (Ontario) grant because of these accusations.

[4]   Some institutions provide both—Capilano is moving in this direction. It should also be noted that union representation on a board of studies is the norm for these institutionally provided labour studies programs.

[5]   This definition—which treats union and labour education as almost synonymous—is different from that of Verner and Dickenson (1974, p. 6) who considered workers' and labour education as "interchangeable" terms.

[6]   It should also be remembered that union terms and conditions directly and indirectly influence contracts of other non-union workers. More than half of all Canadian workers are affected by union-negotiated terms and conditions.

[7]   Aronowitz (1990) has argued that American unions have become "service" providers for members rather than cultural, ideological organs.

[8]   Most labour education has traditionally been non-credential and could be defined as a prime example of non-formal adult education. However, under the UNISON program students can choose to do the courses with or without the credential.

Lumber camp worker resting in class, 1950 (location not known).
Courtesy of Frontier College.

Part 2
Education for Transformation

14

An Overview of Transformation Theory in Adult Education

Sue M. Scott

Too often the term *transformation* is used indiscriminately to mean any kind of change. Transformation includes change but connotes a particular kind of change. Determining if something has transformed requires looking at the nature of the change, the theoretical framework of self and society, and whether or not it meets the criteria for transformative change. In adult education there are primarily two kinds of transformation, social and personal, and a third that attempts to merge these two. The social derives primarily from social theory and the personal has its origins in psychology. In recent adult education literature, transformation is increasingly being situated in the notion of transformative learning, something that individuals and people do to bring about a process of change. In this chapter a framework is developed that can be used to determine to what extent change is transformative.[1]

A Criteria for Assessment

There are specific criteria that one can use to decide if a change is transformative. To be called transformation there must be structural change, either social structural transformation or personal structural transformation or both. The aim of the change is to catalyze a fundamental shift in people's beliefs and values and must include a social vision about the future based on a value system that includes the struggle for freedom, democracy or equity, and authenticity. A third criterion is a shift in what counts as knowledge. Basic conflict in values and what counts as knowledge in an open and free society are usually debated in a lifeworld, a civil space, and often are put forth as statements or "actions" from various interest groups which attempt to influence and change structures, institutions and policies. Fourthly, transformation is based on conflict theory, not consensus or accommodation/adaptation theory as explicated by Talcott Parsons. The assumption is that for transformation to occur, there must be something that unsettles us, shakes us up. Conflict theory assumes there are different interests present when humans act to change either personal meaning or social structures. A kind of clarity emerges which promotes enlightenment through a sense of struggle for freedom. In sum, the four criteria for assessing if something is transformed are: (1) there must be structural change; (2) the aim or intention must be grounded in a future vision that includes freedom, democracy and authenticity; (3) there must be a shift in what counts as knowledge; and (4) the change must be based on conflict theory.

The following sections involve a discussion and application of the criteria above to both social and personal transformation. A discussion of transformation and how it is to be learned, pedagogy, follows each of the sections. A final section includes the merging of the two. (For a comprehensive review of personal transformative learning theory, see Patricia Cranton's chapter "Transformative Learning: Individual Growth and Development through Critical Reflection" in this volume.)

Social Transformation

The orthodox usage of *structure* tends to refer to the institutional macro features of society as opposed to the micro features of face-to-face interactions. Structure is the social organization (including assumptions about race, class and gender), institutions and cultural products (like language and knowledge) of society, or the external social context of behaviour. Some social theorists (Parsons and Althusser) regard structure as if social processes were detached from, and independent of, people's activities. This simply leads to "a view of social behaviour (as in role theory) whereby it is treated as a mechanical outcome of objective social relations" (Layder, 1994, p. 156). Most theorists, however, include a theory of action attached to structure theory where through human agency individuals have the capacity to act to change structures in society. While structures are human-made to maintain a sense of order and generate their own history and traditions, they are nevertheless products of human agency past and present and are subject to change.

In Canada, social transformation has had a critical orientation. Based in critical theory, education with an emancipatory pedagogy advocates for freedom of expression, individual and collective rights and diversity of opinion as healthy in a pluralistic culture. Canadians have appropriated the work of Jurgen Habermas (Welton, 1993; Collins, 1991) as a profound thinker in critical social theory. Habermas is one of the newest members of the Frankfurt School of critical theory that was set up in 1923 to deal with the ills of society, the things that kept people from being fulfilled. The school attempted to identify the social changes that are necessary in order to produce a just and democratic society.

Habermas draws on the work of Max Weber who, writing at the turn of the twentieth century, maintained that the ability to "rationalize" in the modern world is founded on the development of rational knowledge. This led to the decreasing importance of myth and religion as ways of interpreting physical phenomena. As the growth of bureaucratic organizations developed in response to capitalism, increasing rationalization was manifest in technological mastery which is dependent on reason and scientific knowledge. As a consequence there is a loss of meaning since the knowledge claims are based almost exclusively on what is useful for technical or instrumental advancement. This instrumental or technical reason and action is the basis of behaviourism. Habermas views this kind of reasoning as one-dimensional, as in a person applying knowledge to achieve particular personal goals.

When critical theorists in adult education talk about individualism or individualistic actions it is in reference to this instrumental/technical orientation to knowledge. There is also a vehement belief that analysis and critique must be "structural" in origin; introduction of the individual or humanist orientation, the micro perspective, is viewed with suspicion. Individualism is also tied to the dominant economic platform. As Marchak notes, "political ideologies ultimately boil down to these decisions, to the relative emphasis placed on individualism versus collectivism, and on egalitarianism versus elitism" (Marchak, 1988, p. 6). On the individual end of the continuum, the collective society has no claim on the individual who in turn has no responsibility to the collective whole: "The preservation of individual liberty and of the 'free market' become the major concerns for advocates of these positions" (Marchak, 1988, p. 6).

Habermas says that the above view of rationality is limited because it denies that humans communicate through interaction and seek consensus through the use of language. Any adequate theory of society must take into account that action is based on the achievement of shared meaning and understanding. This is what distinguishes humans from animals. He maintains that through the "ideal speech situation" where no one is coerced and everyone is free to participate fully in discourse, the *potential* for rationality exists. Knowledge, then, is constructed with shared meanings among people who put forth "validity claims" and try to persuade each other with their views backed up in various recognized ways.[2]

Since adult educators have historically sided with the poor and the outcasts, our value system includes what will most contribute to just social conditions and equitable relationships that further democracy, authenticity and freedom among the majority of the people. An adult education example from Canadian history that is clearly transformational is the Antigonish Movement. To contest exploitation within the fishing industry, the fishers in Nova Scotia took action to open a banking co-op and a cannery and to break away from their feudal dependency on growing capitalism. Some have called this more reformist in nature rather than transformist, since the form of structural change was in the relationship between the exploited and the exploiters through a conflictual process, but capitalism itself was not changed. However, the fishers were able to construct their own knowledge by re-defining their own experiences; they came to a new meaning and understanding and were able to gain freedom from dependency and servitude, economically and psychically.

More recent examples of change include the governmental shift from a liberal stance of openness and tolerance of difference to one of supporting more narrow economic interests. Hence budget cuts have systematically eroded the social safety net, including health and education. Structural shifts in the corporate sector, such as downsizing, affect workers by overburdening remaining employees and displacing others, creating substantial personal and social upheaval. To what extent do these structural-change examples support freedom, democracy and authenticity? While they are significant changes, which many may call transformation, they harbour a value system that is couched in neo-liberal economic policies which privileges a free market over social goals. "Liberal economic arguments for the free market [are] joined with political arguments about individualism and a reduced public sector" (King, 1987, p. 8). Thus, the maximization of a particular kind of individual freedom (those who have economic wealth) is proposed through the limiting of state intervention: "freedom must be market-based freedom rather than state-imposed" (King, p. 9). Private property and corporate rights are valued over social programs and there are attempts to eliminate equity and individual freedoms. These examples do not fit the criteria for transformation.

To extend this line of reasoning further, the postmodern condition has called into question a quest for truth and freedom, as a guiding meta-narrative. Really useful knowledge, in the original sense, was emancipatory; it supported freedom from constraints that inhibit progress. But, as Edwards (1994) argues, "progress" seems to have gone array. The Holocaust, nuclear arms threats, urban blight and decay, crime and environmental degradation have called into question our progress towards truth and liberty and no longer can be used to legitimate knowledge, postmodernists claim. The postmodern era criteria for what constitutes knowledge revolves around "performativity" of the system. Edwards (1994) maintains it is the systematic usefulness of knowledge, not progress of truth and liberty, that is based on skills rather than ideals, that characterizes the postmodern condition. "This suggests an inter-relationship between the individualizing discourses of learner-centredness, an emphasis on identity and lifestyle and trends toward a market in learning opportunities (Edwards, 1991a, 1994; Kenway, 1993) in which the 'real use value' of knowledge is tied in increasingly complex ways to optimizing the efficiency of the system" (Edwards, 1994, p. 167). Again, this is an example of the encroachment of instrumentalists and neo-liberal thinking on education.

Where can social transformation be learned? The traditional setting is through non-formal education, in community development and action groups that utilize praxis or an action-reflection model. Skillful pedagogy includes dialogue on fundamental premises which have formed worldviews and must be differentiated from andragogy which involves a teaching-learning transaction where knowledge flows fundamentally from teacher to learner. While critical-thinking skills are encouraged in andragogy, there is an absence of engagement with the social in an action process where the learners and teachers are in collective solidarity on issues.

Personal Transformation

Personal theories in the transformative process are helpful in explicating further the micro aspect in the macro-micro debate. The micro theorists focus on the individual as the fundamental unit of analysis in society. "Most importantly, the term 'structure' seems to neglect the 'meanings' with which people imbue their lives and which colour their relations with others" (Layder, 1994, p. 57). These humanists, called symbolic interactionists (SI), believe that a person's self and mind are intrinsically social processes; they are imbued from birth in the social customs and habits of culture and the social group. Primarily from the Chicago School, SI theorists, such as Blumer and Becker, stress that researchers and practitioners should try to unravel the "meaningful worlds" of the social groups they study in order to give an insider's account of what it's like being in a particular group. "Social interactionists attend to the delicate interweaving between the institutional features of society and the creative capacities of people" (Layder, 1996, p. 65).

Thus, the introduction of psychological processes is approached in the micro view. For adult educators, at least in the North American tradition, psychology permeates the curriculum issues regarding teaching and learning. Considering individuals as the primary learning unit, not groups, is a traditional view. Yet the collective social nature of many adult learning programs in Canada, however, more readily demonstrate that groups, in fact, learn, act and grow together. Nevertheless, the personal and the social have been inherently intertwined. We have a long tradition of personal transformation that comes primarily through the church and religious conversion experiences. A burning bush experience (or a bolt of lightening) that changes one forever is certainly a kind of personal transformation. Jacques Pasquier (1978) describes it this way:

> It is always difficult to schematize a phenomenon which is not and cannot be described in logical terms. And yet in every conversion there is a pattern which cannot be avoided. I would describe it as the passage from one certitude (or set of values) to an openness to another reality. The key word is "passage." It evokes the breaking through a wall of resistances in a free act (p. 195).

The four criteria for assessing transformation can be applied in the personal realm as well. For personal transformative learning, structural change occurs in the psyche of individuals. The structure of the psyche involves an awareness or conceptual understanding of the "self." In a structural view, the self usually involves recognition of a tripartite notion which includes the ego, the personal unconscious and the collective unconscious (Boyd and Myers, 1988). In postmodern terms there are multiple selves, each one of which may hold different interests, respond differently to conditions and contribute to a decentred self (Briton, 1996) or divided self (James, 1978) in a fragmented society which no longer holds agreed-upon standards or mores. Thus, at any one time there is conflict among the various structures of the self, or opposing selves. The aim of personal transformation is to align various disparate parts of the self to gain coherence, peace, and a sense of wholeness. This promotes a sense of freedom and authenticity which can contribute to meaningful work and activity in the social sphere.

Various theorists in adult education focus on different aspects of the self structure. Jack Mezirow (1991) proposes a primarily cognitive restructuring of the ego. His view is that we hold various worldviews or perspectives as they relate to a number of personal and social issues, such as democracy, beauty, education, and he calls these meaning perspectives. We can transform our perspectives in a safe environment where reflection through dialogue on the fundamental premises that guide our lives are challenged by the group members. Mezirow suggests this can only be done in a group or in social interaction as we often need help uncovering heretofore undisclosed meaning schemes. They have been lodged in the unconscious and for Mezirow that is the personal unconscious, just below conscious ego awareness. Usually conflict is required to challenge habits and assumptions that have dulled our senses and become like old shoes, comfortable but not particularly meaningful anymore. As a theory of transformation, Mezirow attempts to explicate the personal side of Paulo Freire's more holistic notion of transformation.

There is another kind of personal transformation whose leading proponent is Robert Boyd (1991). Boyd and his followers call personal transformation in adult education transformative education. He uses the broader word, education, to connote a deeper notion which includes an expansion of consciousness that is more than just cognitive. The aim of personal work is to attain self-knowledge which leads to a congruence between the inner and outer parts of our lives and what emerges is a more authentic person. Using the framework of analytical depth psychology, Boyd explicates what the social micro theorists call the emotional, and he calls this extra-rationality. For depth theorists, the unconscious is the collective unconscious where "emotional" work originates. That is, the collective unconscious is the repository for historical, ancient and primordial material and governs the energy and soul life of the individual.

Criticism of the analytical depth orientation includes a dwelling on the personal which takes the individual away from the concerns of the social. Proponents, however, maintain that without the work of self-knowledge, action can be skewed, vulnerability is a possibility and inappropriate eruptions into conscious awareness and speech shake confidence and focus in the heat of social action. Furthermore, without internal work, it is possible for the ego to think it is in control of situations when in fact what governs a collective milieu and/or action is a collective phenomenon deeper than just our awareness. We have all experienced when a rhythm exists in a group and when it does not; the group "clicks" when it does. The breath of life and energy, a quickening, is felt in the group.

A transformative pedagogy from the personal perspective is highly reflective. That is, dialogue is present in both perspective transformation and in transformative education. The first is social dialogue, inter-subjective, on premises that compose a meaning perspective (Mezirow, 1991), and the second is intra-psychic dialogue among the two dynamic parts of the psyche, the unconscious and the ego (Boyd, 1991). Both kinds of personal transformation can be facilitated in formal classrooms where instructors give substantive time to dialoguing on premises as well as images that are found in dreams, fantasies and speech eruptions. The work in the underworld is mythic and poetic, not instrumental or communicative action in the social sense. It is social in that intra-psychic dialogue emanates from persons in dreams and fantasies as they are given attention and consideration by ego consciousness. It is critical in that there is an unrelenting questioning of what is going on, what it means and what difference it makes to the learner. This requires ego action in the form of critical thinking. However, it is not the same as critical social theory; it derives from a different paradigm, from the practical or wisdom orientation. The language is in images, the action is phantasmic and the meaning unfolds in time.

Intersection of the Personal and the Social

Finally, there is considerable interchange between the social and the personal (Scott & Schmitt-Boshnick, 1994). That is, where there is a social upheaval, the personal is affected and vice versa. Paulo Freire was first to recognize this in his dialectical notion of self and society. Based on the premise of a class structure where the poor are kept illiterate, Freire shows us that changing individuals structurally (their self power and self-concept when they learned to read), has massive connotations for changes in society. It is socially a collective phenomenon, as well as a collective unconscious shift and a cognitive change within the egos of individuals. Friere's theory of self involves a process he calls conscientization which is a constant movement between the action and the reflection on the action. While the self in the person changes in dialogue and in action, it is fundamentally a social process that transcends an individualistic concern for knowing. It involves the notion of praxis as the action of moving back and forth between action in the world and reflection on the action in a growing depth of understanding. Sometimes this has been called the hermeneutical circle, which emphasizes new levels of interpretations with a set of new questions which challenges the former interpretation. "Liberation is a thoroughly social process with ... implications for the freedom to develop our individuality within the support and commune of others. Therefore liberation is a social, not an individual, effort which recognizes and celebrates the fact that we are social beings, not isolated, self-striving monads" (Allman, 1996, p. 347).

In problem-posing education, "the oppressed learn to develop the necessary critical tools that will enable them to read their world so they can apprehend the globality of their reality and choose what world they want for themselves" (Freire & Macedo, 1995, p. 389). For instance, Ira Shor describes his classroom experiences: "When the students spoke to me or to others about their reality [in class], their animation became more intense ... The reality-themes we looked at were saturated with critical inquiry so that we wound up inside and outside everyday life at the same time, studying the ordinary with extraordinary scrutiny" (Shor & Freire, 1987, p. 23). There was also a "democracy of expression," which not only encouraged the students to talk openly but also changed the words and language of the teacher. Knowledge, again, was constructed from the students' own reality, sorted through, perhaps labeled, but at least legitimized by student colleagues and the instructor.

Freire maintains that both the teacher and the students have to be learners and be critical agents in the act of knowing. Once people begin to understand how society works, they begin to have a different relationship to knowledge and to society. Study of the power interests in society clarifies one's own interests which might be the same or different.

> Transformation has to be accomplished by those who dream about the re-invention of society, the recreation or reconstruction of society. Then, those whose political dream is to reinvent society have to fill up the space of the schools, the institutional space, in order to unveil the reality which is being hidden by the dominant ideology, the dominant curriculum (Shor & Freire, p. 36).

In other words, an internal vision shared collectively must be captured before we go into action. The vision is captured by unrelenting critique on the social dynamics and construction of structures in society.

A paper distributed by Budd Hall defines his understanding of transformative adult education:

> Transformative adult education is about supporting shifts away from the Global Market Utopia and toward other visions. It is about contributing to the transformation of structures of power and domination whether discursive, electronic, mechanical, social, or physical. It is about self-awareness, critique and creation. Adult education and intentional adult learning has an important role to play in the strengthening of global civil society (Hall, 1997).

Summary

There is a framework that can be used to decide if something has transformed or has just changed. Questions to ask are: Is there structural change? Is the aim grounded in a future vision that includes freedom, democracy and authenticity? Is there a shift in direction for what counts as knowledge? Is the change based on conflict theory which assumes different interests are present when people act to bring about change? I've attempted to show through a brief description of social theory, personal theory and a merging of the two that transformation in adult education must have a formed theory of society as well as a theory of self. Adult education is primarily interested in people, the changing of people to become better citizens, better workers, better contributors to society. Mixed in with this is a concern for education as an institution itself, particularly those adult education agencies and institutions that perpetuate lifelong learning with adults throughout their lives. Education for transformation, however, is intentionally towards a vision of society that is socially responsible, for those work situations that promote humanization and freedom for creativity.

There are some questions still remaining after this discussion, however. To what extent is the intent or value orientation to the structural change a determining factor in calling it transformational? If it does not have a really useful knowledge claim, i.e., it is emancipatory in some way, can it be called transformation? Is it possible for transformation to be accomplished in formal classroom education or does it better suit non-formal education in the social context? Critique is a fundamental tenet of transformation and there is a difference between critical social theory and critical thinking. The first is the unrelenting critique of social structures that are keeping people from being human while the other is a method of analysis and can be politically neutral.

In relation to personal transformation, is there a core to the self with some sort of subsidiary selves that sometimes are divided and create a decentred self? We still haven't determined this. What role does language play in centering the self? For the depth theorists, the language is different, mytho-poetic, and what does that actually do for the soul-work necessary for transformation? (See Dirkx, 1997.) For the British, transformation is almost always in community, is liberatory, participatory, and highly emancipatory and social in nature. For those in North America, particularly the United States, there is a growing interest in what happens to the person in these social endeavours. Transformation historically is both social and personal; it is a centuries-old concept derived from religious life primarily, and experienced as a personal phenomenon. In Canada, however, we have focused on social transformation with the individual embedded within the social. Within the framework of a socially oriented understanding of transformation, the "individuation" of the person is possible as the group matures; he or she is both an active member of the group but autonomous to contribute freely to its and her/his own development. As despair reigns over the demise of treasured programs, such as the social safety net (Miles's chapter, "Learning from the Women's Movement in the Neo-Liberal Period"), and as the environment of the planet is being destroyed (Clover's chapter, "Adult Education within an Ecological Context"), there is an opportunity to spiral to another level of development, another way of being, which is essential if we are to continue, as adult educators, to inspire transformation, both personal and social and a merging of the two.

Endnotes

[1] Thanks to John Dirkx for dialogue on the content of this paper.

[2] For a more substantive discussion of Habermas's ideas, please refer to the chapters in this book by Michael Welton, Michael Collins, and Patricia Cranton.

15

Transformative Learning: Individual Growth and Development through Critical Reflection

Patricia Cranton

When people experience changes in their lives, find themselves in a dilemma or encounter new information that contradicts what they have always believed, they may revise their beliefs and perspectives. Mezirow (1991) developed his transformative learning theory to explain the process individuals go through when transformation takes place. In this chapter, transformative learning theory is reviewed, emphasizing individuals' learning processes rather than the broader issues of social change (see the chapter by Scott "An Overview of Transformative Theory in Adult Education" and the chapter by Haughey "From Passion to Passivity: The Decline of University Extension for Social Change" in this volume). The concept of transformative learning is placed in the context of related theories, and the different ways in which individuals go through transformative learning experiences is described, including the importance of group processes. The nature of the educator's role is highlighted.

Defining Transformative Learning

Transformative learning theory is complex, as it draws together strands from diverse fields. At times, these strands are not fully integrated in Mezirow's thinking, making it difficult for the practitioner and the student of adult education to see how the theory can be applied. In this section, some of the basic concepts of the theory and their interrelationships are described and illustrated.

Meaning Schemes and Meaning Perspectives

Mezirow (1991) drew on the work of George Kelly (1963) among others in the development of his theory. Kelly noted that individuals see the same event in different ways; there is no universal system of constructs, he argued, only personal constructs. Based on the experiences we have, we form expectations about what will happen next. If my friend is consistently kind and considerate, it would be my expectation that she will be kind and considerate the next time I meet her. If she were cold and brutal, I would be shocked. These habitual expectations are called *meaning schemes* by Mezirow. We do not live based on a random set of expectations and assumptions: our meaning schemes are interrelated in ways that are unique to our individual experiences. Further, my many encounters, for instance, with women as friends, colleagues and teachers have led me to develop a set of expectations about women, labeled *meaning perspectives* (Mezirow). We have many meaning perspectives related to our work or profession, our culture and our personal lives.

Types of Meaning Perspectives

In order to define types of meaning perspectives, Mezirow considered theories and frameworks from a diverse set of disciplines. Among others, he reviewed Roth's (1990) notion of perceptual filters, Kuhn's (1962) important description of shifting scientific paradigms and Wittgenstein's (1958) focus on the way we use language to understand each other and learn. Mezirow (1991) lists three kinds of meaning perspectives. *Epistemic* perspectives pertain to the way we come to know things (for example, our learning styles) and the way we use knowledge (for example, whether we focus on the details of an issue or the global picture); *sociolinguistic* perspectives are our understanding of social norms, culture and the way we use language (for example, political views); *psychological* perspectives are the way we see ourselves personally (for example, self-concept). These types of perspectives are not sharply distinct from one another but rather overlap and influence one another. The way we use knowledge may come in part from our cultural background. Our psychological meaning perspectives are likely to be influenced by the way the media portrays men and women in our culture. The way we see ourselves can, in turn, have an impact on the way we use knowledge.

Distorted or Undeveloped Assumptions

Mezirow (1991) defines a distorted assumption as one that "leads the learner to view reality in a way that arbitrarily limits what is included, impedes differentiation, lacks permeability or openness to other ways of seeing, or does not facilitate an integration of experience" (p. 118). His use of the word *distorted* disturbs some people and leads to a misinterpretation of his definition; alternatively, one might refer to "undeveloped" rather than distorted meaning perspectives (Cranton, 1996). What is meant here is that we hold many assumptions and perspectives, based on our previous experiences, which we have never questioned. If I have always lived in a community where prejudices against people of colour are the social norm, I may not ever have questioned the assumptions that make up the prejudices. If I was told by my parents and teachers that I was a slow learner or an unattractive child, I may not have ever seen a reason to question those views. It is only when I have experiences in another community or with a different group of individuals who hold different perspectives that I might become critical of my previous beliefs and begin the process of transformative learning. When this happens, I am becoming free of the constraint of not knowing that there are other perspectives. This is Mezirow's (1991) intent in his description of distorted assumptions.

Critical Reflection: The Central Process

Questioning our assumptions is a process of critical reflection and forms the heart of transformative learning. Reflective thinking is now a general goal of education and the topic of considerable research and debate. Interest in reflection can be traced back to Dewey (1933), who sparked the transition in our schools from memorization to learning how to think. Critical reflection leads us to change our assumptions and perhaps transform our perspectives.

Mezirow (1991) describes three kinds of reflection. *Content reflection* is the consideration of the content of the problem. "What is going on here?" a learner might ask when encountering a new piece of equipment, a different procedure or a change in group structure. *Process reflection* is reflection about how things came to be the way they are, an examination of the process of problem solving being used in the situation. "How have I come to have this perception?" a learner could ask when experiencing a fear of failure or anxiety about trying something new. *Premise reflection* take place when the problem itself is being questioned. "Why does this matter, anyway?" the learner asks, and the very premise of the reflection itself is challenged. Content, process and premise reflection take place in relation to our epistemic, sociolinguistic and psychological meaning perspectives, and the nature of the questions varies somewhat from one domain to another (Cranton, 1994).

Instrumental, Communicative and Emancipatory Learning

There are different kinds of knowledge and therefore different kinds of learning. Not all learning is transformative. We may acquire new meaning schemes or learn based on given assumptions. Moreover, learning processes can be fundamentally different from each other—the way we learn to increase productivity in a grain field bears little resemblance to the way we learn to understand our spouse.

In order to explore different kinds of knowledge in relation to transformative learning, Mezirow uses a theoretical framework developed by Habermas (1971), a contemporary German social theorist. Habermas believes human beings have three basic interests. They have a technical interest in controlling and manipulating the environment, a practical interest in understanding each other and their social group and an emancipatory interest in becoming free from ignorance.

Each of these fundamental interests leads to a type of knowledge. Our interest in controlling the environment leads us to acquire instrumental knowledge, a knowledge of how to build shelters for ourselves, grow food, develop transportation systems and create computers to ease our processing of information. We accumulate such knowledge through *instrumental learning*. Habermas (1971) is critical of how people attempt to view all knowledge as instrumental. People try to explain, for example, social relationships, human nature and learning processes as though they were scientific cause-and-effect phenomena.

Our practical interest in understanding each other leads us to acquire practical knowledge through the use of language, according to Habermas. We want to know what others intend and to make ourselves understood. We do this through conversation and discussion, listening to others, watching television and reading books. We gain a knowledge of social norms, values, beliefs, political issues and philosophical concepts. When people in a group, community or culture agree on an issue—monogamy is right, communism is bad—they see this knowledge as valid or sanctioned. Mezirow (1991) calls the acquisition of practical knowledge *communicative learning*, and argues that most of the significant learning in adulthood falls into this domain.

Our emancipatory interests come from our desire to grow, develop and increase our self-awareness. We want to improve ourselves, understand ourselves, become better human beings, and we work towards this goal by trying to free ourselves of self-distortions and social distortions. Mezirow (1991) describes *emancipatory learning* as freedom from "libidinal, linguistic, epistemic, institutional, or environmental forces that limit our options and our rational control over our lives but have been taken for granted or seen as beyond human control" (p. 87). This definition indicates that emancipatory learning can influence both instrumental and practical knowledge. Critical reflection is the central process in emancipatory learning and the outcome is often transformative.

Content, process and premise reflections can take place in each of instrumental, communicative and emancipatory learning (Cranton, 1994). However, the application is not as straightforward as it initially seems. Premise reflection in the instrumental domain takes the form of "Why is this knowledge important to me?" and, in the communicative domain, leads to questions such as "Why should I believe in this conclusion?" These critical questions can lead to emancipatory learning, which is why Mezirow argues that emancipatory learning has implications for the other two domains.

Unfortunately, the terminology used in transformative learning theory can overwhelm the student of adult education and mask the powerful simplicity of the concept. When we are led to reflect on and question something we previously took for granted and thereby change our views or perspectives, transformative learning has taken place. The change can take place in how we understand ourselves, others, our culture or knowledge itself.

Transformative Learning in Context

The concept of learning as transformation is not new or exclusive to Mezirow's work, although it was Mezirow who gave us the framework and language for seeing the concept as a theory of learning. In this section, transformative learning is related to some of the thinking in which it is grounded as well as other familiar perspectives.

Social Theory and Philosophy: Habermas

Habermas's (1971) three basic human interests and the resultant types of knowledge provide a framework for Mezirow's thinking. Although he has been criticized for his "selective interpretation and adaptation of Habermas" (Collard & Law, 1989, p. 102), Mezirow (1989) indicates that he used Habermas's framework only as a guide and that some aspects of transformative learning theory have "nothing to do with Habermas" (p. 175).

Habermas's (1984) theory of communicative action also strongly influences Mezirow's conceptualization of the process of transformation. *Communicative action* takes place when one person communicates with another with the goal of arriving at a mutual understanding about an experience or situation. If you and I both attend the same lecture, then discuss its quality with the intent of coming to agreement, this is communicative action. During this process, *validity testing* takes place. That is, we provide evidence in support of our arguments and use reason to persuade the other. I might refer to the poor organization of the lecture, and you might comment on the dazzling use of audio-visual materials. Rationality is central to communicative action: we reason rather than cajole, appeal to authority or use brute force. *Communicative competence* is necessary for transformative learning. That is, we must be able to negotiate meaning and question others' views rather than accept things because "they" say it is so.

This leads us to the importance of three further concepts from Habermas's (1984) theory of communicative action. The *lifeworld* is made up of all the daily things we take for granted. It is a culturally transmitted set of patterns or perspectives that allows us to go about our everyday activities in an unquestioning way (Welton, 1995). Habermas (1984) says, "the lifeworld always remains in the background" (Vol. 2, p. 131). We can think of a traditional village society, for example, where individuals routinely provide for their need for food and shelter without wondering why they are doing so. Similarly, I assume that the person I pass on my daily walk will not attack me with a gun. I assume that my place of work will be there tomorrow morning.

One's lifeworld depends on an inter-subjective understanding: others must make the same assumptions for the taken-for-granted perspective to be possible. Through *discourse* we test the validity of the lifeworld. Once an experience has been translated into a speech act, it can be questioned; when I say no one will attack me with a gun, this becomes a judgment and another person may question that judgment. In ordinary dialogue, we describe experiences and express opinions. In discourse, one raises questions of truth, justice and self-deception. Habermas (1984) refers to three kinds of discourse (theoretical, practical and therapeutic) pertaining to different domains of knowledge, but in each, the central process is the challenging of common beliefs. It is through discourse that distorted or limiting assumptions are revealed and transformative learning is possible.

There is another dynamic at play. A self-regulating *systems world*, including bureaucracies, political systems, the organization of the economy and many other institutionalized systems, stifle our ability to question. Our lifeworld is dominated by systems, both large and small, that we do not question. From the policies and procedures in our workplace to the legal, political and educational systems of our culture, we are subjugated to unquestioned and seemingly unquestionable systems.

From this brief overview, one can see how Habermas's theory development could be easily drawn into Mezirow's work on transformative learning. The concepts of unquestioned assumptions, critical reflection, rational discourse and learning through challenging those things commonly taken for granted are themes in both.

Conscientization: Freire

Freire's (1970) definition of conscientization precedes Mezirow's (1975) initial presentation of perspective transformation by only a few years. Freire describes a process in which people "achieve a deepening awareness of both the sociocultural reality which shapes their lives and of their capacity to transform that reality through action upon it" (p. 27). Based on his work in Brazil, Freire outlined a process through which individuals move: (1) a preoccupation with survival; (2) seeing life as out of their control or ruled by fate and destiny; (3) some questioning of their lives, but remaining vulnerable to the persuasion of popular leaders; and (4) participation in dialogue that focuses on the critique of ideologies that foster oppression.

Although the contexts of Freire's and Mezirow's work differ sharply—Freire working with the oppressed people of Brazil and Mezirow's imagination being sparked by the experiences of his wife returning to college—the parallels between the two approaches are remarkable. Mezirow (1991) acknowledges the influence of Freire's work on his thinking.

Reflection: Dewey

Critical reflection is the central process in transformative learning theory and it is Dewey's name that comes to mind when we consider the emphasis on reflection in modern education. Dewey's definition of reflective thought as "active, persistent and careful consideration of any belief or supposed form of knowledge in the light of the grounds that support it" (1933, p. 9) is what Habermas (1984) calls validity testing and what Mezirow (1991) calls critical reflection on meaning schemes. Dewey was interested in reflection as it is used in problem solving. In solving a problem, "we have to turn upon some unconscious assumption and make it explicit" (Dewey, 1933, p. 281). Similarly, Mezirow, when defining the three kinds of reflection (content, process and premise), describes them in terms of problems to be addressed.

Reflection-in-Action: Schön

Schön (1983) takes a slightly different perspective on reflection, one that Mezirow does not clearly integrate into his theory but that could contribute to our understanding of how individuals go through transformative learning in different ways (Cranton, 1994; 1996). Schön is critical of the model of technical rationality. He describes practitioners as intuitively adjusting their responses, strategies and behaviours while they are "in action," while they are practising. He sees professionals as innovative, creative and artistic in their work and delineates this process as reflection-in-action.

Through reflection-in-action, we build up a repertoire of examples or themes upon which we draw in further practice. Such a repertoire Schön (1983) calls a theory-in-action and describes it as framing our professional roles. Mezirow (1991) sees this theory-in-action or frame as equivalent to a meaning perspective on our practice—a socio-linguistic meaning perspective. Although we may not consciously or rationally question a theory-in-action, it develops and transforms with further experiences.

Developmental Perspectives: Tennant

Mezirow (1991) clearly sees transformative learning as a developmental process. In one description of transformation, he writes, "This is what development means in adulthood" (p. 155), and then goes on to argue that transformation could be seen as the central process of adult development. By definition, as we question, revise and validate our beliefs and perspectives, we are developing.

Mezirow's theory is congruent with most of the views of adult development (e.g., King & Kitchener, 1994). However, Tennant (1993) provoked an interesting and lively debate with Mezirow (1994) on how, or if, transformation and development are different. Tennant argues that individual development is both a social and a psychological process and claims that Mezirow has neglected the social forces that shape the lives of individuals. Secondly, he contends that some transformations are part of a normal progression through life phases and as such do not require critical reflection. Bringing these two points together, Tennant and Pogson (1995) claim that development implies growth and progress towards some end point—a healthy or mature personality—and that this "conception cannot be divorced from issues of social value" (p. 113).

In a provocative response to Tennant, Mezirow (1994) comments that he sees "no good reason to differentiate between transformative adult learning and adult development" (p. 228), and he reiterates his view that "learning is profoundly social" (p. 230).

The Process of Transformative Learning

Mezirow (1991) describes the central dynamic of transformative learning as a rational, cognitive process of critical reflection. As discussed earlier, the reflection may take three forms. We reflect on the content of a problem, on the processes or strategies we are using to deal with the problem and on the basic premise underlying the problem. Content and process reflection can lead to either a confirmation or a transformation of meaning schemes; premise reflection can lead to a transformation of a meaning perspective. Not all individuals learn or transform in this way; "reflection" may be a different process for different people (Cranton, 1994; 1996). In this section, individual differences among learners, the group processes that support transformative learning and the role of the educator in the group are discussed.

Individual Differences

Transformative learning theory is grounded in constructivist thought, as Mezirow (1991) clearly outlines. He calls on the work of Kelly (1963) and Candy (1989) to describe constructivism. Simply put, individuals perceive or construe the same event in different ways, as we know from reading about witnesses' accounts of a crime. That we have different expectations or meaning schemes as well as meaning perspectives is an underlying assumption of transformative learning theory. However, we also have commonly accepted understandings (for example, families are important; murder is evil) within communities and cultures. These are socially constructed perspectives, ones with which groups of people agree.

If we accept that individuals construct their own perspectives about the world around them and that people learn by changing those perspectives, we also come to the conclusion that the learning process takes place in varying ways for different people. There has been a considerable amount of research and writing on learning styles verifying this conclusion (e.g., see Kolb, 1984). Jung's (1921: 1971) theory of psychological types provides a powerful way of understanding individual differences in transformative learning (Cranton, 1994). We do not all "reflect" in the same way, nor are we equally likely to revise our values, assumptions and perspectives. Some of us work through thoughts and situations best by ourselves or by writing in a journal; others need to talk to friends or colleagues. Some of us stand by strong principles, while others easily adapt their views. Some of us are interested in all of the possibilities and alternatives, while others are more practical and down to earth. These kinds of individual differences cannot help but lead to varying transformative learning processes.

Not many researchers in adult education have addressed the issue of individual differences in transformative learning, in spite of the general interest in learning styles in the field. Boyd and Myers (1988), writing from a Jungian perspective, suggest that *discernment* rather than critical reflection is the means to transformation. They define discernment as an inner journey and dialogue with the unconscious. Being receptive to this journey can lead to the disintegration of prior ways of knowing, or transformation. As interesting as this approach is, it is implying that all people would engage in an "inner journey." It could still be argued, based on psychological type theory, that this is unlikely. Further attention needs to be paid to individual differences in the transformative learning process.

Group Processes: Challenging and Questioning

How does the process of transformative learning start? We know that the process is one of critical self-reflection kindled by an experience that is discrepant with our expectations, assumptions or values. This may happen by chance, of course, but if we agree with Mezirow that transformative learning is a goal of adult education, it cannot be left to chance. Neither can it be intervention, imposition or indoctrination on the part of the educator. It is the power of the learning group, of which the educator is a part, that is most likely to lead individuals to critical reflection. Seventy years ago, Lindeman (1926) described adult education as a co-operative venture in non-authoritarian learning. The emphasis on discussion, discourse and collaboration has remained a theme in the literature from that time. Mezirow (1991) claims that full and free participation in critical discourse is essential to critical reflection.

In group discourse, learners can question each other and challenge each other's assumptions and perspectives. Mezirow (1991) refers to "reflective discourse through which learners can examine the justification for their meaning schemes and perspectives as well as focusing on the new data presented" (p. 201). It is difficult to question our assumptions in isolation. Another person provides another viewpoint, asks for justification or challenges our evidence. In a group, the kinds of questions that stimulate content, process and premise reflections can be encouraged (e.g., see Cranton, 1994, p. 51). Brookfield (1987) argues that "skilled critical questioning is the most effective means through which ingrained assumptions can be externalized" (p. 92).

Group Processes: Support and Caring

Challenging and questioning can only occur in a supportive and caring atmosphere. Group members must trust each other, respect alternative views and understand that there are valid differences among individuals. Boyd (1989) especially emphasizes the learner group as a social system that "can provide supportive structures that facilitate an individual's work in realizing personal transformation" (p. 467). In the references to group members here, the educator is included as a member of this group, as is elaborated on in the next section of this chapter.

A learner group can build cohesiveness and supportiveness by engaging in activities that bring people together—sharing journals, acting as a unit to write a letter of protest, collaborating on projects, meeting outside the classroom and sharing leadership roles in group activities. Brookfield (1990) provides several examples of practical exercises that serve to build group trust as well as foster critical reflection, such as critical incidents, crisis decision simulations, role plays, role reversals and critical debates.

When individuals question their beliefs and values in a learning situation, there can be feelings of disorientation, loss, anger, or guilt as well as joy, understanding or peace. Two Canadian studies, one by J. Taylor (1989) and one by M. Taylor (1987), describe these reactions vividly. The role of a supportive and caring group becomes pivotal to the process.

The Educator's Role

Mezirow (1991) describes the educator in transformative learning as

an empathic provocateur and role model, a collaborative learner who is critically self-reflective and encourages others to consider alternative perspectives, and a guide who sets and enforces the norms governing rational discourse and encourages the solidarity and group support that is necessary when learners become threatened because comfortably established beliefs and values have been challenged (p. 206).

The educator needs to give up position power that has as its sources formal authority, control over resources and rewards, control over punishments, control over information and ecological or environmental control (Cranton, 1994). However, the educator maintains personal power that has as its sources expertise, friendship, loyalty and charisma. We remain authentic, true to ourselves, and we do not deny our experience and knowledge. At the same time, we become a member of the learning group, letting go of the power that comes with the position we hold.

The educator's role in transformative learning is a complex and sensitive one. As Mezirow (1991) asks, Do we intentionally stimulate transformative learning without the learner fully understanding that such a transformation may result? Do we decide which beliefs of learners should be questioned? Do we present our own perspectives, knowing that these may be unduly influential? Self-awareness about our practice, making our own assumptions explicit, engaging in critical reflection on our practice, talking to others about our practice, and continually questioning and revising our theory of practice are the crucial elements in our role (Cranton, 1994; 1996). It is not a matter of choosing the right method or stance, but rather a matter of ceaseless, critical self-reflection.

Summary

Transformative learning theory draws on research and ideas from philosophy, psychology, sociology and education. The result is a rather intimidating array of concepts and interrelated processes. Meaning schemes are our expectations of what will happen, based on what has happened. Meaning perspectives are the broader views we hold about the world around us. We have meaning schemes and perspectives about knowledge, culture and ourselves, that is, epistemic, sociolinguistic and psychological perspectives.

Often our perspectives have gone unquestioned. We do not know where they came from and have never examined their validity. When we are led to question our assumptions, critical reflection, the central process in transformative learning, takes place. We can question the content, the process or the premises of our assumptions.

Human beings have three basic interests: (1) controlling the environment (technical interests), (2) understanding each other (practical interests), and (3) becoming free from self- and social distortions (emancipatory interests). Learning in the emancipatory domain is transformative, but this learning can, in turn, influence our knowledge in the other two domains.

Transformative learning exists in a broad context. It is related to social theory and philosophy, Freire's concept of conscientization, Dewey's understanding of reflection, Schön's notion of reflection-in-action, developmental perspectives and self-directed learning.

The process of transformative learning varies from individual to individual, based on the preferences of psychological types, learning styles, or other personal attributes. For all learners, though, dialogue and discussion with others is critical. A learning group helps us to question and challenge our assumptions, values and perspectives. This means that the group must be supportive and caring of each other, creating an atmosphere of openness and trust. As a part of the group, the educator plays a vital role in maintaining a democratic process.

16

From Passion to Passivity: The Decline of University Extension for Social Change

Denis Haughey

I was prompted to write this chapter because I felt both puzzled and ashamed that the Canadian university extension movement has lost its former prominence in the promotion of adult education for democratic social change. My disappointment at the lack of a credible alternative voice by extension, and indeed the university at large, was deepened by my recollection of the formerly distinctive Canadian tradition in education for social change, of which citizenship education—the development of an informed and involved public voice—was such an important strand (see the chapter by Selman "The Imaginative Training for Citizenship" in this volume). I was struck by the passion, creativity and dedication of those adult educators of the 1930s, 1940s and 1950s in particular, as they struggled to promote social justice and change in Canada. Many of those women and men were from extension departments. In their time, they accepted the challenge of helping to develop an informed citizenry capable of understanding and countering the oppressive social and economic conditions of their day. And while the particular contexts have changed, Canadians today still find themselves having to contend with a society in crisis.

Increasingly though, and perhaps different from the conditions of the earlier decades of the century, the forces affecting Canadian society have taken on a global character. In his discussion of the democratization of education, Pannu (1996) refers to the rise of neo-liberalism and globalization. He shows how over the past twenty-five years the market has evolved "as the central organizing principle of social relations and collective life" (p. 87); when combined with the dominance of multinational corporations and finance in a world unfettered by economic borders, he sees a threat to "shift national control over political and economic developments to trans-national forces" (p. 88). Cruikshank (1995) has highlighted the importance of Canadian university extension educators informing themselves about the issue of globalization and understanding the role of significant elements of the media in promoting it. Nevertheless, the Canadian extension movement seems content either to largely ignore the most pressing questions concerning the crises in our society or to abrogate responsibility for confronting these issues. At the very time when credible policy alternatives are becoming more essential yet increasingly difficult for public interest groups to sustain, the university's voice seems to be absent.

Canadian University Extension Work for Social Change

Laidlaw (1961), former associate director of St. Francis Xavier (SFX) University's extension division, has observed that despite the early entry into extension work by the University of Saskatchewan in 1910 and the University of Alberta in 1912, most Canadian universities were slow to follow "and when they did it was as a result of pressure and influence from outside rather than conviction and interest within" (p. 54). But by the period 1915-1939, according to Selman and Dampier (1991), "university extension was begun at many universities, the best known project being the co-operative education project of St. Francis Xavier in Nova Scotia, often referred to as the Antigonish Movement" (pp. 65-66). They note, among others, the contribution of the University of Alberta's extension department to the founding in 1933 of the Banff School of Fine Arts, now the Banff Centre, and the influence of university personnel in the founding of the Canadian Association for Adult Education (CAAE) in 1935. The first director of the CAAE, E.A. Corbett, was the former director of the University of Alberta's Department of Extension. This department was very active in innovative outreach activities that used travelling libraries, slides, magic lanterns and moving pictures. In fact, in 1927 the department initiated a unique Canadian venture into non-commercial educational broadcasting with the establishment of the radio station CKUA (Cormack, 1981). Cormack notes that besides broadcasting locally produced drama and public affairs programs, CKUA reached a broad rural and largely isolated audience with network programs. One of these was "Round Table," a CBS current affairs radio program.

In his account of the work of the outstanding Canadian adult educator David Smith, Jackson (1995) refers to "the Canadian wave of popular education in the 1930s and 1940s [which] was associated with a worldwide folk school movement of study groups and independent learning centres" (p. 155). By *popular education* he means education for social change, and he notes that "resisting and proposing alternatives to the neo-liberal policies of the corporate elite and their political allies has come to be seen in Canada as a task of popular education" (p. vii). Notably, he claims, this movement enjoyed an upsurge in the 1930s when workers and the poor were "under siege from the effects of an international capitalist economy in crisis" (p. vii). The crucial role of SFX University's extension department is discussed elsewhere in this volume.

There are many other examples of the enabling work of university extension in programming for social change. Fast (1991) describes the close involvement of E.A. Corbett, former director of university extension at the University of Alberta, in the formation of the National Farm Radio Forum in 1940. The Extension departments played an important facilitation role in co-operating with the CAAE in the Farm Forum's listening and discussion groups. Fast (1991) mentions the "social reform" character of this program and many of its organizers, as well as its willingness to risk offending even the prime minister of the day because of its perceived socialist and political stance. Thus there were many extension personnel willing to risk being associated with an innovative and somewhat controversial social movement.

In her study of Canadian educator Watson Thompson, Fast (1991) reviews the work of the University of Manitoba in rural adult education from 1936 to 1945. Most of this work incorporated study groups, drama and crafts, the first stream being very much in Thompson's own radical social reform tradition. He subsequently became director of the study group program and advocated taking away decision making from government and placing it with the people. Fast's account describes how this program encountered significant internal resistance from conservative faculty suspicious of its social reform intent. Furthermore, the program had to contend with the conservative tendencies of its financial sponsor, the American Carnegie Foundation. On the other hand, it had the support of a charismatic university president, Sidney Earle Smith, who was deeply committed to serving all Manitobans and, according to Fast, "although he was a university president, he advocated, if he did not actively promote, a radical approach to adult education similar to that of leaders in the adult education movement" (p. 56). In fact, Smith collaborated with Corbett and seems to have shared his social reform vision for adult education. Fast reports that Smith became president of the CAAE in 1943 and, at its London conference that year, showed his commitment by urging the group to action, stating that "convictions however, must not lead to insipid inaction, but instead, adult education should be a dynamic entity for creating social change" (p. 56). Fast goes on to show how Smith was able to advance a somewhat radical view of adult education, akin to Corbett's, while successfully pursuing his goal of establishing an extension program at the University of Manitoba;

at the same time, he was able to placate the more conservative strands of the institution.

Watson Thompson, who had worked in the extension division of the University of Alberta, joined the University of Manitoba in 1941 with a considerable expertise in and commitment to the study group as a technique of adult education for democracy. In itself, this was quite radical for its time. Following the university's receipt of a Carnegie Foundation grant, he became the instigator and manager of an imaginative rural education program that bore his strong and enlightened stamp of democratic socialism. Thompson's conception of the power of the study group to enfranchise local communities and transform Canada was also part of his broader vision of adult education for social change (Fast, 1991). This perspective encompassed the interrelated nature of local, national and international issues and emphasized the crucial importance of informed discussion and small-group co-operation.

Thompson and his university and non-university collaborators crafted a program of adult education aimed at the structural reform of society as opposed to its mere social reproduction. Furthermore, Fast contends that at that time the Canadian adult education movement largely differed from its American counterpart in that it sprang from social gospel roots and emphasized social change, as opposed to the latter's more conservative and politically neutral programs of liberal education. Nevertheless, Thompson's pursuit of a quite radical form of citizenship education and its reconciliation with the more conservative academic demands of the University of Manitoba for dispassionate and university "quality" standards in its conduct undoubtedly required considerable risk, persistence and ingenuity on his part. However, Fast (1991) reports that what evolved was "a program of social adult education, written and delivered at a fairly rigorous level" (p. 173). Although in 1945 this program was closed by the university's board largely because of its political character, it nonetheless represents a daring and visionary attempt by a particular extension department and its allies to mount a major program of radical rural adult education.

This particular program demonstrates how creative adult educators with a singular vision of the transformative character of adult education were able to stretch and extend the role and programming boundaries imposed on them by the relative conservatism of their institutions and by external funders. Fast states that "their vision for adult education provides an example from history for modern adult educators to consider" (1991, p. 178).

There are many other examples of creative university extension work in the area of education for social change during the 1950s and 1960s in Canada. One significant program involving extension departments, notably that of Memorial University of Newfoundland, was the National Film Board's Challenge for Change series of the 1960s. However, Selman (1994) notes a major change of direction in the late 1970s when most universities moved heavily into continuing professional education or de-emphasized their community education work; consequently those characteristics that had made them distinctive began to blur. At the same time, there was a burgeoning of new colleges and universities, an apparent growing emphasis on the "professional" character of adult education, and more stringent financial pressures imposed on extension departments by the university at large. According to Selman, those factors accounted in large measure for the virtual abandonment of a serious community education focus in Canadian university extension work.

Campbell (1977) observes that "adult education in Canada for over half a century has been vigorous in its response to community need, often imaginative in many of its conceptions, usually efficient in its execution and certainly varied in its output" (p. 1), but this assessment may have marked the end of a proud era rather than signalling its continuation or expansion. Selman (1994) contends that most universities have now substantially abandoned community education work. "Much of what in the past has been an important part of university-based continuing education," he says, "is now being passed to other hands" (p. 18). He warns that universities will pay a price for this act of abandonment. In a related vein, Lund (1994) contends that university community education or that which enables learners "to take action beyond the confines of the occupational setting towards the resolution of social, economic, political, cultural and legal problems facing society" (p. 171) has lost its importance in the university. Critically, for her, this is not primarily an economic issue but one of basic commitment by individual continuing education units towards this kind of work.

The Decline of University Extension in Public Education

If in fact there is, as I believe, a serious weakening of the university extension movement's involvement in the promotion of a dispassionate examination of the major social issues of the day, why is this so? What follows are some possible answers to this question. My analysis focuses on the university, political inaction, professionalism, sites of practice and intellectual passivity.

The University

As previously discussed, university extension, especially that part of it directed at public issues and social change, has historically enjoyed an uneasy relationship with the institution at large. There is evidence that contemporary campus arenas, too, have become increasingly conservative. Simply put, the contemporary Canadian university is more reflective of the conservative political and social mood of the day than it is of a radical perspective supportive of moderate, progressive and consensual social reform.

Rather than being an active critic of the prevailing political and economic elites, the university appears to be a large part of the problem. If the prevailing campus ideology is one of uncertainty, fiscal conservatism and entrenchment, then with few exceptions this mood is reflected in the kinds of programs we see extension personnel devising, which tend to be safe, conservative and revenue driven. Though disappointing, perhaps this is not surprising.

For example, Birley (1991), in looking at change in British universities, points out that: "Social reform does not usually stem from the efforts of professionals, especially in a conservative trade-like education" (p. 143). Winchester (1992) speaks of the university as a locus of speech and free thought that undergirds democracy, but at the same time he points out there are tendencies in the university which might appear to do just the opposite: "As an elite organization the university tends to reflect a prevailing climate of social and political thought, as well as to help in the forming of one" (p. 2). Husén (1992) in looking at the apparent paradox concerning the essentially conservative nature of the institution and its radical mission of questioning the prevailing centres of power—state and church—explains this well: "the conservatism is exercised by the institution as a whole in its unwillingness to reform itself, but the radicalism lies with its individual members" (p. 14). The problem is that most of those faculty members who can act with comparative impunity, under the protection of academic freedom, to critique the centres of power are not exercising their responsibility to do so. Some, though by no means the majority of these, are Extension personnel. I can only conclude that their silence means tacit acceptance of the status quo, or that it betrays an indifference to what is happening in our society, or that they are afraid or unable to take a stand. This leads to the issue of political inaction.

Political Inaction

A 1991 Alberta study of educational leadership (Montgomerie, Peters, & Ward) characterized the prevailing provincial government policy towards education as one of "financial responsibility" over "social conscience," and this approach appears to have taken root in many university extension operations throughout the rest of Canada as well. In Alberta, too many university extension leaders and practitioners have complied with provincial and institutional pressures for downsizing and program rationalization. They have, without much opposition, allowed themselves to be tied up in protracted negotiations concerning the narrowing of the scope of the extension function, its right to equitable support and, indeed, its very legitimacy as a proper function of an institution in the throes of major fiscal and program reform. In stark contrast to their predecessors, who themselves struggled against enormous odds on and off campus to advance their vision of a more just society in Canada, many of today's extension practitioners have allowed themselves to become cowed, out-manoeuvred and complacent.

There seems to be two major reasons for this decline. First, as Ilsley (1992) puts it, while many adult educators espouse and officially embrace critical thinking, they refrain from identifying and acting on specific political plans of action. Second, and for me more alarming, university extension personnel appear to have largely accepted the "compliance culture" referred to by Shore and Roberts (1995) through the often unwitting internalization by university staff of externally imposed norms focused more on form than content. The mood on Canadian campuses is of accommodation rather than resistance.

There may be some excuse for those Canadian extension practitioners worn down by continual financial and reorganizational pressures, which have left extension divisions gravely weakened and demoralized. Nonetheless, too many with senior academic rank and tenure appear to be much less willing than their predecessors to engage in political behaviour, either intramurally or extramurally. Internally, this may be attributable in part to the failure of the extension movement to truly integrate itself into the fabric of the university. Although this is not always the fault of extension, some extension leaders must take responsibility for their failure to position their department's function internally so as to minimize its vulnerability in times of cut-backs and to speak out vigorously in its defense when it is under threat.

Most recently, these threats involve the proposed debasement by senior campus administrators of the extension function by touting it as a "born-again" solution to the public relations problems of the university, a not infrequent but deliberately cosmetic interpretation of a proud educational tradition. And even when undervalued, the university often equivocates with respect to extension's proper support. For example, *Broader Horizons*, a University of Alberta task force report on the overall extension function (1994), called for the strengthening of the university's policy commitment to continuing education and extension activities. It also stated, however, that "most [recommendations] would not be feasible without radical changes in our existing operations, and a shifting of priorities away from our mainstream programs, which we do not advocate" (p. 5). This report went largely unchallenged, and the Faculty of Extension could call on no internal allies with muscle to assist it to question the hypocrisy of the report's conclusions.

In its dealing with the politics of external relationships, the extension movement has made some errors. Notably, despite their often-cited contention that the nature of their work puts them in direct contact with a broad cross-section of society, few university extension units appear to have succeeded in forging effective political alliances with their constituencies. The test is whether, when budget cutting and downsizing predominate, as they do now, the extension function can effectively enlist the assistance of the public in defending its interests on campus. For the most part, I think the movement has been unsuccessful in doing this. Some would attribute this inability to work in effective political alliances with its public to the extension movement's growing professionalism and loss of a sense of social commitment. Let us now look briefly at this issue.

Professionalism

Professionalism is an important and controversial issue in Canadian adult education, especially in university extension work. It is, however, of great relevance to younger practitioners, since they are now entering a field where advanced degrees and formal training in adult education are the norm. This is undoubtedly to the benefit of the field, for at the university level at least it theoretically guarantees extension's acceptance as a legitimate academic undertaking of the institution. Many questions remain about the overall rating of university extension work compared with other disciplines on campus. Nevertheless, younger practitioners are also heirs to a more radical tradition in university extension work in Canada, and they need to be aware of this, especially since current practice has often been described as almost a polarization between the more social reform or "historical" tradition and an alleged "professional" or apolitical stance.

Selman and Kulich (1995) trace this creative tension between the professionalization and the social movement trends in adult education back to the 1930s when neither trend was dominant. Selman (1995) asserts that now the social reform tradition has faded into the background, and "the field is becoming professionalized and institutionalized" (p. 24). To a large extent Selman attributes this trend not primarily to financial stringency but to "a more professionalized staff who accept and promote this approach" (p. 15).

From Cruikshank's perspective (1995), there are two main camps among adult educators in Canada, social activists and entrepreneurs, with the latter predominant. Alexander (1991) corroborates this view. She also claims that "many adult educators do not even know about early beginnings such as Antigonish" (p. 21). Drawing on similarities between the process of socialization in adult education and in social work, Alexander discusses the trend towards increasing instrumental rationality in practice. In effect she considers that this trend away from "emancipatory social practice" in social work to a more antiseptic stance has led to the diminishment of a critical social perspective. She warns that similar tendencies in the field of adult education need to be monitored, especially if those in the field wish to participate actively in shaping its future. Finally, she cautions that "one may conclude that organizers and program planners supplant social animators during times of increased activity towards professionalism" (p. 130).

David Smith's (1995) critique of the demise of socially conscious extension education, or "popular education" as he terms it, is devastatingly blunt. He terms what we have now as "establishment adult education" and laments that since the days of the Antigonish Movement and Farm Radio Forum "adult education has become a major business" (pp. 73-4). While acknowledging the pivotal contribution of extension departments to the founding of CAAE in 1935, he asserts that, since then, the passion has declined as the adult education movement has become institutionalized; even when establishment adult education does engage in education for change, Smith says it is only to help people adjust to change, not to make changes.

Welton (1994) offers a critique of the contemporary field, stating that "one of the key criticisms of the modern practice of adult education is that it has abandoned its once vital role in fostering democratic social action" (p. 286). Many adult educators, he contends, are playing a troublesome role "in accommodating men and women to prevailing institutional and societal needs" (p. 287), whereas in his view we ought to be assisting citizens "to develop political knowledge, enhance political competence and develop skills to act prudently, or disobediently, when necessary" (p. 289). Whether this apparent lack of social activism on the part of significant segments of university practitioners can be attributed mainly to the alleged ideological neutrality of the professional is hard to say. Surely the truth lies somewhere between Smith's damning indictment and the more temperate views of Cruikshank, Welton, Alexander and Selman. In any case, it appears that both younger and seasoned university extension practitioners need to reflect on the possible negative consequences of the growing professionalism of the field.

New Sites of Practice

One of my main criticisms of the university extension movement, regardless of its ideological orientation, is its failure to adjust to what Mayo (1994) calls the new "sites of practice"—the spheres of life where the struggle occurs. This failure has both practical and theoretical aspects for practitioners; though the two dynamics are complementary, the theoretical side is the more important.

Welton (1994) has stated that currently the main sites of emancipatory learning are the new social movements (ecology, peace, women, among others), and that it is there that people are transforming the way they see themselves, nature and others. Cruikshank, too, (1995) identifies the necessity for adult educators to network extramurally, and Alexander (1991) contends that it is outside the boundaries of formal adult education that most of the activist adult education is occurring. Media is also a key site of adult education practice and a power to be reckoned with in its influence upon social and political issues and agendas. To this extent the modern practice of adult education for social change may differ enormously from that of the earlier part of the century. While the early movement was conscious of the power of the media to influence social questions, and many practitioners recognized the necessity to master their use of it as a tool for learning and instruction, this was by no means as complicated or crucial a task as it is today.

Ironically, many individuals throughout the world are gaining at least a preliminary involvement, mainly through computer technology, with the big issues of the day. The university sector of the adult education movement can only applaud this electronic enfranchisement of individuals and learner initiative, but I think it is ill prepared for its consequences. A clear one of these is that the university extension movement no longer wields the same kind of influence over the conduct of public issues education as it once did. I don't think that university extension personnel have fully recognized this reality, and even when they have, they have been slow to work in new partnerships with those community-based groups that have significant influence. This unwillingness may be due to extension's inability to accept a new relationship where it often has more to learn than contribute; or it may be because many university extension practitioners have become intellectually passive.

Intellectual Passivity

Intellectual passivity is an important issue to examine. Effective university extension education demands not only a moral commitment to social change but also an accompanying and perhaps even more demanding commitment to personal intellectual renewal.

No one could accuse the best of our extension predecessors of a lack of moral or intellectual courage and determination. They had not only passion, commitment and skill, but also the versatility to adapt to the changing conditions of their day. Many current practitioners share these qualities, but the demands placed upon the contemporary practitioner require more from them on the intellectual side than previously. As the role of university extension educators becomes more restricted, they must rethink what they are doing. Increasingly, this will necessitate a reconstruction of their work in social action as a more intellectual pursuit.

For example, Johnson-Riordan (1994) points out the failure of the adult education movement to keep pace with contemporary developments in cultural theory: "To date, adult education theory-practice shows few signs of engagement with a constellation of theoretical work that constitutes contemporary cultural theory and has been available for at least the past decade" (p. 10). She goes on to discuss movements such as poststructuralist critiques of the social sciences, postmodernism and feminist theoretical work, pointing out that they offer "the possibility of more powerful explanatory tools for the contemporary movement than those available through the traditional social sciences as well as the possibility of a radical left critique of the liberal-conservative politics which still dominate the adult education arena" (p. 10). What is required, she states, is a challenge to the traditional frameworks of adult education pedagogy and research both from the existing, traditional social science perspectives and from these newer perspectives.

Many contemporary practitioners are not well versed in these alternative perspectives. This may be related to underrepresentation of such content in modern graduate programs; to the inability of "seasoned" practitioners to re-orient their more pragmatic approach to practice to a more intellectual one, despite what I believe is the increasing efficacy of the latter; or simply to the disarray of much Canadian university extension work in the face of the massive fiscal and organizational changes on campus. Ironically, the failure of extension professionals to recognize the necessity for, and to successfully engage in, their own intellectual "retro-fitting" may be a key factor in their current lack of impact.

How the Extension Movement Might Benefit from New Theory

Mayo (1994) discusses the implications for a radical theory of adult education largely based on the theories of Gramsci. His theory, greatly simplified, depicts adult education struggling against dominant groups that seek to impose their ideologies on society through a combination of coercion and consent. According to Mayo, "mainstream cultural and educational activities help generate such consent through the process of legitimating ideologies and social relations" (p. 140). Wide-ranging social forces and global influences such as multinational capitalism, the media and conservative power blocks are currently exercising disproportionate and often repressive power in our society. The task of those working for social transformation, as Mayo invoking Gramsci puts it, is to engage in a "war of position" (p. 128) or a process of broad social organization and cultural influence as a counter to these pervasive influences. Two key issues arise here: What must these resistors, in this case adult educators, do? Can they do what is required?

Mayo (1994) describes Ransome's (1992) idea that we need to conceive of intellectuals as either "organic intellectuals," who as committed cultural or educational workers are experts in legitimatization and emerge in response to particular historical developments, or as "traditional intellectuals," whose organic purpose is over as society enters a new stage of development. Building on Gramscian theory, Mayo continues with Ransome's idea of adult educators as intellectuals organic to the "subaltern" groups aspiring to power, with their main task being to engage in a war of position that enables it (the subordinate class) to secure the alliances necessary to succeed. Mayo's conception allows for the "assimilation" of traditional intellectuals, and one of their key competencies—critical, and in my view largely lacking in contemporary adult education practice—is the ability to function fluently in the language of the dominant culture so as not to be relegated to the periphery of political life. In contemporary times this means, for example, an ability to analyze and counter the propaganda and slanted messages about the economic and social future of our society disseminated by conservative economic groups and governments.

It also means understanding Ball's explanation (cited in Tett, 1996) of the way a particular ideology comes to be dominant in policy making by, for example, using the postmodernist concept of discourse. Tett describes Ball's (1996) concept of "discourse" as something that "provides a vocabulary, a set of concepts and understandings, a systematic way of seeing, thinking, and acting, without appearing to do so" (p. 25). According to Tett, Ball argues that the substantive views of the new right, in particular, have "served to constrain the possibilities of policy and policy debate through the imposition of a particular political discourse which he has called the discourse of derision" (p. 25). Tett goes on to show how the media play a central role in the creation of particular discourses "by articulating the dominant myths and bringing opposing myths into derision" (p. 27). In an examination of the role of the media's influence over educational policy making, Wallace (1993) corroborates Tett's view. He quotes Bailey (1977) on "context stripping" or the way in which "much of the context of a situation depicted in the media is repressed in order to present an unequivocal (but distorted) message" (p. 324). Tett shows how community education needs to create "alternative discourses" which enable the oppressed (the poor, the unemployed, the marginalized) to give voice to their legitimate concerns and counteract oppressive ideologies. She contends that, for the most part, traditional adult education fails to do this, and that there is little likelihood of a radical model of intervention originating from conservative institutions such as the university. I largely agree, but I also contend that even when committed adult educators do engage in social action programs, many operate from relatively obsolete models of practice infused more with the fervor of tradition than informed by the intellectual and socio-political realities of today. This must change. To be successful in the long run, extension personnel must recognize that a major part of the solution to many of the complex social issues confronting them lies in their own intellectual regeneration. This will require new ways of framing and addressing issues, and not all extension practitioners will be capable of such a radical shift in their philosophical and operational styles.

The Future of Canadian University Extension

Given that many contemporary problems are global in nature, Canadian university extension practitioners should ally themselves with international movements that transcend the more parochial concerns of the traditional movement in Canada. Extension practitioners need to develop the skills to enable them to counter the global forces against which they are now pitted in the struggle for a just society. Most of these skills involve the development of a heightened intellectual understanding of the roots of injustice and new, more subtle ways of responding to these less patent but pervasive influences. Ironically, this may involve the de-emphasis of the Canadian model of small-group, local and community-based action in favour of a more global approach.

Certainly it will require a re-definition of the role of the university extension professional from that of program initiator, architect and provider to that of intellectual provocateur, collaborator and political activist, both within and outside the institution. This gadfly role will increasingly require practitioners to be competent in the fields of politics and cultural theory, and it will be high-risk for them and their universities. To be successful they will need to ally themselves internally across disciplines with committed faculty. Externally, they will need to re-define their relationships with those social movements that have already moved their sites of practice into the global arena. In so doing, Canadian extension practitioners must confront not only the increasing fragility of the university as an effective and committed agent of social change but as a stable educational and cultural agent. As the university itself stumbles towards a re-definition of its intellectual and social role, extension practitioners need to consider whether the institution even has a meaningful role any longer in the conduct of adult education for social change in Canada.

Brooke and Waldron (1994) contend that "university continuing education has a social and community mission that must be fulfilled if it is to be true to its cause" (p. 2), and have observed that extension units must not be treated by the university merely as revenue centres, but I am pessimistic about Canadian universities listening. Currently I cannot see any Canadian university willing to commit stable financial and human resources to this kind of work. Undoubtedly the current allocations are but a shadow of what they once were, and they reflect a clear and purposeful shift of university priorities away from this kind of community involvement at the very time when it is most needed.

If this is, as I believe, the final decade of the socially committed, full-time, Canadian university extension educator, then perhaps the greatest contribution those who are still committed to social change may make will be to oversee the transfer of our radical tradition to those as yet unclear but hopefully creative structures that will surely arise to compensate for the university's virtual abandonment of its formerly proud role in this field.

17

Adult Education within an Ecological Context

Darlene E. Clover

The origin of human concern for nature, and the realization that it must be better understood, preserved and protected, not just for its resource potential, but also its emotional and spiritual value are difficult to pin-point because they have no single root and did not emerge at any one time or in any one country (Tilbury, 1994). What is certain is that concern for the planet is taking on a greater importance in the field of education. However, traditional adult education discourse in Canada has been slow to take up environmental issues. In fact, within the best known examples of adult educa tion traditions and institutions in Canada, such as the Antigonish Movement, the Mechanics' and Women's Institutes, college and university extension programs and the Canadian Association of Adult Education, the environment as a theme has been largely ignored. Although adult education research has tended to "spill out beyond conventional and narrowly defined educational considerations into those which encompass welfare, employment, race and gender issues" (Bryant & Usher in Thomas, 1991, p. 302), it has tended to overlook environmental issues as integral to other social issues. However, an examination through a more ecological lens of past adult education traditions reveals a foundational base of thought and action which invites a more comprehensive weaving of environmental issues into the theory and practice.

Naturalist organizations, clubs and societies across Canada are important sites of adult education that focus on nature and the environment. They have provided an education for adults with, for, about, in and through the natural world. In many cases, they have pushed for social action when humans and nature have been threatened. Since the early twentieth century, these societies and organizations almost exclusively have been the sites for what may be called environmental adult learning in Canada, certainly in terms of non-formal adult learning. These organizations, which embrace thousands of members and are located in each of Canada's provinces and territories in one form or another, are a critical space from which has sprung the contemporary environmental movement, a pervasive and growing mode of consciousness that is searching for a more precise articulation of its own ideals, its institutional form and effective programs of action (Berry, 1988). Why has this huge area of adult education been excluded from mainstream Canadian adult education theory, practice and history?

This chapter explores the relationships between environmental issues, environmental education and adult education in Canada, beginning in the 1920s, in order to make a case for a more systematic inclusion of environmental issues in the Canadian adult education movement. "Environmental issues" in traditions such as the Antigonish Movement, the nationwide Farm Forum and the labour education movement are examined and the ideological and methodological foundations of environmental adult education within naturalist organizations across Canada are described, specifically, within the Toronto Field Naturalists' Club. Lastly, the social construction of nature is briefly examined.

The basic orientation of adult education has been anthropocentric or, as many feminist educators have argued, andropocentric. The focus on raising the quality of life for individuals and communities that is inherent in critical adult education is admirable, but there has been a failure in recognizing how the natural world contributes so fundamentally to the spiritual, physical and mental well-being of humankind and not just their economic well-being as a resource for exploitation. The problem, Rodger Schwass (1972) argues, is that the traditional "history of Canada has been to some extent the story of the discovery and exploitation of the four major resources: fish, fur, forests and agricultural land" (p. 5). It is against this backdrop that nature has been understood and education has been shaped.

Nature in Adult Education

In spite of the anthropocentric nature of adult education, there has been within some traditions a cognizance of the need to better understand and work with the natural world. Three examples from key adult education traditions in Canada are the Farm Radio Forum, the Antigonish Movement and the labour education movement.

The Farm Radio Forum

The Farm Radio Forum began in the 1930s as an initiative of MacDonald College at McGill University and eventually was broadcast nationwide. Its primary purpose was to raise the quality of life of farmers across Canada by providing information and a forum for debate about important issues. Topics in the radio broadcasts that related to environmental care or awareness were limited; the primary focus of programs was on issues such as prices, merchandising, community building and farm organization. However, throughout the

1940s and 1950s, broadcasts provided some impetus for discussions about soil and forest conservation, health and nutrition, and, in 1954, there was an entire session on natural resources entitled "From Under the Earth" (Schwass, 1972). Titles that pointed to a focus on soil and forests included "Poor Soil Produces Poor Food," "Conservation is Everyone's Business," "What About Chemurgy?" (using organic raw materials as fertilizer) and "Forests—Slash or Save?" (Schwass, p. 339). There were also several broadcasts on nutrition and health that linked them directly to healthy soil and farming practices.

On the other side of the adult education equation, the agricultural colleges and extension programs were moving away from advocating mixed or organic cropping used in the early years of Canadian settlement by Europeans and towards chemical fertilizers and heavy equipment. The primary purpose of their educational programs was, like the Farm Radio Forum, to raise the standard of living of farmers. But these institutions believed that a better quality of life was to be had by moving away from the traditional agriculture that held farmers back and towards a more chemically based way of raising crops. Increased use of chemicals resulted in the contamination of soils and groundwater as crop "predators" acquired resistance to chemical agents. Stronger cocktails of chemicals were needed, and led indirectly to the destruction of forests for food production.

The package of adult education activities in agricultural colleges and extension programs did not advocate balanced or mixed agriculture. Moreover, as noted in Brewster Kneen's *From Land to Mouth* (1989), "farmers [began] working just to be consumers, whether it's bigger cars, tractors and trucks or CBs or whatever ... [There has been] a huge change from working to produce to working to consume" (p. 68). Under some circumstances, the more contemporary farming based on chemicals and heavy equipment did help farmers, but more often farmers were still pressured into leaving the farms, and the legacy of contamination will be with us for generations to come (Schwass, 1962).

The Antigonish Movement

A second example of an adult education tradition that recognized that "the health of human beings [depended] on the health of plants and animals, and the health of plants and animals [depended] on the health of the soil and the earth" (Laidlaw, 1971, p. 148) was the Antigonish Movement, based in Nova Scotia (see Selman's chapter "The Imaginative Training for Citizenship" in this volume).

A review of literature shows that references to nature are strewn throughout some of the speeches Father Moses Coady made during his lifetime. In an address to the Home Economics Association of Nova Scotia in 1948, for example, Coady focused on working with nature and, in particular, putting humus back into the soil in order "to preserve the organic life of the soil" (Laidlaw, 1971, pp. 148-149). A second example comes from an address made to the United Nations Conference on Conservation and Utilization of Resources in 1949. In this speech Coady noted that certain profit-seeking individuals were plundering and destroying the earth, that which "was intended for all people" (Laidlaw, p. 44). He also noted that:

> The story of man's misuse of and failure to conserve his natural heritage should also guide us in arriving at a scientific procedure for the future. Past performance should be terrifying to us all ... If we get clearly in mind the reasons why man abused, rather than used, the natural resources of the earth, we have the answer we are looking for (p. 44).

Coady articulated the need to continually replenish the raw materials from the earth that were being overused and overconsumed. However, it can be argued that his focus was primarily anthropocentric. For example, in the opening of his speech in 1949 he noted that "it is in the very nature of things that the earth and the fullness thereof, is for man. Natural resources, therefore, fulfil their purpose when they minister to human life on this earth. This is their manifest destiny, so to speak" (Laidlaw, 1971, p. 43).

Many environmental adult educators today argue that this concept of nature as slave to human beings has helped to create numerous contemporary environmental problems and to widen the gap between people and nature. As environmental educator Thomas Berry notes, what we need is to "change from an exploitative anthropocentrism to a participative biocentrism" (Berry, 1988, p. 169). Berry believes humans are physically and spiritually "woven into this living process" and therefore must "join the earth community as participating members, to foster the progress and prosperity of the bioregional communities to which we belong" (p. 166).

Labour Education

Examples of an environmental awareness and educative action can be found in the labour education movement. In *Thinking Union* (1995), D'Arcy Martin writes that in 1978, although Newfoundland asbestos miners had "known for years, long before the medical establishment was forced to admit, that their own direct exposure to asbestos fibres would kill them ... [they now had evidence] ... that the fibres were damaging their children as well" (p. 17). Asbestos fibres clung to the workers' automobiles and clothing. Once these fibres entered the home, they quickly spread throughout the house "by the laundry machines" (p. 18). Equipped with this knowledge, workers went on strike and were awarded "a car wash, so their vehicles wouldn't carry fibres home from the mine; a sprinkler and shelter system to prevent fibres being blown from the mine into the town and a proper dry, and change room so asbestos-laden clothes would not be taken back" (p. 18).

However, as Bruce Spencer points out, "environmentalism provides an interesting test for labour" (Spencer, 1995, p. 59) because there is a perceived conflict between the environment and jobs. The Canadian Labour Congress (CLC) has tried to resolve this tension by developing an argument for sustainable development that "growth be revived, nationally and globally, while conserving and enhancing the resource base on which growth depends" (Schrecker, 1993, p. 10). The CLC has developed a series of education courses, such as Union Environmental Action, Workers and the Environment and Pollution Prevention, to explore this possibility. (For a fuller discussion, see Spencer, 1995.)

Summary

In spite of the generally anthropocentric bias, environmental themes and issues have been a part, albeit limited, of these foregoing adult education traditions. Perhaps there are other examples, an interesting research project in itself. The important point is that environmental adult education exists and has already been woven into the adult education mosaic. And what is already established can be built upon!

In addition to these examples drawn from the adult education tradition are the many examples of naturalist societies, organizations, clubs and outdoor education institutions scattered across the country, which have been taking up environmental and social issues and educating adults about the natural world for many decades. They are important sites of adult learning that have never found their way into mainstream adult education literature and discourse in Canada.

Naturalist Organizations as Poetic/Historic Sites of Environmental Adult Education

Nature is a theatre for interrelations of activities.
— Whitehead in Griffin, 1988.

Outdoor and/or environmental education has taken on different shades of meaning over the past decades, but the two key premises of this type of teaching and learning have remained constant: an understanding and appreciation of and a relationship with the natural world should be the heritage of every human being, and the outdoors is a rich community resource of individual and social learning.

Beginning in the 1920s, a variety of naturalist societies, clubs and organizations that operated on the above premises emerged. Many of these organizations established in the 1920s through to the 1940s have maintained a sole emphasis on educating their adult (and youth) members about the flora and fauna of a region; others, however, have extended their educational work to incorporate an analysis of contemporary environmental issues such as land

and waterfront development and pollution, deforestation, the abolition of green space and the link to human well-being, links between pollution and poverty and a push for political action. Below are brief introductions to some of these organizations across Canada followed by a fuller examination of one such organization, the Toronto Field Naturalists' Society.

The Hamilton Naturalists' Club, founded in 1950, currently has more than one hundred members. The primary purposes of this organization are to promote the enjoyment of nature, to conserve and preserve nature and to actively engage members and others in the clean-up of streams and rivers. The club offers field outings, monthly members' meetings, lectures and presentations on a variety of environmental and scientific topics. A second example is the Ami-e-s de la Terre in Quebec, founded in 1977. This organization uses popular education, seminars and radio broadcasts to engage people in discussions on local and global ecological issues. Western Canada offers a third example, the Mother Earth Healing Society. This society works with women to rediscover Native traditional values through Women's Healing Circles. Through storytelling, song and the sharing of rituals and experiences, women learn about the fundamental beliefs and values inherent in the culture. A final example is the Yo Who Chas Outdoor Education Centre in Alberta. This club provides adult outdoor recreation programs in order to create respect for self, others and the environment as a way of transforming the human-nature relationship.

All these organizations have in common their belief in the intrinsic value of nature and the informal use of nature as teacher and site of learning. The methodologies are experiential. While some are more critical or political, others focus more on spiritual and sensory re-connections between humans and nature. This last element is extremely important. As John Mohawk of the Seneca Nation noted in *Resurgence*, "the problem is that our relationship [to nature] is not poetic enough" (1996, p. 10). Without regaining a sensual or poetic relationship to nature, true change will not come. The philosophies, practices and methods of these ecologically based organizations are critical elements of newly emerging theoretical, philosophical and methodological frameworks of environmental adult education in Canada and around the world.

Toronto Field Naturalists' Club

The Toronto Field Naturalists' Club was founded in 1923. It is a purely volunteer organization, with organizational, educative and informational activities carried out by its members. There have been and continue to be a variety of key aims behind the work of this club: to instill an appreciation for the wonders of nature; to provide nature-lovers with the opportunity to meet together to exchange observations and increase their knowledge of natural species and processes; to give the public opportunities to hear authorities speak on subjects of natural history and environmental issues; to conduct field excursions with a view to acquiring greater knowledge of and a deeper connection to Toronto; to work with the local, provincial and federal governments towards protecting and conserving nature; and, last, to publish field observations in a Toronto newspaper in order to communicate information and knowledge to a broader constituency.

In the beginning, the club "was much more clearly built around special groups representing particular interests" such as flower, reptile, geological and wildlife preservation groups (Saunders 1965, p. 5), and leaders of the field excursions organized around these specific topics tended to be experts in the field. However, after World War II, leaders became scarcer and field trips became more general in character. This tendency has continued, with a fluidity between the roles of learner and facilitator.

The club took its "first direct action ... on behalf of conservation" in 1924 (Saunders 1965, p. 4). Following a field trip that wound along either side of the banks of the Humber River, members observed the unnecessary human destruction of natural green spaces. Placards were attached to trees in sundry parts of the Toronto region that read: "SPARE THE FLOWERS. Don't pull them up by the roots. YOU CAN DO YOUR PART ... Help to preserve them for future years" (Saunders, p. 4).

The club made its first appeal to its members to engage in political action around environmental issues in 1949, in connection with the dumping of earth from the building of the subway into the Don Valley and River. Members were asked to write to local politicians about the disruptions and pollution this activity was causing. By 1964, the club was fully engaged politically with environmental matters, and in 1968 an Ecology and Conservation Group was set up. In the 1970s, the group prepared briefs about the impact of the Waterfront Airport and about inner and outer waterfront plans (Toronto Field Naturalists' Club, 1974).

In response to the rapid development taking place across Metropolitan Toronto, a report entitled *Toronto the Green* was submitted to politicians in 1992. The purpose of the report was to make "policy recommendations for the conservation and management of natural areas in and around Metropolitan Toronto" for politicians and planners (p. 28).

Currently, the Toronto Field Naturalists' Club organizes about 150 walks a year in various parts of the city and organizes presentations, seminars, workshops and lectures. At the heart of the education process lies the concept of participation and group learning. The outings centre particularly on the latter, promoting active discussion and drawing on the knowledge and experiences of those in the groups. Groups are led by members who have been on the outings before but who do not necessarily have any expert or scientific knowledge. According to Helen Juhola, former president and current newsletter editor, the learning that takes place in natural areas and the community is very experiential.

The excursions explore the good and bad of the city in order to expose the impact of human intervention—in particular the repercussions of overdevelopment and industrial pollution—on the quality of human and wildlife in Toronto. Juhola says the club's work is "about democracy": "it is about learning what democracy should be but what it is not, who really has the power, and what ordinary people can do to make a difference. Once people have seen what is happening, they can't pretend it's not happening" (Juhola, interview with author, 1996).

Members are encouraged to write to politicians about what they notice on these outings, such as the choking of streams, garbage in green areas and on the streets and the disappearance of birds.

Today, the majority of members, educators and group leaders in the club are women. Juhola thinks woman are "more interested in group activities and learning together." It should be noted that in fact it is women across Canada who are the backbone of environmental initiatives. Women are most often the first environmental educators in their families as well (Clover 1995).

In addition to imparting a better awareness of political issues focusing on the environment, naturalist organizations also explore and develop greater appreciation for the intrinsic value of nature. Naturalist societies, clubs and organizations work to help people re-connect with the natural world and gain a greater understanding of place, of the green space around them that they are often too busy to notice.

A major criticism of environmental education and the environmental movement centres on their being apolitical (see, for example, Orr, 1992), and in fact not all naturalist societies have political orientations. The adult education philosophies and methodologies espoused in organizations such as the Toronto Field Naturalists' Club are based on some of the fundamental premises of critical adult education. These include examining relations of power such as humans over nature and one class over another, drawing on people's knowledge and experience and roles for the educator as facilitator and resource rather than the role of "expert."

Emerging Theories and Practices of Adult Environmental Education

> *Environmental education cannot be taught simply from a pulpit or podium—it must be experienced; it must be made personal.*
> — Deri & Cooper, 1992, p. 5.

Never before in the history of human habitation has the life-support system been so in jeopardy. This contemporary crisis is not an environmental crisis but a growing crisis of society. The environment has not created these problems—human beliefs and behaviour have. Education has not alleviated this problem and has often contributed to it. A world concerned primarily with the extraction and use of natural resources is programmed to promote an education that focuses on the management and use of these resources. A world that views natural spaces as places solely for human recreation and pleasure provides an education based on preservation for human use. A world based on reductionist science provides education that links the cause of tuberculosis to a bacillus rather than to slum housing, and the cause of cancer to oncogenes rather than to industrial pollution (Rowe, 1990). People who do not feel the natural world sensually or spiritually or believe it has intrinsic value develop an education that teaches that parks are for people, animals are for shooting, forests are for logging and soils are for mining (Rowe). But a different worldview is beginning to emerge, and adult education must keep pace if it is to reach its professed goal of societal transformation.

The field of adult education is being challenged to take on new intellectual, emotional and spiritual energy in order to keep pace with the devastating urgency of environmental problems. It is beginning, albeit slowly, to incorporate a deeper recognition of the environment and its associated social problems. In fact, adult education is being re-defined and shaped. Newly emerging concerns within communities across Canada today have meant a re-conceptualization of environmental education by educators in order to give "greater prominence to the root social, political and economic causes of the environmental situation" (Tilbury, 1995, p. 197). Guiding principles are being developed and the role of educators articulated. The educational framework appropriate for today's world must be visionary and transformative and go beyond the conventional educational outlooks that have been cultivated over several centuries (O'Sullivan, 1998).

Learning within an ecological context is both a vision and a process. The vision revolves around building economic prosperity, health and social justice and not simply the protection of the environment. The process involves an effort to explore how the dominant cultural understanding of nature is created from our own experiences, understanding that cultural beliefs are at the root of how people understand and relate to nature. It is about exploring the impact that culture has had on human-nature relations. Different sets of values work to shape how individuals see and interpret nature (Evernden, 1992).

Understanding views, cultural traditions and artifacts and values has major implications on the development and delivery of environmental adult education activities and programs. Educating within an ecological context is also about expanding existing analyses of relations of power to include humans over nature. Achieving social justice does not necessarily mean that nature will be treated as anything more than simply a resource, something that exists only in relation to humans and their needs. A renewed understanding of and relationship with nature is needed, a more spiritual and sensory relationship. John Mohawk (1996) believes fear is a major stumbling block to connecting with, protecting and celebrating nature: "People who are afraid of nature have much more difficulty defending it than people who are not. All of those negative emotions give you permission to enact violence on nature" (p. 10).

With all the above factors in mind, educating adults within an ecological context or environmental adult education will have to deal with these fears and more negative views of nature as its starting point. Understanding and working with the "us against nature" relationship is a difficult but necessary challenge of adult learning.

All Canadians are by now more fully aware that the planet is slowly dying (Weston, 1995). What to do about it is one of the biggest challenges humans will face in the next century. Including a focus on the environment within the field of adult education is timely and relevant. A primary challenge facing educators who work within an ecological context is that, according to Hall and Sullivan (1994), "all education, up to our present moment, has never fully countenanced the possibility of planetary destruction [in this way]. This viability of planetary existence has never been an issue for educators because it was not, until now, part of our cultural understanding" (p. 6). In light of this challenge, re-shaping adult education could be an effective tool to secure change.

We in the present cannot predict fully the future of our planet, but adult education, both formal and non-formal, is an important factor in influencing views, behaviour, attitudes and actions that in turn will affect our future. As Kaplan and Kaplan (1989) note so eloquently, "viewed as an amenity, nature may be readily replaced by some greater technological achievement. Viewed as an essential bond between humans and other living things, the natural environment will find no substitute."

18

Adult Education in Transition: The Influence of Social Context on Teaching Prisoners

Howard S. Davidson

The rise of the penitentiary in the modern era is the most important development in the history of crime and punishment in the last two hundred years (Garland, 1990).[1] The introduction of the prison in the eighteenth century removed torture and execution from the public sphere, sequestered them behind walls, and added time served in an isolated, austere, and despotic environment to those more ancient forms of punishment.[2] With the advent of the modern prison, the state did not forsake punishment by pain and execution; it did, however alter the telos of punishment.[3] The prison and the prison sentence created the pre-conditions for methods to emerge that would attempt to normalize the deviant. Using practices that were subject to the growth of bureaucratic controls and of an increasingly professionalized array of treatments, prison reformers endeavoured to transform prisoners into law-abiding citizens by integrating them into "a society of labourers or job-holders" (Cosman, 1981, p. 38). From the very beginning, adult education was intimately connected to this transformative enterprise.

With few exceptions, in prison the adult learner is defined as a cognitively deficient, anti-social *inmate* needing correction, hence the term "correctional education." Educational authorities have retained control over every aspect of curricula. For more than a century the primary subjects have been literacy, numeracy, and employment-skills training, using functionalist curriculum designs to teach convicts the basics for making an honest (if meàgre) living. While this authoritarian, corrective mission has not contradicted the ethos of the penitentiary, the place adult education has occupied in the penal regime has been problematic from the beginning.

In 1840, regulations for Upper Canada's jails made provisions "for the religious instruction of prisoners of both sexes, and also for their instruction in reading and writing" (Weir, 1973, p. 40), but reports in 1845 indicated that these provisions were limited and "results [had] not flowed from education such as were anticipated" (p. 40). The Archambault Report of 1936 was one of several commission reports produced throughout the first half of this century to express a belief in the ability of vocational and academic programs to prepare prisoners to become law-abiding citizens, while at the same time condemning the prison service for failing to implement these programs effectively (Cosman, 1981, p. 39). In the 1950s, a senior administrator for the Canadian Penitentiary Service concluded:

> [C]orrectional education programs received only grudging and halting endorsement, frequently in response to temporary pressures, rather than from any real faith or understanding of the rehabilitative motive and the importance of the role a meaningful adult educational program can play in the social regeneration of society's outcasts. The result was, more often than not, a patchwork of courses and academic programs which permitted little more than the three R's to pass as a valid educational objective (quoted in Griffin, 1978, p. 27).

By the 1970s programs emerged which promised a more meaningful role for adult education "in the social regeneration of society's outcasts." For example, in 1972 the University of Victoria initiated the Prison Education Program at Matsqui Institution in British Columbia. This program, which was subsequently taken over by Simon Fraser University in 1984 and expanded into four British Columbia prisons before it was closed down in 1993, supported the development of a humanities curriculum and offered university-level credit. According to one of its founders, the intent of this program was "to encourage critical thinking, mature thought processes and a greater understanding of and response to the complex social issues which are such an integral part of 'getting on' in the world—without resorting to crime" (Duguid, 1996, p. 3).

Beside such accomplishments, the mainstream programs running throughout the 1970s and 1980s continued to be a "patchwork of courses and academic programs" with an explicit emphasis on teaching functional literacy and numeracy skills to enhance employment opportunities.[4] In articles and staff meetings, educators complained about their marginal status in the institution, where schooling occupied a subordinate role to other treatment programs, work placements and security requirements. Classes were cancelled without prior notice; students were withdrawn from school to attend other treatment programs or perform institutional maintenance jobs; studies were terminated if a person was placed in segregation for punishment, transferred to other institutions or released on parole. In a frequently cited article that spoke to the experiences of adult educators throughout North America's prisons, Goldin and Thomas observed that administrators gave schooling symbolic support to satisfy themselves, policy makers and pressure groups that something was being done to rehabilitate offenders, but substantive support for programs was lacking, and schools' requirements were inevitably passed over to satisfy custodial demands (Goldin & Thomas, 1984; Corcoran, 1985; Gehring, 1995). In his preface to the first issue of the *Yearbook of Correctional Education*, its editor, Stephen Duguid, observed that:

> we walk a thin line in correctional education—serving our students, the state, society, and grand theories. As educators we empower our students by helping them acquire knowledge, skills, perspective, and autonomy. But, as components of the correctional enterprise, we *correct*, restrain, inhibit, and reform. We may even be linked (consciously or inherently) to the apparatus and ideology of punishment (Duguid, 1989, p. vii).

Discourse in the field's major research forums (i.e., *Journal of Correctional Education* and the *Yearbook of Correctional Education*) refers to prisoners' characteristics, educators' objectives and organizational conflicts—especially conflicts between educational and custodial objectives and ideologies—to explain the historical features of prison education and the pressures which push educators into becoming "components of the correctional enterprise." Limited recognition is given to the influences of larger economic, social and political forces on the setting in which adult educators plan and teach. In this chapter, the conventional explanations for what adult education in prisons has become are set aside in order to give sufficient attention to how these larger structural forces are influencing the contemporary features of prison education. The central thesis of this chapter is that the transformation of educational practices in prisons, as in any context (for example, workplace training) cannot be adequately understood without situating that transformation within a wider terrain of structural relationships.[5]

The chapter begins by focusing on the structural forces that are creating a prison overcrowding crisis, the single most important condition affecting adult education in prisons today and the reasons why prisons are filled with people who read and write poorly. Then, a strategy is examined involving adult education that is being used to manage that crisis. Finally, some contradictions are discussed that limit this strategy and some possibilities suggested for realizing an alternative approach for prison education.

A Context for a Crisis in Prison Management

Vast quantities of capital, estimated at $14 trillion by the World Bank in 1994, move quickly around the world seeking favourable investment possibilities (Chomsky & Barsamian, 1994). In order to maximize profits, directors of integrated multinational corporations move this capital from one country to another, favouring those governments that are prepared to relax trade barriers, restrict unions, eliminate environmental regulations and reduce corporate taxation (pp. 5-32). As smaller capitalists strive to compete in this "global economy," they mimic multinationals by replacing workers with technologies, reducing wages and benefits, degrading working conditions and limiting job security. This has resulted in a dramatic growth in unemployment and poverty, which in turn exacerbates racism and sexism. In Canada, the official unemployment rate among youthful workers was more than 16 percent in 1997. Among Aboriginal youth, and in certain regions, the rate exceeded 25 percent (Waldie & Bourette, 1997). As incomes decline, governments collect fewer taxes, but popular demand for social services to ameliorate growing hardship increases. The contradiction between the growing demand for services and the declining revenues produce a fiscal crisis of the state (O'Connor, 1984).

Governments in North America have responded to this crisis by dismembering social services—forgetting, perhaps, that these services were originally put into place not merely to ameliorate economic and social problems created by capital accumulation, but to avoid workers organizing for more radical alternatives (Holloway & Picciotto, 1978). In place of costly social services, the state turns to less expensive repressive policies to maintain order.[6] Meanwhile, the failure of welfare policies in the twentieth century to reduce poverty and racism is not attributed to the haphazard, contradictory ways in which these policies were funded and administered; instead, their failure is used to support the rhetoric that poverty is impervious to government initiatives, and that everyone, including the poor, would be better off without the state meddling in her or his affairs. A conservative corporate discourse popularizes the premise that social problems should be left to the operation of the free market for their "natural" resolution (Fischer et al., 1996, p. 4; George & Wilding, 1985) despite overwhelming evidence that the free-market exacerbates social inequality (Fischer et al., 1996).

This anti-state, free-market ideology legitimates cut-backs in social services by shifting responsibility for poverty and crime onto individuals and the decisions they make. Poverty and criminal activity are blamed on single parenting, a lack of family values, the absence of a sufficient work ethic and on the individual's failure to learn skills that will enable her or him to cope effectively in the "new world order." In this conservative discourse, adult education is touted as a panacea for resolving people's economic and personal problems. A percentage of individuals adapt to change by improving their education; others invest heavily in retraining without gaining any rewards; many cannot overcome structural or personal barriers to participation in adult education, "fall out" of the labour market, take minimum wage part-time jobs, or join the ranks of the working poor; still others "choose" theft, selling drugs, and prostitution as a source of income, and use violence to resolve interpersonal conflicts. Some of these people are imprisoned, often repeatedly.

In the 1980s, North America entered an era of incarceration unparalleled in its history. In the United States, the prison population increased by more than 250 percent from 1980 to 1994. In 1993, 2.6 percent of the United States' population, five-million adults, were either on parole, probation, or in prison; an increase of three million in twelve years. Of these five million, 1.4 million were incarcerated (U.S. Department of Justice, 1996). In the 1990s, the United States had the highest incarceration rate per 100,000 people in the world.

The magnitude of imprisonment in Canada does not compare to the United States; nonetheless, Canada has the second highest incarceration rate in the Western world. The number of people under custody or in community corrections programs (for example, halfway houses) rose from 110,117 in 1988 to 147,960 in 1993, an increase of 34 percent. The majority of these people (86 percent) were under probation or other community service orders, but the prison population rose as well (Foran & Reed, 1996). For the same ten-year period, the federal penitentiary population increased by 27 percent, rising from 9,745 to 12,342 (Solicitor General Canada, 1990).

The relationship between poverty, racism and imprisonment is readily apparent from the overrepresentation of people of colour in North American prisons. In the 1990s, the incarceration rate for African-Americans in state prisons exceeds the White rate by almost seven to one; on average about four out of every hundred Black men are in prison (U.S. Department of Justice, 1996). In Canada, Aboriginal people make up about 3.8 percent of the Canadian population but account for 12 percent of the federal prison population and 17 percent of the provincial prison population (Foran & Reed, 1996).

Criminologists have shown that the disproportion of people of colour to Whites in the prison system occurs in part because poverty and unemployment breed criminal activity, but discriminatory criminal justice practices are a serious contributing factor. At key decision points, the criminal justice system weeds out educated middle-class and upper-class offenders, and convicts the undereducated poor, especially poor people of colour. Criminal activity is ubiquitous across class boundaries, but crimes committed by visible minorities living in low-income districts are more likely to be noticed by police and to result in arrests than the same criminal activity in middle-class districts. Once arrested, indigent defendants with limited education are more likely to be convicted, to receive longer sentences and to be denied probation or parole than are middle-class defendants charged for similar offenses (Reiman, 1984; MacLean & Milovanovic, 1990).

Situating criminal activity in its social context is not done to denigrate the harm crime causes or to excuse criminal action. Crime does not solve the

problems poverty creates; it merely exacerbates them. The intent is to understand that the way in which people become prisoners is a process influenced
greatly by a fiscal crisis of the state, managed by reducing spending on social
services and increasing the use of repressive measures. Political decisions
have created a dramatic increase in the population supervised by the criminal
justice system in the United States and Canada. The prisons are filled not with
educated, middle-class offenders but with the poor. Among these offenders,
there is a disproportionate representation of visible minorities and a high rate
of "functional illiteracy," estimated to be between 40 percent and 60 percent
(Williamson, 1992).

In their efforts to cope with this crisis, prison authorities are using managerial strategies that involve adult education.[7] In Canada, the most important of
these—what criminologists have called "the new penology" (Feeley & Simon,
1992, 1994)—is having a major influence on the transformation of adult
education in prisons.

The "New Penology" and Adult Education in Prison

The newest and most significant strategy being used by the federal prison
system, the Correctional Service of Canada (CSC), is a combination of risk-
assessment technology and correctional treatments, including education. The
objective is to minimize and thereby manage overcrowding by placing "low-
risk" offenders in community correction programs and reserving high-security
prisons for those most likely to re-offend. High-risk prisoners are placed in
treatment programs in order to reduce their risk. As one of these programs, the
aim of adult and/or correctional education in this context is to help reduce
risk.

In 1991, the Chairman of the Canadian National Parole Board announced
at a conference on the future of corrections that the board was "committed to
the principle that its business is the management of risk" (Gibson, 1991, p. 7).
The board wanted prison authorities to identify when a prisoner's risk of
re-offending was low enough to parole him or her to a community-based
program. CSC and the board co-operated on the development of a selective
incapacitation strategy that would detain high-risk offenders in prison, where
they would receive treatment programs to lower their risk. Low-risk offenders
would receive fewer programs and be paroled to community-based programs
as soon as the conditions of their sentences permitted. In a paper on innovative alternatives to community corrections, delivered at the 1993 American
Correctional Association conference, an assistant commissioner of CSC
wrote:

> Part of the basis for pursuing a more aggressive approach to community correc-
> tions lies in the establishment of a sound system of measuring and managing
> risk effectively. Much of our effort has gone into devising reliable risk-assess-

ment tools and prediction models that reflect state-of-the-art research (Reynolds, 1993, p. 120).

Criminologists call this focus on risk management the "new penology" or "actuarial justice" (Feeley & Simon, 1994, 1992). It is actuarial because the aim is to identify, classify and manage groups of people according to their risk of recidivism. It is "new" because unlike the rhetoric of the last two hundred years, it is disinterested in rehabilitation for the sake of making a difference in prisoners' lives.

The new penology is a system of selective incapacitation (Feeley & Simon, 1994) in which the length of imprisonment is determined not only by the severity of the offence but by the risk of re-offending. The higher the risk, the longer the period of incapacitation. Assessment techniques designate certain characteristics as criminogenic factors (for example, criminal history, illiteracy, and substance abuse). Using court records, interviews and standardized tests, an assessment determines which criminogenic factors are present in each prisoner and to what degree of severity (or deficiency). The results place individuals in a high-, medium- or low-risk category and assign them to treatment programs that are targeted to reducing the criminogenic factor to a level that places the individual in a lower risk group. When that occurs, the person may be transferred into a lower security prison or a community-based custodial setting (for example, halfway house).

The incentive for using community corrections for low-risk offenders is financial in the first instance. In Canada, the average annual cost for incorporating one individual was $41,245 in 1992-93 (Foran & Reed, 1996). The total cost of all prison services and community-based custodial options in the same year was $1.88 billion. About 74 percent of that cost was spent on prisons that held only 21 percent of the total number of people under supervision, while 36 percent of the budget was spent on 79 percent of the population supervised by community-based programs. Thus, enormous savings, not to mention reductions in control problems, are to be gained by moving the maximum number of people into a risk category that makes them eligible for less expensive, community-based custodial options.

Decades may pass before the "lingering language of rehabilitation and reintegration" (Feeley & Simon, 1992, p. 465) that characterized the discourse of the "old penology" is replaced by an actuarial discourse that is disinterested in rehabilitation altogether and focuses entirely on calculating the risk of re-offending and assigning an appropriate form of custody. For example, as recently as 1988, CSC's Mission Statement commits CSC to "the protection of society by actively encouraging and assisting offenders to become law-abiding citizens" (Vantour, 1991, p. 47). Feeley and Simon would point out, however, that the "old penology" tone of this Mission Statement is translated into policies and procedures that are decidedly actuarial. For instance, according to CSC's Correctional Strategy, the aim of programming is to ensure "that offenders receive the most effective programs at the appropriate point in their sentences to allow them to serve the greatest proportion of their sentences in the community with the lowest risk of recidivism" (Correctional Service, undated, p. 1).

For educators, the objectives of the new penology are most consequential. While many educators adopt correctional aims that focus on functional skills, a significant group of liberal educators have expressed a genuine concern for promoting self-actualization, autonomy and individual empowerment (Duguid, 1993a; Morin & Cosman, 1989; Werner, 1990). In 1990, for example, the Council of Europe's report on prison education expressed the concern that "the prison context should be minimized and the past criminal behaviour of the student should be kept to the background, so that the normal atmosphere, interactions and processes of adult education can flourish as they would in the outside Community" (Council of Europe, 1990, p. 17).

The new penology takes education in the opposite direction. In the CSC, model participation in school is rationalized as part of a correctional plan. On admission, a prisoner is assessed to determine "the exact circumstances which brought the offender to prison; the nature and extent of the criminal career; the pattern of criminal involvement; and ultimately, an accurate sense of the risk posed by the offender" (Correctional Service, June 1994, p. 9). If illiteracy is a high-risk factor or likely to interfere with effective participation in other treatment programs, the prisoner will be placed in a literacy program. The primary purpose of the placement is not individual empowerment or self-actualization but to assist prisoners "in addressing needs relating specifically to their criminal behaviour so that the likelihood of recidivism is reduced" (p. 28).

In meeting these objectives, there is pressure to integrate literacy with other programs, especially cognitive skills training. The cognitive skills model is based on the assumption that prisoners make bad judgments or fail to consider the consequences before they act. Thinking skills deficiencies have been identified as criminogenic factors not because anyone has shown a causal relationship between poor decision-making abilities and crime but because prisoners score low on tests of problem-solving abilities and because the use of cognitive treatment programs seems to reduce the recidivism risk (Ross & Fabiano, 1985). Thinking skills programs have become popular in prison education because they resonate with an ideology that stresses individual accountability and choices while dismissing societal conditions affecting incarceration patterns as excuses to avoid holding criminals responsible for their actions. Ross and Fabiano write:

> We suggest that, like most people, the offender has some role in determining his own destiny. His environment may drastically restrict the number of choices he has but, with rare exception, it does not prohibit him from choosing not to

engage in criminal behaviour. We suggest that most offenders are responsible for their behaviour and that they choose to commit criminal acts (Ross & Fabiano, 1985, p. 157).

In 1993, Correctional Programs for the Prairie Region of CSC argued for an integrated curriculum that would incorporate cognitive skills, value clarification and academic programs into a "holistic" approach to adult education that would place them all "under the umbrella of education." The justification for doing so was that the school is "the one area of most institutions which has both the ... space and the administrative framework within which the program can be most effectively implemented" (Correctional Programs, 1993, p. 17). By 1996, Excalibur Corporation, a private, for-profit organization that operates most of CSC's schools, was actively engaged in producing a "correctional curriculum to address the social, cognitive and critical thinking skills of offenders" (Excalibur, 1996).

Behind the rhetoric of efficiency is a competitive strategy to protect education from losing its foothold in prisons during the transition to the new penology. With the introduction of several treatment programs in the mid-1990s, literacy has lost some of its glitter as a primary rehabilitative initiative. From 1987 to 1989, the Solicitor General's Annual Report highlighted educational programs, but in the early 1990s, literacy had to share the spotlight in the annual report with treatments for sexual offenders and special programs for women and Aboriginal prisoners. Meanwhile, data from the United States shows a decline in prison school enrollments, with at least half of all state prison systems increasing their use of prison labour and cutting their educational programs between 1991 and 1996 (Barton & Coley, 1996; Ryan, 1995; U.S. Department of Justice, 1994). These indications must give corporate providers of prison education in Canada reason for concern. Literacy as a stand-alone program, is less vulnerable to cut-backs than if it is integrated with other treatments. Private corporations that have invested heavily so that they can profit from prison education cannot have missed this point.

Limitations and Possibilities

Having stressed the influence of the new penology on the contemporary features of adult education in prisons, it is necessary to point to several limits on that influence. The first of these is public tolerance for community-based custodial options. Without cultivating excessive fear of and a punitive response to criminal activity, it would be difficult to justify spending tax dollars on prisons and police. But the rhetoric that legitimates high prison populations contradicts the more permissive discourse required for accepting the transfer of low-risk offenders to community-based custodial centres. In short, after watching *Law and Order* on television and reading the morning newspaper, no one wants to learn that a halfway house is coming to the neighbourhood.

This public resistance creates consequences throughout the risk management system. When prisoner-students are convinced that achieving a Grade 5 reading level and completing other programs will result in transfers to lower security levels and community custody, but prison authorities and parole boards refuse to approve these transfers fearing public reaction if they should make a mistake, the legitimacy of the risk management strategy is undermined and its operation seriously compromised.

Fear of public and political reaction feeds into a tendency for conservative decision making among prison authorities. Studies in the United States suggest that when there is doubt about how much supervision is required for a given person, administrators will make a conservative decision and place the prisoner in a high-risk category. In jurisdictions with very high incarceration rates, this tendency is exacerbated (Lauen, 1988). The legitimacy of education programs linked to risk management strategies is bound to collapse under such constraints.

Another limitation is occupational culture. The complex processes by which people identify themselves as belonging to an occupational group involve extended periods of education and affiliations with associations and colleagues in social and working relationships. These experiences create an occupation's culture. Policy makers may exert tremendous influence on the tasks occupations perform. However, their ability to transform an occupation's culture is more problematic. Values clash. More often than not, the introduction of rationalized forms of management do not change the values of different occupational groups but force people to devise strategies that will accommodate, if not subvert, policy. Over time, opposition may become muted, but rarely will it disappear (Garland, 1990).

Attempts to get educators to take on the identity of risk managers when they are socialized to see themselves as "making a difference" in students' lives will be problematic at best. It is unlikely that the ethos of risk management will ever be successful at fully monopolizing how educators relate to their students. Of course, this limitation may be overcome by replacing certificated educators with guards or volunteers who are less resistant to prison policy while being capable of supervising students working with computerized, competency-based literacy materials. Yet even here, advocates for professionalizing correctional educators have encouraged prison staff and volunteers to participate in their conferences in order to introduce them to a correctional educational ethos that includes a range of philosophical positions on what constitutes learning.

A review of the proceedings of the American Correctional Association from 1986 to 1995 and attendance of sessions at the Correctional Education Association's annual meetings reveal the persistence among educators for writing and/or speaking about learning as a transformative process that prepares prisoners for successful reintegration and a productive life. While this discourse may be little more than the "lingering language of rehabilitation" that one would expect to find among educators, its existence suggests that the new penology can not emerge unscathed from the process of grappling with educators' cultural forms. It would be naïve to suggest that the norms and value systems of educators would not be altered significantly by their encounter with the actuarial discourse of the new penology. It is equally naïve to assume that the actuarial discourse would not have to accommodate the occupational cultures that will be expected to implement the new penology.

Tersely put, managerial strategies tend to ignore the culture of policies and procedures, which ultimately affects how these strategies are actually administered and interpreted in everyday practice.

An Alternative Vision for Adult Education with Prisoners

For a relatively small number of adult educators working with prisoners, modifying the policies, procedures and day-to-day operation of risk management is not enough. This group shares a vision of adult education that I find expressed eloquently in the Manifesto of the Archambault Guys, written during a prisoners' strike at Archambault prison, Quebec, in January 1976: "To us, talking about education means talking about the chance to acquire an intellectual and practical formation that increases understanding and decreases alienation from things, from reality and from life. A step toward a liberated spirit" (quoted in Gosselin, 1982, p. 179).

If the objective of modifying the formation of adult education's role in current managerial strategies is problematic at best, surely it must be ridiculous to contemplate the more radical perspective captured by the Archambault Manifesto or related perspectives (Collins, 1995; Faith, 1995). However, if one radically re-conceptualizes what adult education in prison includes, an entirely new terrain emerges in which the vision expressed by the manifesto becomes a possibility. This terrain is adult education organized by prisoners.

This form of adult education includes the "educational meetings" organized by socialists and anarchists at Auburn Prison, New York, in 1914, and Cook County Jail, Chicago, in 1917 (Legere, 1914; Chaplain, 1948), and African-American and Latino prisoner-educators in the United States who have been teaching literacy, Black history and how to organize in prison and in communities (Sbarbaro, 1995a; Rivera, 1992). It also includes prisoners' efforts to publish a penal press that for more than fifty years has provided information on legal assistance and health issues, critical commentary on prison policies, forums for the exchange of prisoners' political views and a format for reading prisoners' prose and poetry (Gaucher, 1989).

Adult educators should realize that for the last twenty years there has been a supportive relationship between prisoner-educators and progressive adult educators from outside, especially the teachers working for prison higher education programs. Prison higher education programs in Canada were eliminated by the Solicitor General in 1993 and seriously curtailed in the United States in 1994 by legislation that prohibits prisoners from qualifying for financial grants to cover tuition and books (Duguid, 1993b). Prior to these prohibitions, university programs—fought for and defended by prisoners (Attallah Salah-El, 1992; Bell & Glaremin, 1995)—brought feminists, sociologists, social historians, philosophers, literary critics, critical criminologists and artists in contact with prisoners in educational exchanges that often surpassed the best moments in conventional university classes (Devor, 1989; Heberle & Rose, 1994; Linebaugh, 1995; Sbarbaro, 1995b). Limitations on these programs were significant at the best of times (Thomas, 1995), but from the mid-1970s to the dates of their demise, they provided opportunities for prisoner-students to engage in dialogues that promoted a critical, historical consciousness among the prison population and the educators. From these contacts both prisoners and teachers were politicized, and several prisoner-operated adult education programs were supported and introduced to a wider audience (Rivera, 1992; Stone, 1995).

The destruction of prison higher education coupled to the subjugation of literacy education to the status of managing risk does not bode well for ongoing contacts between prisoner-educators and educators from the outside; nonetheless, possibilities remain for contacts to continue.

For example, Julian Stone, a prisoner in Massachusetts, has described how he worked through the prisoners' legal committee to organize courses to teach prisoners to become jailhouse lawyers who in turn help to defend indigent prisoners wrongfully convicted and to protect prisoners' constitutional rights (Stone, 1995). Support for these courses by university law students contributed to their credibility and kept them current and effective. This program and others like it (Rivera, 1992) must be supported with prisoner-organized literacy programs that can function relatively independently of programs operated by the prison. Collins and Niemi (1989) have outlined the structure for prisoners' literacy councils that train and organize peer tutors and define curriculum. And Kathy Boudin's efforts as a prisoner-educator to create a participatory literacy program that focused on AIDS education provides an excellent example of what this approach can achieve and the constraints it faces (Boudin, 1993).

The important point here is that these cases of prisoner-organized adult education provide concrete alternatives that adult educators can engage critically. The alternative to becoming a "correctional educator" is to resist being assigned the role of managing risk (hoping to modify this objective as best as one can) and supporting critically prisoner-organized programs at every opportunity.

The limitations and possibilities described here will, I hope, remind adult educators that social and political forces affecting the formation of the contemporary features of adult education in North American prisons are never one-sided. It is essential to illuminate limitations in order to find in them concrete possibilities for resistance and alternatives. Limitations alert us to the fact that neither the global economy—which is driving the shift to repressive forms of control—nor the managerial responses being used to make prisons more effective repressive instruments are without their contradictions. We must understand and organize politically to exploit these contradictions to their fullest. In this way, adult educators can strive towards an objective worth the effort: "to acquire an intellectual and practical formation that increases understanding and decreases alienation from things, from reality and from life. A step toward a liberated spirit" (quoted in Gosselin, 1982, p. 179).

Endnotes

[1] I want to thank Stephen Duguid, Marcia Stentz and Jon Marc Taylor for their critical comments during the preparation of this chapter.

[2] For excellent surveys on the history of penal punishment, see Garland (1990, 1985).

[3] On the continuous use of force in Canadian prisons, see Arbour (1996). On the use of the death sentence in the United States, see Abu-Jamal (1995).

[4] In 1978 about 20 percent of the federal prison population attended a prison education program (Griffin, 1978). By 1983, the typical province (for example, British Columbia and Ontario) had these programs in about 25 percent of their prisons (Nixon & Bumbarger, 1983, Table 1). With the exception of Ontario, no provincial authority had produced an official statement on the purpose of prison education.

[5] For the importance of examining the influence of larger structural forces on adult education, see Cervero & Wilson (1994), Collins (1991) and Forester (1989).

[6] The operation of the criminal justice system is expensive—about $9.6 billion in 1992-93 (Besserer & Grimes, 1996)—but prison budgets at under 5 percent of public expenditures compare favourably to the 12-15 percent spent on public welfare (Carter, 1991).

[7] Historically, prison education has been used as a substitute for prison labour whenever the latter has been restricted to stop prisoners from competing with non-penal labour. Typically, restrictive legislation has been passed during periods of economic depressions when unemployment has been high and prisons overcrowded. The combination of restricting the use of prison labour and prison overcrowding created serious problems of "idleness" for prison officials. Many of the famous reforms in the history of prison education were instituted as ingenious management-educational strategies to keep prisoners occupied while being rationalized as enhancing released prisoners' employment opportunities, improving their self-esteem and altering their criminal disposition towards life (Davidson, 1995; Gildemeister, 1977). This history is being repeated in the late 1990s. For evidence on the current relationship between prison labour and mandatory literacy education as alternative means to control idleness, see Allison and Royal (1991); American Correctional (1989); Bell & Glaremin (1995), Elliot (1995) and Littlefield (1993).

Kay Desjardins and Ellen Arsenault; March 1956.
Courtesy of the Archives, St. Francis Xavier University.

Part 3

Education for Diversity

19

Women in the History of Adult Education: Misogynist Responses to Our Participation

Joyce Stalker

This chapter has its origins in my experiences as a teacher of adult basic education in northern British Columbia in the early 1980s. One day near the end of term, a young woman who had been successfully upgrading herself from a Grade 6 level to a Grade 10 level came to class with a horribly bruised face. She explained it away as an infected tooth, and in my naïveté, I accepted that explanation. Years later, as abuse and violence against women became more openly discussed issues, I rethought that episode. I combined it with the stories I was then hearing about women locked in rooms by their partners so that they could not sit for university exams, about women who had their books and essays burned by irate partners and about women on continuing education courses who returned to find their homes in sudden and inexplicable chaos after their brief absences. It became clear to me that our field does not fully acknowledge the problematic nature of women's participation in adult education. I realized too that this is not a new problem but that there has been a tendency throughout our history to ignore this issue.

There is little doubt that women have played an important role in shaping the rich history of Canadian adult education, and in framing the foundations of the field within Canada. As our stories emerge (see for example, Selman & Dampier, 1991; Welton, 1987), adult educators can proudly point to women's place in the struggle for social justice. Although many of our stories have yet to be told and explored extensively,[1] there is, nonetheless, a sense that our history is in part a her-story and richer for the leadership of its strong, active and articulate women. The participation of these women too often has been treated as a given, and our involvement in educational organizations, agencies and social movements often do not include our stories of the struggle to be present and active. As Bennett suggests, in explaining the historical experiences of women, "we have focused our main efforts on other factors that can be more readily isolated, defined and analyzed" (1991, p. 167)

This chapter problematizes women's participation in educational organizations, agencies and social movements. In doing so, I hope to provide a framework for understanding and conceptualizing in new ways women's participation in adult education both in the past and in today's context. I first briefly highlight the problematic nature of literature concerned with participation, as exemplified by Cross's (1981) classic model. I explore particularly the richness in acknowledging macro-level factors related to gender. I then explore the nature of misogyny, a particular barrier that flows from those factors and which is un-named and ignored in the participation literature. I examine the three interwoven and related elements that construct the day-to-day practice of misogyny; namely reification, vilification and subjugation. After exploring the ways in which women experience these elements and their possible relationship to women's participation in adult education, I conclude with a brief summary and some reflections on research implications.

Barriers to Women's Participation

Studies into participation have formed a cornerstone of the adult education field's research for decades. The data from that research have revealed consistently that women are active participants in adult education as both learners and leaders. Our history shows us that women have often enrolled in, engaged with and completed many different kinds of adult education activities.

For some time, studies of participation have been fragmented into research of particular kinds of activities, participants and providers. The resulting plethora of literature available on the topic makes it difficult to generalize about who participates and who does not or what the rationales are for participation. The research continues to be guided by classic works. Patricia Cross's work (1981) is particularly relevant to this chapter. Her model presents institutional, dispositional and attitudinal barriers as explanatory categories for non-participation. As she explains,

> situational barriers are those arising from one's situation in life at a given time ... Institutional barriers consist of all those practices and procedures that exclude or discourage working adults from participating in education activities ... Dispositional barriers are those related to attitudes and self-perceptions about oneself as a learner (p. 98).

Cross's model is problematic in three ways that relate to the gender concerns of this chapter. First, the model is presented as gender neutral and thus by definition is andro-centric (Stalker, 1996). Second, a closer look at the model reveals that her situational and dispositional barriers fundamentally "blame the victim" (Ryan, 1972). These two categories assume that potential learners are responsible for their non-participation. Although Cross maintains that she has placed items where they seem "most direct and straightforward" (1981, p. 100), her discussions have a moralistic tone in which the non-participant is deemed to be somehow inferior and deviant relative to the participant. There is a sense that the individual has the ability but not the desire or motivation to overcome barriers. Items are stated in individualistic terms, such as "not enough time," "home responsibilities," "no place to study" and "afraid that I'm too old" (p. 99). As is the case in many participation studies, these items are labelled in a way that allocates responsibility to the individual. It is of little comfort to think that the items and categories were derived from survey questionnaires. Indeed, it just deepens the nature of the problem.

The third criticism of this classic model lies in its tendency to give little consideration to the impact of macro-level pressures. Although Cross's category of institutional barriers does shift the responsibility from the individual to the institution and includes items such as "courses aren't scheduled when I can attend," and "no information about offerings," it does not make clear connections to the social, economic, political and cultural contexts that create barriers to participation.

Today, these macro-level concepts continue to be ignored in empirical research in favour of more observable, measurable and predictable micro-level factors related to the individual and the institution. There is much to be gained by basing an exploration of these micro-factors in macro-level concepts. Although those concepts might appear overly abstract, they are operationalized in real practices and are experienced on a day-to-day basis in ways which foster or inhibit participation in adult education. In terms of women's participation, important and often ignored macro-level barriers can be identified as patriarchy, androcentricity, sexism and sex discrimination in general. From these macro-level barriers flow the lived experiences women encounter as obstacles to participation. They form the barrier which is never named yet which strongly influences the participation of women: misogyny.

Misogyny

The term *misogyny* is not new. It is a "cultural force" (Bennett, 1991, p. 167) based on the Greek word *misognunes*, from *misein* meaning hate, *misos* meaning hatred and *gune*, meaning woman (Mills, 1989). It is generally taken to mean hatred of women. The practice of misogyny has been traced to seventh and sixth centuries B.C. (French, 1989; Gordon, 1990). Its written usage in the English language dates from 1620 and precedes, by several centuries, the use in 1946 of the word "misandry" meaning hatred of men (Kramarae, 1985; Mills, 1989). The concept has appeared primarily in the study of literature and its misogynist characters and themes. Rogers (1966) has shown that it is evident in ancient, medieval and renaissance literature of the West and in the Eastern writings of Confucius.

Usage of the term had a resurgence in the 1970s (see Dworkin, 1974). Although popular usage of the term has subsided, the idea behind it has not. Indeed, a recent best-seller was a self-help book directed to women, entitled *Men Who Hate Women and the Women Who Love Them* (Forward & Torres, 1986).

As suggested by its origins, misogyny is based on a fundamental theme of hostility to women and is expressed in acts of "denigration and intimidation" (Dworkin, 1983, p. 201). These actions can be placed on a continuum that ranges from suspicion, displeasure and discontent with women to abuse, brutality and violence against them. Misogyny is a relational term; that is, it occurs within the context of relationships between and among individuals. Although usually assumed to be practices of malevolence by men against women it also can be practiced by women against women (Gubar, 1994). The usual interpretation of this phenomenon is that ideologies based in class, race, heterosexuality and ability run more deeply than ideologies based in gender. Graham's explanation (1994) is more thought provoking. She argues theoretically and empirically that under conditions of domination, women's aggression against women is a survival strategy through which, like hostages, we attempt to bond with our oppressors.

Regardless of the gender of those practicing it, misogyny is shaped by its context. Certain social, economic and cultural contexts have encouraged particular practices of misogyny. In industrialized societies, for example, women traditionally were dependent on men for financial support. This in turn fostered a vision and treatment of women as grasping and mercenary. The intensity of misogynist practices also is context bound. In contemporary times, the increase in women's power and independence located within a context of decreasing economic and political stability have caused an increase in actions of contempt and cruelty against women (Faludi, 1991).

Fundamentally, misogynists view women in terms of either how they desire us to be or how they fear us to be (Laws, 1979). The tension between these two views constitutes a basic characteristic of misogyny (Kahn Blumstein, 1977). It represents the dis-ease between views of women as virgin and whore, between attraction and repulsion, between desire and dread and between exaltation and degradation. In this chapter, the former view is labelled reification and the latter view, vilification. Together, these views create and are sustained by subjugation.

There is, of course, a much more unstable discourse about what women are or should be than this falsely tidy triadic representation presents. It can be argued that the specific nature of these views differs according to one's ethnicity, race, sexual orientation and ability. However, the three elements presented below shape the *dominant* discourse of misogyny in Westernized, industrialized nations. Thus, a counter-argument can be made that for women in these groups, these elements create, not a different, but a "double dilemma" (Torton Beck, 1991, p. 19).

Arguments and counter-arguments do not form the basis of this chapter. Instead, I have chosen to present these three elements in a stark manner. By doing this, I hope to reclaim the vile nature of misogyny in its classic sense and throw into sharp relief issues relevant to women's participation in adult education activities. I hope this will foster discomfort, reflections and actions that will re-shape our understandings and analyses of these issues.

Misogynistic Responses to Women's Participation

Reification

As noted above, misogynists view women in terms of how they desire us to be through a process of reification. This process creates an enduring and restrictive representation of women's characteristics and roles. Misogynists present the characteristics of "Woman" not as an entity of social construction, but rather as one of biological destiny. Collectively and individually, women are fixed as a particular kind of woman. The basis of our identity supposedly is lodged in the characteristics of femininity, love of men and heterosexuality (Graham, 1994). There is an adulation of women that seems antithetical to a hatred of women. Indeed, it partly explains the view that "misogyny is generally recognized as an abnormal feeling, not to be expressed directly" (Rogers, 1966, p. 265).

There is a hint of the delicate woman of the Victorian era in the idealization of docility, poise, grace and charm. The attributes of modesty, gentleness, compliancy, beauty and affection are stressed. We are represented as "naturally" sensitive, nurturing and caring as well as industrious, thrifty and quiet (Rogers, 1966; Russell, 1925). Although in and of themselves these characteristics may have value, manipulation of them by misogynists creates a repressive situation.

Embedded in these "virtues" is women's location of "lovely inferiority" in which our primary role is to "adorn [our] male relatives" (Steele, cited in Rogers, 1966, p. 274). There is a vision of a "feminine" woman who is subordinate in the minds of men and women alike (Baron McBride, 1976; Graham, 1994). This view is not unexpected, given that "Buddhism, Christianity, Hinduism, Islam, and Judaism all explicitly stress to a greater or lesser degree the natural inferiority of Woman and her lawful, right and proper subjection to Man" (Boxer, 1975, p. 97).

This weaker and subordinate position of women locates us as helpmates who have submissive roles as mistress, partner and mother. These roles ensure that we take care of the domestic needs of the household and that the home is a sanctuary of reasonableness and stability in the midst of an irrational and chaotic external world. We become the primary keepers of morality, cleanliness and order. Simultaneously, we willingly provide domestic, emotional, reproductive and sexual services. In those roles we are respected and applauded for our domestic achievements and abilities.

What, then, are the implications of the reification of these particular characteristics and roles for women's participation in adult education? In part it depends on the extent to which women integrate these expectations into their behaviours, norms and beliefs. On the one hand, we are not merely passive victims of such idealizations. On the other hand, the hegemonic nature of misogyny is subtle and difficult to resist. Thus, to the extent that a society is not able to permeate it, a misogynistic hegemony creates an environment in which women enact and are expected to enact the characteristics and roles described above. In the day-to-day lives of women, this means that we experience and act out experiences and actions that are different from those of men. Throughout this chapter, those experiences and actions are highlighted rather than women's resistance to them. This approach is not meant to denigrate women's ability to be active agents in shaping their environments. Rather, it is meant to sharpen the discourse around the issue of women's participation in adult education and the barrier of misogyny.

Behaviours based on the characteristics noted above are unlikely to foster participation in some kinds of adult education activities. It is not probable, for example, that Victorian characteristics of fragility and delicacy will be helpful in successful enrollment in, engagement with, or completion of, formal and non-formal adult education activities. There are elements of passivity and submission in those niceties that are incongruent with the robust, competitive environment of the activities. As well, since typically feminine characteristics are equated in the minds of men and women with subordination (Graham, 1994), women may seek out particular kinds of adult education activities that do not accrue the rewards, status and power of others.

Attributes of sensitivity and caring are equally as inhibiting. They have built into them a tremendous expectation for women's energy and time to be focused on others and others' concerns. This in itself may create a barrier to women's participation in adult education. As well, the very act of focusing on one's own concerns by participating in an adult education activity may create self-recriminations and condemnations from others. If that activity is not oriented to developing "normal" women's attributes, there may be additional hostilities to overcome.

The powerful archetype represented by these reified characteristics creates an ideal against which ordinary women are measured and will inevitably fail. Recalling that the perspective here is of the bleakest scenario rather than one of resistance, one can project that women may participate in particular kinds of adult education activities in an attempt to achieve those characteristics. Participation in activities concerned with making relationships work, parenting skills, appropriate assertiveness and caring for others may follow. Similarly, courses may be created to ensure that there are opportunities to attain this ideal. However, since the objectives of such courses represent an idealization rather than a realistic end, they prepare the potential participant for ongoing disillusionment and failure. Thus, it is no surprise that there is a high failure and drop out rate from learning activities.

If women are placed in the role of helpmates to our partners as our primary function, there may be resistance to anything that interferes with the excellent execution of that role. To break away from these demands and to challenge the ownership implicit in the concept is to be unwomanly. In the context of an asymmetrical power relationship, such breakaways may be viewed as unsafe. Thus, we may create and are encouraged to create restricted goals for our participation.

The roles for women embedded in attitudes of misogyny may inhibit women's participation in adult education. Integral to the roles are continuous demands for a wide range of services that require much time and energy. Viewed as the stable centrepiece of the domestic sphere, women must ensure that the home base is unshaken by our absences. Thus participation in adult education activities requires not just motivation but considerable pre-planning and organization.

Assumptions of intellectual inferiority and dependency are also built into the notion of helpmate and are similarly restrictive. They suggest that women do not have the ability or the right to self-determination. Participation thus may be viewed as an other-determined activity that is a privilege.

Vilification

The second dimension of misogynistic responses to women's participation in adult education activities, vilification, represents how men fear us to be. It has two interrelated dimensions. In the first instance, women may be denounced for our weaknesses. In the second instance, we may be scorned for our strengths.

In our weaknesses, women are portrayed as idle, inactive and of insubstantial spirit. We supposedly suffer from lack of self-respect and are vain, prideful, jealous and haughty. Fundamentally weak of spirit, woman is an indolent, "changeable, fickle and treacherous moon relative to the male constant, proud and dependable sun" (Rigolot, 1994, p. 225). Open to ridicule, censure and indignation, this weak and undependable woman is an ungrateful, greedy person who is basically self-serving, extravagant and eager to spend her partner's hard-earned money.

This view of women's paucity of moral integrity meshes nicely with the vilification of women's strengths. Portrayed as weak in morals and less capable of control, women represent potential danger. We are linked to unrestrained sexuality, sin, temptation and ruin. This theme is a strong one. Throughout history, women have been said to be, in varying degrees, "a hindrance to the thinking man. We are proud, irascible, adulterous, materialistic. We are governed by animal passions, are given to abandoning their children, and aspire to rule and thereby usurp powers which by right should be exclusively male" (Kahn Blumstein, 1977, p. 24).

The Old and New Testament stories warn men against the strength of women's wiles and seductive powers. Women are presented, after all, as the instigators of Christianity's original sin. We presumably possess violent and uncontrollable passions and the power to entice through our sexuality and attractiveness. In the New Testament, "women are depicted as seducers of men, an evil and sinful influence which distracts men from their true purpose" (van Vuuren, 1973, p. 21), while male celibacy is linked to the Kingdom of Heaven. In sum, this kind of vilification of strengths presents women as not completely human, lustful, pagan-like villains who wish to take a man's sexual powers and to use him for our own ends.

Similarly, the stories of monstrous Amazons (Doane & Hodges, 1987) and witches (Hester, 1992; Ross, 1995) seep into current misogynistic views. Once again, women are portrayed as dangerous beings with unnatural energies and desires. Amazons were identified as too militant, too strong and too possessive of a "ruinous power which [they] can exercise over men" (Rogers, 1966, p. 13). Witches also were identified as playing an overly active and domineering role in society. They were active in religious activities assigned to men, acted in an independent sexual way (for example, unmarried, widowed) and competed with men for economic resources (Karlsen in Hester, 1992). Against these backdrops, it is not surprising that some argue that misogyny has its origins in a fear of women and of being ruled by our unworthy and corrupting motives (Tibbetts-Schulenberg, 1989).

Potentially, all women who do not fit the reified stereotype may be vilified. This clear division between two types of women fosters misogynistic practices (Berleth, 1995). When we express our power through un-stereotypical behaviours, like the curious Pandora in Greek times, we may be judged as rebellious. We may be labelled as harsh and domineering with a desire to rule. This portrayal of women can be used in anti-feminist explanations for the abuse of women, since it suggests that through our enticements and our aggressions we invite our own victimization.

There are several implications of these misogynistic views for women's participation in adult education activities. Once again, to foster debate on the issues, I will focus on the bleak possibilities rather than a more hopeful scenario of resistance. Van Vuuren (1973) created a tidy model of how women act out the experience of these subversive pressures. She speaks of the tendencies of women to respond in either intro-punitive or extro-punitive ways.

In the first instance, given a portrayal as idle and weak of spirit, we may feel insecure and incapable, want to depend on others and assume that others should have power over us and our decisions about participation. In the context of participation in adult education, active participation becomes something entered into hesitantly if at all and is viewed as other-determined, rather than self-determined. Further, since women presumably have much to gain from men and their higher aspirations, an agenda for women's participation may model itself on male norms, values and concerns. In the second instance, women may extend the characterizations of women as manipulators and view ourselves and others as untrustworthy. This in turn may create a sense of dislocation, isolation and alienation antithetical to full and active participation in adult education activities.

The vilification of women's strengths may be as inhibiting to women's participation as the vilification of our weaknesses. It may signal an underlying antagonism between the sexes since it fundamentally presumes that men are wronged and used by women. This may make equitable participation in mixed-sex activities problematic, or indeed, from the perspective of either sex, undesirable. There may be an atmosphere of opposition to women's realization of their strengths, given the danger to men inherent in them.

Concurrently, vilification may create among women a fear of accusation or violence as we step outside reified roles into ones in which we display more strengths. In the face of this threat of hostility, women may display gratefulness for freedoms and kindnesses which foster participation. Again, the activity of participation may be viewed as a privilege rather than a right.

As well, an atmosphere of hostility against women's strengths may foster a desire for a return to the reified female. Women may attempt to dissociate themselves from the "bad" component which is apparently within ourselves and create an identity that rejects these vilified attributes (Torton Beck, 1991). Women's choice of adult education activities may reflect this as we "choose" processes, content and activities congruent with the reified woman. Conversely, we may make choices that avoid certain kinds of adult education congruent with the vilified role.

Subjugation

Subjugation is the third way in which misogyny is expressed. It is an outcome of reification and vilification and is also the process that maintains them. Fundamentally, subjugation is about controlling women (Smith, 1989). At one level it operates under the guise of protection; at a second level, it is about suppression of women's unruliness.

The vision created by reification of the delicate woman with her lovely inferiority lends itself nicely to the view that women need to be protected. Softly veiled in the notion of love, misogyny survives as an "eroticized construct of inequality between men and women" (Hester, 1992, p. 198). Under the guise of "courtly romance" (Kahn Blumstein, 1977), the woman is reduced to an "emotional and intellectual non-person" (p. 311) who must be provided with security and safety.

Chivalry and courtly love "certify a male heroics that restores 'natural' sexuality and cultural stability" (Doane & Hodges, 1987, p. 20). These heroics reinforce women's role as the keepers of homes, which are sanctuaries of reasonableness and stability. In seeming harmony with this role, men are linked to presumably honourable notions of protection, defence and guardianship. Embedded within these terms, however, are repressive concepts of supervision, possession, custody and ownership. In other words, gallantry may be more motivated by men's desire to master women than it is by their desire to protect us (Kahn Blumstein, 1977).

Subjugation is expressed also through the suppression of women. In this instance, suppression is a reaction to the view of women as unruly and as a threat to men's greater power, authority and control. Since women are seen as potentially dangerous and in need of control, the task becomes to constrain us. This constraint can be acted out in both explicit and subtle ways. An obvious constraint of women is made through violence. The details of pornography, abuse, rape and murder fill our newspapers daily. These areas are increasingly well researched, analyzed and publicized as areas of women's suppression. It is a suppression that is effective because it generates fear, a deep fear that constrains women from breaking away from the norms, values, beliefs and behaviours deemed to be appropriate for a woman. It is based in force and discipline and presumes women's submission.

A more subtle form of subjugation also exists. It complements the more overt form and appears as a more social and acceptable exercise of power (Hawkesworth, 1990). It can be expressed as satires and jokes. These are frequently hidden behind criticisms of an admittedly obnoxious type of behaviour. Misogyny results, however, when no distinction is made between the admittedly obnoxious type and the particular woman. Satire is a particularly effective tool of repression, since it allows its authors to separate from an emotional bond with women and yet express anger, violence or patronage (Nussbaum, 1984). In the same vein, satires against women's failings or statements of our mental and moral differences from men become the basis of ostensibly harmless jokes (Kahn Blumstein, 1977; Nussbaum, 1984). Together, satire and jokes express sentiments of disrespect, dismissal and distrust. They are a canny way to limit, demean and stifle women's power.

There are many implications of subjugation for barriers to women's participation in adult education. Since subjugation is both the process and the outcome of misogyny, many of the implications have been noted in the discussions above. Courtly love may reduce women to an expectation that we will be grateful for chivalrous responses. It may restrict our sense of our own margins of freedom and of our breadth of choices. It may replace our own views with those of the supervising male who is presumed to be better placed to make caring decisions for us about what constitutes our "best" kind of participation in adult education activities. This form of subjugation also defines female-male relationships in a dualistic manner and further fosters the view that women and men have, or should have, different needs, desires and ambitions in relation to their participation in adult education.

The notions of protection and suppression foster a fear of repercussion. Jointly, they create a milieu in which it may appear unsafe to break away from stereotypical expectations, unsafe to venture into territories (both physical and intellectual) that are not a "woman's place," unsafe to challenge or threaten existing male norms, values, beliefs or hierarchies through our participation in adult education.

Conclusion

In this chapter I have explored the relationship of macro-level factors particularly related to gender and barriers to women's participation in adult education activities. I have based my analysis in a stark interpretation of the lived experience of those factors, namely misogyny. For the most part I have ignored the active agency of women. Although I have struggled to retain the idea of misogyny as a gender-neutral practice, much of the literature has forced me into presenting it as a male practice. I am aware that I have not explored the dynamic interplay and the shifting boundaries among the three elements of reification, vilification and subjugation. I am aware, too, that this chapter contains essentialistic and deterministic statements. Each assertion has called out to be softened by the complexities, variations, heterogeneity and differences inherent in it. Yet there is something within me which says that this chapter, at an important level, has it right. Perhaps it is the vision of that woman's battered face or the stories, too many to tell here,[2] that dovetail perfectly with these theorizations. Perhaps it is the congruency between the implications floated here and the studies that identify barriers such as "not enough time," "home responsibilities," or "not enough energy."

There is a perplexing incongruence in this chapter, however. As noted at the beginning, women throughout our history have been active participants in adult education as learners and leaders. If we accept even part of the above scenarios, these data become all the more remarkable. Women who pushed past the barriers of an oppressive misogynistic hegemony must have exhibited an incredible strength, forced themselves forward, refused to be used, dismissed or denied. They were able to differentiate between who they were and who others wanted and expected them to be. An important question for the future thus becomes: "Under what conditions and in what ways does a misogynistic hegemony prevent, inhibit or foster women's participation in adult education activities?".

As much as our generation might like to believe that the practice of misogyny no longer exists, it is unlikely that these deep rhythms[3] of our society are so easily erased. There is much to be gained by uncovering and confronting the real lived experiences of women in relation to misogyny. It gives us the opportunity to actively re-define the nature of women's participation and non-participation and to dismantle old barriers in new ways. Perhaps equally important, it gives us a new and deepened appreciation for those women in our past whose commitment and vigour strengthened the field.

Endnotes

[1] For a starting place, see A. Prentice et al., *Canadian Women: A History* (Toronto: Harcourt Brace Jovanovich, 1988).

[2] I am currently conducting an empirical study (at the University of Waikato, Hamilton, New Zealand) which parallels this paper.

[3] I am indebted to Michael Law (University of Waikato, Hamilton, New Zealand) for development of this concept through his own work on the radical traditions of adult education.

20

Learning from the Women's Movement in the Neo-Liberal Period

Angela Miles

A dult education has always been an enterprise too broad and diverse to be contained within any professionally defined field.[1] It is deeply rooted in all the projects of our lives and communities and in all our social, economic, political and cultural institutions. Self-education and mutual education are at the heart of all individual and collective activities, whether or not structured education plays a part; and where structured education is present, it is often done by "non-educators," by those who do not primarily identify themselves as adult educators. Nurse-educators, for instance, are generally nurses who educate rather than adult educators who nurse.

Much of the vitality and creativity of Adult Education as an academic discipline, professional field of practice and movement lies in the rich diversity among participants and their complex, multi-layered loyalties and locations. It is crucial to the health and relevance of Adult Education as a professional and academic field that we recognize, respect and foster this diversity. Our task is not to shape educators of adults in all their splendid variety into any single mould of "adult educator" or to assimilate them to any established professional identity. It is rather to keep our sense of Adult Education open and permeable to all its practice; to develop a multi-centred, dynamic sense of the adult education world, with no margins and no single centre; to provide for its practitioners spaces and contexts for critical reflection, research and skills development enriched by dialogue across the breadth of their heterogeneous experiences and perspectives. It is in these stretching exchanges that skills develop, knowledge is created and communicated and theoretical understandings emerge.

This chapter examines the current neo-liberal economic context of adult education and the significance of feminist knowledge and the feminist movement in these circumstances. A case will be developed for:

- an inclusive, dynamic and multi-centred conceptualization and practice of adult education; and
- the close association between Adult Education in the academy and adult education practice in diverse, non-professional contexts, in particular the context of social movements.

The Neo-Liberal Agenda and the Role of Adult Education

Much is said about the importance of adult education in the current neo-liberal context. This section addresses two questions: What is the neo-liberal economic agenda and its global effects? And, within this, how is the role of adult education conceptualized?

Modernization, Globalization and Neo-Liberalism

So-called progress or development not only brings an enormous increase in production and in the incomes of middle-class and working-class men (and the standard of living of their families) in the "developed" nations, it also brings relative and/or absolute deprivation to women and marginal groups and communities. The expansion of the market and of production for external exchange at the expense of production for local use has the impact of: (1) removing the means of subsistence from individuals and communities; (2) compromising sustainable production practices; (3) institutionalizing men's dependence on wages and women's dependence on men; (4) reducing human and non-human life to a commodity, valuable only in so far as it contributes to profit for a few; and (5) fuelling the concentration of wealth and power, ultimately in the hands of non-accountable transnational corporations.

The current neo-liberal economic agenda of "globalization" is an intensification of this process of homogenization, control and commodification. Everywhere, the exigencies of global competition and the global market are used to enforce policies that put priority on unfettered transnational profit making at the expense of people and the planet. The spectre of debt and deficit is used to impose these policies (called *Stabilization* or *Structural Adjustment Programs* (SAPs) in the South and *restructuring* in the North) throughout the world.[2]

In Canada, the federal government and most provincial and local governments are privatizing public goods, offering tax reductions to business, subsidizing highly capital-intensive production by large corporations and weakening environmental and labour laws, industry regulations, and pay equity programs and their enforcement. Cuts have been made to public broadcasting, health care, childcare, welfare, education and research, transportation, housing and other social services. At the same time, corporations are relocating production to cheaper, less-regulated venues and imposing wage reductions and drastic downsizing.

Centuries-old sustainable livelihood for local communities has been destroyed by the capital-heavy approach favoured by government policy. Succumbing to debts, family farms are being bought out by agribusiness in all regions. In-shore fisheries in the Atlantic provinces and on the West coast are no longer viable. The plight of those who do not share in the minority advantage of highly skilled, highly paid work is bleak indeed. Between 1972 and 1992 the value of the minimum wage dropped 48 percent. Dramatically altered criteria for unemployment benefits mean that in 1996 only 40 percent of jobless Canadians were eligible, compared to 87 percent in 1989. There were 51 percent more poor children in Canada in 1994 than in 1989. Such stories are legion and their impact cumulative.

The Role of Adult Education

Recognition of the importance of adult education is widespread these days, and not only among adult educators.[3] Within the neo-liberal context, adult education plays a dual role in both enhancing competitive competence and in containing its social costs. Competitiveness in the job market and the global economy requires that adult education become an integral part of individual and corporate life. At the same time, Adult Education is increasingly called upon to ameliorate the consequences of the very policies designed to support this competitiveness at the expense of the general population and the environment. Crisis mediation and management of the fall-out from the neo-liberal agenda have become central roles of Adult Education today as adult educators pick up the pieces of destroyed lives and communities.

General cut-backs in government spending have hit adult education along with other social and cultural areas, while corporations are increasingly providing education for employees within their own walls. Ironically, these developments threaten Adult Education in the academy despite the growing multi-faceted importance of adult education within the neo-liberal context.

One response to the tenuous position of adult education in the academy is to support current moves towards a situation closer to that of, for example, school teachers or social workers, where academic degrees are not just highly respected but are required qualifications for many jobs. A more systematically structured and credentialized field would ensure a continuing role for Adult Education in the academy and would greatly enhance the job value of an Adult Education degree for students. This would be an eminently sensible evolution if Adult Education's role were simply to fulfil growing government and corporate training needs. However, Adult Education's history and commitment in Canada has been larger than this.

As a field, we need to do more than serve the lifelong learning needs of those in demanding jobs and to go beyond the contingency agenda that simply ignores the structural underpinnings of the neo-liberal paradigm in its haste to offer literacy classes for those whom poverty and underfunded education has left without reading and writing skills; English as a second language classes for migrants and refugees displaced by the consequences of SAPs and the militarization required to force those policies on unwilling populations; "retraining" for fishers and farmers whose traditional livelihood has been destroyed and workers who have lost their jobs or young people who have never had jobs; support for women who have been abused by their partners and left destitute at the end of their relationships.

Adult Educators need to cultivate among themselves and those they are working with the critical capacity to understand the meaning of these educational needs and to envision how they might be overcome or supplied in a more just and life-enhancing world. In this period of transnational corporate ascendancy, when government policies (nationally and internationally) support the rapid concentration of wealth and power and the continuing impoverishment of communities and degradation of nature, it becomes particularly important to protect and enhance a critical and visionary capacity in the academy and the field. For without this capacity, individual adult educators can easily and unknowingly become tools in the implementation of unjust policies, and Adult Education as a professional field will be contained in and complicit with the destructive neo-liberal agenda.

The field would gain short-term protection at the expense of long-term relevance, power and integrity. The credentializing route holds this danger as it potentially ties the practice of the academy into a close and direct dependence on corporate and government hiring institutions in all matters, including curriculum and program. At the same time, it introduces a sharp qualitative difference between credentialized Adult Education practice and all other adult education, possibly narrowing the range of participants and breadth of dialogue and exchange. These developments would limit the autonomy and diversity of Adult Education in the academy, two elements that must be protected as fiercely as its physical and financial survival, or we will be left with only the husk of what we seek to preserve.

Social Movements: Sources of New Knowledge in Adult Education

To avoid this containment and retain an autonomous and progressive role, Adult Education in the academy must be able to challenge neo-liberal definitions and values and to envision alternatives. Social movements are important sources of new thinking and new knowledge for Adult Education. Indigenous, women's, Black, youth, farmers', fishers', workers', lesbian and gay groups as well as environmental, peace, community, health and literacy activists are (with many others) naming the costs, resisting the global neo-liberal economic agenda, and implicitly (or often explicitly) articulating alternative values and naming and/or creating new possibilities. If adult education in the academy is open to these diverse voices, it can make an important contribution by providing spaces for dialogue and mutual learning, by encouraging and legitimating the resulting research and by supporting its dissemination.

In order to do this, academic Adult Education must be physically accessible to these groups and be open to the major paradigm shifts they are proposing. This implies an Adult Education that is not simply about retraining workers, fishers and farmers to chase fast disappearing opportunities, but about working with these groups to challenge the commodification of land and sea and labour, to enhance protective labour and environmental legislation and workplace and community democracy in ways that move us towards a society that prioritizes human and non-human life rather than profit. It requires not just equal access to existing programs and credentials for Indigenous learners, women and people of colour but close and respectful attention and integration of Indigenous, women-centred and Afro-centric perspectives and values into Adult Education's core constructions of the world.

The Women's Movement

In the remainder of this chapter, some of the alternative values being articulated in feminism today will be briefly outlined, as just one example of the rich new thinking offered by and required of serious engagement with social movements, and of the crucial contribution of this thinking to Adult Education's ability to challenge neo-liberal ascendancy and retain an independence of self-definition and program.

Women in Canada and around the world are struggling for autonomy and equality—for equal access to education, employment, promotion and politics; for equal pay, equal respect and for the recognition of women's equal humanity. Achieving this will require major structural and value changes, for our current social and economic arrangements and dominant worldview institutionalize women's subordination.[4] The trivialization, marginalization and devaluation of the work, characteristics and concerns associated with women in patriarchal industrial society is currently being resisted by women everywhere. This women-defined, women-affirming movement is presenting a major challenge to the neo-liberal agenda, in particular its individualistic and competitive presumptions and its valuing of individual profit over human and non-human life.

Women's work around the world has always contradicted such market-oriented values and assumptions. Women have long done the unrecognized, traditionally unpaid, and now also poorly paid, nurturing and co-operative work of individual and community reproduction. Women's concerns and values across many diverse cultures and communities generally have been built around this life-sustaining work and responsibility.[5] Women's struggle for autonomy and equality is necessarily a struggle for the revaluation of their work and the life it sustains, and the generalization of responsibility and effort from women alone to the whole community.

Feminists are fighting for recognition of the value of the goods and services women produce in the home;[6] for men's equal participation in this work; for social support in the form of childcare, income support, health and education, housing and transportation services; and for decent wages for chronically underpaid "women's" clerical, service and caring work. At the same time, women in embattled communities in both the South and North are struggling to maintain traditional patterns of subsistence in the face of devastating development processes.[7]

Women's struggle for their rights is at the same time a struggle to transform social priorities and re-distribute social resources, all of which runs directly contrary to neo-liberal received wisdom which misleadingly equates prosperity with the "growth" of market production and transnational profit while condemning any resources that do not serve this end as insupportable "costs."

Hilkka Pietila has shown the falsness of these claims.[8] Her analysis reveals that, far from being the bulk of economic activity even in advanced industrial societies, production for international exchange is a tiny shell of activity around a large core of production for local use, a substantial amount of which is women's unpaid work. Pietila divided the Finnish economy into three spheres which she called Free, Protected, and Fettered and calculated the proportion of time spent and value created in each:

- The Free Economy, made up of all non-monetary production for local use, accounted for 54% of total work time and 35% of total value of production;
- The Protected Economy, which includes all production for the home market, including such services as transportation, health, and education, accounted for 36% of work time and 46% of value;
- The Fettered Economy, which is production for international exchange, accounted for only 10% of work time and 19% of value of production.

The tyranny of policies that sacrifice all other interests and needs to the dictates of international competitiveness becomes evident. Current neo-liberal policies and resulting globalization are revealed as a concentrated and ruthless attempt to capture ever more production for this sphere regardless of the huge social and environmental costs. Women are most at risk from these policies that belie their reality in the economy, and for this reason their resistance is strong all over the world. Their interests, in both the short and long term, require that the production for local use that Pietila demonstrated be recognized and supported as the major economic activity that it is, rather than sacrificed to enhance the competitiveness of production for international trade and the profit of a few. Women's empowerment requires a general shift towards life-centred values and social organization; at the same time, this shift requires the empowerment of women.

Feminists are not just seeking to be recognized as human like men, but to transform/feminize the dominant notions of humanity and the world, as the following quotation demonstrates:

> We refuse to enter that society on its own terms ... The human values that women were assigned to preserve [must] become the organizing principle of society. The vision that is implicit in feminism [is] a society organized around human needs ... There are no human alternatives. The Market, with its financial abstractions, deformed science, and obsession with dead things ... must be pushed back to the margin. And the "womanly" values of community and caring must rise to the centre as the only human principle (Ehrenreich & English, 1979, p. 342).

Patriarchal Western dualism historically constructs the world as a series of unequal opposites such as reason/emotion, mind/body, spirit/flesh, mental/manual, society/nature, public/private, production/reproduction, individual/community. The first set of each familiar pair is associated with maleness and humanity, and the second with its undermining. Feminists cannot simply claim humanity by abandoning their association with the latter set of each pair without accepting their devaluation. Instead they are posing alternative, holistic conceptualizations that reject the androcentric, hierarchical and separative logic at the root of these oppositions and revalue the much-maligned, female-associated side of each pair. For feminists, individuals realize themselves in community; the connection between society and nature can be honoured and fostered; reason and emotion are human capabilities which enhance each other. Flesh, the body, emotion, manual work, co-operation, nurture and community are integral, not inimical, to the full realization of individual human status. Concepts of humanity that exclude these elements are impoverished.

Life-centred feminist visions are thus grounded in alternative values whose very enunciation requires the re-definition of key concepts such as work, value, wealth, development and humanity. These are revolutionary re-definitions that are timely, appropriate and essential. Women are not born with these alternative understandings and values. Their articulation is the political achievement of a movement. In this struggle women are drawing on diverse women's work and embodied life experiences as resources in articulating holistic, egalitarian, and life-centred aspirations and possibilities.

I have written elsewhere about the daunting challenge this kind of transformative equal integration of women into Adult Education represents for the academy (Miles, 1989), despite its social justice traditions. Feminist vision and the women's movement is not easily integrated into a field that is threatened and co-opted by neo-liberal policy agendas. Adult educators must be vigilant that our responses to these external threats do not cut us off from women's new feminist knowledge and the knowledge of other groups who challenge this agenda.

Conclusion

In these times of increasing commodification, competition and globalization, the space for Adult Education to serve liberatory ends is under threat. Yet a vibrant and powerful network of social movements remains active in resistance and solidarity. It is from these diverse locations of community-based and movement-based education that Adult Education in the academy can draw fresh thinking and ideas. By being physically accessible and philosophically open to the new paradigms proposed by groups such as environmentalists, feminists, Indigenous peoples, Adult Education can be strengthened in its ability to challenge neo-liberal ascendancy and retain an autonomous self-definition that does not fall into the easy traps posed by credentializing and formalizing a field that is necessarily and preferably broad, diffuse and diverse. In this chapter, I have argued that the women's movement offers vast possibilities for such linkages. The critiques and the visions proposed by women throughout the world create spaces much needed by an embattled field that is historically connected to cultural and social life.

Endnotes

[1] I use "adult education" in lower case to refer to the myriad diverse activities of educating adults; "Adult Education" in upper case refers to adult education activities that are part of a distinct (professional and academic) field of endeavour, and the field itself.

[2] For a discussion of the genesis and impact of the debt crisis on the South and the role of trans-national capital, the governments of the North and such multilateral agencies as the World Trade Organization, World Bank, and International Monetary Fund, see Isla 1993a, 1993b. For a comparative description of SAPS in the South and restructuring in Canada and the North generally, see Isla, Miles & Molloy, 1996.

[3] The Premiers Council on Lifelong Learning, established by the NDP Government in Ontario in 1993, is just one example of this recognition.

[4] A widely cited United Nations' study has estimated that women do between 66 percent and 75 percent of work in the world, earn 10 percent of the earned income, and own 1 percent of the property.

[5] For a more detailed and fully argued presentation of this somewhat controversial claim, see Miles, 1996.

[6] Campaigns to gather data on housework in the census have been successful in Canada, one of the first countries to take this step. At the same time, women were successful internationally at the Fourth World Congress on Women in Beijing in 1995 in gaining a recommendation that governments' record the value of the goods and services produced in the home in addenda to their national income accounts.

[7] For feminist critiques of dominant forms of "development" or "maldevelopment," see Mies, 1986; Shiva, 1989; Bhasin, 1992.

[8] Waring (1988) reports this research on pages 300-301.

21

Senior Learners: Optimizing the Learning Community

Dorothy MacKeracher

An understanding of how a society values and treats its senior citizens tells us much about how that society values and treats all its citizens. An understanding of how we conceptualize senior learners and their learning tells us much about how we do the same for all learners. In this chapter characteristics of senior learners and two paradigms—one which currently exists and one which is emerging—are examined for understanding how we treat older adults and conceptualize them as learners. The existing (and predominant), welfare-based paradigm rests on paternalistic assumptions, hierarchical organizations and concerns about educational attainment and participation in formal programs; it views education as preparation for a competitive market-place and adult learning as the consequence of autonomous activities. The emerging, partnership-based paradigm rests on assumptions of equality, empowering partnerships and concerns about learning skills and interactivity in the home, workplace and community; it views education as preparation for a collaborative market-place and adult learning as a consequence of integrated and relational activities.

Lest you should mistakenly believe that this chapter about senior learners is not relevant to you or your understanding of adult education in Canada, remember that, by the year 2031, one in four Canadians will be a "senior learner." If you are between 35 and 55 years old in the year 2001, then you will be between 65 and 85 years in 2031, well within the life expectancy of the average Canadian. If you are younger, likely you will be working with senior learners.

Characteristics of Current and Future Senior Learners

Defining a senior learner is problematic because no single definition satisfies everyone. When Canada introduced universal old age security benefits, the term *senior* came to signify anyone sixty-five years and over (Chappell & Prince, 1994). The terms *senior* and *older* will be used interchangeably in this chapter and will refer, unless specified otherwise, to persons sixty-five years and older; the term *elder* will be reserved for those eighty years and older.

Canada's population is aging. The senior population has grown from 8 percent of the total population in 1951 to 12 percent in 1991 and is projected to reach 23 percent by 2031 (Statistics Canada, 1992). Desjardins (1993) contends that projections made in 1971 about the 1991 population underestimated the senior population by 8 percent. Thus it is possible that the one-in-four figure projected for 2031 is also underestimated. Canada's senior population is also aging. Those who are "elderly" (80 years and older) increased from 5 percent of the senior population in 1951 to 9 percent in 1991 and are projected to increase to 12 percent by 2031 (Desjardins, 1993). This aging of the older population will create new concerns for society.

Factors that help characterize older adults as potential learners include:

Gender ratio. There are many more women than men in the ranks of senior learners. On average there are seventy-two older men for every one hundred older women. Learning programs for older adults, therefore, should be designed with particular concern paid to accommodating women's learning preferences and needs.

Living arrangements. The majority of older women (59 percent) are unattached (i.e., single, separated, divorced or widowed), while the majority of older men (75 percent) are married (Statistics Canada, 1992). To accommodate those who are unattached or who live alone, learning programs for older learners should include a strong social component and should be offered at times and in places that encourage them to leave the security of their own homes.

Financial resources: More than 56 percent of older women and 38 percent of older men have low incomes composed of Old Age Security (OAS), Guaranteed Income Supplement (GIS) and, for some, Canada Pension Plan (CPP) (Statistics Canada, 1995). The combined OAS/GIS payment represents about 61 percent of the low income cut-off (or poverty) line for unattached persons living in large urban areas. Older couples and unattached older persons living in small urban and rural areas are somewhat better off (NACA, 1996). Thus the majority of older adults, particularly women, are unlikely to have the discretionary funds necessary to participate in educational activities for which fees must be paid, for obtaining essential transportation services or for purchasing learning resources.

Health status. About two-thirds of older adults describe their health as excellent or good, with reported health status declining with age (Statistics Canada, 1993). A more interesting characteristic is *disability*, a term defined as any restriction on normal daily activities. About 45 percent of all older adults report a disability, with 16 percent reporting a mild level (can perform daily activities without assistance), 15 percent reporting a moderate level (some restriction on daily activities) and 15 percent reporting a severe level (cannot perform daily activities without assistance) (Statistics Canada, 1994). The severity of disability increases with age and slightly more older women in all age groups report disabilities than older men (Statistics Canada, 1995). The most commonly reported disabilities are: mobility (74 percent), agility (65 per cent), hearing (42 percent), seeing (27 percent) and speaking (9 percent) (Statistics Canada, 1994).

The 55 percent of older adults who report no disabilities and the 15 percent who report a mild disability level are the most likely participants in learning activities outside the home. The remaining 30 percent may be interested in participating provided the learning activities could be conducted inside the home. Well-designed learning activities could and should assist older learners to compensate for their disabilities.

Cognitive impairment. The majority of seniors suffer <u>no</u> impairment in their abilities to attend, concentrate, think, remember, plan, decide or co-ordinate thought and action. The normal forgetfulness experienced by some older adults is not a symptom of cognitive impairment, which results from organic or physical disorders (for example, Alzheimer's disease, Parkinson's disease, stroke, alcohol or drug abuse or misuse) and/or functional or behavioural disorders (for example, depression, anxiety, fear, sleep problems). The best estimate is that, on average, between 5 and 10 percent of all older adults suffer from some form of cognitive impairment, with the average rate low among seniors in their sixties, rising to about 20 percent among those in their eighties (NACA, 1991). Cognitively impaired older adults often have other health problems and disabilities, and are unlikely to participate in organized learning activities.

Public Policy and Senior Citizens

In the first two decades of the twentieth century, older adults were supported through kinship and community-based networks. In the next three decades, urbanization, industrialization, economic conditions, and two world wars greatly reduced the family unit's capacity to support and care for its senior members (Chappell & Prince, 1994). In 1927, Canada introduced a means-tested old age pension for its most needy senior citizens; and, in 1951, universal OAS benefits for persons 70 years and over. With the subsequent introduction of the GIS (1960), the CPP (1965) and Medicare (1966), and the reduced eligibility age for OAS, spending on seniors increased to become the largest portion of the federal government's income security budget (Novak, 1993).

With the economic downturn of the last two decades of the century, questions were raised about universal entitlement to public benefits and the state's ability to support all its needy citizens. The hierarchical public organizations that manage the welfare state were seen as having marginalized those being served who came to rely on a secondary welfare system of food banks, emergency shelters and voluntary services. A health care system designed to deliver acute care services proved inappropriate for treating the chronic health problems of older adults, problems which respond better to improved self-care, fitness, prevention and community support services.

In 1972 Health and Welfare Canada developed New Horizons, a program to support community programs and services that help seniors meet needs beyond those addressed by medical services and social benefits. New Horizons funds partnerships between community-based organizations and senior-led and senior-dominated committees and groups. Funds must be used to support programs themselves rather than to meet the administrative costs of the partnering groups (Novak, 1993).

The success of the New Horizons program has led the government to rethink its methods for funding services to seniors. The new buzz words are *partnerships* and *empowerment* (Chappell & Prince, 1994). A partnership offers the government a means for serving the public better while spending fewer public dollars. Empowerment, from the government's point of view, involves fostering local solutions through policies that strengthen the mediating structures between individuals and the larger society. Large, remote, hierarchical and patriarchal organizations are out; local solutions to local problems through networking, mutual aid, self-help groups, volunteerism and community-based partnerships are in (Chappell & Prince, 1994).

This shift from paternalism to partnerships and from marginalization to empowerment has introduced new problems. The responsibility for funding support services for seniors has been shifted to local communities; but community-based services are shifting from publicly-funded, not-for-profit organizations to private, for-profit businesses, with increased competition for service dollars and reduced wages and benefits paid to, and training provided for, service workers. Services delivered in the home must be "purchased" by seniors who become, in effect, "employers" with responsibilities for hiring, supervising and indemnifying service providers, new skills for most older women (MacKeracher & Mersereau, 1995). Competition among service providers fragments the support networks available for seniors, networks that work best with multiple linkages among providers (Biegel, Shore & Gordon, 1984).

As the partnership-based paradigm emerges, many seniors have become frustrated by gaps in services, shifting expectations and incomprehensible means-based criteria for entitlement to public funding. Seniors are increasingly squeezed between the two paradigms as one replaces the other. Adult educators can help bridge the gap between the existing and the emerging paradigms through timely informative resources for both seniors and their families, well-designed learning programs for seniors and new service providers and participatory consultations to help communities improve services for their senior citizens.

Conceptions of Senior Learners

In the existing welfare-based paradigm, senior learners are defined and classified by their educational attainment. For example, anyone with less than a Grade 9 education is defined as "functionally illiterate," even though many persons within this group have good literacy skills. In 1991, 45 percent of older adults were reported as not having completed Grade 8 (Statistics Canada, 1993). If we accept this definition of "functional illiteracy," then we are apt to believe that nearly half of older adults probably have some difficulty writing letters, reading newspapers and magazines and using print materials to obtain information. Such learners probably will not participate in formal educational programs, particularly those that rely on print-based learning resources.

Furthermore, the educational institutions most likely to offer educational programs for older learners, the post-secondary institutions, are those in which the majority of senior learners, particularly the women, have little or no experience. Research suggests that the educational institutions in which learners have the most experience are those to which they turn for educational programs (Thomas, 1991).

Between 1 percent and 4 percent of senior learners participate in formal educational activities (Statistics Canada, 1993; Devereaux, 1985), with participation higher in western provinces than in eastern provinces, higher with increasing educational levels, higher for older women than older men in all provinces and higher for senior francophones than for senior anglophones (Denton, Pineo & Spencer, 1988). By the year 2010, a participation rate among older adults of between 7 percent and 10 percent has been predicted (Denton, Pineo & Spencer). However, the well-educated seniors I have encountered over the last twenty years inform me that, while they are interested in learning, they have little interest in the educational activities that typify formal educational institutions. In particular, they do not wish to become involved in activities that emphasize testing, grading and credentialling and that encourage competition among learners, traits which unfortunately characterize many post-secondary programs.

The emerging partnership-based paradigm places emphasis on the skills of individual learners, such as literacy skills, learning-to-learn skills and critical thinking skills, and on the informal learning activities taking place in the home and community. In 1989, Statistics Canada completed a survey of the literacy skills used in daily activities. Each participant was assessed at one of four literacy levels with Level 1 including those who were unable to read most print materials and Level 4, those who were able to meet most daily reading demands (Statistics Canada, 1991). The survey did not include adults older than seventy years, and the category of "older adult" included persons between fifty-five and sixty-nine years. Within this group, 36 percent were assessed as having major problems with literacy skills (Levels 1 and 2) and 64 percent as having minor or no problems with literacy skills. We can assume that if individuals seventy years and over had been included, the proportion assessed at Levels 1 and 2 would have been higher.

In contrast, only 10 percent of persons between thirty-five and forty-four years were assessed as having some problems with literacy skills while 90 percent had few or no problems. As succeeding age cohorts reach sixty-five years, the literacy skill levels of older adults will rise. However, the skills which typify the literate person today are different than those which typified literate persons fifty years ago; and there is every reason to believe that the skills required in the future will not be the same as today. Seniors invariably find themselves in the position of having literacy skills which may be unsuitable for new literacy tasks. Today's senior learners need literacy skills to ensure adequate access to health and pension-related information and resources; to assess information and reject what is misleading, inaccurate or irrelevant; to satisfy their own leisure needs; to be informed advocates; to keep abreast of the technological changes affecting their lives; and to act as informed consumers and supervisors of essential home-based services.

While their participation in formal educational programs is low, senior learners are more likely to participate in informal learning activities and community-based programs (Hiemstra, 1975; Merriam & Lumsden, 1985). For example, a 1991 study reported that among the people in its sample, 75 percent of older men and women obtained information about social and civic matters through radio and television (non-print media), while 25 percent preferred newspapers and magazines (print media); 11 percent used their local libraries; 57 percent worked on arts and crafts projects; 39 percent participated in the activities of various clubs and community centres; 23 percent attended plays and concerts, galleries and museums; and 14 percent learned through travelling (Statistics Canada, 1993).

If we focus on informal learning activities rather than participation in formal educational activities and on personal skill development rather than educational attainment, our perception of older adults will change from "functionally illiterate, non-participants" to "competent and engaged learners."

Educational Programs for Senior Learners

As part of the development of the welfare state, educational institutions took on some responsibility for supporting senior learners. In the 1970s, most educational institutions developed policies that waived tuition fees for senior learners wishing to enrol in university credit programs. However, even tuition waivers did not attract many senior learners into such programs (Novak, 1985). Few credit programs are designed to make the participation of senior learners easier. Many universities and community colleges developed gerontology programs for training younger and middle-aged learners to work with seniors and the elderly.

At about the same time, two national organizations emerged that encouraged a shift from a welfare-based to a partnership-based paradigm. The Canadian Association on Gerontology (CAG), formed in 1971, supports academic study and research into all aspects of aging, including education and learning, publishes the *Canadian Journal on Aging* and other materials and holds scientific and educational meetings. The National Advisory Council on Aging (NACA) was created in 1980 to advise the federal Minister of Health and Welfare on issues related to the aging of the Canadian population and the quality of life of seniors. The advisory board is composed largely of seniors representing each province and territory. NACA publishes position papers, special reports, other writings in gerontology, a thematic quarterly (*Expressions*), a statistical bulletin (*Info-age*) and other materials.

NACA's position paper on lifelong learning advocates a move to a partnership-based paradigm for developing learning activities for senior learners:

> The Council recognizes that many adult learning opportunities for older adults currently exist. Yet more needs to be done to adequately serve all seniors. NACA also considers that the involvement of seniors is vital in initiating, promoting and, in some instances, managing educational programs to ensure that their learning needs are met (NACA, 1990, p. 1).

By the 1980s, some post-secondary institutions were developing programs in collaborative partnerships with senior learners. A full review of the programs available across Canada is beyond the scope of this chapter.

Typical of partnership-based programs is Elderhostel, which began in the New England states in 1975 and was imported into Canada by the University of New Brunswick in 1980. The program was originally conceived as a combination of the European hostelling and Scandinavian folk school traditions.

Each program is designed to make the participation of senior learners easier and the programs more relevant to participants' interests and more accepting of their life experience.

Over time, the concept of Elderhostel grew well beyond the universities that spawned them and the original academic focus of the programs. Between 1984 and 1991, participation in Elderhostel programs in Canada increased 400 percent (NACA, 1993). By 1996, Elderhostel was an independent organization funded through fees paid by learners, with programs operating in all Canadian provinces and both Territories, in some fifty other countries and in more than eighteen hundred institutions. Each program is developed by an educational institution, voluntary agency or community organization with the advice of a committee of senior learners. Most programs are designed as residential experiences, which run from Sunday evening to Saturday morning, with relatively formal "classes" in the morning and early afternoon, and informal learning and social activities in the late afternoon and evening. Persons fifty-five years and over, who are retired or about to retire, can attend for a fee which, in 1996, averaged $400 per week, including room and board, all learning activities and some social activities (Elderhostel Canada, 1996). "Hostelships" are available for financially needy seniors.

Typical of the educational programs developed under New Horizons funding is Creative Retirement Manitoba (CRM). In addition to providing extensive learning opportunities for older learners, CRM uses seniors' talents to deliver talks to school children about Manitoba's history. Another CRM program, Homebound Learning Opportunities, meets the learning needs of homebound adults, 50 years and over, through visits from trained facilitators or a series of educational videos.

Other senior-organized groups act as advocates concerned about the quality of life of senior citizens and the impact of government policies on seniors' lives. The most active national advocacy groups are Canadian Pensioners Concerned, the Canadian Association of Retired Persons (CARP), One Voice—the Canadian Seniors Network, l'Assemblie des aînés et aînées francophones du Canada and the National Pensioners and Senior Citizens Federation.

Finally, new types of educational programs are emerging as more and more seniors become computer literate. Computer networking enables seniors to interact with their peers even when the Canadian weather keeps them homebound. Two sources of information about such programs are worth exploring: *Internet and E-mail Resources on Aging*, compiled by the Philadelphia Geriatric Center, offers a listing of a wide range of North American internet programs; and *Senior Computer Information Project (SCIP)*, operated by CRM, provides a website especially for seniors.

Since governments discovered the benefit of partnership programs, community-based learning programs have proliferated. Such programs are flexible, creative, responsive to the special needs of the community and often very practical. They tend to focus on expanding wellness rather than treating illness, encouraging interactivity and independence rather than passivity and dependence and thinking globally but acting locally.

However, such programs have some problems which are not immediately apparent to the uncritical observer. First, the founding group is usually composed of persons with common interests. The emerging organization may focus on these interests in a way which narrows its goals, thereby limiting long-term viability. This is particularly true when the focus is on a relatively new public issue (for example, elder abuse) for which long-term interest within the community is difficult to sustain.

Second, while the seniors involved have all the skills and interests necessary to organize programs for themselves, in the long run they need additional funding to purchase the necessary resources (for example, office assistance) to keep the program operating. While governments will fund start-up activities, they are loathe to get into long-term, core funding to maintain administrative activities. This problem, in turn, means that the organization must expend as much energy searching for new sources of funding as running the planned activity.

In addition to programmatic and financial concerns, for the seniors' group to be successful over time it must find ways to bring in new and younger members from the senior population. As founders of the group age, their personal resources for participating (for example, energy, funds, health) tend to decline and each person is able to do less and less. The work must be taken over by younger seniors with similar interests and skills. If the group was founded on narrow interests, finding new members may be difficult. Bringing in new members requires some administrative support, and if the organization has not been able to obtain core funding, the work of the founding members may come to naught in the long run.

Organizations run by older adults involve a paradox. While members have the energy and time in the immediate present to do the work of the organization, they often have less energy and time in the long term to sustain the work of the organization. Sustaining the organization always turns out to be harder than running the learning programs for which the organization was developed.

The Purpose of Learning Programs for Senior Learners

Sometime during the evolution of the welfare state in Canada, the purpose of publicly funded education shifted from the preparation of "educated persons" to the preparation of "productive persons." While it is difficult to point to policies which explicitly state this shift, there is considerable implicit evidence that learners, programs and institutions are increasingly being funded with an eye on the extent to which programs turn out "productive" citizens who can contribute to society in some way (Myles & Boyd, 1982). Government funds to support educational programs for older learners tend to go to those programs which can demonstrate, not that older learners become productive, but that, as a consequence of their learning activities, they make fewer demands on social and health care services.

Moody (1988) describes four patterns for providing education for older learners: rejection, social services, participation and self-actualization. These four patterns correspond to four different views of aging and later life. The rejection pattern views old age as a time of obsolescence and post-productivity. The perception that older adults are not contributing productively to society is accompanied by the assumption that they don't need to learn anything and there is little need to educate them. The social services pattern sees older adults as dependent and in need of services. In this pattern, education serves two purposes. First, educational activities fill time and give individuals private satisfaction; programs of this type are a very low priority for public funding. Second, education provides remedial instruction so that older individuals will be able to comply with societal expectations and medical treatment, thus requiring less public funding on expensive social and medical services. In the report on the 1990 Literacy Survey of Canada, the following statement reflects this type of thinking:

> It is important as aging people confront conditions of deteriorating health that they have the ability to read materials informing them of healthier practices ... Curative and acute health care also require literacy, such as being able to find proper medical services, reading prescriptions and other medical instructions, understanding what is available under provincial health care schemes, reading contracts and forms for extended health care services, and so on. *Expensive institutional care is the most likely alternative available for [illiterate] people unable to care for themselves* (Statistics Canada, 1991, p. 67, emphasis mine).

The welfare and social service patterns typify the educational approaches found in the welfare-based paradigm.

The participation pattern views later life as a time to take part in community life. Educational activities provide opportunities for such participation, assist older adults to continue to live independently in their own communities for as long as possible and help seniors develop new relationships with each other and with members of other generations. The participation pattern emphasizes interpersonal and inter-generational learning activities. The self-actualization pattern emphasizes individual development and sees old age as a time to develop wisdom through learning opportunities which can free the older person to discover new possibilities, leading to ego integrity and personal fulfilment (Erikson, Erikson & Kivnick, 1986). This pattern relies on individual learning projects which can be carried out alone or through collective activities. The participation and self-actualization patterns typify the educational approaches found in the partnership-based paradigm.

An underlying problem with the participatory and self-actualization concepts of learning and education is that, in spite of our humanitarian tendencies, many of us still have a sneaking suspicion that learning just for the sake of learning is an indulgence which only the wealthy can afford. Any older learner who learns on this basis must have money and therefore does not require funding. Further, the andragogical principles espoused by many adult educators (e.g., Knowles, 1968) may lead us to assume that learning without an immediate and practical application is somehow "impractical," even "immature" for an adult learner. Sinnott (1994) suggests that seniors who engage in broad exploratory learning are rarely offered opportunities by their societies to apply their new knowledge or skills to practical problems, thus perpetuating the myth that they are "impractical" and their learning activities are "inconsequential."

Conceptions of Seniors' Learning

The traditional view of learning is based on a dichotomy. "Mature" learning processes are perceived as involving non-emotional and objective forms of knowing, analytical and logical forms of reasoning and propositional forms of understanding leading to general, context-free principles; while "immature" learning processes are perceived as involving emotional and subjective forms of knowing, holistic and metaphoric forms of reasoning and narrative forms of understanding which seek to establish general themes that typify human life (Labouvie-Vief, 1990). In this tradition, teaching, instructing and training are perceived either as remedial processes which correct immature learning processes, or, more benevolently, as facilitating development from immature to mature learning. This view is consistent with the welfare-based paradigm. By claiming one type of learning as immature, a teacher or instructor can lock older learners into dysfunctional teaching-learning interactions which do not meet their needs.

Recent writers have suggested that this traditional view provides an incomplete view of human learning and a distorted view of the functions of the human mind. Such writers as Sternberg (1988) and Bruner (1986) propose that learning should be viewed as being grounded in the duality of both objective and subjective knowing, logical and holistic reasoning, propositional and narrative understanding. Labouvie-Vief (1990) reminds us that, although often in competition, subjective and objective forms of knowing "ideally function in a dialogic relationship [in which] one mode provides experiential richness and fluidity, the other logical cohesion and stability" (pp. 52-53). Integrated learning is both empirical and emotional, and is grounded in both abstract reasoning and concrete personal experience. Because it encourages learners to use personal experience, integrated learning is empowering and is easiest to develop in co-operative and collaborative relationships with other learners. The integrated view of learning is more consistent with the partnership-based paradigm.

In studying the cognitive skills of older adults, researchers tend to use measures which are consistent with logical reasoning and which draw on school-based information-processing skills. Schaie (1977-78) questions the use of such tests to assess the cognitive functions of middle-aged and older adults. He reasons that if the tests are consistent with the school contexts in which younger persons function, then they are inconsistent with the family, work and community contexts within which middle-aged and older adults function. Since that time, researchers have reconsidered their understanding of seniors' cognitive abilities. For example, Berg, Klaczynski, Calderone and Strough (1994) report on research which tested younger and older typists and found that, while the older typists showed a decline in specific cognitive abilities associated with typing (for example, memory span and reaction time), they demonstrated no overall decline in typing ability. The older typists adopted strategies which allowed them to compensate for specific losses, such as anticipating words to be typed. Labouvie-Vief (1990) tested older and younger adults on their ability to recall stories to determine whether recall style could account for the poorer memory performance of older adults on text-processing tasks. She found that younger respondents tended to recall the propositional content of the story, content well suited to the scoring schemes used to measure text-processing tasks. Older respondents, however, tended to use an interpretive strategy to recall the metaphorical and psychological implications of the story, content which was not measured in the scoring scheme. Labouvie-Vief argues that the interpretive or narrative style has adaptive significance for older adults by providing a more efficient means for storing and transmitting information to other generations.

The conclusion of these and other researchers (e.g., Baltes & Smith, 1990; Sinnott, 1994) is that, while some age differences in performing cognitive tasks can be perceived as evidence of cognitive deficits, the different strategies used by older adults may have adaptive functions in old age which have not yet been identified. If, as educators, we assume that the cognitive strategies used by seniors represent deficits we are likely to encourage them to correct these deficits through training or we may simply give up working with them as learners. Both approaches are consistent with the welfare-based paradigm and Moody's rejection and social service patterns for delivering educational services. If, on the other hand, we view seniors' cognitive strategies as adaptive for old age, then we are more likely to use our understanding of these strategies to help individual older learners capitalize on their strategies, an approach consistent with the self-actualizing pattern; or to re-design our programs to encompass these strategies in working with groups of older learners, an approach consistent with the participation pattern (Moody, 1988).

Research into women's and men's ways of learning and reasoning (Baxter Magolda, 1992; Lyons, 1987) indicates that a focus on autonomous and independent learning behaviours, a focus associated with objective knowing, analytical and logical reasoning, and propositional understanding, tends to facilitate the learning of more men than women. Since we know that the majority of older learners are women and that older learners frequently use narrative knowing for making sense of text-based information, we can assume that facilitating strategies which encourage autonomous and independent learning behaviours may be counter-productive for most older learners, most especially for senior women (Sinnott, 1994).

Optimizing the Learning Community for Senior Learners

We need to design programs, in partnerships with older learners, using an integrative view of learning. What follows are some salient points to keep in mind when working with senior learners:

- Competitive, individualistic approaches to learning run counter to the developmental goals of senior learners. We need to avoid teaching seniors as if they were identity-creating adolescents or identity-maintaining younger adults. Rather we should work with them as selves-in-relation or selves-in-interpersonal-contexts, as contributing and integral members of families, communities and cultures. For example, most senior learners need dialogue with small groups of learners or one-to-one interactions with someone who can facilitate their learning.

- Learning activities designed for and with senior learners need to observe at least two of Kidd's three R's (relevancy, relationship and responsibility) (Kidd, 1960). Content should be relevant to seniors' current and future needs and interests. Service providers cannot know about such needs and interests unless they interact through partnerships with the senior learners they serve. Relevant content is more easily connected to and integrated with existing knowledge. Relationship refers to both the need to use past experience as a resource for current learning and the need to learn in relationships with others. Connecting past experience to current learning takes longer for senior learners than for younger learners because they have more experience to examine reflectively and their knowledge tends to be more integrated.

- Learning activities need to use senior learners' strengths rather than attempting to remediate their deficits. For example, learning should never be equated with memory or speed of response. At the same time, the learning environment and activities need to be adjusted to compensate for such age-related changes as declines in visual and auditory acuity and such chronic conditions as loss of mobility and agility. For example, seniors with even minor declines in auditory acuity are rapidly demotivated in poor acoustic environments. Excessive noise, white "noise" (for example, from electrical appliances), and poor seating arrangements all exacerbate hearing problems.

- Facilitating activities that do not work well with senior learners are those which attempt to maintain objectivity through adopting a frame of reference centred solely on a discipline (for example, history, political science) or an authority figure (for example, the instructor) to the exclusion of other disciplines or authorities, or which lie outside the context of the seniors' personal experiences.

- An exclusive focus on instrumental learning or technical knowledge to the exclusion of communicative learning or practical knowledge is dysfunctional for all adult learners, and particularly so for senior learners.

- Narrative understanding lends itself to autobiographical and story-telling activities which in turn are essential components of life-renewing and self-confirming activities for all adult learners, most particularly for senior learners (Birren et al., 1996). When such activities lead to writing and publishing stories, younger generations also benefit.

Conclusion

If, by now, you have come to the conclusion that improving learning opportunities for senior learners is not vastly different than improving learning opportunities for all learners, then you have reached the same conclusion I have. Research and experience tell us that, in the area of public policy for seniors, we need to integrate the welfare-based and partnership-based paradigms in order to provide a co-ordinated continuum of appropriate services. In the area of learning opportunities, we need an integrative view of learning if we are to understand how best to work with senior learners.

We, that is those who work with senior learners to develop a learning community, need to become more aware of the assumptions which underlie our attitudes and actions. We need to keep in mind that senior learners were us ten, twenty or thirty years ago; and we, the service providers and facilitators, will be them in the rapidly approaching future. Words and actions which separate them from us and us from them are just as likely to create obstacles as poor transportation services, means-tested eligibility criteria, educational fees, poor scheduling, administrative red tape and hearing difficulties. We need to see them and us as an integrated, whole group, the parts of which may vary in age and expertise but which must function interdependently if we are to optimize the learning community for all group members.

22

Spiritual Lessons from the Antigonish Movement

Marie A. Gillen

Adult education has evolved through efforts to assist people in their search for a better life. What people need in order to achieve a better life was and still is related to the context in which they live. Early adult educators addressed the spiritual needs as well as the economic and social needs of people. In an always changing world, these needs also seem to change, yet aspects of life at the end of the twentieth century are surprisingly similar to aspects that characterized the early part of the century. People's search for values to which they can remain faithful, values that remain constant, is a spiritual aspect of living in a complex society that changes rapidly.

We are living in times whose materialistic and temporal context confounds individuals who seek a vision of a full life to which they can be faithful. Throughout our society today, there is a rising interest in spirituality and a remarkable level of faith in God, even as attendance at traditional places of worship declines (*Maclean's*, July 1, 1996). This search for a vision of life that transcends contemporary social conventions is not unique to the current decade.

Historical Background

The Antigonish Movement of the late 1920s and early 1930s was founded at a time when people in eastern Nova Scotia were searching for a way of overcoming obstacles they encountered in their everyday life. The movement was founded by educators at St. Francis Xavier University, Father Jimmy Tompkins and Father Moses Coady, who had a deeply religious, humanitarian perspective. They advocated a non-formal approach to education; they wanted to "help the people to build greater and better democratic institutions than we ever had before" (Coady, 1939, p. 3). The main thrust of the Antigonish Movement was education for economic development through projects such as co-operatives and credit unions (Brookfield, 1984; Cameron, 1996; Laidlaw,

1961). However, both Tompkins and Coady believed that the Antigonish Movement should meet the spiritual as well as the material needs of persons:

> We have no desire ... to create a nation of mere shopkeepers ... We want our people to look into the sun and into the depth of the sea ... We want them to live, to love, to play and to pray with all their being ... Life for them shall not be in terms of merchandising but in terms of all that is good and beautiful, be it economic, political, social, cultural, or spiritual (Coady, 1939, p. 163).

In the last fifty years or so, the field of adult education has gradually become professionalized and its grassroots aspect has diminished (Collins, 1991; Welton, 1987). Its former aspirations for social change have been replaced by a focus on individual change. As Merriam and Cafferella (1991) lament, today there exists a gap between the adult education rhetoric of access and equal opportunity and adult education practice and outcomes. Government funding today is often tied to adult education activities that support job training and basic skills, confining adult education to a relatively narrow sphere. Collins (1991) concurs. He considers current mainstream adult education practice to be so preoccupied with individual learners and their deficiencies that it neglects to critique the social system, thus unwittingly supporting the status quo in society and perpetuating a social system that is creating an impoverished way of life for many Canadians.

The Antigonish Movement relied on practical educational activities, such as mass meetings, living-room study groups, kitchen meetings and community refresher courses. The essence of its philosophy is contained in six principles. In this chapter the importance of continuing these principles in adult education today is examined, in particular two of them—the primacy of the individual and education through group action—as an integrated concept. Unfortunately, adult education has tended to segregate these two principles into two educational domains, with emphasis on the individual in the formal domain and emphasis on group action in the non-formal domain. I believe the integration of these two principles is important to the development of the spiritual aspects of adult education. This chapter also examines how reforms can occur. I argue that effective reforms require fundamental changes in social and economic institutions. Also examined are the spiritual dimensions of a full and abundant life for everyone.

Social, Economic and Religious Context

The strong connection between adult education and spiritual concerns is well grounded in Canadian history and eloquently expressed by the words of Moses Coady (1943):

> We are thankful that in the whole course of our Canadian history we have had a religious and pious people. God meant in a special way that the Canadian people should be good. He showed it in the very creation of the land we have inherited. Canada is a great terrestrial cathedral. The mosaic of the Maritimes is

its facade. Its nave and aisles are the long corridors of Quebec and Ontario. Its transept is the great prairie provinces. Its sanctuary is the coastal province of British Columbia. Its high altar is the Rocky Mountains over which hangs the white baldachino of its snowy peaks. The colourful background of this sanctuary is the verdant slopes of the west coast merging into calm and blue Pacific. We are living in a terrestrial temple. To keep it undefiled and exclude everything that is unholy—this is our manifest historic destiny (pp. 81-82).

The pioneers in the field of adult education, consciously or not, drew on thousands of years of religious thought in formulating their operational principles and sets of assumptions. They realized that all citizens of Canada should have the opportunity to develop socially, morally and spiritually and to benefit economically. Their ideas were not the product of only their generation but grew from our past. The ideals of justice, service, caring, co-operation and the dignity of the person are the bedrock on which the field of adult education is built.

The Antigonish Movement was linked to the spiritual aspects of adult education by several factors: Moses Coady and Jimmy Tompkins were Catholic priests; the movement began in a small Catholic college, St. Francis Xavier; it was built on a solid base of Christian beliefs and precepts; and the Catholic clergy of the diocese were keenly aware of the great economic and social changes taking place and wanted their diocesan college to develop an educational program for the benefit of the common people. However, Coady did not see the movement as a specifically Catholic movement. In fact, the Antigonish Movement was not affiliated with any single religious denomination, although certainly its founders drew from the wisdom of their religious past.

Coady reminds the reader in his book *Masters of Their Own Destiny* (1939) that the Christian church embraced the philosophy of pagan Aristotle, not because it was Christian but because it was a philosophy grounded in a system of principles for guidance in leading the good life. He believed the movement should address both the spiritual and material needs of persons and that these needs should not be compartmentalized but rather be integrated. He also believed that every social problem is an educational problem. As he explained, "Education goes beyond economics. It is as comprehensive as life itself" (Coady, 1943, p. 16).

The Antigonish Movement provided a channel through which poor Cape Breton farmers, fishers and workers gained control over their lives and brought about social change. It provides an excellent example of the radical vision, scope and practice of early adult educators (Delaney, 1985; Laidlaw, 1961). The movement grew quickly in its early years, and news of its success rapidly spread across Canada and beyond, where it inspired others to organize to help themselves and to achieve collective aims. The movement is an excellent example of adult education with a spiritual foundation.

During the time the Antigonish Movement was developing and flourishing, other activities involving adult education also were underway in Canada, leading to the formal establishment of the Canadian Association of Adult Education (CAAE) in 1935. Edward "Ned" Corbett was the first director. Selman (1995) characterizes him as "one of the great charismatic leaders in Canada" (p. 121) and a man who had "strong views about society and the role adult education should play in moulding it" (p. 122). Like Coady, he had a strong theological background, but he had decided after graduating from a Presbyterian theological college that the ministry was not for him. He continued to be passionately driven throughout his career by the social gospel teaching of his theological days, during the same period as Coady struggled to put into practice the ideas presented in the social encyclicals of the Catholic Church. Coady and Corbett found in each other kindred souls. Between 1935 and 1959, thanks to the efforts of these two men and other pioneers, the social dimension of adult education thrived.

Adult education in Canada has flourished over the years, and has "gained a considerable reputation internationally for imagination and excellence" (Selman, 1995, p. 63). This growth, however, has had negative as well as positive consequences. Collins (1990) and Welton (1987) contend that adult education has lost its way, has lost sight of what Coady referred to as the "big picture" (MacLellan, 1985). Today co-operative values of self-help, self-sufficiency, democracy, equality and solidarity are threatened, and values of honesty, openness, social responsibility and caring for others are being called into question by business and government leaders who view any threat to profit and control of the economy with dismay and disfavour.

Co-operative values are the spiritual roots of adult education. Like the good seed in the gospel parable of the sower, these roots have been planted in fertile ground by pioneers such as Corbett, Tompkins and Coady and fortunately continue to flourish in the minds and hearts of many who today are trying to pull together for the common good. Witness the work going on in soup kitchens, food banks and volunteer agencies, not to mention fundraising for worthy causes and community involvement in the running of hospital boards and school boards. People are cutting across political and ideological lines to find pragmatic solutions to their problems.

Adult educators can assist people to make sense of and act on the personal, social, occupational and political environments in which they live—either in formal or informal educational settings. By helping people to help themselves and others through educational interventions, the adult educator helps to foster values such as justice, charity, mercy and a sense of togetherness. One reason volunteerism is attractive today is because it has spiritual significance.

Table 22-1: Six Principles of the Antigonish Movement

1. The primacy of individual needs—such needs to be met and capacities to be developed in social contexts.

2. The root of social reform lies in education.

3. Individuals are most concerned with economic needs—therefore education must start with the economic dimension of life.

4. Group settings are those most suitable to education.

5. Social reform both causes, and is dependent on, basic change in social and economic institutions.

6. A full self-actualized life for all in the community is the aim of the movement.

Summarized by Laidlaw, 1961, and Conger, 1974; see Brookfield, 1984.

Primacy of the Individual within Group Action

The principle of the primacy of the individual is based on both religious and democratic teaching: religion emphasizes the dignity of the person, created in the image and likeness of God; democracy stresses the value of the individual and the development of individual capacities as the aim of social organization. As Coady (1945) put it, "Any sound philosophy should teach that education is an instrument to unlock life to all the people" (p. 10). He dispelled the notion that the rise of the masses meant the demise of the rich; to the contrary, the good life for all in an age of mass production made sense from a humanitarian as well as business perspective. He continues, "but this worldly consideration should not be the chief reason for our solicitude for giving the good and abundant life to the people." He explains that "the spiritual and cultural life of the nation depends upon it." He put great emphasis on the balance between the economic and the spiritual and constantly strove to harmonize the two dimensions. "Any people who rise high in the realization of their possibilities and have symmetry in their development," he said, "will be a great people and will achieve a great civilization" (pp. 10-11).

Coady rooted his philosophy in a solid conviction in the essential goodness of democracy and its role in liberating the human spirit. He had unwavering faith in God, faith in people and faith in the power of ideas. He challenged people to move from the economic, through the social, to the cultural, esthetic and spiritual.

Today many adult educators feel the principle of the primacy of the individual has led to intense individualism and that people no longer know how to create, maintain or protect community. How can one promote respect for both individuals and community? Somerville (1996) suggests that the world needs a new form of individualism that will articulate individual responsibility equally with individual rights. She says, "Our strong focus on individual rights in the recent past was necessary and has achieved great good." She then cautions that in losing "sight of the correlative requirement of individual responsibility, not just as individuals and to individuals, but also to the intangible reality of community itself," people have lost sight of some fundamental truths. She believes the Canadian challenge is to "evolve and develop an integrated structure that will accommodate both individual rights and individual responsibilities such that [we] will promote respect for all individuals and will be able to form community at whatever level this is required, whether in our families, cities, our country or our planet" (p. 8).

Humans are social beings, and thus group action is a natural choice. People commonly are organized into groups, and their problems are usually group problems. Any effective adult education program must therefore fit into this group organization of society. Moreover, group action is essential to success under modern conditions; one cannot get results in business or civic affairs without organization. The challenge faced by adult educators today is how to integrate the individual and the collective.

Habits for the Heart: Individualism and Commitment in American Life (Bellah et al., 1985) asks questions such as, How ought we to live? and Who are we, as citizens of wherever? Although the authors did not address the diversity of citizens found in the United States and Canada today, focusing instead on those people who have traditionally dominated American culture, the book offers many ideas for thought on the integration of the individual and the collective. In brief, Bellah et al. point out that the ideal of the self-made person, in which the self is the centre of wants and the definer and evaluator of what is good, has run its full course. This ideal resulted in a separation between the private and the public, the material and the spiritual, the past and the future. To change such habits of the heart, Bellah et al. call on religious and civic groups to engage citizens in ways to link together the life of the individual to the community and to the consideration of the common good.

Similarly, Fowler (1982) acknowledges that growth towards a mature self and a mature faith involves a stage of independence and self-ordering. He cautions, however, that one can get stuck in this stage and not move on to the next stages of openness to diversity within the community and to seeing the universal within the specific. The challenge to religious and public institutions is to create adequate structures and strategies for helping people give up the myth of their detached and independent lives and to establish new (or renew old) habits of the heart that value intimacy, diversity, compassion and an unreserved adherence to the common good.

Effective Reform Involves Fundamental Changes in Institutions

Coady (1939) refers to the "great default of the people" (p. 17), meaning their blindness to the economic system in which they live. The consequences of living within this system have been loss of dignity and "poverty of thought and inspiration" (p. 22). Coady deplored the indifference and lack of foresight in people who relinquished their consumer rights, became victims of ignorance and exploitation and of big business. He called for a rebuilding of the economic system, and viewed this task as formidable because "there will be mind-sets to be broken—habits to be changed" (p. 25).

The establishment of the extension department at St. Francis Xavier University in 1930 was a pivotal event in the university's history and a departure from its rather elitist previous position. This shift involved fundamental changes, and so it was no surprise that Coady, as the new department's first director, faced opposition and difficulties as he moved forward Jimmy Tompkins' ideas, first set out in a pamphlet entitled *Knowledge for the People* (1921). Many people, however, supported the university's efforts, as bold programs were conceived and carried out. Coady's approach was anything but gentle and participatory, as he himself attests: "To blast these minds into some real thinking is the first work of the adult educator" (1939, p. 32). This was not the time for needs assessments. As Brookfield (1986) noted many years later, people like Coady were right, given the context in which they worked. Simply responding to the felt needs of people unaware of alternatives would be "to condemn such adults to remaining within existing paradigms of thought and action" (p. 124).

Coady was a mover and a shaker. He worked with great vigour in mobilizing the people through adult education and involved himself in fundamental changes in institutions. As the movement spread, consumer co-operatives and credit unions were formed and co-operative marketing was established. Coady fostered material success, but he never lost sight of the spiritual: "the great accomplishment of the new age will be to restore the spiritual by using the material as it ought to be used, a means to a higher end" (1939, p. 143).

Today, as the world at large is struggling, so too are religious organizations. Many believers are striving to give form to a renewed model of the faith community that can provide hope and inspiration for humankind. In 1993, the Canadian Conference of Catholic Bishops released a report based on the findings of a broad consultation with many people and groups across Canada involved in adult faith development. The report pointed out that work with adults is on the cutting-edge of a new movement with the church; it also stated that there are "challenges calling forth more commitment and creativity in the way we meet the faith development needs of adults" (p. 5).

A Full and Abundant Life for Everyone

When the prosperity era of the 1920s collapsed in a spectacular manner in 1929, many people were left living in poverty and misery, in insecurity and fear, able to concern themselves only with the grim struggle to survive. Coady and Tompkins were well aware that the hardships the rest of the country experienced during the Depression years had been going on in eastern Canada for a long time. The quality of life of those who caught fish, planted seed or mined coal was deplorable. In 1929, when Jimmy Tompkins was sent to Canso as parish priest, he found poverty and despair. His bedraggled constituency were good people but also were ignorant, passive and diseased. Before he could preach and prod about the full and abundant life, he had to feed and clothe. He had to get the people reading and thinking. Slowly, the ideas of co-operative ownership took hold as the people began building their own factories, processing their own lobsters and establishing a credit union and a co-operative store. Tompkins put it strongly and eloquently: "Ideas have hands and feet, they will work for you. Have faith. Work together. You can't teach an old dog new tricks. But lobstermen are not dogs. They are men. And men [sic] can read and think and learn new ways as long as they live" (Tompkins, see Arnold; last page, pages unnumbered). Coady was adamant that Christian leadership should work towards improving the prevailing economic and social order. To neglect these issues was a great danger, causing an erosion of confidence of the people. They would rationalize that if Christian leadership failed in addressing the economic problems that were obvious to the people, then why should the people have any confidence in those who preach spiritual doctrines one cannot see or understand? Coady (1943) cautioned, "History confirms us in the conviction that if religion and Christianity are to flourish we must not overlook the well-being of men [and women]. We should learn well its lessons" (p. 6).

Coady's idea of the full and abundant life for everyone was based on a belief that a person's life cannot be compartmentalized. He believed in a vital and intimate connection between a person's material livelihood and the spiritual question of saving their souls. "Fixing up the economic," asserted Coady, "is a main way and perhaps the only way to ensure law and order and decency and religion in the world" (Cameron, 1996, p. 230). This perspective, which unites the material and the spiritual, calls for a broad education that foremost takes into consideration the spiritual and moral formation of a person and then all the other dimensions: the physical, intellectual, social, civic, vocational, domestic and aesthetic. All these parts have an organic connection so that the neglect of one affects and is affected by the others.

Griffin (1988) compares the neglect of a holistic approach to learning to playing a guitar with just one string. She calls attention to the limitations of such an approach and suggests learners would learn more fully by using more than their rational capability; by drawing on their five other capabilities as well: relational, emotional, physical, metaphorical and spiritual. She makes clear that one's spiritual capability does not necessarily develop out of a religion and is often difficult to define. Spiritual capability is best understood in terms of its characteristics: "Spirituality is an awareness, wonder, deep sense of awe of the present, the potential, of person or nature. It is an awareness and awe of connectedness of what is and what could be. It includes your vision of what could be for yourself—your purpose in life—for others, for nature" (p. 121). Spirituality has inner and outer dimensions. It provides a link between a person's inner life and the infinite. Miller (1983), in his discussion of transcendence and spirituality, points out that spirituality is "experienced through relationships—relationships which form a whole" (p. 164). This wholeness is what leads to the full and abundant life for all. One task for the adult educator is to make a difference; that is, to work towards a full and abundant life today.

The trend to community is very much the Canadian way, harkening back to the days when our ancestors colonized the land. Today people are trying to pull together for the common good. Never before have communities and organizations in Atlantic Canada been at such a point of profound change. Government restructuring, growth of trans-national corporations, technology and globalization are affecting the economy and health, education and social services. These changes, in turn, are affecting rural, urban and ethnic communities and influencing unions, co-operatives, and religious and community organizations.

In the midst of all this chaos, adults need a vision of the full life to which they can be faithful. Vision, as the prophet Habakkuk points out, is not static but rather needs to be alive—a dynamic, vibrant force propelling all to a common end. It requires the individual to integrate with the collective.

Some Thoughts about the Future

Almost sixty years separate the thoughts on the future that Coady (1939) and Selman (1994) express, but the similarity of their ideas is striking. Both men refer to the continued growth of the field, the significance of lifelong learning, the importance of releasing human energy, the opportunities for colleges and universities to move the field ahead, the creation of great and good citizens, a vision based on hopes and expectations and global peace, grounded in the passion of individuals and groups who care and who view adult education as a force for achieving this goal.

This vision for the future points out enduring questions and calls for a holistic approach to adult education. It is one that invites balance among the various aspects of a person's life: economic, political, cultural and spiritual. The spiritual part of people is their soul, the animating principle that gives them life; it is the essential part of their being. As adult educators continue their search for the full and abundant life for everyone, especially "in those places in our society where the struggle for social betterment intersects with the knowledge and empowerment which can flow from adult learning" (Selman, 1994, p. 226), addressing the spiritual aspects of adult education remains a perennial challenge. The answer might be in the search itself, for as Coady tells us, "the formula by which the good society of the future can be built will be found when we discover how to release from commonplace relationships of man to man the forces that lies hidden in them." Coady continues this thought in his usual poetic way: "When we do this, we can put a universal rainbow on the social horizon that will flash a ray of hope to all mankind" (see Laidlaw, 1971, pp. 194-5).

> What is wrong with the world now is that there are too many obstacles in the way of sanctity. We have to remove these and build in the world a runway where the whole human race can take off to new flights of culture and spirituality ... It's going to call for a deep and unalterable faith in the eternal truths and a courage that is seldom found in the world of today. We need something more than little innocent activities within the framework of present society ... We need a new dedication and a new sense of realism (taken from an address by Moses Coady to the Catholic Women's League, June 30, 1953; see Laidlaw, 1971, p. 191).

23

English As a Second Language for Adult Immigrants

Barbara Burnaby

Immigration has been and still is a central part of Canada's existence. About 97 percent of the current population is descended from people who came here after 1500. The majority are of British or French origins, but in 1991, 31 percent of the population reported their origins as neither British nor French (Statistics Canada, 1993). Recorded immigration levels have fluctuated greatly over the years from a high of more than 400,000 in 1913 to fewer than 8,000 in 1942 (Whitaker, 1991). Current levels are about 200,000 per year. According to the World Refugee Survey of 1992, Canada has the highest proportion among the countries surveyed of re-settled refugees in its population (one refugee to 82 in the general population compared, for example, with the United States at one per 171; Immigration Canada, 1992a). In the 1991 Census, 13 percent of the population stated that their mother tongue was other than English or French (Statistics Canada, 1992) and about 1 percent reported speaking neither English nor French (Statistics Canada, 1993, p. 1).

In the current enterprise of adult education in Canada, then, the teaching of official languages to newcomers has a role. What that role is depends on several factors, including the pressure by the majority society for the use of official languages, the extent that newcomers are prepared (in several senses of the word) to learn the new languages, and opportunities and conditions provided to support such learning. In this chapter, the teaching of English as a second language (ESL) to adult immigrants is considered. I do not address the teaching of a *second* official language to Canadians who already speak one (for example, English to francophones) because that undertaking is greatly regulated and supported under provisions following from the *Official Language Act* (1969 and subsequent) and is carefully kept apart in policy from the learning of a *first* official language by immigrants (Burnaby, 1996). Nor is the teaching of French to immigrants in Quebec or elsewhere included, because although its history is in many ways similar to that of ESL in English-speaking Canada, it has also had special circumstances and events too complex to cover within the scope of this chapter (D'Anglejan & De Koninck, 1992).

Despite these exclusions, there is plenty to consider here. The needs of and provisions for adult immigrants learning English include specific consideration for:

- those recently arrived
- those in a wide variety of work situations
- those entering or re-entering post-secondary education
- those starting literacy for the first time
- those undergoing cultural adjustment to the new country legally, economically (for example, as consumers) and civically (for example, getting citizenship and taking part in governing systems)
- those facing life changes (for example, mothers with pre-school and school-aged children facing relations with the school system, women recently widowed, older immigrants in retirement).

Language training provisions for such a range of learning are highly complex and virtually unco-ordinated; therefore, the description of the field here is made with examples rather than a comprehensive picture of the variety and extent of the coverage.

Language learning, like most other kinds of learning, usually has a period of intense concentration of effort and then a lifetime of further learning from experience at a slower pace as changing environments offer new data and challenges. Most learning of English by non-English-speaking immigrants takes place in informal contexts without the benefit of any instruction. As Alan Thomas has said, "The educational enterprise in Canada, as in other countries, floats in a sea of learning" (Thomas, 1987, p. 109). This is certainly true of adult ESL in Canada, and we must acknowledge and value the vast amounts of language learning immigrants achieve in their efforts to manage and succeed in our country. Our governments and citizens, especially in earlier times, have taken this factor for granted and have assumed that, for the most part, immigrants will either learn official languages on their own without the public expense of training them or suffer the consequences of isolation and exploitation. The following description, therefore, is of the small amount of formal training offered to immigrants for language learning relative to the vast amounts they accomplish on their own.

The chapter is organized in two parts. First, an historical sketch of major periods in ESL in Canada from Confederation until the present is offered, followed by a discussion of ESL for adult immigrants in relation to the whole field of adult education, paying special attention to relationships to adult basic education and/or literacy.

Confederation to World War II: Non-Governmental Organizations

Discussions on the history of Canadian public services usually start with the division of powers between the federal and provincial governments in the *British North America Act* of 1867. With respect to ESL for adult immigrants, the crucial factors in our constitution are that education is a provincial responsibility and that immigration is divided between the federal and provincial levels. There is room, however, for negotiation at the borders of these categories, and definitions have been altered as situations change. The federal government deals with citizenship registration but has worked out various relationships with provinces regarding selection of immigrants and services for immigrants. As discussed below, changing economic considerations prompted the federal government to encroach on what could be considered education.

In the early years of this century, immigration levels went up and down in waves depending on world economic and political conditions, reaching a peak of more than 400,00 just before the First World War (Whitaker, 1991). The percentage of foreign born in the Canadian population between 1900 and 1930 stayed at about 22 percent (compared with about 16 percent in the 1970s) (Hawkins, 1989).[1] Although most previous immigrants had been British and French, the great wave included large numbers of central and eastern Europeans. Agricultural settlement was a major goal of the government, but the need for men to build railways and work in extraction industries grew quickly. Thus non-English-speaking immigrants tended to be dispersed to areas of the hinterland to do manual work of various sorts. Especially in the climate of the Great War, there was considerable xenophobia in the Canadian population, which resulted in racist immigration policies, particularly against the Chinese. There certainly was no question of providing publicly funded social services for immigrants.

As with many facets of adult education in the earlier part of this century, what organized activities there were to teach English to adult immigrants were carried out by voluntary, non-governmental organizations (NGOs). Perhaps the most enterprising was Frontier College (see "The Imaginative Training for Citizenship" by Selman in this volume), which provided ESL and basic education for men in frontier work camps (Cook, 1987). Fitzpatrick may have written the first Canadian English-language learning book for immigrants, *Handbook for New Canadians* (1919). Selman (1987) describes Canadian adult ESL activities in this period as follows:

> Some of the earliest adult education activities of which we have record, most conducted under private auspices (churches, ethnic groups, organized labour,

and so on), were aimed at assisting immigrants to learn about and adjust to Canadian society and to the conditions of life in Canada. Frontier College (which began as the Reading Camps Association) conducted its work, beginning at the turn of the century, in mining, lumbering, construction, and other isolated camps and communities. Most of the people it served—and the same is true of the "railway camps" of the YMCA, which began about the same time—were men, many of whom needed language instruction and basic education. Beginning in the 1920s, especially in the Prairies, increased efforts were made by school authorities and the Canadian National Railway, among others, to assist immigrant individuals and community and ethnic groups to learn the dominant language of the area and to adjust to Canadian ways, at the same time retaining a pride in their native culture (p. 38).

Despite the participatory aspect of Frontier College, one suspects that there was more work among the men on "adjustment" to Canada than on retaining ethnic pride. The 19th annual report of Frontier College (1919) lists the objectives of the labourer-teachers as: "(1) to educate the worker and give him a fighting chance; (2) to educate and citizenize the immigrant; (3) to meet the 'Red' agitator on his own ground" (quoted in Cook, 1987, p. 47).

1945 to the Late 1980s: Governments Get Involved

In 1940 the Canadian Council of Education for Citizenship (later the Canadian Citizenship Council) was formed, which advocated for immigrant services. From the end of World War II into the 1960s, several structural changes were made in the federal government so that, in the end, the Department of the Secretary of State held responsibility for the *Citizenship Act* (1946) and the Department of Manpower and Immigration dealt with the *Immigration Act* (Pal, 1993, ch. 4; Whitaker, 1991). Immigration rose after the war, and policy was formed in 1947 to manage especially the influx of "displaced persons" (war refugees); people with suitable occupations from southern Europe were permitted to enter along with those from the countries previously favoured. Refugees from Hungary came in the 1950s and from Czechoslovakia in the 1960s. Not only was the ethnic mix becoming greater, but the geographic spread of immigration was different from before, with many more immigrants coming to the cities and to provinces from Quebec westward, but not to the Atlantic provinces. An assimilationist policy under the aegis of the *Citizenship Act* prompted grants to NGOs (for example, the Canadian Citizenship Council) and later to provinces to support services promoting citizenship, including costs for teachers and textbooks for language training (see Pal, 1993, pp. 92-93 for a list of such NGOs). In 1961, Ontario created a Department of the Ontario Provincial Secretary and Citizenship, which financed language training for adult immigrants through NGOs. Most provinces responded separately over the years through their school boards and/or provincial policies.

In 1967, the *Immigration Act* was substantially revised, foreshadowed by changes in regulations in 1962; discrimination on the basis of race, colour, and religion was to be eliminated and instead a point system based on individuals' characteristics of interest to the Canadian economy (including skills in English and French) was established.[2] The federal government, concerned about human resources for the country's booming economy, built an emphasis into the *Immigration Act* not only on the selection of the most suitable workers and on their dispersal to places around the country where they were needed,[3] but also on co-operation with the provinces in bearing the costs of immigration. In 1966, it passed the *Occupational Training Act for Adults*, which survived until the late 1980s under various names and reformulations. It provided funding for a range of occupational and pre-occupational training for adults. In taking this step, the federal government came close to trespassing on the provincial governments' educational territory; it side-stepped confrontation by calling the services "training" rather than "education" and by having the provinces provide the training through classroom seats purchased for students chosen by federal officials (Thomas, 1987). English as a second language comprised a large proportion of the training offered. Adult basic education (below high school level) was also included originally but was soon dropped. Students received about twenty-four weeks of full-time training with a living allowance. To some degree as a response to this federal program, community colleges were developed to house and staff it.

Meanwhile the *Official Languages Act* of 1969 was enacted, creating a backlash among non-official language communities about recognition of their issues. As a result, then-Prime Minister Pierre Trudeau declared in 1973 that the country was to be by policy multicultural, but while non-official language speakers were encouraged under the policy to learn an official language, no funds were attached to further this end. Thus, entering the 1970s, the federal government had two ESL programs for adult immigrants: it funded provinces (and through them, NGOs and school boards) to provide teachers of English and textbooks to promote citizenship, and bought seats in community colleges through provinces to enhance immigrants' value in the workforce. It also gave money to NGOs beginning in 1979 to help in the general settlement of immigrants (particularly refugees) in their first year; this money and the growth of immigrant communities gave rise to more ethnic-specific NGOs and to NGOs serving immigrants from any background. Provinces from Quebec westward created their own policies and services. Quebec negotiated control over the selection of immigrants to that province and all immigrant services, with federal financial compensation.[4] In the Atlantic provinces, immigration was relatively low, and those provinces largely left the federal government to deal directly with NGOs and educational institutions to provide services.

Most of the language training under these provisions was generic, basic language training in educational institutions, although a little federal funding and some money from certain provinces went to training for English in the workplace. As sources of immigration changed radically and new waves of refugees arrived (for example, Chileans in the 1970s and boat people from Southeast Asia in the 1980s), special needs arose, such as the teaching of English to people who were not literate in their first language. In larger immigrant receiving cities, bilingual ESL and ESL literacy programs were started. There was an impetus in the 1980s for large school boards and post-secondary organizations to partner with immigrant-serving NGOs to provide language training. With so many players and programs involved, brokerage of language training and other immigrant services became an issue; in response, for example, Ontario created Ontario Welcome House, and Alberta supported two consortia of service-delivery agencies to direct immigrants to suitable language training and other services.

ESL teachers and other workers joined in provincial ESL organizations that affiliated to form TESL Canada in 1979. Umbrella organizations of NGOs serving immigrants also were established in some provinces along with national advocacy organizations. In 1984, under pressure from such organizations, the House of Commons Special Committee on Participation of Visible Minorities in Canadian Society published its report *Equality Now!*, the first recommendation of which was for more ESL/FSL. Universities, colleges, school boards and private institutions developed programs in which fee-paying students (some coming from overseas just to study English) could improve their English skills, especially to help them gain access to post-secondary education.

Although ESL programs were burgeoning throughout these decades, so were criticisms directed towards them. General concerns included the uniform and non-specific goals of the majority of programs, the lack of special programs for those with very low or very high levels of education and English language skill, and the lack of programs outside of the main, immigrant-receiving communities. More specific complaints were made about the big federal program offered through Employment and Immigration Canada: that it was sexist in its choice of students because of its policies on only sending "the head of the household" and only serving independent class immigrants (Doherty, 1992); that federal officers were not trained to make judgments about immigrants' language needs (Belfiore & Heller, 1992); and that community colleges were using the programs as a milk cow in siphoning off money for other programs and exploiting the teachers. The federal government was not satisfied with the program it was running through the provinces for citizenship training because it was not getting any credit for the expenditure and because at least one province was trying to manipulate it for more control over spending on immigrant language services. There was an underlying current of concern about teacher qualifications because so many institutions and services were related to ESL. A problem arose when school boards started making a distinction between the qualifications and employment conditions of teachers who taught non-credit rather than credit courses. All governments were worried because ESL delivery was becoming so complex that it was incomprehensible, let alone accountable (see Burnaby, 1992a).

From the Late 1980s to the Present: Government Pulls Back

Conditions in the mid-1980s and onward set the stage for some major changes in ESL teaching. The economy went through several recessions. The international economy moved towards service industries and away from manufacturing, and industrialized countries became worried about the basic skills of their workforces. In response, Ontario, in 1985, followed by the federal government in 1986, announced programs for the first time to support adult literacy instruction (Burnaby, 1992b). Also, the end of the baby boom meant a significant decrease in the numbers of young people entering the labour market. Thus, largely for demographic reasons, the federal government decided to raise immigration levels in order to balance the age groups in the Canadian population (Immigration Canada, 1992a), despite criticisms that it was bringing new immigrants into a situation of growing unemployment. The need to reduce the national debt became a central political issue, starting a strong trend towards the downsizing of programs and the shifting of responsibilities from higher levels of government to lower levels or to the private sector.

In this climate, the federal government began to experiment. In 1986, from the immigration side of Employment and Immigration, it set aside a small amount of money to fund language training programs aimed at women who were not in the workforce. Rather than working through the provinces, it sought out proposals directly from NGOs and individual educational institutions across the country. It made no pretence of giving provinces decision-making power over the educational value of the contracts, although it did establish advisory boards in most provinces, composed of provincial authorities and representatives of NGO umbrella groups. Each project funded was unique, with the delivery agency deciding on the target population and structure of the program. The results showed that many new groups of clients were reached (for example, homebound mothers and seniors, people who did not have the literacy skills or confidence to go to regular ESL training and people in areas with few immigrants), mostly in effective ways. But the delivery agencies found the time frame and the short-term funding arrangements highly frustrating (Burnaby et al., 1987). The experiment indicated to the government that it was possible to bypass the provinces, with their strong negotiating positions and unionized teaching forces, and get individual NGOs and other institutions to compete for short-term funds to deliver ESL services.

After several years of work on this model, the federal government withdrew both its funding programs for ESL and replaced them, in 1990, with a new program associated with its plans to raise immigration levels. Called Language Instruction for New Canadians (LINC), it is provided through one-year contracts with NGOs, educational institutions, unions, and organizations to offer language training for immigrants, but only for those who have not yet taken out citizenship. Five levels of proficiency have been determined in co-operation with the provinces (Citizenship and Immigration Canada, 1996), and prospective students are tested and placed at suitable levels in programs available in their communities. Presumably, setting and testing such levels allows the potential for more co-ordination and accountability across training sites. A separate level is described for ESL learners who are not literate in any language. No training allowances for students are given, but other supports such as child care and transportation can be written into the contract where appropriate. Some students are eligible to go on to more sophisticated and job-centred training in another program called Labour Market Language Training (LMLT).

The federal government made it clear that it was creating strict limits on the extent to which it would fund ESL for adults in the future, as the following statement demonstrates:

> The government's increased funding represents a significant commitment. However, EIC [The Employment and Immigration Commission] never has and never will act as the sole provider of language training. EIC is counting on sponsors and on training providers to continue to make other opportunities available. The federal government wants overall training opportunities increased. It does not want its increased expenditures to replace existing sources (Immigration Canada, 1992b, p. 1).

It leaves all other stakeholders responsible for language training for refugee claimants and those newcomers who have taken out citizenship. The federal government is in direct control of each LINC program and has a means of dealing with accountability issues.

In the meantime, provinces, NGOs and educational institutions are experiencing their own financial problems. Within them and among them, ESL for adult immigrants is no better co-ordinated than before and is under fire in every sector. Immigrants, as they have always done, are finding support for their language learning wherever they can—in extension classes of school boards, colleges and universities, in academic upgrading classes, in literacy programs, in workplace training, in community agencies and through self-study. It is impossible to know the extent to which levels of opportunities for formal language learning have changed or the extent to which language learning has been incorporated, by necessity, into a wide range of other kinds of programs.

Summary of Historical Factors

NGOs have been key players in this story all the way through; indeed, they were the only real players until the 1960s. After that, big government initiatives overshadowed their work, but governments found, by the 1980s, that NGOs were essential in linking immigrants' needs and interests with governments' intentions. The NGOs' focus was mainly social development. At first, the NGOs were patronizing and assimilationist in many ways, but they have always been well ahead of governments in advocacy for immigrants' rights and support and have strongly influenced government policy on multiculturalism, non-discrimination in employment and anti-racism, as well as language training. The federal government has mainly confined its support to its legislated mandates in citizenship (1950s on), labour force development (1960s to 1980s) and multiculturalism (1970s on, with the *Multiculturalism Act* passed in 1988). Provincial support has varied considerably, partly due to the density of immigrants within their respective populations. Most use their regular and post-secondary education systems to provide language and other training, and some involve a considerable number of other departments as well (for example, social services, labour, and consumerism). Thus, we see a constant and complex mix of motives such as xenophobia, racism, assimilation, citizenship participation, economic development, demographic manipulation, social development and justice at play in the interface between immigrants and Canadian institutions. Interventions mostly assume low profiles, but their relevance is so far reaching in Canadian society that it is virtually ubiquitous.

ESL in Adult Education in Canada

Content

The following discussion addresses three aspects of ESL for adult immigrants—content, learners' perspectives and mainstream agendas—in order to relate it to aspects of the larger field of adult education in Canada. The content of ESL learning for adults is vast, since language pervades not only all aspects of our social relations but is also critical to our thought processes. Therefore, when people in the community do not speak the mainstream language, this fact becomes an issue in many facets of life. The major initiatives to resolve such communication problems in Canada have been attempts to isolate language and teach it as a generic skill in the naïve hope that the learners will end up having enough in common with us for practical purposes. But language cannot be divorced from content and language teaching can never be other than a highly political process. Thus, many ESL programs have been criticized as being both naïvely assimilationist and ineffective in preparing immigrants for the real challenges that they will face in the community.

In addition, as far as one can estimate, only a small proportion of immigrants receives any language training at all, however generic. Therefore, efforts to deal specifically with immigrants' lack of mainstream language skills through formal language training inevitably become surrounded by other initiatives on the parts of other stakeholders to influence immigrants' language learning. One type of such an initiative is to provide materials and train teachers to teach language specific to certain aspects of life. For example, several newspapers are published especially for ESL learners so they will become accustomed to reading Canadian newspapers; industrial councils and government ministries produce language learning kits about their areas of focus; ESL programs are combined with life skills, parenting, workplace training and academic upgrading classes for immigrants. ESL becomes part of every public service and every private institution that relate to a significant number of immigrants.

In practice, weaving ESL into all facets of life means that ESL services are hard to define, much less co-ordinate. This becomes a problem in several ways. First, it is a major obstacle when it comes to assessing the need for and adequacy of services in ESL. We will probably never have a suitable measure of the extent to which we are meeting needs, a situation that is frustrating to funders and advocates alike. Second, it is very difficult to provide brokerage so that potential learners can get in touch with the learning opportunities they need. Brokerage problems are especially severe when lack of communication in the mainstream language is the point in the first place. The few programs we had that attempted this were marginal, and most have fallen to funding cuts. Third, it is a challenge to provide for and ensure suitable training for teachers. Even within formal education, ESL takes many forms and appears in every type of educational institution, making standards of teacher preparation challenging. But ESL is also part of many other kinds of informal and non-formal education. How can those teachers and facilitators be prepared to support language teaching? Tensions arise in the ESL field over this matter; for example, there are debates over the relative value of a facilitator being able to speak the learners' first language versus having training in second language teaching methods.

To wind up this discussion of ESL content, it must be noted that there has been a degree of distance between ESL teaching and other kinds of adult education in Canada for several decades, especially since the rapid expansion of generic ESL classes began in the 1960s. A major reason for this separation has been the strong influence on second language teaching of linguistics and psychology directed at the behaviour of individuals rather than at social and power relations between groups (see, for example, Rodby, 1992, ch. 1). Teacher training and professional development for ESL teachers was dominated by such individual-centred perspectives, showing signs of other influences only in the past decade. Thus, lines of communication and apparent mutual interest between the ESL profession and other related adult education groups have been weak. Perhaps the most closely related adult education undertaking, adult literacy and basic education (ABE), has been influenced as much by social and economic theory as by the psychology of reading. Since ESL and ABE share an interest in the development of communication and social relations, one hopes for continued and growing co-operation between the two in the future.

Learners' Perspectives

The one thing that immigrant ESL learners in Canada have in common is that they have come to this country unable to speak one of our mainstream languages. Otherwise, they are as widely varied as any other large group of people, so their needs are just as diverse. A comprehensive picture of appropriate ESL teaching to meet their needs, then, is complex. First, adult ESL learners differ with respect to the amount of English they speak when they come for training. This factor creates a moving target, since they need different levels of language training as their experience with the language increases, not only within the scope of one episode of training but also as they enter and re-enter training over the years. Second, learners differ considerably with respect to their experience in language learning; those who come to Canada already speaking several languages have effective strategies and confidence. Third, learners may have very little experience with formal education. This factor is crucial to the design of learning opportunities for them since their experience with and confidence in learning in a formal classroom situation is largely based on the success of such previous experiences. When ESL training was almost exclusively generic, linguistic and print oriented in regular classrooms, many learners were completely excluded. Some went to literacy programs that were or were not prepared to address their particular needs. Recent programs in ESL literacy and mother-tongue literacy have begun to fill these gaps.

Finally, immigrants come to Canada and to the prospect of learning English with many different goals in mind. Indeed, some do not come to class at all because they can meet their needs within their own families, workplaces or communities. Many accept survival-level language skills and continue learning on their own while others want access to jobs and relationships that require high levels of English proficiency. This latter group's needs are often ignored because they do not fit the generic language teaching pattern, because they are seen as a threat to native-born Canadians who fear competition from them or because these immigrants *seem* to be managing so well in the language that their needs for specialized language training are not recognized. Immigrants go through stages as they gather more experience in this country and as they mature as individuals. Therefore, one person may go through all of these scenarios in his or her lifetime. Not only is a variety of kinds of language training needed to suit the range of characteristics of the immigrant population, but also such variety must be planned to address changes that individuals go through over the years. One-shot language training is often not enough to meet immigrants' needs.

In terms of adult education as a whole, this last point in particular means that adult educators in various venues may find themselves working with a group that includes immigrants, but on projects where language is not the focus. An important aspect of the target learning for the immigrants may be the task-specific language involved. Often, the special learning required is not extensive or linguistically sophisticated, but the educator must be alert to the potential need in order to make the most of the learning opportunity. In this way, all adult educators are language and literacy teachers.

Mainstream Agendas

In the earlier discussion of the history of ESL in Canada for adult immigrants, a variety of goals for immigration and language training on the part of government were examined, from total assimilation to mainstream norms permitting various forms of discrimination, to multiculturalism and social equity. Policies within governments are frequently contradictory, with one faction or policy promoting Draconian assimilation and another the celebration of differences. Society as a whole demonstrates a similar range in approaches to immigrants in the workplace, the media, political activities, commercial enterprises and so on. Education is particularly ambivalent in its insistence, on the one hand, on the goal of a standard of English proficiency that virtually no one could achieve, and, on the other, for its support and valuation of multilingualism and creative expression (Rodby, 1992; Baynham, 1995). To what extent is mainstream society forcing immigrants to learn English against their will, holding out language training as a key to doors that actually are nailed shut to them? To what extent are we creating false conceptions of the purity of our language(s) and refusing to accept the changes that immigrants will inevitably make in our ways of communicating? Is the middle class closing ranks and deliberately using language that those who are not native speakers and those with low levels of literacy cannot understand? (See Tollefson, 1991; Phillipson, 1992.) When the 1997 immigration level targets were being set at the time of writing this chapter, it was clear that there was a widening gulf in the response to such questions. It is the stated policy of this government to increase annual immigration to one percent of the total population. However, it has pulled back substantially from that target in recent years because of indications of strongly divided public opinion over the value of immigration.

In this climate, adult education is permeated with ESL and with the variety of attitudes to immigrants and their language needs that exist in our society as a whole. We need better communication and co-operation between the specific enterprise of ESL and the more general one of adult education in Canada, with plenty of stretching and re-assessment on both sides. Each group has much to teach the other about the place of immigration in Canada and the role of language within it. ESL is just beginning to learn from adult education how important the whole social context of immigrants and immigration is to its activities, and adult education more generally would benefit from specific sensitivities to the nuances and power of language itself in our multilingual environment.

Endnotes

[1] The 1981 Canadian Census showed immigrants to be 16 percent of the total population, which can be compared with 5 percent in the United States and 20 percent in Australia at the time (Hawkins, 1989, p. 259).

[2] Independent class immigrants are assessed on this point system, but they are in the minority relative to family class immigrants and refugees, who are not so assessed.

[3] Chiswick (1992, p. 5) notes that "economics was more important for shaping immigration policy in Canada than in the United States, and American policies were more closely tied to foreign policy questions than were Canadian ... [I]mmigration has been dealt with in the same ministry as manpower or employment matters in Canada, whereas most immigration issues are handled by the Justice Department in the United States."

[4] Through the Cullen-Couture Agreement, 1978, and the Canada-Quebec Accord, 1991.

Lumber camp workers in class (location not known).
Courtesy of Frontier College.

CHALLENGES AND FUTURE VISIONS

Radio studio exhibit, Department of Extension, University of Alberta, 1929.
Courtesy of the Archives of Ontario (Collection Identification Number: CAAE F1205, E11-8; Ref AO3949).

Part 1

Current Challenges

24

Self-Directed Learning: Highlighting the Contradictions

Donna M. Chovanec

Some of the most influential authors in the field of adult and higher education have devoted considerable attention to self-directed learning (SDL) in recent decades. The explosion of research and theory regarding SDL since the 1960s is well documented. Many suggest that SDL as a guiding principle holds substantial promise for the field of adult education and for the adult learner (Brockett & Hiemstra, 1991; Knowles, 1975; Tough, 1979). Some, however, are more skeptical. For example, Caffarella (1993) notes an "almost cult-like quality to the extent that self-directedness is viewed as the essence of what adult learning is all about" (p. 25). Still others are undeniably cynical as exemplified in Collins' (1991) reference to the reification of SDL.

In view of its strong presence in the study of the teaching and learning of adults, SDL merits thoughtful review and reflection. This chapter is a critical review of the prevailing literature to which many students of adult education will have been exposed. It focuses on the contradictions, paradoxes and unanswered questions surrounding the issue of SDL and concludes by challenging the concept's position and usefulness within adult education. The paper is organized around four themes commonly addressed in the literature on SDL: history and philosophy, definition, professionalization and methods.[1]

History and Philosophy of SDL

Malcolm Knowles and Allen Tough are generally regarded as the forefathers of SDL in adult education. The impetus for their concerted studies of SDL was provided by the theoretical groundwork laid by Cyril Houle in his book *The Inquiring Mind* (1961), combined with studies on participation rates of adult learners that affirmed that adults engage in many learning activities outside formal institutions. Although the theoretical attention to SDL is relatively recent, there is a long and rich history of interest in self-directed learning. For example, the Greek philosophers Aristotle, Plato and Socrates advocated self-directed learning, and early written works from the nineteenth century (for example, *Self-Education* by Hosmer, 1847) discuss self-initiated learning activities. Moreover, it is commonly recognized that self-study was the primary means of learning prior to the advent of formal schooling, albeit these learning endeavours often took root within the society of other learners such as in associations and discussion groups. Later, SDL was often heralded as a means to ensure learners some control over their learning environments within or, more commonly, outside formal educational institutions.

Applying the Paradigms to SDL

Like much of mainstream adult education, SDL is primarily influenced by the premises of humanist, behaviourist and developmental psychology. Although the roots of these psychologies are primarily located in two competing paradigms (for example, the technical and the interpretive), Knowles' version of the "modern practice of adult education" is a resolute attempt to bridge such disparate elements.[2] He and his proponents contend, for example, that learning contracts, objectives, techniques and outcome evaluations (technical paradigm) promote the development of increasingly higher levels of self-understanding and self-actualization (interpretive paradigm). Critics, however, lament "the colonization of the territory of adult education by psychology and the intrusion of individualism into the conceptual framework of adult educators" (Welton, 1987, p. 52). Notwithstanding the obvious humanist influence, some adult education scholars specifically criticize the increasing formalization and technisization of SDL methods and structures (Candy, 1991; Collins, 1991). Such critique points to the encroachment of the premises of the technical paradigm into the more interpretive (or meaning-based) orientation of humanist education. Some suggest that this is evident in the chronology of publications by Knowles and Tough, which demonstrate an increasing reliance on prescriptive techniques for the adult educator (Collins, 1991).

Some adult educators attempt to link SDL with a critical perspective. Mezirow (1996) and Garrison (1992), for example, focus respectively on transformative learning and critical thinking, while Brookfield (1985; 1993) proposes a process of critical reflection and action intended to question and change social, political and economic circumstances. He contends that SDL ultimately undermines the hegemony of the formal education system: "Radical change in social, moral, aesthetic and political affairs is often the outcome of a process of self-directed learning in opposition to the educational message imposed from without" (Gelphi cited in Brookfield, 1993, p. 229). Taking a radically oppositional stance, Collins (1991) vehemently opposes what he calls "psychologism" and proposes instead an emancipatory practice of adult education "informed by social theories of action rather than by psychological learning theories" (p. xii) within which the current technical preoccupation with SDL would be re-directed to "emancipation as a core concern" (p. 32).

Definitions of SDL

Nowhere is the philosophical diversity of SDL more apparent than in the explications and criticisms of the meaning of the concept itself. Readers of the literature on SDL realize immediately that they cannot assume a universal definition of the term; the definition is contested terrain, fraught with ambiguity and contradictions, and no clear consensus exists. Brockett and Hiemstra (1991) argue that SDL is a "misunderstood concept." While more recent multi-dimensional definitions have attempted to accommodate these variations, still there are significant and convincing critiques of the prevailing definitions. Collins (1991), for example, recognizes the obvious self-initiating capacities of adult learners, yet he questions whether this observation "merits such a clear-cut distinction" (p. 21) as that delineated by the study of SDL within adult education.

Dimensions of Process and Personality

Within the literature, authors differentiate between definitions that focus on SDL as a *process* of learning and definitions that promote SDL as a desirable learner *personality* trait or characteristic. Illustrating this distinction, Candy (1991) argues that conceptions of SDL typically conflate means (process) and ends (personality).

The original propositions of Tough and Knowles are generally considered to be process oriented (Brockett & Hiemstra, 1991) as is evident in Knowles (1975) oft-repeated definition:

> In its broadest meaning, "self-directed learning" describes a process in which individuals take the initiative, with or without the help of others, in diagnosing their learning needs, formulating learning goals, identifying human and material resources for learning, choosing and implementing appropriate learning strategies, and evaluating learning outcomes (p. 18).

The above definition implies that the learner carries out the activities more commonly assumed by a teacher or instructor. While process definitions focus on the individual learner, instructional realities often contradict this ideal. Candy (1991), Cranton (1992), Grow (1991) and Schuttenberg and Tracy (1987), for example, suggest that many learners are ill-prepared for the SDL process. Additionally, process more typically focuses on institutional requirements such as curriculum, grading, methods and teacher skills rather than on the learners themselves.

Some theorists believe that undue attention has been paid to SDL as an instructional process, thereby focusing too much on discreet skills and not enough on internal personality characteristics. Oddi (1987), for example, advocates "moving beyond the focus on self-directed learning as a set of activities in a self-instructional process to a study of the motivational, cognitive and affective characteristics or personalities of self-directed learners" (p. 27). Brookfield (1985) likewise suggests that the process dimension is overly "mechanistic" and contends that SDL is an "internal change in consciousness" which "occurs when process and reflection are married in the adult's pursuit of meaning" (p. 15).

Multi-Dimensional Definitions

Many adult educators do not accept a "unidimensional" view of SDL (Kasworm, 1983) but propose instead a variety of conceptualizations intended to capture both process and personality elements. Frequently, definitions with two (or more) parts are proposed that form the basis of a theoretical model. For example, in the article mentioned above, Brookfield (1985) proposes that in SDL "the external technical dimension is fused with the internal reflective dimension" (p. 15).[3] Models developed by Kasworm (1983), Brockett and Hiemstra (1991) and Candy (1991) are reviewed below.

A developmental view of SDL has considerable support. Sometimes, hierarchies of development are represented by "transformations" (e.g., Kegan, 1994; Mezirow, 1996). One such orientation is provided by Kasworm (1983), who suggests that "a broader lifespan, cognitive development framework" would contribute to the development of SDL characteristics in learners. Incorporating the interdependence of both process and personality elements in a pyramidal model, she depicts a process of "movement" in the learner from one set of values and behaviours to another seemingly more advanced cognitive, behavioural and affective state; for example, from extrinsic to intrinsic motivation. She argues that process then must be translated into a set of instructional activities ("actions of process"), which would generate the internal change process and engender the desired personality outcomes at each level.

Using "self-direction in learning" (rather than SDL) as an umbrella concept, Brockett and Hiemstra (1991) propose the "Personal Responsibility Orientation Model (PROM)," an easy to understand model that neatly incorporates the two primary definitional components of process and personality as follows: "Self-direction in learning refers to both the external characteristics of an instructional process and the internal characteristics of the learner, where the individual assumes primary responsibility for a learning experience" (p. 24).

The definition of each component of "self-direction in learning" is as follows:

> *Personality.* "Learner self-direction" refers to the personality characteristics of the learner. It is the internal, psychological component.
>
> *Process.* "Self-directed learning" refers to the characteristics of the teaching-learning process. It is the external, methodological component.

In his highly regarded critique and re-conceptualization of SDL, Candy (1991) further subdivides these two components, thereby meticulously distinguishing among *four* distinct concepts.

Personality/Goal.

1. self-determination (autonomy): to be in control of one's destiny.

2. self-management: willingness and capacity to conduct one's own education.

Process/Method.

3. learner-control: a mode of instruction in formal educational settings whereby the learner assumes increasing levels of control over the instructional process; for example, independent study.

4. autodidaxy: the individual, non-institutional pursuit of learning.

Characteristics of the Self-Directed Learner

As is evident above, many authors incorporate learner characteristics into their definitions of SDL. But what exactly are these characteristics? Literature review of this domain reveals another philosophical and definitional quagmire and further contradictions. Although Candy (1991) appends a comprehensive list of SDL characteristics he has extrapolated from many studies, his orientation towards personal and contextual differences (to be discussed later) leads him to conclude that "the search for the definitive qualities of the self-directed learner is doomed to fail" (Candy, 1991, p. 300).

While earlier writers assumed SDL to be a sign of adult maturity, levels of which would increase over the lifespan, this has been contested by others (Caffarella, 1993; Candy, 1991; Ellsworth, 1992; Kegan, 1994). In her study of adult learners, for example, Ellsworth discovered that educational experiences, not age, were more important indicators of self-directedness. Inconclusive results regarding field dependence and/or independence have been reported, again challenging the assumption that self-directed learners would necessarily be less dependent on external sources of information and support (Brockett & Hiemstra, 1991; Candy, 1991). Some speculate that the reverse may be more accurate, i.e., that learners who require more structured forms of support may respond well to some SDL methods such as pre-packaged, self-paced learning materials (Collins, 1991).

"Personal autonomy" is an essential concept and/or component in virtually any understanding of SDL. It is a valued social ideal that has long been reflected in the goals of education. Autonomy has been variably characterized as including independence, free choice, will-power and control. Brockett and Hiemstra (1991), for example, declare that "within the context of learning, it is the ability and/or willingness of individuals to take control of their own learning that determines their potential for self-direction" (p. 26). Yet, many challenge the individualism that pervades these concepts (Brookfield, 1985; 1993; Caffarella, 1993; Candy, 1991; Chené, 1983; Collins, 1991; Welton, 1987) or question independence as the desired aim (Brookfield, 1985; Candy, 1991; Kegan, 1994).

Caffarella cites feminist authors, including herself, in arguing that "autonomy must be coupled with interdependence and interconnectedness" (p. 29). In Chené's (1983) critique of the prevailing individualistic notions of autonomy, she suggests that what constitutes independent autonomous behaviour is ironically highly *dependent* on socially mediated norms. Foreshadowing a similar view expressed by Candy (1991), she charges that "the value of independence or self-reliance is an illusion and adults are trapped in other forms of dependence if they are not aware of the necessity of mediation by others" (p. 46). Welton (1987) adds that self-direction or autonomy cannot be understood apart from historical and social contexts or separate from "the capacity to exercise control over social life" (p. 53).

The Social Context of SDL

Thus, significant criticism has been levelled at many conceptualizations of SDL that have focused solely on the individual learner and paid scant attention to the social aspects of the learning environment. Some have attempted to compensate for this omission (Brockett & Hiemstra, 1991; Candy, 1991), and others claim that the "individualistic" foundations of SDL preclude adequate attention to socio-political structures (Collins, 1991; Welton, 1987). Two general streams of response to this critique are evident in the literature: interactional and structural.

From an *interactional* perspective, adult education authors generally refute the erroneous perception that SDL necessarily implies a solitary, isolated experience. Both Tough (1979) and Knowles (1975) acknowledged the mutuality, association and assistance sought by learners in the self-directed learning process. Candy (1991) is unequivocal on this point.

> Adult education is distinguished by the extent to which it arises naturally as a result of, and takes place within, social contexts. Even truly independent and solitary learning activities are the result of the learner's membership in some

group or society, and although the learning process itself may be largely solitary, its intention and justification is social (p. 22).

Based on a study of non-institutional learners, Brookfield (1985) likewise
concludes that "it is evident that no act of learning can be self-directed if we
understand self-direction as meaning the absence of external sources of assistance" (p. 7). Particularly influential in Candy's (1991) "constructivist"[4] approach to SDL is an unshakable assumption in the social nature of learning
itself. Similarly, Chené (1983) declares "autonomy starts with heteronomy,"
that is, the "relation to others is fundamental to knowledge" (p. 43).

Structural perspectives typically introduce societal issues based on the critique of an enduring inequitable distribution of power and control. It is commonly perceived, for example, that institutions have more power than
individual learners. Thus, many would concur with Chené's (1983) observation that the external constraints of the learning situation (for example, organizational issues, evaluation and grading, and content requirements) "will
determine the power that learners may have over their learning activity" (p.
42).

> Furthermore, in an institutional context, the contradictions often found between
> established norms and individual norms will limit the area over which the
> learner may have power ... Similarly, skill performance is evaluated according
> to a standard which, at least at the beginning of the learning process, is outside
> the self ... [and must] conform to certain criteria (Chené, p. 42-43).

In contrast to humanist approaches, which tend "to conceal the fact that the
pedagogical relationship is a power relationship" (Chené, 1983, p. 44), feminists and critical adult educators are also quick to point out the asymmetrical
or "manifestly unequal" power relationships between teacher and learner
within the classroom (Candy, 1991; Chené, 1983; Collins, 1991; Scott,
Chovanec & Young, 1994).

Those adult educators who are most critically attuned to social structures
and inequalities accent the often ignored implications of socio-economic
class, gender, region, race and ethnic community. Such issues are not discernible within the SDL frameworks proposed by theorists such as Brockett and
Hiemstra (1991), Grow (1991), Knowles (1975) or Tough (1979). Welton
(1987) argues that both Knowles' and Tough's "decontextualized and abstract
concept of the self forgets that we are social individuals, [and forgets] that we
cannot understand the socially constructed self apart from class and gender
structures" (p. 52). For Candy, such socio-cultural issues have a profound
effect on topics of learning chosen by learners, depth and amount of learning
and perceived and actual barriers to learning.

While Brockett and Hiemstra (1991) very nearly ignore the issue, Candy
(1991) and Brookfield (1993) clearly assume that these structural issues *can*
be incorporated into the theory, study and practice of SDL by questioning

underlying assumptions and through sensitivity to teaching strategies. In contrast, Collins (1991) and Welton (1987) believe that SDL can no longer be salvaged from the individualistic and technicist paradigm to which it has become wedded. In so saying, however, they do not discount the value of autonomous learning nor of technical skills but only that the concept has been co-opted by institutional interests which do not serve the ideals of an emancipatory education.

The "Self" in Self-Directed Learning

In addition to the many confounding problems with the definition of self-directed learning, the "self" has not been clearly explicated in the literature. There is an implicit assumption within the adult education literature that SDL is a cognitive, conscious and unified phenomenon.

There is, however, a growing body of literature that leads us to question theories of a unified self and that introduces the notion of unconscious learning processes. Theorists concerned about the soul (Sardello, 1995; Moore, 1984; Singer, 1972) or the spirit (Fenwick, 1996; Wilbur, 1996) postulate that feelings, emotions, motivations and dynamics emerge from either a transcendent or an unconscious core which actually fuels the rational decision-making abilities of the learner. Theories of psychoanalysis on the other hand, analyze how "elements of social structure ... are appropriated and transformed internally through unconscious processes and come to influence affective life and psychic structure ... [and which then] are imposed upon and give meaning to external situations" (Chodorow, 1978, p. 50). Thus, the prevailing notions of "self" as an independent and fully conscious actor are challenged.

The Professionalization of SDL

In view of this definitional confusion, the persistent affinity to the concept and/or term within the field of adult and higher education is puzzling. Many claim that SDL operates as a crucial rationale for the establishment and maintenance of adult education as a profession and/or discipline. By maintaining that self-direction is a distinct and abiding characteristic of adulthood and that SDL methods set andragogy apart from pedagogy, university programs in adult education have been able to delineate the unique domain of adult education and proceed towards professionalization. Many praise these efforts, but others say that the foundational assumptions about the distinctiveness of adult knowledge, needs and methods of instruction provide a justification for SDL that is ideologically rather than empirically based (Candy, 1991). Others, such as Welton and Collins, are vocal critics of what they view as the professionalized manipulation of adult learning activities: "From the insight that an individual is the primary source of her or his own learning experiences, an array of techniques (largely under the rubric of 'andragogy') has emerged for ready deployment on to the vast arena of formal and non-formal adult education" (Collins, 1991, p. 22).

Skeptics point out the self-serving nature of much of the research and discourse on SDL (Brookfield, 1985; Candy, 1991; Collins, 1991). Indeed, it seems ironic that most of the theory and studies on SDL focus on the educator and the educational process rather than the learner. "What [SDL research] gives us, instead, is an explanatory framework that tells us more about the perspectives of professional educators than it does about autonomous learning" (Collins, 1991, p. 23). Thus, Collins argues, the *meanings* that adults bring to their learning endeavours are neglected. This is an incongruous oversight in view of the allegedly humanist base of much of adult education, including SDL. Moreover, SDL research has relied heavily on two primary quantitative measures, the Self-Directed Learning Readiness Scale (SDLRS) and modifications of Tough's SDL projects method (Oddi, 1987). Critics charge that these ignore quality and effectiveness for individuals and society, focus on individual activities to the exclusion of the collaborative and social aspects of SDL (Brookfield, 1985; Candy, 1991) and persistently avoid a critique of the wider social context within which SDL is situated (Collins, 1991). Criticizing also the linear, simplistic cause–effect (Candy, 1991), and reductionistic (Collins, 1991) logic that pervades the technical research paradigm, Candy argues that much of SDL research is methodologically and philosophically incompatible with SDL.

SDL Methods and Strategies

As is evident throughout this review, the concept of SDL is fraught with inconsistencies and contradictions. The theoretical confusion that thwarts a representative understanding of the concept is again apparent in a discussion of methods. It is here that the technical paradigm is most influential. A brief review of the methods shared by mainstream authors is included here followed by the challenges and critique.

Types of Methods and Strategies for SDL

Candy (1991) outlines several perspectives educators hold on the methodology of enhancing self-directed learning. The first group believes SDL is a natural and universal characteristic of adults and advocates learning environments with minimal constraints. Another group believes SDL skills can be identified and discreetly targeted for instruction. "Learning how to learn," competency-based instruction, study skills sessions, time management seminars and assertiveness training may fall into this category. Others disagree, believing instead that "autonomous behaviour is not taught or learned as ordinary content in the curriculum ... We must provide a learning environment in which [the learners] are encouraged to make autonomous judgments"

(Dittman cited in Candy, 1991, p. 319). This approach advocates encouraging increasing levels of learner control over the instructional process. This is the most commonly advocated form of SDL methodology evident in the literature and will be discussed at some length here.

Proponents of this perspective often suggest that two interrelated themes must be taken into account in the optimal learning environment, namely, learning styles and/or situations and developmental progression. Grow's (1991) "Staged Self-directed Learning Model" and Schuttenberg and Tracy's (1987) "Model for Fostering Self-directed Learning" are two examples. Both conclude that instructional difficulties are often caused by a mismatch between learners and teachers. Like others (e.g., Brockett & Hiemstra, 1991; Candy, 1991; Kegan, 1994), they advocate congruence between the level of learner self-direction and the conditions of the learning situation. Therefore, many models propose that the instructional strategies of the teacher should match the style, skills and expectations of the learner. This highlights the common-sense notion, shared by many, that "individuals will vary in their readiness for self-direction thereby requiring varying degrees of assistance by facilitators" (Brockett & Hiemstra, 1991, p. 10). Consistent with the importance he attributes to social context, Candy (1991) argues that SDL is a "person-situation variable." By this he means that "no one ever *becomes* fully self-directed in any final sense, but in certain circumstances, or at certain times, people may behave more autonomously than at others" (p. 300).

Despite such recognition, it is evident that SDL is a highly valued commodity both as a personality trait and as an instructional process. Thus, along with an understanding of learning styles and situational factors, it is the contention of many that the instructional process include methods and strategies that facilitate the progression of learners through increasing levels of self-directedness. Generally, adult educators are viewed as facilitators with varying degrees of control and direction over the learning situation. For example, Grow (1991) has developed a matrix model based on varying levels of teacher directedness on the horizontal axis and learner self-directedness on the vertical axis. He proposes that in the optimal learning environment there is: (a) a match between dependent learners and authoritative teachers and self-directed learners and delegating teachers, and (b) the instructional process should facilitate a progression towards the latter. In this type of orientation, the suggested methods and strategies are intended to move the learner through a series of instructional "stages," beginning with lectures, course outlines and drills, progressing to facilitated discussion and teamwork and, finally, to independent projects, discovery learning and student-led discussion.

The concept of individual differences implied in this perspective introduces a challenge to institutionalized attempts to establish, prescribe and even dictate particular SDL teaching methods. An alternative methodological perspective held by Candy (1991) views learning as "the construction of personal structures of meaning" (p. 321). Here, content and process are viewed as inseparable and meta-reflection of the learning process itself is encouraged. Candy suggests that this is accomplished by methods which, for example, make use of learners' existing knowledge, increase question asking of learners, develop critical thinking and create a supportive climate.

Important Challenges and Critique

Before adult educators can fully tackle the question of methods and strategies, they must address the many compelling contradictions, incongruencies and paradoxes in the study of SDL. Perhaps the most important and foundational critique of SDL methods questions the assumption that SDL can be taught. This question in turn raises the issue of the role of formal or structured adult education in SDL.

Can SDL be taught? Since the earlier work of Knowles (1975) and Tough (1979), adult educators have simultaneously held the conflicting beliefs that adults are naturally self-directing and that self-direction is a goal of adult education. As Candy (1991) put it, "adult educators are confronted with a paradox: How can they assume the existence of certain circumstances at the outset, and at the same time hold those circumstances to be the desired goal or outcome of their activities?" (p. 122).

That SDL needs to be taught is a notion that is taken for granted and is difficult to challenge; yet it is inherently contradictory. As Collins (1991) observes, "many adult educators and learners are prepared to accept, on expert authority, specific directions on how to manage, and how to be, self-directed learners. *Techniques that enable us to be what we already are"* (p. 26, emphasis in the original). Such sentiments prompt Chené's (1983) view that "we cannot help seeing a paradox in the adult education discourse where the adult is led down the path of autonomy" (p. 43). These comments illustrate the embedded tension in the assumption that one can *direct* the self-directed learning of another.

With such a critique in mind, the contradictions within a methodological focus become transparent. For example, based on an early foundational study of self-taught historical figures, Gibbons, et al. (1980) make the following pronouncement about "teaching for self-education": "The systematic implementation, evaluation and modification of self-directed learning programs will continue until we have a set of principles which generate practices that enable people to become expert without formal training" (p. 55). The assumption that adult educators can "translate these theoretical principles into strategies we can teach to people" (p. 53) might suggest that this is no longer *self*-education.

Another paradox is revealed in the following representative quotation of Caffarella (1993): "What differentiates SDL from learning in more traditional formal settings is that *the learner chooses to assume the primary responsibility for planning, carrying out, and evaluation of those learning experiences.*" (p. 28, emphasis in the original). Such views prompt the adult educator to ask: In what situations are adults: (a) so *free* as to be unrestrained by dominant cultural practices and socio-political processes or (b) so *directed* that they are not able to choose?

Is SDL possible within formal educational institutions? While the plethora of publications on SDL in adult and higher education would suggest that it is possible, many of these publications' authors express doubts as well. Still others are more overtly skeptical. Some identify the "hidden" forms of external control within formal settings which work against SDL. Candy (1991) suggests that even in independent study, the "ghost" of a teacher is evident. Chené (1983) addresses teacher-learner power relationships, the limits of the institutional setting and the norm-setting role of the teacher. She states: "The teacher cannot disappear without reappearing in another form, since learners have to test their knowledge against somebody else" (p. 43). In his analysis of socio-political power structures, Collins (1991, 1995) claims that SDL materials such as pre-packaged, self-paced curricula are well suited to an increasingly commodified, market-oriented culture.

> The transformation of autonomous learning into a methodology for SDL undoubtedly can work to the advantage of management in business and industry, professional organizations and large-scale institutions when individuals who depend upon them appear to be voluntarily directing their educational projects through formal learning contracts and in accordance with institutional purposes ... [SDL] permits the learner to choose between options already defined by formal systems (Collins, 1991, p. 24).

Candy (1991) again distinguishes between learner-control and auto-didaxy in understanding the methodological process of SDL. While he accepts that formal instructional settings play a partial role in enhancing autonomous learning behaviour, he maintains that different learning skills are needed for formal versus natural learning situations. "In view of these discontinuities, there may be something incongruous about attempts to enhance the ability of learners to function independently outside the structures of formal institutions, from within the institutions themselves" (Candy, p. 338). In his view, adult educators who use techniques to relinquish partial control over the instructional environment, such as individualized learning modules, are often unwittingly practicing "pseudoautonomy." Evaluation and grading of so-called self-directed learning activities are cogent examples of such contradictions (Candy, 1991; Kegan, 1994; Scott, Chovanec & Young, 1994).

Despite the skepticism, there is widespread recognition that even self-directed learners sometimes choose formal learning environments, "expert" instruction or classroom lectures within their self-directed learning endeavours. Candy (1991), for example, quotes: "Autonomy is the quality of being able to choose dependence or independence" (p. 91).

Summary and Conclusion

A review of the complex issue of SDL suggests it is imperative for any scholar, researcher, policy maker, program planner or practitioner to be clear about the definition of SDL to be used in any learning project. Furthermore, the absence of a coherent and mutually understood or accepted definition of the term raises the question of the feasibility of its use. In view of the credible critique within the field, consideration must also be given to the gaps in the prevailing definitions, which often (a) limit the phenomenon to an individual activity, ignoring social and/or contextual factors in the learning process, and (b) assume an engagement only with cognitive skills while disregarding unconscious processes.

What does all this mean for adult educators? This critical review suggests that adult educators remain critically reflective about the concept of SDL. Claims to be facilitating self-directed learning or using self-directed learning approaches must be carefully scrutinized for philosophical premises, definition, assumptions and procedures. More fundamentally, we are challenged to ponder the usefulness of the term in the study and practice of adult education. If meaning is a socially constructed and mutually shared understanding, does the absence of an accepted definition within the discipline of adult education render the term *self-directed learning* meaningless?

Endnotes

[1]   The original version of this chapter is a segment of a research report entitled *Self-directed Learning in the Classroom*, written for the Alberta Heritage Scholarship Fund (Scott, Deneff & Chovanec, 1996). Many thanks to Sue M. Scott and Bill Deneff for their contributions.

[2]   Germaine to this section is Habermas's three paradigms—technical, interpretive and critical—which are discussed in the chapters by Collins, Scott, Cranton and Fenwick in this volume.

[3]   Here we witness the merging of elements of all three paradigms as Brookfield incorporates critical reflection, meaning making and instructional strategies into an educational process.

[4]   Mediated by the interpretive paradigm, constructivism asserts that human beings *construct* reality by attaching meanings to their experience and that these meanings are determined through social interaction.

25

Dimensions of Competence-Based Learning

Geoff Peruniak

C ompetence, like motherhood, seems like an inherently good notion. It has a solid and reassuring feel to it. Competence-based learning builds on this aura of dependability, adds a ring of precision and further bolsters it by an allusion to depth and focus. Somehow ordinary learning pales in comparison. It is small wonder, in a climate of fiscal restraint, that organizations, agencies and other groups across Canada appear to be enamoured with the concept.

Currently, there is a boom in competence-based initiatives across the country. These initiatives are found in school curricula, in college and university programs, in government training programs, in professional associations and in industry. And it is being hailed by high-profile groups such as the Canadian Conference Board of Canada (1994) as an index of acceptability in program planning. But is there more to competence-based learning than hype? What is competence in the first place, and how is it related to competence-based learning? Is it really different from and better than what has been done before? What are the implications for accountability using this new system?

This chapter looks at competence and the tangle of terms related to it in competence-based learning and reviews some of its key contributions and limitations. It presents a range of approaches to competence and attempts to identify some of the key issues that arise in the application of such approaches. It argues that some of the assumptions made about competence-based learning are not only unrealistic but potentially dangerous, such as the assumption that human judgment can be standardized and maintained independently of the framework that it created.

Historical Threads and Context

From the prehistoric flint knapper to the latest computer programmer, people have been concerned with the ability to carry out a task well. Competence is basically a reflection of a value system. At the turn of this century, when disciplines such as psychology patterned their value system more closely to the scientific method, education fell under the influence of empiricism. Applications to education were sought from more controlled laboratory settings. The influence of B.F. Skinner's work in operant psychology became evident in education in the 1960s and programmed learning materials began to multiply. Through contemporaries of Skinner such as Fred Keller, new operant-based methods began to be explored, such as "mastery learning" which Keller started in his own classes at the university level (Keller, 1968).

A strong military influence on competence-based learning arose in the United States, stemming from the urgent need to train vast numbers of personnel for each of the world wars. Neumann (1979) traces some of the early military influences on competence-based learning in ideas such as job analysis activity analysis, and trait analysis from the 1920s. Prominent psychologists such as Robert Gagné and Robert Glaser were closely involved in this training and introduced to education ideas such as performance objectives and task analysis (Gagné, 1962; 1970).

A major and more recent influence on ideas of competence came with the American panic over their education system in light of the Russian Sputnik success. The call for accountability for teachers led to a movement in competence-based teacher education (Houston, 1974; Houston & Howsam, 1972) in which the influence of behaviourism was evident in notions such as task analysis and in the flood of behavioural objectives. However, competence-based reforms in the United States had limited influence in the overall educational system in the 1960s and 1970s, and even less influence in Canada. Certainly there were individual competence-based initiatives at the course and program levels, but at an institutional level, these curricular reforms usually had little impact.

Larger forces came into play as governments began large-scale initiatives to pressure the education system into more explicitly addressing the economic concerns of industry and training in the 1980s. Britain, led by Thatcher's New Training Initiative, was an early advocate of this new impetus (Manpower Services Commission, 1981). The prospect of global standardization in education and industry was enhanced as countries such as New Zealand and Australia began their own revamping programs (Robson, 1994; New Zealand Qualifications Authority, 1991; Gonczi, 1992). Canada's effort in this direction has been less centralist than in Britain or New Zealand, but the prevailing attitudes in government are blowing in the same direction (Alberta Advanced

Education and Career Development, 1994; Canadian Labour Force Development Board, 1995).

Terms

Competence seems like such a straightforward idea. But beneath its serene surface, there is a quicksand of competing approaches, murky technological jargon and a glutinous host of personal and contextual factors. *Webster's Third International Dictionary* (1986) defines competence, or competency, as: "the quality or state of being functionally adequate or having sufficient knowledge, judgment, skill, or strength (as for a particular duty or in a particular respect)" (p. 463). It is in the determination of functional adequacy that competence becomes less straightforward. Like learning in general, competence-based learning is both a means and an end. Competence-based learning is a means for determining competence. In the end it consists of a system of procedures for that determination. The system sets parameters on factors such as the identification of tasks, how these tasks are categorized, and the criteria and devices to be used during assessment. Competence implies scrutiny, and competence-based learning provides a process for that scrutiny. Competence-based systems occur in various sectors and agencies outside of formal education and thus I have taken competence-based learning to be the more comprehensive term.

Again from *Webster's*, "learning" is defined as: "the process of acquisition and extinction of modifications in existing knowledge, skills, habits, or action tendencies in a motivated organism through experience, practice, or exercise" (p. 1286). So what exactly does "competence-based" add to the meaning of "learning?" Isn't all learning involved with achieving some kind of competence? While this is probably true, learning does not have quite the same formality. Part of the formality of "competence-based" comes from its connection to accountability. No doubt it can be argued that learning also has accountability built in, at least in some general sense, since learning does not happen in a vacuum. However, "competence-based" is a descriptor that specifically alludes to learning in relation to a role, task or duty. Competence-based learning has come to suggest a set of expectations about the kinds of evidence that will be accepted for learning. These expectations are evident in the definition provided by Grant et al. (1979):

> Competence-based education tends to be a form of education that derives a curriculum from an analysis of a prospective or actual role in modern society and that attempts to certify student progress on the basis of demonstrated performance in some or all aspects of that role. Theoretically, such demonstrations of competence are independent of time served in formal educational settings (p. 6).

Several terms have developed in the competence-based movement. Some of them describe overlapping interests in competence and are confusing as a result. The most common of these terms include competence-based assessment, competence-based standards, competence-based measurement and competence-based performance. Competence-based assessment is contained within the usage of competence-based learning for current purposes. Other terms have lent further confusion to the area by exacerbating the technical jargon. In addition to competence-based learning and competence-based education are closely related terms such as performance-based teacher education (Houston, 1974; Houston & Howsam, 1972), mastery learning (Bloom, 1976), personalized system of instruction (Keller, 1968), precision teaching and outcomes-based education (Baron & Boschee, 1996; Towers, 1994). All of these terms can be subsumed under the broad category we saw earlier of criterion-referenced learning that emphasizes a system of clearly specified objectives, frequent feedback and reliable assessment usually accompanied by identifiable minimum standards. Wolfe (1995) has observed that criterion-referenced systems are closely linked to the school curriculum, while competence-based systems tend to be associated with broadly based vocational or occupational settings.

Dimensions of Competence in Competence-Based Learning

At first glance competence is the fairly straightforward concept of being "up" to a task. Our definition specifies "functionally adequate" in handling a particular task. However, under closer examination some complex questions are posed in even the most elementary case of learning:

1. What is the approach to, or notion of, competence-based learning, including the attendant assumptions?
2. What is the purpose of the competence?
3. What is the content domain for the identification and assessment of the competence?
4. What is the level of generality or specificity of the competence?
5. What are the criteria for determining functional adequacy?
6. What are the characteristics of the assessor?
7. What are the characteristics and role of the person assessed?
8. What is the general climate and what is the setting where the competence is considered?
9. Does this activity have heart?

Each dimension presents a slightly different view of competence and emphasizes different aspects of it. Lest this appear to be another form of reductionism, a few cautions are in order. These dimensions are not additive and neither are they presented in an order of priority or developmental sequence.

It will quickly become evident that they can only be separated conceptually and that in fact they all work together simultaneously. Each of these dimensions will now be discussed in turn.

Approaches to Competence-Based Learning

There are several approaches to competence-based learning, and thus to the particular conception of competence being considered. These approaches are part of the general setting or context but because they have such an important role in setting expectations and assumptions, they need to be highlighted separately.

The Behavioural Approach

Some of the major assumptions of this approach include:

1. Empirical methods of natural science apply equally well to the study of humans.

2. Complex tasks can be broken into meaningfully discrete categories and arranged in a rational hierarchy.

3. Inner states of being are only important insofar as they can be operationalized in terms of performance (behaviour).

One of the main contributions of this approach has been the idea that complex tasks can sometimes be broken into smaller, more manageable steps. For instance, learning about cursive handwriting for a learning-disabled child in elementary school can be made more manageable if the child is first encouraged to practise holding the pencil and to begin by drawing large circles and lines on big blank sheets of paper. This idea is not new, but behaviourism gave some fresh recognition to what good teachers were already doing. Second, the explication of learning objectives and achievement levels at least was an attempt, if sometimes overdone, to publicly clarify purposes. If you have ever progressed through a Keller Plan, you may not have found it to be the most exciting learning experience, but you would have had a good sense of what content was being covered and that what was taught was indeed what was tested. Third, the emphasis on performance or behaviour was a welcome break from a heavy dose of normative personality inventories and characteristics. Fourth, the emphasis on continuous feedback, or positive reinforcement, was useful for instructional purposes.

In spite of these contributions, there continues to be a vociferous opposition to behavioural notions of competence, particularly among educators. Criticisms have included excessive reductionism and quantification, prescriptive and mechanistic methods and a rush to premature closure. In the behavioural approach there has been a singular lack of reflection accorded to the social context. Where countries such as Britain have implemented national standards of competence, criticisms specifically directed at the behavioural heritage of these standards have been launched against the excessive bureaucratization and centralization and the misplaced claims for objectivity (Hyland, 1994; Norris, 1991; Wolfe, 1995).

There is a certain neglect of personal characteristics of the person whose performance is being examined in behavioural approaches. In fact, worse than neglect, Short, cited in Norris (1991), has charged that sometimes achievements in performance have been taken for qualities of the person. Furthermore, there has tended to be an excessive emphasis on individual performance in assessment schemes for competence, such as in the English National Vocational Qualifications, to the detriment of co-operative performance. Where co-operation is considered, it tends to be conceptualized narrowly, such as on-the-job teamwork rather than more broadly as in the sense of citizenship which Raven (1984) has argued must be part of competence. A similar point was made by Ashworth and Saxton (1990) in their critique of competence as developed by the then-British Training Agency. These authors argued that successful teams often originate from a balancing of characteristics within a group and not by educating people to the same standard. Finally, behavioural approaches often have neglected the ongoing developmental changes in the person.

The Functional Approach

The largest impact on competence in the past forty years has undoubtedly been from notions of a functionalist approach (Department of Industry for Scotland, 1988; Grant et al., 1979; Manpower Services Commission, 1981; New Zealand Qualifications Authority, 1991; Raven, 1984). I will not endeavour to distinguish the varieties of functional approaches here, but only point out that some have modified elements of earlier functional approaches and called it an integrative approach (Hager & Gonczi, 1993; Chappell & Hager, 1994) and even a holistic approach (Gonczi, 1992).

A functional approach derives elements from both the behavioural and trait approaches. The trait approach recognizes the inner qualities or characteristics of a person as these influence the determination of competence. While often difficult to identify, most of us recognize the importance of attitudes, beliefs, energy and other inner states of personality. Essentially, the functional approach attempts to identify the specific tasks and functions of what is deemed to be competence by experts in that role. An investigation takes place of what competent individuals do in particular job situations and these performances are considered as evidence of characteristics that distinguish competent from less-competent individuals. These elements are field tested through questionnaires to practitioners and further refined in statistical analysis or sometimes in conjunction with feedback and dialogue with stakeholder groups.

Klemp (1979) talked of incorporating traits, motives and self-concept into the analysis of functions. Raven (1984) constructed an ambitious model of competence based on his research in the Scottish workplace, in which he stressed the importance of attitudes and the pursuit of valued goals such as citizenship as critical to an assessment of competence. More recently, Chappell and Hager (1994) and Hager and Gonczi (1993) have used the word "integrated" to convey their emphasis on underlying attributes being as important as the identification of key functions. Thus, although earlier functional analyses may have emphasized the role of tasks over all else, there has been a clear recognition that some combination of tasks and traits is more appropriate.

Among the pre-eminent premises of this approach are:

1. There exists an agreed-upon notion of competence for each role.

2. Assessment built upon a functional approach to competence can "guarantee" information about a person's competence that is accurate, specific, reliable and valid.

3. Content domains can be precisely and unambiguously specified.

4. Occupations or experts agree on what constitutes appropriate roles and performance standards, and this agreement is relatively stable.

5. Past performance is the best indicator of future performance.

6. There are sufficient resources available to provide adequate sampling of the competence domains.

7. Assessment of performance in the regular course of carrying out one's work is the best form of evidence of competence.

8. Differences in value judgments can be worked out technically.

9. Clarity resides in standards written on paper and may be made clear for everyone to see.

10. A system for assessing competence in one occupational sector or domain will transfer to another setting.

There are several positive aspects to the behavioural approach. First, substantial evidence amassed by Wolfe (1995) from the English and Welsh experiences with National Vocational Qualifications indicates that assessment of competence-based learning in this functional approach does have a demonstrable validity in measuring occupational performance over more traditional methods. Related to this is evidence that past performance is, indeed, a more accurate predictor of future performance than other measures (Klemp, 1982). Second, as in the case of the behavioural approach, the clarification of what is to be learned has been useful in determining how it will be assessed and in what form it will be recognized. Third, in the very nature of the explication of content and criteria for determining standards, the functional approach has ironically laid bare the fundamentally arbitrary nature of its assessments. Fourth, the functional approach, by its emphasis on performance rather than acquisition, has eased open credential access through Prior Learning Assessment to learners who may have gained learning outside of formal educational systems.

Most assumptions of the functional approach are questionable. The shortcomings of these assumptions have been catalogued at length by many writers, including Ashworth (1992), Ashworth & Saxton (1990), Collins (1983), Hyland (1994), Norris (1991) and Wolfe (1995). The following is an overview of these criticisms.

Assessment requirements have often been methodologically oppressive, time consuming and expensive. This is a sweeping generalization, but doing "authentic" assessment in the workplace has been found to have all of these features when compared to administering a simple multiple-choice test. Furthermore, with all of the checklists and time sampling, there is the impression that a great deal is happening. This is the mesmerizing effect of the well-oiled system. Collins (1983) referred to this tendency as the "busyness syndrome": "Security is gleaned from 'actually doing something' regardless of the quality of its effects ... [I]nasmuch as competency-based systems serve as conduits for mere 'busy' work, they tend to discourage users from identifying and critically evaluating problems within their own learning situations" (pp. 178-179). High levels of stress are often associated with all this activity as more and more data are generated, collected and analyzed in the name of accountability. After a certain point, I believe that quality actually goes down in proportion to the empirical demand for quality indices.

This approach seems to promise precision, but ultimately its assessments still rest on norms and the arbitrariness of human judgment. Part of the illusion of precision comes from the technical jargon associated with various systems of competence. This is most clearly seen with the National Vocational Qualifications (NVQ) system in Britain (Department of Employment, 1989).

The atomistic requirements for reliability result in a need for more and more specification in a downward spiral of reductionism. Wolfe (1995) outlines this phenomenon in her description of attempts to produce unambiguous criteria on the English Graduate Certificate of Education examinations written by sixteen-year-olds at the end of compulsory schooling:

> First of all, the attempt to specify domains led, in every subject group, to the further elaboration of sub-domains, sub-sub domains—and no doubt sub-sub-sub-domains too. There were two (related) reasons for this. The first was the attempt to pin down the ever-elusive comprehensive list of criteria which differentiated levels of performance, and which could somehow never be made long or explicit enough to preclude false ascription ... [The second was] the issue of "compensation" [where assessors try to compensate for what they perceive to be inadequacies in the performance criteria], and the ambiguity this imports into any summary of grade descriptors (p. 73).

There has been an overemphasis on skills to the detriment of theory in functional approaches (Smithers, cited in Wolfe, 1995). This was a definite bias in the re-design of the British vocational qualifications.

Towers (1994) has charged that the functional approach in outcomes-based teacher education emphasizes minimal standards while virtually ignoring maximum learning expectations.

There is an underestimation of the role of social issues and context in the operation of the functional approach. This is why many authors see competence-based learning as reinforcing the status quo (Magnusson & Osborne, 1990).

In the predetermination of performance standards there is the danger of precluding new or hitherto unseen criteria in the development of competence in an occupation or in an educational setting. Do we really know where we're headed?

There seems to be a failure to recognize the importance of the beliefs and values of the assessors. This has been mentioned already in relation to their compensation for perceived flaws in the assessment system. This is also related to the social issues and contingencies criticism already mentioned.

A problem occurs in functional approaches such as the British NVQ when 100 percent mastery is required before the candidate can proceed to the next step in certification. For instance, in a ten-unit course, learners cannot proceed to further learning until they have mastered each sequential unit in turn. This, in effect, can hold learners hostage to the weakest link in their learning and imposes tremendous inflexibility and perhaps unrealistic expectations on the candidate's learning experience.

The Humanistic Approach

There would seem to be an inherent contradiction in relating competence-based learning to humanistic notions of learning. This has been the source of much debate in Britain in publications such as *A Liberal Vocationalism* by Silver and Brennan (1988). In the United States, a humanistic theme has continued to linger in competence-based learning in contrast to the more prominent behavioural and functional approaches. The humanistic theme, for example, has been evident in many small liberal arts colleges, including Alverno, Stephens, Rollins and Mars Hill, which have used a competence-based learning approach to achieve a more integrative and broadly conceived ideal of the full development of the individual.

Since this approach lends itself to higher education more readily than some of the others, it will be discussed here within the context of liberal education. Several prominent premises are operating here: (1) education is preparation of the whole person for life in all its facets; (2) liberal education can be extended to incorporate elements of the practical without diminishing the idea of knowledge for its own sake; and (3) related to the above, theory plays a dominant role but it is informed by practice.

The humanistic approach has provided a moderating influence in some of the debates on competence-based learning. In an interesting analysis of the affects of competence-based learning on liberal education, Ewens (1979) suggested that the emphasis on the practical has tended to subvert the primary theoretical orientation of "traditional" liberal education.

There are at least two arguments on the critical side. First is the argument that liberal education simply cannot accommodate the competence-based learning emphasis on practical concerns. Second, and in contrast to the first, is the familiar cry that this approach is too theoretical and has less applicability than other approaches.

The Constructivist Approach

This approach emphasizes the interpretive role of the person in making sense of competence. It borrows from Kegan (1982) in his description of the individual as a meaning maker within a state of human development and within a "life-surround." Candy's (1989) discussion of assumptions of constructivist thought is also very pertinent. The creation of meaning can take various forms, including knowledge, skills, attitudes, values and feelings. The role of meaning schemes in the interpretation of reality figures prominently within this approach (Mezirow, 1991).

Hodkinson (1992) has likewise given prominence to the role of schemas in what he has termed an "interactive" model of competence. He states: "From this perspective, what we learn depends at least as much upon our beliefs and existing understanding (schemas) as it does on what we are taught. Learning is a dialectical process, where our use of schemas filters experience as we know it" (p. 33).

The constructivist approach is based on the following assumptions *to a significant extent*:

1. People create their own reality.

2. Reality is socially constructed.

3. Construction of reality reflects an interaction between the unique biographical experiences of those involved; the social context including historical, cultural, economic, and political antecedents; and the physical context.

4. Explicating the framework of values and beliefs that constitutes one's meaning perspective or worldview offers a means to its revision and is therefore a useful exercise.

5. Reality is under constant change and development.

One advantage to this approach is the alternative view it gives to a functional approach such as that used in the NVQ scheme. Hodkinson (1992) states it this way:

> From this perspective, the search for the definitive elements of competence to fit an occupational role becomes little more useful than the hunt for the holy grail, because there will be no absolute and objectively defined role in the first place. Rather, the role will be defined by the perceptions of different people, which in turn will be the product of their culture, history and interactions with others. The nature of role also depends on the context in which it is placed, including the unequal power relations between participants. Views of the role will often be contested (p. 32).

The constructivist approach is ultimately optimistic in outlook because the reality being created can be changed with alterations in meaning perspectives or worldviews. The constructivist approach is generally holistic in outlook and would not look favourably on assessment practices that try to separate elements of competence from the important referents that give meaning to the competence. In all these ways, the constructivist approach emphasizes the central role of the person in the determination of competence.

This approach is often seen as unrealistic, as a flight of fantasy. It paints an overly optimistic view of change and ignores the given parameters of reality. Furthermore, when reality can be so subjective, it makes prediction, control and accountability very difficult to pin down.

Purpose

The intent of establishing competence is a significant consideration that represents particular values. One of the major criticisms of competence-based learning is the tendency to spend an enormous amount of time and energy on the measurement issues of competence to the detriment of a broad discussion and critical analysis of purpose (Collins, 1983; 1991). This is ironic, since clarity of purpose has always been at the heart of competence-based learning, albeit in a narrower sense. At this point, it may useful to review some of the major uses for which competence-based learning has been touted:

1. clarity of intent and evaluation in learning and curriculum development;
2. fairness, equity and accessibility to training and education based on learning however acquired;
3. standards clarification and responsiveness to market conditions and competition;
4. accountability.

The purpose of competence-based learning usually makes sense only in relation to a content area or domain of learning and the level of generality.

Content Domain

The content domain is the "what" of competence. For what do we need functional adequacy? Competence-based learning has proven easier to apply in the vocational field than in the academic domain. There are inherent and intangible characteristics of each content domain that bend and shape the meaning of competence. One of the problems with competence has been the propensity to become mired in its measurement and thereby deflect attention from the more fundamental question of, competence for what?

Levels of Generality and Specificity

In most systems that try to capture competence and set criteria for functional adequacy, there is an attempt to specify levels of generality or specificity. With respect to specificity, we can still remember the onslaught of behavioural objectives that plagued the curriculum in the late 1960s and early 1970s, and I have already referred to the observations by Wolfe (1995) regarding the endless spiral of specificity that has been revealed in attempts to provide perfect clarity in the NVQ. On the other hand, a more general competence such as "willingness to think for oneself" may lend itself to a wide variety of interpretations and projections when it comes to determining functional adequacy.

The generality of competence varies with different purposes. Raven (1984) tackled the problem as follows:

> For certain purposes, it is possible to use the term *competencies* to refer to the motivated abilities—the entire package of motivated cognitive, affective, and cognitive behaviours—which are conjured up by such terms as 'initiative', and to use the term 'components of efficacy' or 'components of competence' to refer to the narrower behavioural tendencies which make up the competencies—such as the tendency to bring to bear past experiences or to obtain the co-operation of others in the pursuit of the goal (pp. 171-172).

The National Vocational Qualifications system lays out competence in a much more differentiated set of levels, identified here in order from the most general to the least: title, module name, element (learning outcomes), performance criteria, range statements, and prerequisite knowledge and skills. Avoiding some of this obsession with detail, Gonczi (1992) and Chappell and Hager (1994) explain a broader conception of competence, closer to the approach by Raven, in its application to the professions in Australia.

The Search for Generic Competence

The behavioural approach has emphasized generic competence in a limited way by what instructional designers have referred to as "transfer" (Gagné, 1970). This is the ability to take a skill learned in one situation and apply it in different contexts and at different times. When such skills include critical thinking, called "higher-order" thinking by advocates of this approach (Bloom, 1956), then the behavioural approach is about as close as it gets to generic competence. On the other hand, generic competence is exactly what the trait approach is about, since the idea is to discover those deep, underlying structures that substantially account for competence.

The search for generic competence in the functional approach has never progressed very far beyond the behavioural approach, probably because the functional approach was founded on similar beliefs that have highlighted the role of stimulus or environmental control. Raelin and Cooledge (1996) have pointed out that the failure to find generic competence across industry is largely because of the vast differences between organizations in terms of history, language, purpose, culture, and private or public sector orientation. The Quebec government made an attempt to find generic competence in some of its Manpower initiatives, but without apparent success (Drolet & d'Amour, 1987). Ashworth (1992) emphatically pointed out that the use of competence statements to describe learning in the NVQ had never properly addressed the issue of transfer.

The humanistic approach has focused on theory and liberal education in an effort to secure generic competence, as we saw earlier. The arguments for liberal education reside in many sources and will not be elaborated here. The constructivist approach has usually treated competence as inseparable from context and the people involved. Thus, this approach does not readily lend itself to generic analysis.

Characteristics and Role of the Assessor

Insofar as we recognize that competence, like beauty, lies mainly in the eyes of the beholder, or assessor in this case, we will limit unwarranted claims of objectivity or even omnipotence. The identification and assessment of competence is an act that reveals a mutuality between assessor and those assessed. It indicates as much about the assessor as those assessed since the establishment of competence is grounded in the value and belief systems of the assessor, which in turn are part of a larger social and cultural context. For example, in her review of competence-based assessment in England and Wales, Wolfe (1995) states that:

> all the research evidence that we have on assessors' behaviour emphasizes the very active role that their own concepts and interpretations play … Assessors do not simply "match" candidates' behaviour to asesssment instruction in a mechanistic fashion. On the contrary: they operate in terms of an internalized, holistic set of concepts about what an assessment "ought" to show, and about how, and how far, they can take account of the context of the performance, make allowances, refer to other evidence about the candidate in deciding what they "really meant," and so on (p. 67).

There is a close relationship between the assessor, the one assessed and the context.

Characteristics and Role of the Person Assessed

Who are you? The trait approach exists to address this question. The behavioural approach, on the other hand, has the least to say about this. The other approaches lie somewhere in between, with the humanistic and constructivist approaches having relevance to both assessor and assessed, since they emphasize the central place of person in the whole equation of competence.

Role is an important part of this discussion, since it begins to set the parameters for competence and thus the pre-eminent framework of values. Competence, like an arrow, can be aimed in many directions. Are we looking at a person's competence at the worksite, or are we concerned with his or her competence as a parent or spouse or homemaker? Are we interested in competence as it relates to a hobby such as gardening or competence in keeping fit and healthy? Are we interested in the competence of citizenship? Persons take on multiple roles in life, and there are elements of competence such as "trustworthiness" or "problem-solving attitude" that can cross role boundaries and sometimes make it difficult to set definitive parameters. One danger in dividing up the kaleidoscope of the whole person into what are ultimately arbitrary roles is the failure to acknowledge that there is a greater whole.

General Climate and Setting

The setting and the general climate of the times set further parameters on competence-based learning. Had the same degree of current fiscal competence, however broadly we might define that term, been applied in Alberta's booming economy of the 1960s and 1970s, we might not ever have experienced the drastic budget slashes to social services, health and education of the early 1990s. The general climate and setting is a grab-bag of variables that may influence competence-based learning. It is this indeterminate mix of contextual influences that makes empirical studies of competence-based learning so difficult. It is virtually impossible to isolate the relevant variables into cause-and-effect relationships. Instead, descriptive patterns are probably more useful. For example, Raelin and Cooledge (1996) cite evidence of substantive differences in what was considered to be management competence between private and public-sector organizations. Argis (1976) gave a stark example of the nearly futile attempts to get top managers to transfer a more humanistic management style from the learning site back to their home organizations.

The Heart of Competence

It will be recalled that the definition of competence was the "quality or state of being functionally adequate." Being functionally adequate is part of being. The concept of heart has to do with "one's innermost being: one's innermost or actual character, disposition, or feelings" (*Webster's Third International Dictionary*, 1986, p. 1044). This is the connection between heart and competence-based learning. Competence without heart is an empty vessel. Our lists of learning outcomes have but passing interest without heart. The recognition of the role of this kind of subjectivity often seems to be missing from occupational restructuring in sector boards or university curriculum revamping. Competence lists that claim to objectify what is important in performance and measurement terms are misguided at best and dangerous at worst. What is important often cannot be objectified or de-contextualized.

Heart is a concept closely associated with the personal characteristics of the person, whether assessor or the person assessed. Yet at the same time, it is not separate from the social and contextual features. I would like to highlight the role of heart by considering it to be a ninth dimension of competence-based learning or a transcendent dimension that contains all of the previous eight.

Part of discovering heart is getting to know the people who exercise the competence in question. There is something artificial and even disrespectful about setting standards of performance or functional adequacy for those of whom you have little knowledge. When government officials from the Scottish Vocational Education Council (Scottish Vocational Education Council, 1988)—the national accreditation agency overseeing vocational qualifications in Scotland—approached North Sea fishermen to begin setting up performance standards, the fishermen insisted these bureaucrats take a fishing trip out to sea with them. I think they were saying, "Hey, learn something about us first! And learn something about what you don't know."

Competence may be understood in a deeper way by first getting to know people. The anthropologist Robin Ridington (1995) tells the story of how his perception of Aboriginal people was permanently affected on his first exploration into the wilderness of central British Columbia in 1959. He had decided to test his skills in the wilderness near Mile 210 on the Alaska highway and was helping a friend build a cabin on his hunting and trapping territory. Soon they were visited by Beaver Indians from a nearby reserve. He recalls:

> Here in the forest north of the Peace River, I found a country still occupied by people whose right to the land was demonstrated, at least in their own thinking, by their knowledge of it [or competence in it]. They had not paid cash for the land or possessed it by changing it, nor could they imagine selling it any more than they could imagine selling a part of their own bodies. Their right was the right of belonging. It was the right of knowing. Their relationship to the land

was more complex, more deeply rooted, more spiritual, than simple material possession (p. 237).

Competence here is rooted in living with the land. There is care for the competence. It has heart. There is something about genuine caring and passion that does not succumb to a readily measurable and straightforward attitude yet greatly contributes to the definition of competence. In fact, it is a little like trying to put a price on love. Competence is encompassed and then eclipsed by heart. It is not the purpose here to explore what type of competence does or does not have heart. Rather, the aim is to point to heart as an important element in the meaning of competence and competence-based learning.

If empirical methods are not well suited to the determination of heart, then how can we tell if a competence has heart? Intuition, or the process of coming to direct knowledge without resort to reasoning, has an underused role to play here. It is underused in the sense that it does not appear as an issue in most of the large-scale functional approaches to competence-based learning. Nevertheless, we saw that in the NVQ, assessors used intuition anyway. Intuitive knowing, with its holistic touch, is one of the ways back to simplicity after the complexity of issues and questions introduced by these nine dimensions of competence.

Conclusion

Competence has a useful role to play in instruction and evaluation. It is not the concept itself that has been a problem but rather the use to which notions of competence have been put and the unrealistic expectations placed on it. Notions of competence cannot by themselves somehow magically resolve questions that are ultimately ones of value and power. Yet as a heuristic device, competence-based learning has a contribution to make to reflective pedagogy.

Many of us together have put effort into deciding which of several learning outcomes should be core or elective, general or more specific, have a more definite action verb, need to be broken into several sub-tasks, whether the outcome can be measured and how and so on. The understandings that result from such discussions can be very significant, for without the deeper meanings and judgments that accompany the lists, they are sails without a ship. It was the dialogue among assessors that led Wolfe (1995) to conclude that networks of assessors were a key to successful implementation of a reliable standard of competence in the NVQ. This relates to the notion of communicative competence described by Habermas (1984; 1987). Therefore, a major contribution of competence-based learning may be to clarify the assessor's intentions at the outset and to thereby alert the learner. Learning outcomes provide a clarity at the starting point rather than the ending point. Through this clarity, competence-based learning can emphasize the teaching-learning process and keep assessment in its proper relationship to this process. It can provide a beacon for reference and for student appeal. In concert with initiatives in Prior Learning Assessment, it has offered more accessibility to formal learning to those with informal learning. However, those who would employ competence-based systems must recognize the inherent limitations or become trapped by them. They will end up assessing the body after the spirit has fled and not know the difference.

26

The Tolerable Contradictions of Prior Learning Assessment

Alan M. Thomas

Prior Learning Assessment (PLA), or Prior Learning Assessment and Recognition (PLAR) as it is more commonly becoming known in Canada, is potentially the most radical innovation in education since the development of mass formal education during the last century.[1] PLAR promises a major transformation in the relationships among informal, non-formal and formal Adult Education in the context of lifelong learning. PLAR is usually defined, and certainly most often discussed, in terms of what it does. We have given less thought perhaps to what it is.

What PLAR does largely has been cast in terms of its use in systems of formal education, rather than in the broader arena of "certification" for which most current definitions allow, and which is, perhaps, best reflected in the French distinction between Prior Learning Assessment (PLA) and Prior Learning Validation (PLV). It is from the encounter between PLAR and formal education that we have drawn most of our experience, and this may be in itself the first of the tolerable contradictions. The addition of "Recognition" to the original term in Canada is simply an indication of the extension of interest in PLAR to groups outside the education system, although a candidate must be identified as a "student" before gaining access to the assessment.

The impact of PLAR has already been felt. It has revealed neglected aspects of our educational systems that tell us something about the nature of teaching and learning, and knowledge and knowing.

CAUCE/OCULL (1995) defines PLAR as follows:

> Prior learning assessment is based on the premise that adults acquire skills, knowledge and attitudes through many means of formal and informal learning. A PLA system evaluates this learning and relates it to the learning outcomes of post-secondary courses and programs for the purpose of granting credit ... Op-

tions for assessing prior learning include the following: challenge exams, oral examinations, skills demonstrations/product evaluation, standardized tests, performance observations, transcripts, licenses and certificates, portfolio review (p. 1).

With the exception of "transcripts and licenses" and the like, which seem a matter of conventional credit transfer, the CAUCE/OCULL definition is as useful as any currently available. This definition allows entry to, and progress through, academic experience on bases other than academic experience, and it is construed principally to be a means of translating learning resulting from other experience into the equivalent of learning resulting from academic experience. It is still too soon to know which of the alternative means of access are being most used or most useful. However there is interesting evidence appearing that the process of "portfolio development," the most novel of the means, has afforded the candidate a liberating sense of the character of the educational journey, which has not been encouraged in the past by educational agencies.

In this chapter, two principal factors are considered: the character of PLAR itself and the dynamics of its introduction into systems of formal education, principally in Canada. How those two things are related presents an additional collection of ironies. Finally we will return to a consideration of some of the meanings of PLAR in the education of adults.

The Character of Formal Education

Consider, first of all, the character of the educational systems in which PLAR is being introduced. Historically, they are closed systems because within them, success is measured in more or less identifiable learning outcomes resulting from exposure to an environment determined by the system itself. Performance with respect to achievement is measured by individuals or groups formally identified as "educators" or "teachers," who have designed the environment in the first place and who have traditionally been granted, and jealously retain, the right to do so.

The term *environment* is used here broadly to include schools, books, buildings, organization of the educational year, programs, courses, even student associations; everything, in fact, that defines and creates the student. In the ideal maintenance of this environment, teaching is inseparable from evaluation, and learning, defined in terms of outcomes, is inseparable from the way it has been taught. It is to the culmination of the effective separation of these three activities—teaching, evaluation and learning—a separation that has been proceeding relentlessly in Western education for nearly half a century, that PLAR makes its spectacular contribution.

The degree to which the "ideal" has been maintained throughout formal education in Canada has varied according to educational levels. In the universities it has been traditionally very high, in the lower systems less so, though the increasing power of teachers during the last half century has raised it considerably. At public schools, that trend has been slowed somewhat recently by the introduction of system-wide testing, though the teachers continue to control the content and evaluation of the tests. The work of the College Standards and Accreditation Council (CSAC) in Ontario, and of comparable bodies in other provinces, is having similar effects on the colleges. Even in the universities, increased demand for access from students and increased demand for outcomes from employers has begun to blur the boundaries of control. Nevertheless, the basic pattern remains: the educational system evaluates on the basis of a learning experience it has designed and controls. A great deal of the current PLAR literature, for obvious reasons, insists on the sanctity of that right.

One might observe in passing that learning accomplished in this setting, that is, learning that results from teaching, is every much as "experiential" as learning accomplished in other circumstances. It is simply that the experience of being a student, of being taught, is so familiar to us that we hardly recognize it as such, thus blinding ourselves to much of the experience of formal education. It might be more accurate if we referred to "sponsored" and "unsponsored" experiential learning.

It is useful at this stage to distinguish between two different connotations of the English word *learning*, both of them legitimate and often, at serious risk, confused. The emphasis on "English" is deliberate since the word *learning* is unique to this language. That fact might serve as a caution to those working in the area of PLAR and foreign educational experience. In English the word is used first to describe a *process,* an *activity*; the second way the word is used is to denote the *results* or *outcome* of that activity. When the two meanings are confused, the resulting misconception suggests that the failure to learn some particular outcome is a failure of the process itself, and therefore a failure of the learner. It is a confusion to which large organizations are particularly prone.

PLAR involves both meanings, and their proper distinction throws a light on its significance. While it is usually considered to be concerned primarily with the second meaning, outcomes, in fact it carries a message of particular consequence with respect to the first meaning, the ability of the specific individual to engage in the process of learning under a variety of circumstances.

The principal characteristic of formal education highlighted by PLAR has to do with the way in which the formal system treats learning that occurs either prior to admission or concurrently, with participation outside the educational environment. The exclusiveness of the formal educational environment has inclined its authorities to either ignore or deplore the learning acquired outside, although the degree to which that is true varies according to different levels of education.

Since by law the public school system must accept everyone, they must take into account both prior learning and concurrent learning. Mostly they try to ignore prior learning, deplore it, or attempt to counteract it.

Post-secondary education tries to eliminate irrelevant prior learning by its control of admission and tries to diminish the impact of concurrent learning by extending the environment as widely as possible and encouraging "membership" as well as "studentship." Hence the deep distaste for the part-time student whose concurrent learning as potentially creative in the usually lengthy educational program is largely ignored, or discounted, except by the student. To be sure, co-operative education and distance education are making inroads on the preservation of these tendencies, but none strikes at the heart of the educational enterprise to the same degree as PLAR.

Educational evaluation was originally designed, and for the most part remains, a prediction of further success or failure within the controlled and special educational environment. It is accomplished by various means, each one involving the development of reciprocal skills on the part of both teachers and students that become the principal preoccupation of students. Various and creaky as it sometimes is, it has served the system very well. Judging the potential of other people is a principal preoccupation of us all.

What was not clearly predicted a century ago was the extent to which these evaluations, which tend to become "certifications" outside the system, would be used for myriad other purposes by the society as a whole, mostly in terms of employment. Recently the usage has become global. So long as the system restricted itself to children and youth and involved a one-time passage from school to the greater outside world, the use of these evaluations for other purposes than for which they were created, and indeed, the self-containment of the system itself, was allowable. Conflict over how the educational environment would be controlled is endemic to such an arrangement, but rarely has it involved society on such a large scale. As our society becomes more complex, however, both in terms of the growth of technology and the movement of people throughout the world, the formal educational systems have begun to include other segments of the population, principally adults, on both a consecutive and concurrent basis. Until the introduction of PLAR, those developments have occurred without radical change in the methods of evaluation or in society's use of them. Add to that the increasing proliferation of knowledge and information outside the educational system and it is inevitable that the control of the formal system itself by a relatively small group of designated, trained teachers and administrators would be challenged.

That challenge comes in various forms, though none so profound and potentially engulfing as PLAR. One of the curious aspects of the traditional "academic" certification is that it travels easily through time and awkwardly through space. A high-school certification and an undergraduate degree received twenty or more years ago within the country in question are valid today, with some exceptions, for admission to further study and are used somewhat recklessly with respect to employment. However, when a degree has been awarded in another country, another culture or sometimes even in another province, regardless of when it was completed, it is often subject to some form of discrimination. It is to the limitations of the current system of evaluation with respect to space—including economic, social and political, and geographical space—that PLAR offers a formidable challenge. In terms of time, also, PLAR perhaps represents a comparable challenge by providing a means for the identification of current skills and knowledge.

The Introduction of PLAR in Canada

The impact of the introduction of PLAR in Canada can be categorized into developments affecting faculty, students and providing agencies, as well as the nature of education, learning and knowledge themselves. It is too soon to grasp the long-term implications of PLAR, but the short-term impact is interesting enough. The existing literature of PLAR has examined its impact on faculty and providing agencies, less so with respect to students and the nature of knowledge. There is in the literature a good deal of polemical, anecdotal and technical how-to-do-it material, but little of the research based or contemplative. There has been recent evidence that some agencies, notably the colleges, are beginning to collect data systematically. A substantial federally supported project recently established at Ontario Institute of Studies in Education/University of Toronto, New Approaches to Lifelong Learning devotes a large segment to PLAR. It is essential that knowledge gained through the project and anecdotal material be shared more widely and consistently.

Faculty

Faculty, meaning teachers at all levels, are key to the success or failure of PLAR. Under challenge is the system they depend on and support, the system of the steady accumulation of grades assigned, programs completed, awards granted and stature achieved. It is that system of evaluation that is, or has, represented the much-vaunted "seamlessness" associated with articulation and systematization in the past. It is precisely that form of seamlessness that PLAR invades. Perhaps for that reason, in Canada and elsewhere there is little evidence of the formal introduction of PLAR being initiated by members of faculty. The overwhelming evidence so far is that the initiative for the introduction of PLAR has come either from senior levels of administration or from government. Curiously, it has not come from any of the outside groups, at least until recently, whose members are likely to be the principal beneficiaries.

It is ironic that the formal grading system, as a basis for admission and advancement, has never been as iron-bound as it has seemed from outside of the formal system or from the stern rhetoric of formal documents. There is evidence that a good deal of discretion has been practiced, but always at the "pleasure" of the faculty. It is the conferring of a right on students to be evaluated independently of how they have been taught, and presumably of the circumstances under which they have learned, that compels existing, intuitive, private practices, imbedded within individual and collective judgments and decisions, to become coherent, systematic and open to public scrutiny. Whatever the arguments advanced for the significance of doing so, and they are many and diverse, we should not be surprised that there is considerable reluctance and hesitation to be found among faculty. Faculty reputation, security and self-esteem are based totally on public and private confidence in the existing predominant system. More open public discussion among faculty and faculty associations about the meaning of PLAR is essential, as is more dialogue about issues such as the identification of new skills in evaluation.

The Canadian Association for Prior Learning Assessment (CAPLA) is a new national association that has already prompted changes in the educational establishment. The essence of the formal system, of the educational "environment," is that it is graded. An overwhelming characteristic of student life is that of "next-year country"; the next course, the next year, the next grade, the next institution—it is inescapably a life of futures, measured in annual or semestered steps. Dominated by successive providing agencies, historically determined for the most part, each stage is a preparation for the next, with the student being the only real link between the steps. Understandably there has always been some distance between agencies at different levels and their personnel. Sometimes acrimony prevails as teachers higher up the ladder deplore the preparation of their students at the previous stages whose sole preoccupation that should have been. For the system, as designed, such distance is endemic. However, PLAR introduces a new factor, because while teaching may be graded, learning, on the whole, is not.

PLAR can only survive if it is system-wide in acceptance, if not in direct practice. The recognition of that necessity has already stimulated more exchange between individuals at various educational levels than we have witnessed for some time. CAPLA cannot succeed unless all levels of education are represented actively and effectively. PLAR itself cannot succeed unless there is even greater confidence in the validity of its assessments throughout the entire system and among the public at large than exists even for the current methods of evaluation. If the attempts to improve university teaching are a useful example, the integrity of the judgments required by PLAR will be better sustained by organizations like CAPLA than they will be by any kind of administrative fiat or regulations. That can only be accomplished if CAPLA sees as its main purpose the systematic facilitation of professional exchanges between the "users" of PLAR at all levels of education in Canada.

An examination of the "portfolio" or "dossier" process in PLAR will reveal a close resemblance to the processes associated with the security and promotion of university faculty. Thus the venue that seems to be the most hesitant about the public acknowledgment of PLAR is also the venue that has developed many of the skills in judgment essential to the implementation of one of its most important mechanisms. All of us, everywhere in the system, have something to learn from this area of university experience.

PLAR has already stimulated innovative co-operation within and across educational agencies and levels in Canada as well as suggesting new links between the processes of education and those of other institutions in our society. Capitalizing on these new relationships is important, since it is precisely these relationships that will contribute more to seamlessness, where it is desirable, than any structural or programmatic changes.

Finally there is the potential of shortening student programs by accrediting external learning, and thereby reducing the need for courses and faculty. Whether the projected increase in numbers of new students or the additional work required for the administration of PLAR will compensate for the decline in conventional hours required is not yet clear, though apprehension has been present since the early stages. Part of the problem is the way in which we collect educational information and part is that the financial implications make themselves felt in different areas of the providing agencies, indeed of the entire system, than do the teaching or administrative demands. PLAR shows as much potential for affecting financial practices within the formal system as it does of affecting everything else. While the re-distribution of tasks and costs will undoubtedly take some time, the net result should lie in a reduction of unnecessary teaching for faculty and in unnecessary "time-serving" by students. At the same time, it will involve the inclusion of students with different backgrounds in learning that will contribute to the vitality—and problems—of teaching. Swedish experience provides interesting evidence of the latter (Abrahamsson, 1984).

We are all painfully aware that PLAR's promise of identifying new constituencies of students manifests itself against a background of relentless reduction in conventional educational resources. The students aged twenty and older for whom PLA is most appropriate have for two decades been the fastest growing source of students at all educational levels. The commensurate promise of PLAR is that it will allow us to increase the efficiency of our educational provision without automatically sacrificing both standards and students.

Students

Despite nearly thrity years of growing experience with PLAR in Western countries, it is the students about whom we seem to know the least. There is as yet no evidence arising from longitudinal studies to address questions such as: Who are PLAR students? How well do PLAR students succeed academically compared to other students? Are PLAR students relating to knowledge differently than those students who have been exclusively taught in formal educational institutions? Most of what we know so far is based on the anecdotal, valuable in itself, but no substitute for the results of disciplined inquiry.

In the United States, with its large number of private post-secondary providing agencies, there has been active recruiting by agencies hungry for new populations or constituencies of students. This has been less true in Britain, France and Canada. But nowhere, it appears, has there been the anticipated avalanche of students from these new constituencies that suddenly have access to formal education in a more efficient way. In Ontario, the discrepancy between the sometimes unstated expectations of the early implementation groups and the reality of demand has been dramatic. Since the period of initiation, demand has grown slowly.

Experience suggests that other factors are at work, not the least of which is the conditioning about the proper nature of formal education that each child receives more thoroughly than anything else provided by the system. While learning may not be graded, education is, and the need to complete it in precisely the way it is provided has long been evident among the adults who have eschewed "mature student" opportunities in order to complete secondary school as God intended they should. Other reports indicate that students faced with the opportunity of challenge exams or portfolios often decide they are too frightening and risky compared to proceeding in the conventional manner.

There may be a distinction to be found here between PLAR used for purposes of admission and PLAR used for advanced standing. That distinction seemed more than clear in the original research (Thomas & Klaiman, 1989). This distinction may be shared as much by students as by educational administrators. It may also be the case that in our concern for "standards," the mantra of educational anxieties, we are making the PLAR route so difficult and unfamiliar that potential students can only see failure and aggravation before them. There is compelling evidence for the need to review the initial procedures. It would be an advantage if those reviews were based on some empirical evidence.

One area of experience with PLAR is producing evidence about problems associated with a *threshold* phenomenon in adult education that is supported by experience in other areas of adult education in Canada. The project underway at General Motors in Oshawa, Ontario, and in a couple of other centres in Canada, resembles the American programs of "Joint Ventures" (sponsored by the Council for Adult and Experiential Learning [CAEL]) and involves a four-way co-operation between employers, unions, educators and students. As in the case of labour education in Canada, individuals are "employees" or "members" before they become students, and become students only as a function of occupying the other roles. Obviously the two roles are closely and psychically intertwined. Japan provides a particularly good example of the large-scale combination of student-employee roles. It is possible that as educators we underestimate the difficulty faced by those who have less formal education in their transformations into adult students, that is, of their crossing the educational threshold. That crossing is made easier and more intelligible for those individuals if it is imbedded in the more familiar role of employee or member.

Perhaps it is only members of the middle class—the class that virtually owns the educational system—that can literally walk in off the street and register as students. In a way we already feel like "members" of that system. It is possible that the major impact of PLAR will be felt through the effective operation of projects and avenues. The administrative, economic and cultural impact of that type of development is beyond our immediate scope, but there is great promise that it will be by those means that we will begin to deal with the "inequitable" characteristics of adult education in Canada.

A final observation drawn from what evidence we have about students and PLAR can be made only tentatively and with caution, but may turn out to be the most important of all implications. Reflecting on the development of PLAR in Canada and the United States, one is struck by the prominent role played by women both in implementation and use. The leading American organization, CAEL, has been predominantly an organization run by women. Leadership in Ontario colleges and elsewhere in Canada also has been provided by a large number of women. Even more cogently, the investigation of the use of "maturity credits" in Ontario secondary schools since their introduction in 1974 (Thomas & Klaiman, 1989) revealed that three times as many women as men applied for the credits, and the same proportion completed the programs to which they were admitted. It is possible that the more personal, individual procedures of PLAR, associated most prominently in the development of portfolios, resembles the learning preferences of women some feminist literature suggests are gender related if not gender specific (Belenky et al, 1986; Gilligan, 1988). The preponderance of women at nearly all levels of formal and informal adult education may be the least visible but strongest support for the development of PLAR.

It is to the students we ultimately will have to turn in order to understand the real significance of PLAR. There is a great deal of accumulated experience of students that needs to be articulated and systematized if PLAR is to realize its full potential, and there is an overwhelming need for systematic inquiry.

Providing Agencies

Obviously anything that affects faculty and students will affect the providing agencies, though to differing degrees. The public school system has the greatest opportunity to address equity issues. A larger portion of the population most in need of educational opportunity turns there first. However, that opportunity is matched by a responsibility to act "beyond" the operating dimensions of the system by recommending potential students out of it, and helping them gain access to the appropriate providers. It is here that the "non-graded" implications of PLAR will make themselves felt most dramatically, since it will become clear to increasing numbers of applicants that obtaining admission to secondary school is not really the point. If PLAR operates at all levels including "certification," the point will be to place the individual appropriately anywhere in the system. While that demand will assert itself at the other levels, it will perhaps be less cogent since colleges and universities are closer to the ultimate goal of the potential student.

Evidence from Sweden (Abrahamson, 1984), arising from its policy of admission to university on the basis of age and years in employment, suggests two immediate impacts on post-secondary agencies: a decline of interest in programs in favour of individual courses, and the lessening of the distinction between being a student and occupying other roles in the society. The latter may be of less consequence to us because of our long tradition of "part-time" study, but the first leads directly to a decrease in control of the student's environment as part of the traditional educational ideal.

Nothing makes this clearer than the debate over "residence" requirements, the most prominent of the vestiges of formal education as "total" institution. Existing evidence indicates that there is no providing agency that will allow a complete program to be accredited by means of PLAR. Percentages of required study vary, but everywhere some experience with the "teaching" program of a particular agency is a requirement. This seems particularly ironic in the light of the steady proliferation of "certification" bodies, such as the National Council of Academic Awards in Great Britain and The British Columbia Council for Admissions and Transfer, where teaching and certifying are separated.

It would appear that both students and administrators believe there is a unique "cultural" quality to the experience of a particular providing agency. The increase in the practice of graduates of attaching the "home" of their degrees to their resumes is indicative of the tenacity of that belief. Is it possible that we simply do not trust methods of evaluation that are not deeply imbedded in instruction itself?

The separation of teaching and evaluation, most clearly signified by PLAR, is growing, and we will have to rethink those relationships. The imposition of formal requirements of somewhat ill-defined "residence" has outlived its usefulness and function. The intriguing suggestion from Australia, that, while the university may not be the source of all university-level learning, it remains the "steward" of that learning throughout its society (CAUCE, 1995), allows for the concept of the separation of teaching and evaluation and should provoke useful discussion of the proper role and function of existing agencies.

Inherent in these practices also are expectations about the degree to which each stage of formal education "conditions" the student for the next one. This is an aspect of the "total" educational environment we only think about when it is patently absent. It has to do, not just with specific knowledge in a specific subject matter, but with more inclusive habits of being a student. When fully operational, PLAR will disrupt these expectations perhaps more than any others, since it will bring into the academy individuals who are without the conventional experience of being taught, whose context for knowledge is quite different. That in itself may be good for our schools, colleges and universities, but it will not be an experience without conflict and misunderstanding.

The initial research (Thomas & Klaiman, 1989) revealed little or no evidence of the development of special offices, positions or personnel associated with the administration of PLAR. By and large, where it was practiced, it was accomplished as part of existing roles and responsibilities. The skills involved were assumed to be similar to those already possessed by the individuals assigned to administer PLAR. As was pointed out earlier, the universities are concerned that there is a strong resemblance between the skills associated with the manner in which faculty evaluate each other and those involved in PLAR. A witness to an evaluation being carried out by a secondary-school assessor is struck by the degree to which the assessor's experience with the community from which the candidate comes plays a part in the evaluation, resembling the experience that university colleague "peers" have of one another. These contextual details, so often unarticulated, suggest that the skills associated with PLAR, with its high degree of individualized assessment, are particular skills we have only just now begun to identify.

In their roles of systems managers, governments such as those of Ontario and Quebec stimulated the creation of specific organizations, roles and designations, but the current trend is to re-absorb these roles and procedures within pre-existing ones. While the desirable long-term outcome is to absorb PLAR into the regular operations of the providing agencies, it is important that the assimilation not occur too early in the process. Specially designated individuals frequently act as "advocates" for PLAR, a critical role particularly when the anticipated student demand is slow to materialize. Such identification serves the additional purpose of insisting that there are new skills or the refinement and extension of old ones required for PLAR. Without those pressures on the system, there is some danger that PLAR, after a brave beginning, will be overtaken by institutional inertia.

Finally, there is the matter of the identification on student transcripts of credits obtained by means of PLAR. Initially, many supporters of the introduction of PLAR argued against any such identification on the grounds that other variants of means of achievement are not so identified, and further argued that recipients of those documents, unfamiliar with or prejudiced against PLAR, would use such information as the basis for negative discrimination. However, it is equally possible to argue that the position that has been generally accepted undermines the special meaning of PLAR. The designation conveys that the individual is capable of learning from both being taught and from other sources of stimulation in a variety of circumstances. That variety of knowledge ought to be a plus for employers given the current rhetoric about the need for employees who are learners, and a plus to academic agencies as well. That reality of PLAR lies at the heart of the different meaning of knowledge that the instrument implies.

Conclusion

In reflecting on some of the contradictions implicit in PLA I have tried to highlight some aspects of what it is, as distinct from what functions it can perform. I have argued that it has implications beyond the system of formal education, implications for the separation of teaching and evaluation and for new relationships between student demands, or needs, and the practices of providing agencies.

The first suggests new relationships between "certification" and measures and symbols of educational achievement; the second, the liberation of teaching from both certification and awards; the third, the liberation of learning from instruction and the last, the extension of what it means to be a student. Our adult population has for some time been making consecutive and concurrent use of our educational systems. In response, grudging adjustments have been made of an educational system that held, and to a degree still holds, the ideal of "total" authority over the environment of the learner. PLAR is, in my opinion, the practical and symbolic instrument for rethinking the entire enterprise.

I began by asserting that PLAR is potentially the most radical innovation since the introduction of mass formal education for children and youth in the last century, and its extension to adults in this one. It is radical because it challenges the vaunted seamlessness of formal education on both functional and intellectual grounds. The assault is functional in the sense that it attacks the maintenance of linear verticality and limited entrances and exits that have characterized formal education until now. PLAR in effect makes legitimate the way in which adults have been making use of the formal system, with reluctant assistance from the authorities, for nearly half a century. It is intellectual on the grounds that it asserts that not all important, essential knowledge comes from instruction, and places hope in a future form of education that is an acknowledged rather than surreptitious combination of the two, assisted rather than divided by formal education. For example, the application of PLAR promises to destroy the distinction between education and training that has corrupted learning in Canada for nearly a century precisely because it does not discriminate among sources of learning. Adult Canadians who have in the past only had access to training, with all of its limited rewards, will be free to move between education and training as their interests and needs dictate, taking advantage of the rewards of both.

While regarding PLAR as an instrument of liberation, it is also true that it can be seen as an instrument of seduction. In current uses of PLAR, learning acquired freely and from an immense variety of experience is obliged to seek evaluation by an educational system, which, like all educational systems, is limited in what it includes and rewards. The reason for that subjection is simply the degree to which educational rewards are used for multiple purposes in our society. It will only be with the effective extension of PLAR to non-educational purposes that its final value will be realized. There is slight but promising evidence that that is already taking place.

When that takes place the results for formal education will be not a huge, historical enterprise increasingly crippled by trying to reconcile the conflicting demands of economy, equity and efficiency, but a new, vital teaching and learning endeavour that can inspire the excitement and commitment characteristic of the origins of the medieval universities and of the "common" schools. What PLAR represents above all is the implications of the iron law that nothing is guaranteed to change an educational system more surely than a change in the composition of the student body. Commensurately, the non-educational use of PLAR will free learning from an exclusive subjection to education and educational certification. Fundamentally, PLAR is a means of providing for the individual's power over his or her own learning, which is the ultimate power of all.

Endnotes

[1] PLA is being experimented with throughout the industrialized world, but is known by different names; for example, the Recognition of Prior Learning (RPL) in Australia and South Africa.

27

Distance Education and the Virtual Classroom

Bruce Spencer

Distance education (DE) has always been associated with adult education, either in the form of the educator travelling to students (Frontier College, university extension) or the educational materials being delivered from the educator, who lives at a distance from the students (Farm Forum Radio, correspondence schools). Newer technologies allow for variations of these possibilities; for example, audio- or video-conferencing projects the educator and possibly some of the educational materials into remote classrooms.[1] Courses offered by computer network can allow students to pull down materials from a remote site as and when they wish. In addition, students in computer-networked courses can "conference" with fellow students or the tutor either in real time or asynchronously and can thus participate in, and create, an electronic or virtual classroom.

Although forms of DE have been part of adult education from the outset, DE has not been a major area of interest within adult education discourse (see Solar's chapter "Trends in Adult Education in the 1990s" in this volume). This omission is perhaps understandable given the individualized focus of most modern DE. Borje Holmberg, a leading exponent of DE, opens his *Theory and Practice of Distance Education* with the sentence: "Distance education is practised in all parts of the world to provide study opportunities for those who cannot—or do not want to—take part in classroom teaching" (1995, p. 1). He goes on to state that "usually students learn entirely individually and at their own pace. They then neither belong to a group or class, nor feel that they do so" (p. 1). While he notes there are many "exceptions to this rule," it nonetheless helps explain why adult education scholars, concerned with adult education as a dialogical and social activity, have ignored DE. If we accept Lindeman's contention that "true adult education is social education" (1947, p. 55), then a form of learning which is individual, usually print based and verbally non-dialogical cannot be considered as a viable form of "adult education." Even a definition of adult education that accepted multiple and diverse purposes for adult education, such as education for economy (vocational training), liberal arts education and others discussed in this book, would not readily recognize the legitimacy of such an individualized and often technologically dependent form of education as adult education. For example, Collins' (1991) plea for all those engaged in adult education to recognize their "vocational commitment" makes scarce mention of DE. Collins questions technocratic innovation and therefore can be read as a critic of DE with its formulaic instructional design and delivery and its obsession with technology.

However, given the development within DE of the electronic classroom, we need to revisit this issue. Questions to be resolved include: Does DE—particularly the electronic classroom—enable open, critical, liberal adult education? Does it facilitate authentic dialogue: the blending of experience with other knowledge and the pursuit of social educational aims (such as the promotion of participatory democracy and citizenship)? This chapter explores these questions by reviewing DE discourse, including DE's claim to critical adult education and social purpose. In particular, I critically evaluate the potential offered by the addition to individualized print-based courses of the "virtual classroom," that is, the classroom made possible by computer networking.

The Nature of Distance Education

Garrison supports a view that "distance education is a species of education characterized by one structural characteristic—the non-contiguity of teacher and student" (1989, p. 8). According to Keegan (1980), this "separation of teacher and student" is the first of six elements present in all well-established definitions of distance education: The others are:

- influence of an educational organization, especially in planning and preparation of learning materials,
- uses of technical media,
- provision of two-way communication,
- possibility of occasional seminars,
- participation in the most industrialized form of education.

This list illustrates that DE is focused on the techniques of delivery, which distinguishes it from most of the concerns of traditional "face-to-face" education. The list does not directly address many of the issues debated within adult education, although there are aspects of DE which are of interest to the field. For example:

- the idea that DE students study at a time and place of their own choosing is linked to ideas of self-directed, lifelong education;

- the target audience for DE institutions is, typically, adults studying part-time, fitting their studies around work, family and community commitments;
- although not all DE institutions describe themselves as "open," most claim "open access", i.e., no or few entry requirements into their main programs (as illustrated by the names of many DE institutions, including the British Open University (OU) and British Columbia's Open Learning Agency).

These aspects of DE—self-directed, lifelong, accessible education, open to all adults—can be considered goals of DE that are shared with adult educators in general (for a more extensive discussion of accessibility and openness in DE see Spencer, 1995).

However, distance educators' concern with the techniques of delivery lead them away from debating broader educational issues. Garrison (1989) argues for an understanding of DE to be located within the broader study of education itself. His discussion of adult and distance education (pp. 103-113) is limited by his concentration on "voluntarism" (students voluntarily enrol) and "self-directed learning" as the key features of adult education, features which ignore adult education's dialogical and social dimensions. He refers to the early experiments in adult education (such as Frontier College) that often had a distance education component, but he does not draw out the social educational methods, social purposes or the accessibility embedded in those experiments.

Dewey was one of the first educators to discuss social learning. He emphasized the use of small groups, dialogue, emotional support, individual and group experimentation and praxis. These are all elements that have been identified with adult education, particularly the kind of adult education associated with Freire, community action and education and the educational practices of new social movements (Freire, 1970; Fraser & Ward, 1988; Welton, 1993). These collectivist and social elements can be seen in juxtaposition to traditional DE's emphasis on serving the needs of individual learners and may explain the popularity of DE among policy makers, particularly among new-right politicians. The challenge for DE is to include social learning within the system, but it must be recognized that one of the obstacles to achieving that goal may be the structure of DE itself.

Overcoming the Structures of Distance Education

The structure of DE has been described by Peters (1983) as an "industrial model" of course production and delivery. Peters contends that DE is similar to a form of industrial production that depends on division of labour (between course authors, editors, instructional designers and tutors, for example), mechanization, rationalization, quality control and mass distribution. It can also be argued that a technologically dependent delivery of DE can entrench existing social and economic forms within that delivery system. Reliance on capital-intensive DE, manufactured within an industrial model, can make that education even more supportive of capital investment and even less accessible to educationally disadvantaged groups. The internal obsession with technologically advanced delivery systems and carefully structured knowledge, referred to as "instructional industrialism" by Evans and Nation (1987), will work against the more creative symbiosis of knowledge and experience necessary for social purpose education. The concentration on technology can mask the way the education is being used to achieve student conformity and adaptation to dominant ideology.

Distance teaching has also been characterized as a "contradiction in terms" (Sewart, 1983) because there is little teaching or student support and counselling beyond the package. If we add that the traditional views of the role of a university or college educator as essentially a transmitter of "banked" knowledge have been absorbed by distance educators, then it can be argued that all of these features have combined with DE's internal interests in delivery systems to push critical adult education to the margins. An exception to this trend should be noted in the way DE is organized in some economically disadvantaged countries. In this context, DE is often targeted at social goals and in many cases experienced in social groups. For example, a women's health group might gather in a remote settlement to be guided in their discussion via a radio link to a health educator. The purpose is not just learning about women's health issues but acting on the information within their community. Other inspiration can be found in historical examples of "distance" adult education such as the Frontier College and the National Farm Radio Forum (see Selman's chapter "The Imaginative Training for Citizenship" in this volume). However, it should be recognized that all these examples involve education that is received in a group context.

Perhaps a social purpose DE that promotes participatory democracy can best be built in collaboration with other educational and community groups not subject to the same internal institutional constraints as DE. Indeed, in a case study of the British Open University, Harris (1987) argued that "every kind of openness associated with distance education seems to have its opposite side, a tendency to closure, which also has to be considered" (p. 3). A simple example of what Harris is talking about may be provided by the increased use of computer networking resulting in greater student interaction but only for those with the equipment and skills.

Critical Distance Education

Three scholars from Deakin University in Australia have adopted a critical perspective on DE similar to that being argued here, which does support its potential as critical liberal adult education (Evans & Nation, 1989; Evans & King, 1991). They locate DE within the subject areas of education and social science. They reject a delivery-centred approach and argue that much DE should be understood as text production and reproduction and that critical theory and critical reflection can rescue DE from the social relations embedded in educational technology and tradition. To achieve this, students need space to engage in discourse with the text, to create their own text and to become more self-directed and independent learners. The Deakin-edited collections include several case studies that address these questions and provide examples of critical practice (some of which are more convincing than others). This kind of work is also proceeding in other locations, with courses designed to include more student choice, more open-ended projects, experientially based assignments and interactive materials. In arguing for critical reflection, for locating study within a broader yet critical understanding of the social context, the Deakin (and other) scholars marry critical theory and practice to some insights gained from postmodernism (see the chapter "Parameters, Pedagogy and Possibilties in Changing Times" by Grace in this volume).

How, then, can DE serve the social purposes of adult education? If DE is consciously combined with more social educational forms (for example, group and co-operative learning), and if it is linked to social movements (see Clover's chapter "Adult Education within an Ecological Context" in this volume, for example), then the social interaction and collective learning potential of an education (including experiential and critical knowledge) leading to diverse social purposes may be possible. For example, instead of emphasizing individual learning in order to fit into the economic designs of a company by becoming a better human resources manager, an individual may be provided with an opportunity to learn how to work with others to establish a genuinely democratic, self-managed enterprise. In these circumstances, the distance learning institution may provide vocational technical knowledge linked to the meetings of a community enterprise group. Although such links are possible, critical distance educators must come to terms with the structural constraints of DE institutions if they are to become a force for democracy.

The Virtual Classroom

In the examples offered for overcoming the limitations of DE discussed above, the spacial dimension of DE were complemented by existing community links or classroom teaching. This may indicate that social education requires interactive learning between students and students and between students and tutor, which may best be achieved face to face. However, it is also the case that some of these elements can be achieved electronically. An argument can be made as to the relative merits of traditional classrooms and computer-network classrooms, but the first emphasis here should be on DE without a classroom compared to DE with a virtual classroom added. The virtual classroom goes beyond the limited possibilities for dialogue with the text and telephone tutoring characteristic of traditional DE to embrace interaction with other students, small group discussion and open dialogue with the tutor. The computer network can also facilitate individual contact between students and between students and third parties (for example, by using links to other sites embedded within the electronic course materials). Thus the educational experience is no longer isolated and individualized but has the potential to be social and diverse. The very nature of DE as described by Holmberg is changed.

Electronic communication allows easier contact within existing community or interest groups and can be a means by which contact may be maintained once the group is established. It can also be argued that electronic communication has called forth new social groupings, but whether these are equivalent to new social movements or narrow interest groups has still to be determined. Our interest here is not so much with the informal learning possibilities of the Internet (the "Information Super Highway" could in any case be viewed as essentially a corporate transmission conduit)[2] but with the non-formal and formal educational opportunities provided by computer-mediated conferencing and learning.

Some might claim that newer technologies can completely replicate the classroom, but in my experience the types of interaction are different.[3] It is too early to be definitive about the strengths and weaknesses of the virtual classroom. Sometimes it may appear to be better, at others worse than a traditional seminar classroom; in any case, the interaction achieved electronically is simply not the same as that achieved face to face—it changes the educational experience. For example, short comments seem to work best in computer conferences, while more expansive and punctuated presentations do not.

Strengths and Limitations of Electronic Delivery

The asynchronous nature of some conferences (with students entering comments on different days) works against focused discussion. As individuals take up and reply to different points, the structure of an argument and the key issues can get lost. However, easier access to the debate may not result in a fuller exploration of an issue: it can lead to students discussing only the easier aspects of a problem, deflecting the tougher questions that would have been dealt with in a classroom. Also, a general invitation by the tutor to discuss a particular issue may go unheeded by the students; as Taylor comments, the skills required to moderate live and electronic conferences are different (Spencer & Taylor, 1994).[4] It should also be acknowledged that computer conferencing privileges those with typing and computer skills over those without (a bias favouring women?) and favours written over oral communication, thus discriminating against those with writing disabilities such as dyslexia.

I focus here on some of the limiting aspects of computer-mediated courses as a counterweight to the gushingly enthusiastic embrace of new technology and exaggerated claims made by some educational administrators and practitioners. For example, the claim that "computer-mediated communication traverses the oral/written continuum and encompasses qualities associated traditionally with both forms of communication" (Harrison & Stephen, 1996, p. 25, drawing on Wilkins, 1991) is simply unsupportable: the form of communication used currently is "written" and therefore the many qualities of oral communication cannot possibly be present.

There are, however, many positive aspects to the adoption of computer networking techniques. For example:

- Class discussion is not cut off by the end of the traditional class meeting or by a coffee break.
- The student does not have to gain the tutor's attention in order to make a contribution.
- It is more difficult for one person to dominate the debate since all participants can enter a comment.
- All electronic courses with conferencing equipment have a dialogical component, whereas many traditional classrooms are non-dialogical.
- Students gain from not being stereotyped by visual clues and may find making a presentation easier on-line than in front of a class
- Students with speech defects are not disadvantaged.
- A written comment in a conference can be read and re-read by tutor and classmates in contrast to a comment made verbally in a traditional classroom, which must be remembered or noted if it is to be recalled.

Many of the "benefits" of an on-line classroom have been claimed but not carefully researched. For example, do shy students find it easier to contribute? Or are students who are shy in a classroom also likely to be shy ("lurkers") in the conference? Is the quality of contributions higher (reflecting the fact that students have more time to construct an answer before posting it) than those made in a traditional classroom? Or are they in fact shallower (reflecting the ease of adding a quick comment when in front of the computer screen)? Can students easily amend a position as they gain more information? Or do they feel bound to defend what was so publicly posted? Students gain from not being so easily typecast by their body shape, skin colour, gender (this is likely to be known but it is not up-front when a comment is being read) and accent; but they may lose from not having visual and tonal clues associated with traditional classroom communication. Further, the kind of fierce debate that can occur in a classroom, the kind which is not personal once the right rapport has been established, may be difficult to reproduce on-line.

The Impact of the Virtual Classroom

Regardless of how all these issues around the relative merits of electronic classrooms are resolved, the virtual classroom has changed DE.[5] It has also made DE a possible method for delivering a fuller range of adult education programs, and doing so across an even wider terrain than previously.

Given the state of current research into computer-networked education, the questions still to be resolved are those outlined in the introduction. Dialogue is different when it is developed electronically, as is the group's social learning.[6] Experience to date supports the view that distance delivery alone is less capable than face-to-face methods of providing for social education, but that is not a reason to dismiss DE's virtual classrooms and hallways.

The virtual classroom is a substantial advance on, and indeed is qualitatively different from, the isolated, individualized learning of traditional distance education. Further, when it is combined with existing community, it can support social objectives and can do so across a wider terrain than is possible by traditional adult education. However, there is also a danger that the virtual classroom and the Internet will be used to support narrow aims, that they may not be critically examined by their advocates. It could be argued that these technologies, which are also being used in traditional educational institutions to supplement other means of education, were developed to help achieve economic goals of training and re-education rather than for social adult education.[7] However, given the shifts in funding and emphasis away from non-formal community-based provision, it is important for adult educators to consider the potential contradictions within the newly developed forms of DE and try to exploit these to achieve broader purposes. They do present opportunities for co-operative learning (McConnell, 1994) and, once the equipment is in place, can be more cost effective than other alternatives.

Social Education On-Line

We should not overlook the issue of differential access to computer-networking. Indeed, some have suggested that computer ownership will become a defining characteristic of the "haves" and "have-nots" in the Information Age. However, this is not an argument for ignoring new technology but rather an argument for making it communally and universally accessible. If we vacate the field, the field will be completely taken over by the privileged.

When students are linked in a community or environmental group, DE (in common with other education for adults) can become social education, can become not just social learning but learning with a social intent. Trying to re-create community in the electronic classroom becomes easier if the students themselves are committed to a real community or shared social purpose. They can then use their "individualized" studies and their remote classroom as a basis for their community-based social action.

There are other examples of the use of DE technology as "social education" in community and economic development (Koul & Jenkins, 1990) and as a component in an educational mix promoting community development (Spronk, 1994) that build on existing community links. In many instances in Canada and elsewhere it is colleges or local educational consortium that are taking the lead in establishing computer facilities in remote areas and using features such as audio-graphics to link students to each other and the instructor.[8] Although this chapter has discussed the limiting nature of individualized DE, it should be acknowledged that a central strength of DE is that it provides access to education in the remote communities in which some students live and work. Students do not have to move away and their learning can be instrumental for social change within their community (even when the emphasis may be on basic math or other credit courses). Indeed, students signing on for a traditional, individualized DE three-credit English language course may only be doing so because they have taken over as secretary of a community group and they wish to improve their communication skills. The educational purpose can be determined by the students alone: they can replace the institution's vocational credential purpose with social goals.

Another example of on-line social education is the Internet course on the World Wide Web offered by Athabasca University and SoliNet (a system created by the Canadian Union of Public Employees; see the chapter by Spencer "Workers' Education for the Twenty-First Century" in this volume). This course uses Hypertext hot-links to other sites, Web conferencing and other features. Labour educators from across Canada and around the globe participate in the course, whose purpose is to illustrate how the Internet can be used for delivering labour education. With its virtual classroom, it provides a timely example of how DE can serve social purpose education when it is linked to a social movement or community (for a discussion of computer conferencing and labour education see Taylor, 1996). It also illustrates how such a course is not constricted by time zones or even national boundaries.

Conclusion

DE can no longer be defined as "an education without a classroom," nor perhaps even as "the separation of teacher and student." Distance educators can now become adult educators and as Taylor suggests (1996), "computer-mediated communications may allow distance ... educators to retrieve this important element [interaction] of adult education" (p. 284).

The new possibilities for an "electronic classroom" offered by dedicated networking systems such as Lotus Notes or by conferencing systems such as First Class, and by the Internet and World Wide Web, must be critically evaluated according to established criteria. A proper evaluation means that critique must replace the gushing enthusiasm of the technology advocates.

Computer-mediated learning is affecting all education. Adults, reachable via computer and video DE techniques, are viewed as a new market opportunity by traditional educational institutions that now see their chance to be distance and adult educators. Adult educators must critically influence this form of education. The inclusion of the DE classroom and the opportunity for interaction within DE calls for recognition by adult educators of the possibilities for dialogical, social learning now offered by new technologies.

While the shift to social purpose education may be aided by these technological advances that allow for social learning, a more important influence will be the distance adult educator's ability to learn from the historical purposes of adult education and accept Collins' challenge to treat adult education as vocation (Collins, 1991). If distance educators accept their responsibility to provide learning opportunities that speak to the social conditions of students as citizens, and if they are prepared to work with other like-minded educational and community projects, then they can displace the traditional individualized focus of distance education with a democratic, social adult education.

Endnotes

[1]   This chapter will ignore tele- and video-conferencing which, although a major part of traditional DE, can be considered as essentially the projection of an existing classroom across space and therefore an "exception" to individualized DE described by Holmberg (1995).

[2]   This is similar to a point made by Harasim (1996, p. 205) who argues the difference between knowledge transmission (the Information Super Highway) and knowledge creation made possible by computer conferencing.

[3]   I taught the same graduate course—"Foundations of Adult Education"—in the classroom (for the University of Alberta) and on-line with only a virtual classroom (for Athabasca University). Annand (1997) is researching the experiences of instructors in computer conferencing.

[4]   These issues need more research. They may reflect the "experiential" aspects of some kinds of knowledge as well as the limits of the current technology. They may also be partially resolved by improved instructional design and instructional practice.

[5]   As a colleague (Marco Adria) commented when asked by the author: "I do not know if the dialogue is authentic or not, but I do know that the possibility for such dialogue now exists." Marco has been involved with developing Athabasca University's Virtual Teaching and Learning (ViTAL) community.

[6]   Sometimes the technology fails and students are discouraged from engaging in extended debate. I have experienced the full range from students withdrawing from courses because of technical problems, to "servers" failing for a week, to phone lines being flooded-out for a day.

[7]   I am referring here to the broad mix of DE methods and DE institutions, such as the OU. Computer networking was primarily developed to serve the US military.

[8]   As illustrated by a presentation made at AU, 7 February 1996, by Alberta Vocational College, Lesser Slave Lake. The presentation discussed synchronous linkages between five sites (primarily in different Cree communities) each with three or four students, combining a tele-conference with a computer link.

Part 2
Future Visions

28

Learning Our Way Out

Alan M. Thomas

When democratic groups, even democratic societies, lose their way, they invariably turn to the learning capabilities of their members. The future of adult education in Canada and in the rest of the world lies in the vitality of a renewed discourse between learning and education and the need to nourish and protect that discourse at all costs.

The hopes, fears and ideas expressed in the chapters in this book represent a considerable variety of Canadians engaged in practicing and thinking about the education of adults and reflect both the presence and the value of such a discourse. Some are preoccupied with the goals and venues of existing and future programs and others with the assumptions about learning that underlie those activities. All those represented here, in one way or another, reflect the existence, however fragile, of the discourse between the two. When minds were gripped by clearer visions and hearts were more certain, the dialogue was barely audible. Now, it approaches its proper volume.

An observer in Canada in the 1990s, especially one with some historical perspective, could be forgiven for seeing only a spectacular present and future for adult education. In general, his or her view could be well summarized by Selman and Dampier's assertion that

> the field has made substantial strides in the last two decades in terms of the general acceptance and understanding of the idea; its acceptance as a basis for public policy in areas such as manpower training, public health, citizenship, and economic development; the development of institutional structures, curricula, and methodology; and the training of professional manpower for the field (1991, p. 284).

In comparison with the grudging interest and threadbare resources of only forty years ago, "spectacular" seems the appropriate word.

Few of the outward signs would have alerted that observer to the degree of turmoil and angst that in fact characterized those people thoughtfully involved in the provision of education for adults in Canada during the same period. In contrast to the trends identified by Selman and Dampier, they were much more conscious of some or all of the following conditions:

- the sharp reduction in public support for education in general, and for "general education," which seemed to be even more severe with respect to adults;

- the apparent failure of new bodies, for example, Sectoral Councils composed of employers, government, unions, educators and equity groups, created for the specific purpose of improving the management of adult training;

- the disappearance or radical alteration of many academic departments of adult education;

- the increasing fragmentation of the provision of adult education among various agencies, between public and private providers and between "establishment" ideologies and those advocating social change;

- the emergence of a lifelong learning movement that challenged many of the distinctive characteristics of adult education;

- the simultaneous rise to prominence of vocational training for adults and the radical dislocation and "downsizing" of industrial workers and managers, comparable to the de-population of agriculture that seems to have accompanied the rise of agricultural extension in the early part of this century;

- the contrast in several Central European countries between a recent past of apparently extensive, humane, well-endowed, programs of adult education (for example, education for self reliance in Yugoslavia) and the outbreak of ethnic hatred and violence.

In short, it seemed that having finally discovered the power of adult learning, and having brought increasing numbers of adults within the precincts of adult education, the latter would now be submerged in the older, pre-existing institutions of society and that society's competing ideologies. The old dream of "movement," of some solidarity of means and values that characterized the visions and writings of adult education during the earlier part of this century, seemed a lost hope (Kidd, 1963; CAAE, 1966). If we confine ourselves to the "goals" or "objectives" of adult education, then the outlines of the future seem already discernible. Many of the fears evident among authors in this volume seem certain to be realized.

To be sure, within the essential, if conventional, concern for goals and programs there are issues that must be addressed, as exemplified in this volume. In addition, the peculiar historical development of adult education in the West, with its high degree of ambivalence towards formal education, has resulted in the neglect of a specific group in society: those in the age group between seventeen and twenty-five years who do not continue uninterruptedly in school. That group has become the most isolated and troubled group in all industrial nations. Acknowledging and remedying that neglect may be the major contribution of the new lifelong learning movement. Similarly, the inclusion of increasingly "older" individuals within formal education, with the result that in all industrial countries the average age of students is moving upwards, has meant a blurring of the existing definitions of adult education (UNESCO, 1985). Finally, adult educators, given their historic claims for the importance of adult learning, should not be surprised that all of the major social institutions, having accepted those claims, now compete for the power that learning embodies among the adult population. The issue of power is one with which adult educators perhaps have had little experience. It is hoped that these readings mark an end to our initiation.

There is little doubt that educational providing agencies will continue to claim increasing numbers of older students and will incorporate more and more of the technical aspects of teaching adults pioneered by adult educators operating in a multitude of varying circumstances. The private sector will continue to grow and to include educational providing agencies and large enterprises that must invest in the training and development of their employees to survive. However, if the concept of the "learning" organization actually materializes (see Fenwick's chapter "Questioning the Concept of the Learning Organization" in this volume), we are likely to see a decline in "formal" instruction in those settings as the structure itself reduces the need for self-conscious intervention in the learning. That development, combined with the expanded use of Prior Learning Assessment and Recognition (PLAR), will radically alter the relationship between the formal educational providing agencies with their singular power of certification and the rest of society, particularly the labour market (see the earlier chapter "The Tolerable Contradictions of Prior Learning Assessment" by Thomas in this volume). Employers and, more important, employees will increasingly become independent of that certifying power for many of the technical areas in which it now is so pervasive and influential.

Technical innovations, particularly the electronic ones that seem to eliminate space, will continue to re-define the role of "student." The concept of "residence," the submerged principle in all current educational thinking and rhetoric, will come to the forefront in the changes that are likely to sweep existing providing agencies as a result of the appearance in the educational heavens of "death star" satellites and other means of long-distance multi-media transmission. The virtual classroom (see Spencer's chapter "Distance Education and the Virtual Classroom" in this volume) in every home (if you possess a home), will continue to challenge the oldest and most cherished of educational ideals—the personal contact of teacher and student, of student and student and, frequently less acknowledged, of teacher and teacher.

But the key to assessing the more interesting and gripping future for adult education lies not in considering present or future substantive outcomes, but in considering the *processes* of the education of adults. That in turn requires a consideration of the phenomenon upon which adult education is based, learning itself. It is crucial to suggest this avenue of enquiry to educators of adults because the nature of their practice makes them more sensitive to learning than is the case for most other educators. Because most of us have worked with adult learners in a great variety of circumstances defined by time, location, selection, numbers and objective, we have become more aware of learning itself. Though there are increasing examples of "involuntary" adult education, the experience of most of us has been defined by the choice of our students to attend, in every sense of the word. We have spent our occupational lives as witnesses to adult learning. That fact creates a special responsibility to the realities of learning in society as a whole. One writer defines the relationship between educator and learner as follows:

> Radical educators would do well to consider the mystical nature of the relationship they enter with their learners, and move beyond the narrow rationality of planned development. The learning relationship is a creative space, known to artists as the sphere of imagination and to sages as the realm of the sacred. Learning is essentially anarchical. It transcends the structure of knowledge from which it emerges. It is antithetical to all hierarchical authority, including that of ideas. It occurs between human beings as they understand together. Experience is personal, but meaning is social and is passed from person to person. It is in encounters with others that we continuously awaken to the meanings of life ... Learning is the extension of the human organism towards completion ... The images we receive are of the world, but through these worldly images we perceive what is beyond the world (Shapiro, 1995, p. 45.)

Unlike a few years ago, it is now unnecessary to defend a distinction between learning and education. The current popularity of learning, found in phrases such as "the learning organization" and "lifelong learning," suggests not only the currency of the distinction but a contemporary abandonment of the convictions that propelled education into the role of panacea that it occupied for the thirty years following the end of World War II. However, there is value in examining the differences between the two, especially when learning is considered in a social as well as a psychological context. The first assumption on which these comparisons are based is that they can both be considered as processes, as activities, which exist independently of any specific content or objective.

Learning

Learning is an essential survival activity, and it manifests itself to varying degrees at all stages of an organism's life span. In the human context, learning demands and releases energy, takes time, is irreversible and cannot be coerced. Learning is most commonly a process that takes place within human groups of all kinds: families, associations, corporations, communities and states, for example. Therefore, the primary role associated with learning is that of "member." The point is significant because, despite the educational boom of the past fifty years, it remains true that individuals learn more as members than they do as students. The context of learning, therefore—as distinct from the source—is primarily collective, a context of action, of passion and engagement. It is a context of an immediacy of means and ends, of a limited freedom to make mistakes in order to learn from them, a freedom which is supposed to be the essence of education. And it is frequently a context of group rivalry, in which the object is for members of one group to learn faster and more effectively than the members of another, or to act so as to curb the learning potential of competitors—the final manifestation of which is to kill them, or at the least eliminate them from further opportunities to learn.

History perceived through the "learning glass" is a chronicle of competitive learning, though, until this century that learning, especially on a lifelong basis, was enjoyed by a relatively small elite, and the social and political structure was defined by who had access, over what period of time, to what opportunities to learn. Now, more and more members of the population worldwide are being systematically "encouraged" to engage in learning throughout their lives for the first time in history, and we can only guess at what the consequences may be. It is likely that the fall of the Eastern European governments in the late 1980s, and the way in which they fell, were a direct result of their failure to "manage" the learning of their citizens.

There is a problem of meaning within the English language that is critical. The *Oxford English Dictionary* (1987, p. 1191) provides two definitions for the word learning: "the action of *learn* (to get knowledge of a subject) or skill, by study, experience or teaching)"; and "what is learnt or taught." Thus, the word can be used legitimately as both verb and noun. To use either meaning of learning, a process or activity, or to indicate a particular outcome, is entirely legitimate. To confuse them as many large organizations do, is not.

Confusing the two meanings is destructive and dangerous, since the confusion implies that failure to learn what has been taught is not a failure of the teacher to convey the significance or the details of the "subject" in question, but the failure of individuals at their most vulnerable and intimate core, *of their capacity to learn*. The confusion is inexcusable in formal education, especially when the contemporary mission of any formal system must be to concentrate on learning how to learn. Whether it is deliberate or not, in the education of adults this confusion represents the attempt by large organizations to exploit and control the capacity of the participants (employees, citizens and so on) for learning by blurring the distinction between dancer and dance and capturing those learning capacities for the organizations' particular objectives. The result is the ultimate capture of the individual self by the collective, which represents an entirely different circumstance than the voluntary participation in groups already identified as the principal context for learning. In a democratic society, with the new dependence on lifelong learning for reasons of economic survival, the confusion must be vigilantly identified and exposed whenever and wherever it occurs.

Education

Education is a collective response to the existence of the human capacity to learn. While it is clearly based on that capacity, its predominant preoccupation is not learning but teaching. Education is a legitimate and necessary attempt to direct and channel the capacity to learn towards collectively decided objectives of knowledge, skill and attitude. Historically, at least until the second half of this century, it has been directed primarily to children. Whatever else it may be known for, the twentieth century will surely be designated as the Education Century for its relentless extension of education, first to all of the world's children, a goal as yet unreached, and then to ever increasing numbers of adults.

The new scale of formal education allows us to see more clearly its essential characteristics. It is a realm primarily of second-hand knowledge; that is, the knowledge disseminated is, by definition, already known by someone else. It is also a realm of hierarchies of knowledge in the sense that one ascends a pre-determined ladder of ordered information from early school to later, from elementary to advanced; and it is a hierarchy of time in the sense that it is measured in time-defined courses and programs, characterized by repetitive weeks, terms and years. It is a world of futures, truly a "next-year country" where progression through time is its essence. It is dominated by measures or evaluations of individuals in a currency of diplomas, certificates and degrees, all of which are implemented and awarded by those who "know." Submission to their judgment is the essence of the educational system.

In addition, formal education is "detached," the learning separate from action, as the traditional school is separated from the community in which it is located. There is almost unlimited freedom to make "virtual" mistakes. Education aspires to be predominantly cognitive, though educators have learned the need to enlist the "whole" organism in the pursuit of cognitive objectives. It is fundamentally individual in focus. While teaching is undertaken in groups, evaluation is, without exception, individual encouraging individual rather than group competition. The ultimate objective is that students should learn something they did not know before.

Finally, formal education creates the "student," the characteristic role that in the last half of this century has re-displayed on a large scale the essential universality that was already evident on a smaller scale in the thirteenth and fourteenth centuries and earlier. Traditionally, students have been grouped in concentrated numbers in clearly designated buildings or collections of build-ings, largely determined by the need for access to centralized sources of information, people and documents. With the development of new modes of making these resources available across large spaces, those groupings may become less central to the enterprise of education, though no doubt they will continue to exist in some form and in some locations. But the other charac-teristics—the hierarchies, time sequences in greater varieties and, most impor-tant of all, the subjection to external evaluation will remain essential to the enterprise.

When education was primarily concerned with children, many of these characteristics seemed to be imbedded in the culture of the child and young person and justified on those grounds. With the extension of education to adults of all ages, we are able to see more clearly what is characteristic of education itself, distinct from the characteristics of its student body or its particular objectives. What we do not know is the effects of extending these formal procedures to an older population made up of individuals who other-wise are independent, responsible adult citizens fulfilling all the appropriate roles and obligations of citizens in a democratic society. Ohliger (1974) be-lieved that student characteristics of dependency and intellectual deficit would permeate the lives of adult students and consequently of adult citizens. Per-haps he meant that the danger in formal adult education lies precisely in the tendency to confuse process with outcome, and thereby to enslave learning capacity by collective goals. Determining whether that is true, or what is true of the combined roles of student, learner and citizen with respect to demo-cratic and other kinds of societies, is an urgent task for the immediate future.

But it is the emerging discourse, perhaps dialectic, between learning and education that will dominate the future and to which we need to turn our attention. To speculate on the future, it is necessary to review the past through the same learning perspective.

Pioneers and Immigrants

The first three centuries of Canada's existence were dominated by pioneer-ing (settlement) and immigration. While the latter attracts little attention to-day, both have profound implications for learning. Pioneers faced a physical environment for which there was no recognized prior experience or authority. The pioneer must, in the words of Finger (1985), "learn his or her way out." Immigration, though mediated until the middle of this century by copious space, demands the two-way dynamics of constant learning about and from "strangers." Both pioneering and immigration involved adult learning, and the early centuries exhibit a proliferation of groups and associations in which those adults combined to share their problems and experience. Predominant were religious groups, but in addition there were rural agricultural organizations and the primarily vocational groups of the growing urban areas. Many of the agricultural groups grew into political parties whereby the action in which the learning was imbedded was translated onto a larger stage and into the established organs of the community.

The voluntary tradition has continued in Canada, as a growing and ever more luxuriant vehicle for adult learning. A good example relevant to immigration are the various "ethnic" groups that provide for the necessary learning for their immigrant members and for the members of the receiving society. The politics of "voluntarism," never far beneath the more apparent and conventional public politics of the modern state, is in essence the politics of learning. The recent change in many large voluntary organizations from acting as agents of the state, with the assistance of public funds, to becoming agents of the community without government financial assistance promises to create substantial changes in the way in which Canada has "managed" the learning of its citizens as citizens (see Selman's chapter "The Imaginative Training for Citizenship" in this volume).

In summary, for approximately 250 years in Canada, up to mid-twentieth century, there was an emphasis on *learning*, not necessarily exclusive to adults, with a limited tolerance for "book learning" or education, which was associated primarily with elites. The spread of book learning was largely carried out by vocational demands as commerce began to compete with agriculture, and the Industrial Revolution swept through Canada. Still, access to education was a powerful dream, particularly for women on behalf of their children. Both pioneers and immigrants brought the idea of schools with them, symbolized by the book. And it was on the basis of the book, rather than of the teacher, that they built Canadian education. Universities were founded throughout the nineteenth century, and there were always some elementary and secondary schools for the children of the well-to-do. But it was the mid- to late-nineteenth century that witnessed the stirring and emergence of the movement for free, compulsory education for all the community's children, the essential instrument of every burgeoning nation state. By the early part of the twentieth century the idea had taken firm root and, by the First World War, elementary, secondary and university education was in place.

However, it was following World War II that a really significant commitment was made to education. Educational expenditures as a proportion of the national wealth, in Canada as in other countries, increased steadily from approximately 1950 to 1975. School populations blossomed at all levels as the post-war baby boom and the belief in the value of education combined. A measure of the inclusive power of both is the fact that Allen Tough's systematic exploration of learning outside of school by adults surprised a society so recently defined as both pioneer and immigrant. Education, in its procedures, its culture and its measures of achievement, had become the surrogate for learning as a means of entrance to most of the rewards in Canadian society. Until the 1970s, when governments discovered that education was a monstrously expensive means of "managing" learning in any society, Canada was on the way to becoming not a "learning" but an "educative" society. The balance between learning and education had been tipped dramatically towards the latter in a very short time. In some respects, the unstated slogan of the period, reflected by the great many new responsibilities assumed by the formal schools, was that if "it isn't taught somewhere, it isn't worth learning."

There is no need here to recite the steady erosion of the relatively short-lived educational empire of the twenty years between 1950 and 1970. The same governments that accepted the "salvation" message of education during the post-war period have been increasingly transferring costs and provisions *back* to the private sector. What is of far greater importance is that they have vastly increased our dependence on the learning domain in a search for the vigour, skills and commitment any society in a changing technological, natural and human environment must develop and maintain in order to survive.

The decline of public resources for education is a relatively new concern for adult educators. It is hardly twenty years since the public education sector, with its sole concern for children and young people, was regarded, if not as an enemy, then at least as an obstacle to the extension of the education of adults. Nevertheless, the seemingly limitless resources accessible during the "imperial" era and the imagination of many conventional educators contributed substantially to the growth of adult education. The growth of adult participation in school board programs in Ontario, with only the most ambiguous leadership from the provincial government, is a fine example. The rapid decline in those resources hit young and not so young alike, but the latter more severely.

However, what is at stake here is not so much the decline in what have been only recently acquired resources, serious as that is, but the balance between support for learning and support for education, and the responsibility of adult educators in being alert to the threats to that balance, and in being effective in maintaining it.

One might think that the two would complement each other, but as we have seen in the past fifty years, that is not always the case. In a changing society, learning outcomes always precede those resulting from education. In fact, that is the case whenever change occurs no matter how small or how few it affects. For the past century it has been possible for enough of the learning of each generation to be translated into education in time for each succeeding generation, or in time at least for a critical proportion of the next generation to be adequately equipped. But when change engulfs entire generations, societies, indeed the world, and when education includes almost all children and young people, at least in the industrial societies, the balance between learning and education becomes a matter of pressing concern. While a clear and definitive understanding of the nature of the balance and its essential characteristics remains unclear, there are clues to be found in the work of Toynbee (1947) and Kennedy (1988).

Conclusion

The new popularity of "learning" in the industrial societies, particularly in the context of lifelong learning, is clearly part of the restoration of the balance that has been endangered since the beginning of this century by the educational revolution that accompanied it. However, that popularity brings with it new risks, particularly with respect to the inadvertent or deliberate confusion of the meaning of the word, whereby learning becomes a mask for education and/or training. That is to say, that the capture of individual learning capability itself by particular, current, social or economic objectives presents a far greater threat of tyranny than ever before. It lies at the root of the tyranny described by Orwell in the novel *1984*. However, we do know enough to involve ourselves with determination in some or all of the following goals and initiatives:

- the maintenance and protection of sufficient numbers of publicly supported "learning" agencies, such as public libraries, museums, art galleries, public broadcasting and wilderness areas;
- a comparative analysis of expenditures on learning and educational agencies needs to be developed and publicized;
- the value of "membership" that most of the learning agencies have developed for their support needs to be examined and extended;
- a national survey of what ordinary Canadians are learning should be conducted on a regular basis. The techniques for conducting such a survey are available (Tough, 1979; Thomas, 1982). The survey would tell us what the future of Canada holds, since what people are learning is what they wish to become. It would also tell us what agencies, sources and mechanisms citizens find most useful in order to learn;
- the support and extension of the use of PLAR in Canada and elsewhere as a means of facilitating easier movement between the learning and the educational domains, invigorating and supporting them both in the most efficient and effective way. The only sure way of maintaining the balance is if it is maintained by individuals themselves becoming the vehicles of the continuing discourse between the two;
- the support of the use of PLAR in employment settings, thus reducing the inordinate and inefficient dependence of the labour market on formal educational credentials;
- the establishment of the study of learning as a field of theory and practice in universities and other research agencies;

- the development of a public means of assessing and evaluating private providers of education;
- the protection of the rights and opportunities of the individual voter in democratic societies, so that political power remains lodged firmly with the source of all learning.

These are only some of the future activities in which adult educators will have to engage if we have paid attention to our experiences and the lessons of the past. The proper balance between learning and education is desirable precisely because of their contrasting processes and the significance of those processes in the meaning of learning in the world. The discourse between the two brings face to face the collective passions and energies of learning and the detachment, deliberation and reflection of formal education, an essential dialogue in a society committed to learning itself.

In writing about the future one is always caught between estimates of what will happen and what one wishes to happen. My attempt is no exception. In acknowledging that all education depends on learning, I have argued that while education tends to focus on the meaning of the word that has learning as outcome, educators of adults have a greater opportunity to witness both meanings, and thereby have a greater responsibility towards learning as process, as the distinctive factor in human life. I have tried to bring forth some of the specific characteristics of learning and education, acknowledging the value of each but emphasizing the primacy of learning, independent of education, and its enlarged, crucial social significance. Continuing discourse (as exemplified in the chapters by Collins and Morin in this volume) is the only way the balance can be maintained.

Perhaps I expect too much from adult educators, more than is fair, but I know of no other group of people who are likely to have glimpsed what is true about learning in the world. All of us know that the pursuit of learning, that is of the understanding of learning, is a lonely business, and that the world has ambivalent feelings about learning that is not safely subject to the accomplishment of some other, familiar, human objective. There is always the suspicion that in embracing learning itself we are, like Faust, making a treaty with the devil. Perhaps we are, but it is a risk that must be taken.

29

Educating for a Deliberative Democracy

Michael R. Welton

...for adult education is essentially the scientific shortcut to human progress. To look upon it merely as a movement to make up for the defects of formal education, or to hand down packaged knowledge to the people, or to be nothing more than appreciation of the dead past, is to misunderstand the whole idea of adult education. It is a sacred agency that should not be perverted to the base business of maintaining a privileged status quo.
—Coady in Laidlaw, 1971, pp. 66-67.

The longing at the heart of the twentieth century has been to create a unified world characterized by the triumph of reason, science, technology and materialism. Perhaps one of the most poignant moments in the twentieth century was the message conveyed in the first photograph of the "one world" taken from outer space. This late-1960s image became the icon of our age; the earth as one body. But as we near the end of this century, we are not celebrating "unparalleled and marvellous progress" (Hobsbawm, 1995, p. 13). At best, we have a kind of modulated, queasy hopefulness; at worst, a sense that "life" has succumbed to the logic of the market-place, and that the world has become more barbarous and hard-hearted. Many authors in this book believe that adult education has become a "base business of maintaining a privileged status quo." We are not a joyful crew.

Our world seems extremely unpredictable and disorderly. It is as if we are standing at the edge of the twenty-first century, holding maps and charts that no longer provide a way through sea, sky and land. Familiar landmarks seem oddly askew; we look up and cannot quite recognize the constellations; we gaze into the future, and it seems foreboding and dangerous. No wonder we walk less easily, think with less certainty and teach more hesitantly. We are experiencing epochal changes in our global civilization. The old andragogical paradigm does not have the theoretical riches and depth of understanding of historical learning challenges and social learning processes to address the current upheaval and to speak to its possibilities (see the chapter "Critical Returns: From Andragogy to Lifelong Learning" by Collins in this volume; Welton, 1995). Yet we do not know how to address the emergent new world order.

Two themes stand out in this troubled text. First, many of us in the Canadian academic adult education community feel that the new world has passed us by. Our main stance seems to be a kind of nostalgia for the old movement days. Historical reflection on the extension movement, Antigonish Movement and prison education movement makes us sad as we think of the clarity of vision and liberating methodologies of earlier projects (see the chapters by Haughey, Gillen, and Davidson in this volume). Nostalgia has both a positive side and a negative one. Positively, nostalgia keeps our memory alive. Negatively, nostalgia is a kind of sweet defeatism. We are so caught up, say, in the way the late modern university scarcely nods towards the poor and neglected that we have little energy to see the "spring hidden beneath the cement" (Touraine, 1981, p. 85). Too much nostalgia makes us melancholy, and a melancholic humour easily succumbs to a kind of "end of history" mentality. As well, most of us believe quite passionately that the system has colonized the lifeworld. We may not all be Habermasians (or even have read him), but we all seem to believe that *laissez-faire* global capitalism subverts the very basis for human development.

If we are unhappy or confused, it has much to do with our sense as Canadian adult educators that, left unconstrained and unregulated, the "market" will ultimately destroy anything worth preserving. Beneath our anguish is the insistence that human well-being is the prime value of our practice. What follows are suggested ways for pushing beyond nostalgia and instrumental reason.

Changing Configurations

I think the main cause of the disorder and confusion within most societies (and the global adult education movement) has to do with the changing configuration of the relationships among economy, state and civil society. The economy has pried itself loose from the constraining effects of the state and has turned a deaf ear to the agonies reverberating through civil society and the life histories of men and women. Systemic deficiencies, we should never tire of reminding ourselves, are always experienced in the context of individual life histories. As the market has become ascendant—almost god-like—over the last decade or so, adult education has been under tremendous pressure to couple its caboose to the corporate training and development agenda. The language of economy, money and market has colonized our public vocabularies, displacing spiritual, moral and social-critical vocabularies. The fundamental strategy of the new right has been to disempower the signifiers of culture by attributing to them denuded economic meanings. "Freedom" becomes absence of "economic restraint," "equality" the opportunity to compete and "efficiency" has become the master signifier of the new right by elevating itself to an end in itself (see the chapter "Paradigm Shifts" by Morin in this volume; Briton, 1996).

In the field of adult and continuing education, we notice that individualistic and pragmatic conceptions of adult learning have become predominant. "Self-directedness" becomes the equivalent of adult learning (see the chapter "Self-Directed Learning: Highlighting the Contradictions" by Chovanec in this volume), and "empowerment" is unhitched from collective action and linked with individual empowerment. This tendency affects adult education as a field of practice dramatically. Adult education plays a decreasing role in addressing public issues. It is re-oriented towards supporting individuals who, because of taken-for-granted globalization processes, must adapt skilfully to new circumstances. Public authorities, obsessed with national competitiveness, are comfortable with this emphasis on the person as human capital (as explained in the chapter "Training and Work: Myths about Human Capital" by Bouchard in this volume). They do not understand adult education as the preparation of citizens to play an engaged and committed role in civic life. Adult education is understood primarily as an instrument to achieve a nationally competitive economy (Wildemeersch, 1995). Why have Canadians and global adult education communities been so unable to resist "market-speak"? Where are Tompkins, Coady, Thomson, Sim, McNaughton and Sister Irene Doyle when we need them?

Today many speak glowingly of finance capital, of physical capital and even human capital. Human Resource Development (HRD) is where it's at! Only rarely do we hear people speak of social capital. But as many people become aware of the way global restructuring is eroding relations of mutuality and trust within our associational lives, this is changing. The American sociologist Robert Putnam defines social capital as the "processes between people which establish networks, norms and social trust and facilitate co-ordination and co-operation for mutual benefit" (in Cox, 1995, p. 15). And it is precisely within the domain of what we are now calling civil society (the social space that includes intimate relationships, friendships, associations, social movements and public spheres) that social capital is produced or depleted. While social capital is only one of the core components of a vitally functioning civil society (the institutions and learning processes of civil society also have the normative task of producing meaning and critically active personalities), if relations of trust and reciprocity are damaged, one can scarcely imagine life making much sense or persons functioning in stable fashion. The unspeakable tragedy of Rwanda illustrates the madness into which humans can descend when trust is stripped from all interactions.

Canadian adult education, particularly the movement tradition referenced widely in this volume, has been knocked off balance in the last two decades largely because the neo-conservative corporatist agenda challenges the foundation of our movement practice; namely, forms of solidarity and the belief that democracy means participation. Decisions made only in terms of economic efficiency neglect the pain that reaches into the human psyche and does not notice the fault lines that appear in our families and associations, workplaces and public spaces, let alone the almost unbearable pressures exerted on the overstressed welfare state. Australian Eva Cox comments:

> Social capital should be the pre-eminent and most valued form of capital as it provides the basis on which we build a truly civil society. Without our social bases we cannot be fully human. Social capital is as vital as language for human society. We become vulnerable to social bankruptcy when our social connections fail. If most of our experiences enhance our sense of trust and mutuality, allowing us to feel valued and to value others, then social capital increases (1995, p. 17).

These insights ought to provide some encouragement for beleaguered, socially responsible adult educators. The "education for social transformation" discourse, with its orientation to strategic action to change the way people think and institutions perform, may obscure the way our educational practice (in and out of classrooms) either produces or depletes social capital. The global adult education movement must consider the extent to which its practices conserve and sustain the social basis for what Habermas called communicative action.

Socially responsible adult education is not simply about "social change." In fact, one could make a strong case that today socially responsible adult education must be deeply preservationist in sensibility. Consider the following learning challenges engendered by globalization: the deprivation of meaning (which confronts consumerism as surrogate god); the depletion of solidarity (which confronts possessive individualism and social fragmentation) and the de-stabilization of the personality (which confronts many pathologizing tendencies in society). In our topsy-turvy world, socially responsible adult education may well emerge as "philosophic conservatism," defined by Anthony Giddens as a "philosophy of protection, conservation and solidarity." He thinks that a "radical political program must recognize that confronting manufactured risk cannot take the form of 'more of the same,' an endless exploration of the future at the cost of protection of the present or past" (1994, p. 10).

A new self-understanding of society at the end of the twentieth century is emerging from the rubble of post-communist and post-welfare societies and from the suffering of millions of people living in societies that lack traditions of liberal rights and vital citizen participation. Twentieth-century late moderns have learned some acidulous lessons. We have learned that political projects that seek to totally re-make the world (creating the new man or woman) have radiated nothing but disaster (the self-limiting nature of transformative ideals). We also learned that both communism and the welfare-state utopias have lost their capacity to mobilize for an alternative future. We now have an unprecedented opportunity to rethink the fundamentals of democracy.

Civil Society and Socially Responsible Adult Education

Civil society is the *privileged domain* for non-instrumental learning processes. This is a normative statement; of course, as actually existing relationships within civil society can be destructive or manipulative. For this reason Habermas uses the phrase "rationalized lifeworld" to capture both the possibility of pathologies within the lifeworld and the necessity of persons arriving at norms, values and procedures that govern their interactions through reflective, deliberative learning processes. Communication within the institutions of civil society is oriented to understanding, and we recognize intuitively and rationally that when a spouse, for instance, coerces a partner into a particular act through force, this is a distortion of what ought to be mutually agreed upon.

The institutions of civil society, which have evolved over time in interplay with the development of complex sub-systems of state and economy, have the task of enabling us to learn what it means to be competent, active persons in our particular world. An important rule of thumb here is that learning and action within the sub-systems tend to be governed by strategic intentions, and learning and action within civil society tend to be governed by communicative intentions. In sociological language, we can speak of the cultural, social and personal reproductive tasks of civil society. This rather flat language does not fully communicate what is at stake. If the reproductive tasks are interfered with, or cannot be carried out for systemically rooted reasons, then the spiritual, moral and social infrastructure of the economy and state will be imperiled.

Our disquiet as Canadian adult educators stems from our sense that "social liberalism," fought for by the pioneering adult educators in the 1930s, 1940s and 1950s is unravelling day by day as the Harrises and Kleins have their flickering moment in the political sun. But the Harrises and the Kleins do not understand that a work-less and care-less economy will ultimately undermine itself.

Canadian adult educators are under enormous pressure to comply, to hop on one of many bandwagons careening by on the way to a high-tech utopia. But there is hope here because people cannot live by the market alone. We are inherently creatures of meaning and sociality. Irrepressibly so. Too much in late twentieth-century Canada makes little sense to far too many Canadians. Current corporate-managed Canada will face its own Berlin wall.

The Canadian adult education community must emerge from its twin crises of confidence and self-doubt to stand with the "neglected citizens" and articulate a new democratic project for the twenty-first century. Our historic commitment to helping Canadians "live a life" and "earn a living" (Coady's metaphor of the "good and abundant life")—good work and active citizenship—must be renewed with vigour. Many authors in this book make reference to the Antigonish Movement. In the words of Cape Breton educator Peter Bushell,

> the "good and abundant life" would allow people to develop themselves and their communities by working and learning as an outgrowth of their base life experiences naturally received through the ordinary stages of their lives. Education then, shouldn't strive to prepare people for life but rather contribute to their unfolding lives within community—it should give people life where they are and through the callings in which they find themselves (1997, unpaginated).

I would argue that the core value structure of socially responsible adult education (or maybe merely "civilized adult education") is compatible with "deliberative" approaches to democracy (Bohman, 1996; Chambers, 1996; Habermas, 1996). This core value structure affirms that the lifeworld is the foundation of meaning, solidarity and stable personality; that we have a commitment to the enlightened, relatively autonomous and reflective learner; that social learning processes are central to the formation of the active citizen; and that we have an obligation to foster discussion, debate and dialogue among citizens. This formulation captures in modern social theoretical language the vision and commitment of our movement tradition.

Three axioms pertinent to our discussion emerge from the extensive literature on civil society. First, the scope and vitality of a society's associational life is a prerequisite for building deliberative democracy. We learn to be citizens not by participating in "politics" first, but in the "free spaces" of school, church, clubs, unions and other associations. Associations are "schools of citizenship": in these associations people learn to respect and trust others, fulfil obligations and press their claims communicatively. That is what our foremothers and forefathers were fighting for when they created Citizen's, Farm and Film forums and organized thousands of study clubs from Prince Rupert to St. John's. We have been a nation that studies together.

Second, in late modern societies the new social movements take on a special significance as action-oriented sites for learning democracy. The peace and ecology movements, the women's movement (see the chapters by Stalker, Miles and Clover in this volume) and the struggles of Aboriginal people, for example, are certainly bound up with identity assertion and can skid into the worst of lobbying politics. But the learning processes inside the movements are generally oriented to bringing up issues relevant to the entire society, defining ways of approaching problems, proposing possible solutions, supplying new information, interpreting values differently, mobilizing good reasons and criticizing bad ones (Habermas, 1996, p. 370).

Third, the creation and maintenance of exuberant public spheres is central to civil societarian adult education (my name for our central traditions as Canadian adult educators). Andrew Parkin (1996) maintains that

> the public sphere and civil society are not identical; rather, the public sphere is a central element of civil society in that it is via the institutions of the public sphere that members of civil society can engage in informed public debate upon matters of common concern, including the way in which power is distributed and deployed within society (p. 3).

A dynamic and vigorous public sphere depends on the "favourable organization of civil society" (Calhoun, 1993, p. 276); the "civil society against the state" movements in Eastern Europe (and subsequent attempts to re-strangulate civil society) bear witness to this statement. For it is in the learning life of associations, organizations and movements that systemically generated problems, which reverberate first in individual life histories, are distilled and transmitted in "amplified form to the public sphere" (Habermas, 1996, p. 367). The new social movements often play particularly salient roles in late modernity, in ensuring that reflective learning processes occur outside the control of government and private corporate interests.

Civil societarian adult educators must be committed to a process of double democratization. The principle of division between state and civil society is fundamental to this outlook on societal learning processes. This is one of the underlying lessons of the struggles in the former Soviet Union and Central and Eastern Europe. The second premise must be that the power to make decisions be free of the inequalities and constraints that can be imposed by an unregulated system of capital (Held, 1993). This means that the learning processes within civil society—the organization of enlightenment in Habermas's terms—are oriented to the generating of influence through the "life of democratic associations and unconstrained discussion in the cultural public sphere" (Cohen & Arato, 1992, p.x). Socially responsible adult education would decry any form of democracy that focused on voting while confining citizen action largely to the "private" sidelines of civil society. There must be institutionalized opportunities to exist and act as citizens, as participants in public life. Without active participation of citizens in egalitarian institutions and civil associations as well as "politically relevant" organizations, there will be no way to maintain the democratic character of any society.

The Canadian adult education community, however, will have to make this vision practicable. To do so, we face some formidable enemies: complexity (the late modern world is too complex for deliberative processes to actually work); pluralism (there are too many different notions of the "good life" to imagine people actually arriving at consensus); and social inequality (the neo-conservative agenda has radically shifted opportunities for dialogue to the rich and powerful and away from the masses) (see Bohman, 1996).

We have learned some important lessons as the twentieth century crashes to a close. The old leftist dream of bringing society as a whole under control lies in ruins. Civil societarian adult educators have lessons to learn from the struggles in Eastern Europe of "civil society against the state," lessons that tell us that any viable project for the further democratization of society must be self-limiting. We cannot abolish the "state" or the "market." Habermas argues that

> democratic movements emerging from civil society must give up holistic aspi-rations to a self-organizing society, aspirations that also undergirded Marxist ideas of social revolution. Civil society can directly transform only itself, and it can have at most an indirect effect on the self-transformation of the political system; generally, it has an influence only on the personnel and programming of this system (1996, p. 372).

The self-limitation of civil society, however, should not be understood as incapacitation or paralysis. Civil society, Habermas reminds us, has the "op-portunity of mobilizing counter-knowledge and drawing on the pertinent forms of expertise to make its own translations" (1996, p. 37). Thus, it be-comes very important to understand the circumstances under which civil soci-ety can acquire influence in the public sphere and have an effect on the parliamentary complex (and the courts) through its own public opinions. It is important to compel the political (or economic) system to open itself to learn-ing emerging from civil society. Collective learning processes emerging within civil society must have their crystallized demands channelled through the gates and into the arenas of formal decision making (within state and economic sub-systems). The Citizen's Forums, for instance, were anchored precisely in such a conception of social change. The listening-study-action clubs, scattered across this huge land, were communicative spaces for the crystallization of public opinion. Each of the thousands of clubs sent their views to the government for reflection and action. The global adult education movement must deepen its theoretical and practical understanding of the cir-cumstances under which a mobilized civil society is able to find receptors for its concerns.

Canadian adult education in the twenty-first century must respond to this question: How can civil society be secured, sustained and invigorated in our time? Moses Michael Coady, that adamantine Irish priest from the Margaree Valley in Cape Breton, taught us that adults are motivated to learn at the points of most acute suffering. It may be, in late twentieth-century Canada, that our deepest suffering lies in the erosion of the lifeworld as the foundation for our capacity to work and act well.

References

Abrahamson, K. (1984). Does the adult majority create new patterns of student life? Some experiences of Swedish higher education. *European Journal of education*, *19*, 238-298.

Abu-Jamal, M. (1995). *Live from death row*. Reading, MA: Addison-Wesley.

Ackoff, R.L. & Gharajedaghi, J. (1985). Towards systemic education of systems scientists, *Systems Research*, *2*(1), 21-27.

Adams, A.V., Middleton, J. & Ziderman, A. (1992). Un document de politique générale de la Banque mondiale sur l'enseignement technique et la formation professionnelle. *Perspectives*, *22*(2), 141-157.

Alberta Advanced Education and Career Development. (1994). *New Directions for Adult Learning in Alberta*. Edmonton: Author.

Alexander, A. (1991). Critical social theory: A perspective for critiquing professionalization in adult education. *The Canadian Journal for the Study of Adult Education*, *5*, 120-132.

Allison, T.L. & Royal, E.A. (1991). The inmate management system: An approach to jail management. *The State of Corrections: Proceedings ACA Annual Conference 1990*. Arlington VA: American Correctional Association, 39-43.

Allman, P. (1996). Freire with no delusions. In P. Allman, E.L. Christensen, P. Mayo, S.M. Scott & D. Schugurensky, In Paulo Freire and Transformative Education Symposium. *Adult Education Research Conference Proceedings (pp. 344-350)*. Tampa, Florida: University of South Florida.

American Correctional Association Program Committee. (1989). *Literacy: A concept for all seasons*. Washington, D.C.: American Correctional Association, Anchor/Doubleday.

Anderson, J. (1997). *Research Paper No. 3*. Canadian Labour Congress National Training Conference, June 25-27.

Anisef, P. & Axelrod, P. (Eds.) (1993). *Schooling and employment in Canada*. Toronto: Thompson Educational.

Annand, D. (1997). *Experiences of instructors in computer conferences*. Ph.D. dissertation, University of Alberta.

Apps, J.W. (1989, Winter). What should the future focus be for adult and continuing education? *New Directions for Continuing Education*, *44*, 23-30.

Arbour, L. (1996). *Commission of inquiry into certain events at prison for women in Kingston*. Ottawa: Canada Communication Group.

Argis, C. (1976). Theories of action that inhibit individual learning. *American Psychologist, 31*, 638-654.

Argyris, C. (1991, May-June). Teaching smart people how to learn. *Harvard Business Review*, 99-109.

Argyris, C. (1993). *Organizational learning*. Cambridge, MA: Blackwell.

Argyris, C. & Schon, D.A. (1974). *Theory in practice*. San Francisco: Jossey-Bass.

Argyris, C. & Schon, D. (1978). *Organizational learning: A theory of action perspective*. Reading, Mass: Addison-Wesley.

Armstrong, D.P. (1968). *Corbett's house*. Unpublished Masters Thesis, University of Toronto.

Arnold, M.E. (n.d.). *Father Jimmy of Nova Scotia*. Chicago: Cooperative League of the U.S.A.

Aronowitz, S. (1990). The new labour education: a return to ideology. In S.H. London, E.R. Tarr & J.F. Wilson (Eds.), *The re-education of the American working class* (pp. 21-33). New York: Greenwood.

Ashton, D. & Greene, F. (1996). *Education, training, and the global economy*. Brookfield, Vermont: Edward Elgar.

Ashworth, M. (1988). *Blessed with bilingual brains: Education of immigrant children with English as a second language*. Vancouver: Pacific Educational Press.

Ashworth, P. (1992). Being competent and having "competencies." *Journal of Further and Higher Education*, *16*(3), 8-17.

Ashworth, P. & Saxton, J. (1990). On competence. *Journal of Further and Higher Education, 14*, 3-25.

Attallah Salah-El, T. (1992). Attaining education in prison equals prisoner power. *Journal of Prisoners on Prison, 4*(1), 45-52.

Bailey, F.G. (1977). *Morality and expediency*. Oxford, UK: Blackwell.

Baker, H.B. (1993). A history of CAUCE: Its formation, development and role. *Canadian Journal of University Continuing Education, 19*(2), 37-65.

Baltes, P.B. & Smith, J. (1990). Toward a psychology of wisdom and its ontogenesis. In R.J. Sternberg (Ed.), *Wisdom: its nature, origins, and development* (pp. 87-120). Cambridge, UK: Cambridge University Press.

Barbier, J.-M., Caspar, P., Chaix, M.-L., Ferrand, J.-L., Lietard, B., Thesmar, C. & Volery, L. (1991, oct-nov-dec). Tendances d'évolution de la formation des adultes. *Revue française de pedagogie, 97*, 75-108.

Barchechat, E. (1988). Éducation et informatique multimédias. Que peuvent donc les technologies nouvelles pour l'éducation? *Éducation Permanente. 93/94*, 9-18.

Bardin L. (1977). *L'analyse de contenu*. Paris: Presses Universitaires de France.

Baron McBride, A. (1976). *The married feminist*. NY: Harper & Row.

Baron, M.A. & Boschee, F. (1996). Dispelling the myths surrounding obe. *Phi Delta Kappan, 77*(8), 574-576.

Barton, P.E. & Coley, R.J. (1996). *Captive students: Education and training in America's prisons*. Princeton: Policy Information Center, Educational Testing Service.

Baum, G. (1980). *Catholics and Canadian socialism*. Toronto: James Lorimer.

Bauman, Z. (1992). Survival as a social construct. *Theory, Culture & Society, 9*, 1-36.

Baxter Magolda, M. (1992). *Knowing and reasoning in college: Gender-related patterns in students' intellectual development*. San Francisco, CA: Jossey-Bass.

Baynham, M. (1995). *Literacy practices: Investigating literacy in social contexts*. London and New York: Longman.

Beaudet, G. et al. (1997, May). *Survey of trends in adult education in Canada, 1985-95*. Canadian Commission for UNESCO.

Beck, N. (1995). *Shifting gears: Thriving in the new economy*. Toronto, ON: Nuala Beck and Associates.

Beck, U. (1992). *Risk society* (M. Ritter, Trans.). London: Sage Publications. (Original work published 1986)

Becker G.S. (1964). *Human capital: A theoretical and empirical analysis, with special reference to education*. New York: Columbia University Press.

Beder, H. (1989). Purposes and philosophies of adult education. In S. Merriam & P. Cunningham (Eds.), *Handbook of adult and continuing education* (pp. 37-50). San Francisco: Jossey-Bass.

Belenky, M.F., Clinchy, B.M., Goldberger, N.B. & Tarule, J.M. (1986). *Women's ways of knowing: The development of self, voice, and mind*. New York: Basic Books.

Belfiore, M.E. & Heller, M. (1992). Cross-cultural interviews: Participation and decision-making. In B. Burnaby & A. Cumming (Eds.), *Socio-political aspects of ESL in Canada* (pp. 223-240). Toronto: OISE Press.

Bell, D. (1967). The post-industrial society: A speculative view. In E. Hutchings & E. Hutchings (Eds.), *Scientific progress and human values* (pp. 154-170). New York: American Elsevier Publishing Company.

Bell, G. & Glaremin, T.A. (1995). On prison education and women in prison: An interview with Therasa Ann Glaremin. In H.S. Davidson (Ed.), *Schooling in a "total institution:" Critical perspectives on prison education* (pp. 43-48). Westport CT: Bergin & Garvey.

Bellah, R.N., Madsen, R., Sullivan, W.M., Swidler, A. & Tipton, S.M. (1985). *Habits of the heart: Individualism and commitment in American life*. New York: Harper & Row.

Benack, S. & Basseches, M.A. (1989). Dialectical thinking and relativisitic epistemology: Their relation in adult develop-ment. In M.L. Commons, J.D. Sinnitt, F.A. Richards & C. Armon (Eds.), *Adult development*. New York: Praegar.

Bennett, J. (1991, Spring). Misogyny, popular culture and women's work. *History Workshop. A Journal of Socialist and Feminist Historians, 31,* 166-188.

Berg, C.A., Klaczynski, P.A., Calderone, K.S. & Strough, J. (1994). Adult age differences in cognitive strategies: Adaptive or deficient? In J.D. Sinnott (Ed.), *Interdisciplinary handbook of adult lifespan learning* (pp. 371-388). Westport, CN: Greenwood Press.

Berg, Ivar & Gorelick, S. (1971). *Education and jobs: The great training robbery*. Boston: Beacon Press.

Berleth, R. (1995). Fraile woman, foolish gerle: Misogyny in Spenser's Mutabilitie Cantos, *Modern Philology, 93*(1), 37-53.

Berry, T. (1988). *The dream of the universe*. San Francisco: Sierra Club Books.

Besserer, S. & Grimes, R.C. (1996). The courts. In L.W. Kennedy & V.F. Sacco (Eds.), *Crime counts: A criminal event analysis* (pp. 271-292). Toronto: Nelson Canada.

Bezdek, R.H. (1974). *Long-range forecasting of manpower requirements: Theory and applications*. New York: Institute of Electrical & Electronics Engineers.

Bhasin, K. (1992). Alternative and sustainable development. *Convergence XXV*(2), 26-35.

Biegel, D.E., Shore, B.K. & Gordon, E. (1984). *Building support networks for the elderly: Theory and applications*. Beverly Hills, CA: Sage.

Bigge, M.L. (1982). *Learning theories for teachers* (4th Ed.). New York: Harper Row.

Birley, D. (1991). Crossing Ulster's other great divide. *Higher Education Quarterly, 45*(2), 125-144.

Birren, J.E., Kenyon, G.M., Ruth, J-E, Schroots, J.J.F. & Svensson, T. (Eds.) (1996). *Aging and biography: Explorations in adult development*. New York: Springer Publishing.

Blais, M., Chamberland, E., Hrimech, M., and Thibault, A. (1994). *L'Andragogie: Champ D'Etudes et Profession, Une Histoire a Suivre*. Montreal: Guerin universitaire.

Bloom, B.S. (1976). *Human characteristics and school learning*. New York: McGraw-Hill.

Bloom, M. (1990). *La voie du succes : La synergie des affaires et de l'enseignement. Première conférence nationale sur les partenariats entreprise-établissement d'enseignement*. Ottawa: Conference Board du Canada. Rapport 57-90-E/F.

Bloom, M. (1991a). *La voie du succès : La synergie des affaires et de l'enseignement. Deuxieme conférence nationale sur les les entreprises et l'enseignement*. Ottawa: Conference Board du Canada. Rapport 77-91-E/F.

Bloom, M. (1991b). *Profils de partenariats. Partenariats entreprise-établissement d'enseignement qui gardent nos jeunes a l'école*. Ottawa: Conference Board du Canada. Rapport 70-91-E/F.

Bohman, J. (1996). *Public deliberation: Pluralism, complexity, and democracy*. Cambridge: MIT Press,

Boreham, N.C. (1992). Harnessing implicit knowing to improve medical practice. *New Directions for Adult and Continuing Education, 55*, 71-78.

Boshier, R. W. (1986). Proaction for a Change: Some Guide-lines for the Future. *International Journal of Lifelong Learning, 5*(1), 15-31.

Boud, D.J., Keogh, R. & Walker, D. (Eds.). (1985). *Reflection: Turning experience into learning.* London: Kogan Page.

Boudin, K. (1993). Participatory literacy education behind bars: AIDS opens the door. *Harvard Educational Review, 63,* 207-232.

Bourdieu, P. (1968). Sociologie de l'éducation. Paris: Centre d'études sociologiques, CNRS. Numéro spécial de *la Revue Francaise de Sociologie,* 1967-68.

Bowles, S. & Gintis, H. (1977). *Schooling in capitalist America: Educational reform and the contradictions of economic life.* Basic Books: Harper Collins.

Boxer, C. (1975). *Mary and misogyny.* London: Duckworth.

Boyd, R.D. (1989). Facilitating personal transformation in small groups. *Small Group Behavior, 20,* 459-474.

Boyd, R. & Associates. (1991). *Personal transformation in small groups.* London: Routledge.

Boyd, R.D. & Myers, J.G. (1988). Transformative education. *International Journal of Lifelong Education, 7,* 261-284.

Bradwin, E.W. (1928). *The bunkhouse men,* Toronto, University of Toronto (reprinted 1972).

Braudillard, J. (1991). La guerre du Golfe n'a pas eu lieu. *Liberation,* March 29.

Brennan, B. (1987). *Hands of light.* New York: Pleiades Books.

Briskin, L. (1990). Feminist pedagogy: Teaching and learning liberation. *Feminist Perspectives, 19.* Ottawa: Canadian Research Institute for the Advancement of Women

Briskin, L. & Coulter, R.P. (1992). Introduction—Feminist pedagogy: Challenging the normative. *Canadian Journal of Education, 17*(3), 247-263.

Briton, D. (1996). Decentering the self in adult education practice. *Adult Education Research Conference Proceedings* (pp. 25-30). Tampa, FL: Florida State University.

Briton, D. (1996). Marketspeak: The rhetoric of restructuring and its implications for adult and higher education. *Studies in the Education of Adults, 28*(1), April.

Briton, D. (1996). *The modern practice of adult education: A post-modern critique.* New York: SUNY.

Briton, D. & Plumb, D. (1993). The commodification of adult education. *Proceedings, Adult Education Research Conference* (pp. 31-36). University Park: Pennsylvania State University.

Briton, D. & Plumb, D. (1993). Remapping adult education: Post-hegemonic possibilities. *Proceedings of the 12th Annual Conference of the Canadian Association for the Study of Adult Education* (pp. 54-59). Ottawa, ON: Faculty of Education, University of Ottawa.

Brockett, R. & Hiemstra, R. (1991). *Self-direction in adult learning: Perspectives on theory, research, and practice.* London: Routledge.

Brooke, M. (Ed.) (1972). *Adult basic education,* Toronto: New Press.

Brooke, M. & Waldron, M. (Eds.) (1994). *University continuing education in Canada* (pp. 1-3). Toronto: Thompson Educational.

Brookfield, S. (1984). *Adult learners, adult education and the community.* New York: Teachers' College, Columbia University.

Brookfield, S. (1985). A critical definition of adult education. *Adult Education Quarterly, 36*(1), 44-49.

Brookfield, S. (1986). *Understanding and facilitating adult learning,* San Francisco, Jossey-Bass.

Brookfield, S. (1987). *Developing critical thinkers: Challenging adults to explore alternative ways of thinking and acting.* San Francisco: Jossey-Bass.

Brookfield, S. (1987). *Learning democracy: Eduard Lindeman on adult education and social change.* London: Croom Helm.

Brookfield, S. (1990). *The skillful teacher.* San Francisco: Jossey-Bass.

Brookfield, S. (1993). Self-directed learning, political clarity, and the critical practice of adult education. *Adult Education Quarterly, 43*(4), 227-242.

Brookfield, S.D. (1995). *Becoming a critically reflective teacher.* San Francisco: Jossey-Bass.

Brooks, A.K. (1995). The myth of self-directed work teams and the ineffectiveness of team effectiveness training: An argument with special reference to teams that produce knowledge. *Proceedings of the 26th Annual Adult Education Research Conference* (pp. 41-48). Edmonton, AB: University of Alberta.

Brooks, C. et al. (1993). Working across our differences—Perspectives on oppression. *Convergence XXVI*(2), 20-37.

Bruner, J. (1986). *Actual minds, possible worlds.* Cambridge, MA: Harvard University Press.

Buchanan, D. (1944). Motion pictures as a spearhead. *Food For Thought, 4,* 5.

Burch, M. (1994 May). Adult environmental education in North America, a paper prepared for the *International Council for Adult Education* (pp. 12-28) and presented in Curacao, Netherlands Antilles.

Burnaby, B. (1992a). Official language training for adult immigrants in Canada: Features and issues. In B. Burnaby & A. Cumming (Eds.), *Socio-political aspects of ESL in Canada* (pp. 3-34). Toronto: OISE Press.

Burnaby, B. (1992b). Adult literacy issues in Canada. In R.B. Kaplan (Ed.), *Annual Review of Applied Linguistics, 12* (pp. 156-171). Cambridge: Cambridge University Press.

Burnaby, B. (1996). Language policies in Canada: An overview. In M. Herriman & B. Burnaby (Eds.), *Language policy in English-dominant countries: Six case studies* (pp. 159-219). Clevedon, England: Multilingual Matters.

Burnaby, B., Holt, M., Steltzer, N. & Collins, N. (1987). *The Settlement Language Training Program: An assessment* (Report on behalf of the TESL Canada Federation). Ottawa: Employment and Immigration Canada.

Bushell, P. (1997). Module seven assignment. *Historical Perspectives on Adult Education,* Halifax: Mount St. Vincent University.

Caffarella, R. (1993). Self-directed learning. *New Directions for Adult and Continuing Education, 57*, 25-35.

Calhoun, C. (1993). Civil society and the public sphere. *Public Culture, 5.*

Callincos, A. (1990). *Against postmodernism.* Cambridge: Polit Press.

Cameron, J.D. (1996). *For the people: A history of St. Francis Xavier University.* Montreal & Kingston: McGill-Queen's University Press.

Campbell, D.D. (1977). *Adult education as a field of study and practice.* Vancouver, BC: UBC Centre for Continuing Education.

Campbell, E. (1995). Raising the moral dimension of school leadership. *Curriculum Inquiry, 25*(1), 87-99.

CANADA. (1986a). *Job creation, training and employment services: A study team report to the task force on program review.* Ottawa: Task force on program review.

CANADA. (1986b). *Report of the task force on federal policies and programs for technology development.* Ottawa : Ministry of State, Science and Technology Canada.

CANADA. (1995). *The 1992 adult education and training survey.* Ottawa: Statistics Canada, Human Resources Development Canada.

CANADA. (1996). *Release of the 1991 follow-up of the 1986 Graduates Survey Report.* Ottawa: Statistics Canada, Human Resources Development Canada.

Canadian Environment Network. (1993-94). *Green list: Guide to environmental organizations*, Ottawa: Author.

Canadian Labour Force Development Board. (1993). *Local boards: A partnership for training: Ottawa*: Author and Ontario and Federal Governments.

Canadian Labour Force Development Board. (1994). *Putting the pieces together: Toward a coherent transition system for Canada's labour force.* Report of the Task Force on Transition into Employment, Ottawa: Canadian Labour Force Development Board.

Canadian Labour Force Development Board. (1995). *Annual Report 1994-95.* Ottawa: Author.

Canadian Labour Force Development Board. (1995, Sept.). *Training standards.* Ottawa: Author.

Candy, P.C. (1982). Personal constructs and personal paradigms: Elaboration, modification, and transformation. *Interchange on Educational Policy, 13*(4), 56-69.

Candy, P.C. (1989). Constructivism and the study of self-direction in adult learning. *Studies in the Education of Adults, 21*, 95-116.

Candy, P. (1991). *Self-direction for lifelong learning.* San Francisco: Jossey-Bass.

Capra, F. (1983). *The turning point.* (French Edition); New York: Simon and Schuster.

Carter, S.A. (1991). The future of corrections in the 21st century. *International symposium on the future of corrections: Program.* Ottawa: Correctional Service of Canada.

Caspar, P., Chaix M.-L., Ferrand, J.-L., Liétard, B., Thesmar, C. & Volery, L. (1991). Tendances d'évolution de la formation des adultes. *Revue française de pédagogie, 97* (oct-nov-dec), 75-108.

CCMD Report No. 1. (May 1994). *Continuous learning: A CCMD Report.* Canadian Centre for Management Development. Minister of Supply and Services Canada.

Cervero, R. (1991). Changing relationships between theory and practice. In J. Peters, P. Jarvis & Associates (Eds.), *Adult education* (pp. 19-41). San Francisco: Jossey-Bass.

Cervero, R.M. & Wilson, A.L. (1994). *Planning responsibility for adult education: A guide to negotiating power and interests.* San Francisco: Jossey-Bass.

Chambers, S. (1996). *Reasonable democracy: Jurgen Habermas and the politics of discourse.* Ithaca: Cornell University Press.

Chaplain, R. (1948). *Wobbly.* Chicago: University of Chicago.

Chappell, C. & Hager, P. (1994). Values and competency standards. *Journal of Further and Higher Education, 18*(3), 12-23.

Chappell, N.L. (1989). *Formal programs for informal caregivers to elders.* Winnipeg, MB: University of Manitoba, Centre on Aging.

Chappell, N.L. & Prince, M.J. (1994). *Social support among today's seniors: Final report.* Victoria, BC: University of Victoria, Centre on Aging.

Chené, A. (1983). The concept of autonomy: A philosophical discussion. *Adult Education Quarterly, 34*, 38-47.

Chiswick, B. (1992). Introduction. In B. Chiswick (Ed.), *Immigration, language, and ethnicity: Canada and the United States* (pp. 1-12). Washington, D.C.: The AEI Press.

Chodorow, N. (1978). *The reproduction of mothering: Psychoanalysis and the sociology of gender.* Berkeley: University of California Press.

Chomsky, N. & Barsamian, D. (1994). *Keeping the rabble in line.* Monroe, ME: Common Courage Press.

Chovanec, D. (1996). Doing interpretive research in a technocratic age: A clash of paradigms. *Proceedings of the 37th Adult Education Research Conference* (pp. 55-60). Tampa, FL: University of South Florida.

Clover, D. (1995). Gender, transformative learning and environmental action. *Gender and Education, 7*(4), 243-258.

Coady, M.M. (1939). *Masters of their own destiny.* New York: Harper and Brothers.

Coady, M.M. (1945). *The Antigonish movement, yesterday and today.* (Part 1 of 3rd ed. published in 1976). Antigonish, N.S.: St. F.X. University, Extension Department.

Coady, M.M. (1945). *The social significance of the co-operative movement.* Chicago: Co-operative League of the USA.

Cochrane, N. et al. (1986). *J.R. Kidd: International legacy of learning.* Vancouver, Univ. of British Columbia/Centre for Continuing Education.

Cohen, J. & Arato, A. (1992). *Civil society and political theory.* Cambridge: MIT Press.

Collard, S. & Law, M. (1989). The limits of perspective transformation: A critique of Mezirow's theory. *Adult Education Quarterly, 39*, 99-107.

Collard, S. & Stalker, J. (1991). Women's trouble: Women, gender and the learning environment. In R. Heimstra (Ed.), *Creating environments for effective adult learning* (pp. 71-82). San Francisco: Jossey-Bass.

Collins, M. (1983). A critical analysis of competency-based systems in adult education. *Adult Education Quarterly, 33*(3), 174-183.

Collins, M. (1987). *Competence in adult education: A new perspective.* Lantham & New York: University Press of America.

Collins, M. (1988). Prison education: A substantial metaphor for adult education. *Adult Education Quarterly, 38*(2), 101-10.

Collins, M. (1990). The potential and pretensions of critical discourse in mainstream adult education. *Proceedings of the 9th Annual Conference of Canadian Association for the Study of Adult Education* (pp. 96-101). B.C.: University of Victoria.

Collins, M. (1991). *Adult education as vocation: A critical role for the adult educator.* New York and London: Routledge.

Collins, M. (1992). Current trends in adult education: From self-directed learning to critical theory. Paper presented at the *6th Annual meeting of the Association of Process Philosophy of Education.* The Galt House, Louisville, Kentucky.

Collins, M. (Ed.) (1995). *The Canmore proceedings. Educating the adult educator: Role of the university.* Saskatoon: University of Saskatchewan.

Collins, M. (1995). Critical commentaries on the role of the adult educator: From self-directed learning to postmodernist sensibilities (pp. 71-97). In Welton, R., (Ed.), *In defense of the lifeworld: Critical perspectives on adult learning.* Albany: State University of New York Press.

Collins, M. (1995). In the wake of postmodernist sensibilities and opting for a critical return. In M.R. Welton (Ed.), *In defense of the lifeworld: Critical perspectives on adult learning* (pp. 195-201). Albany: State University of New York Press.

Collins, M. (1995). Shades of the prison house: Adult literacy and the correctional ethos. In H.S. Davidson (Ed.), *Schooling in a "total institution:" Critical perspectives on prison education* (pp. 49-63). Westport CT: Bergin & Garvey.

Collins, M. (1995a). The critical juncture: Commitment, prospects, and the struggle for adult education in the academy. In M. Collins (Ed.), *The Canmore Proceedings* (pp. 11-20). International Conference on Educating the Adult Educator: Role of the University, Canada: University of Saskatchewan.

Collins, M. & Long, H. (1989). Federal and provincial agencies in the United States and Canada. In S. Merriam & P. Cunningham (Eds.), *Handbook of Adult Education.* San Francisco: Jossey-Bass.

Collins, M. & Niemi, J.A. (1989). Advancing adult basic education in prisons: The recruitment, selection, and training of inmate tutors. In S. Duguid (Ed.), *Yearbook of correctional education, 1989* (pp. 193-208). Burnaby: Institute for the Humanities Simon Fraser University.

Conger, D.S. (1974). *Canadian open learning systems.* Prince Albert, SK: Dept. of Manpower and Immigration.

Conseil supérieur de l'éducation (1992). *Accro-tre l'accessibilité et garantir l'adaptation. L'éducation des adultes dix ans après la Commission Jean.* Québec: Gouvernement du Québec.

Cook, G.L. (1987). Educational justice for campmen: Alfred Fitzpatrick and the foundation of Frontier College, 1899-1922. In M.R. Welton (Ed.), *Knowledge for the people: The struggle for adult learning in English-speaking Canada 1828-1973* (pp. 35-51). Toronto: OISE Press.

Corbett, A. (1957). *We have with us tonight.* Toronto: Ryerson Press.

Corcoran, F. (1985). Pedagogy in prison: Teaching in maximum security institutions. *Communication Education, 34,* 49-58.

Cormack, B.V. (1981). *Beyond the classroom.* Edmonton: University of Alberta. Correctional Programs Prairie Region.

Correctional Programs Prairie Region. (1993, December). *Correctional programs: A proposal for a theory of correctional education for the Correctional Service of Canada.* (Available from Correctional Service of Canada).

Correctional Service of Canada. (1994, June). *The correctional planning process.* (Available from Correctional Service of Canada).

Correctional Service of Canada. (n.d.). *The correctional strategy: An overview.* (Available from Correctional Service of Canada).

Cosman, J.W. (1981). Penitentiary education in Canada. In L. Morin (Ed.), *On prison education* (pp. 34-42). Ottawa: Minister of Supply and Services.

Council of Europe, Legal Affairs. (1990). *Education in prison.* Strasbourg: Council of Europe, Legal Affairs.

Courtney, S. (1989). Defining adult and continuing education. In S. Merriam & P. Cunningham (Eds.), *Handbook of Adult and Continuing Education* (pp. 15-25). San Francisco: Jossey-Bass.

Cox, E. (1995). *A truly civil society.* Sydney: Sydney Australian Broadcast Corporation.

Cranton, P. (1992). *Working with adult learners.* Toronto: Wall & Emerson.

Cranton, P. (1994). *Understanding and promoting transformative learning: A guide for educators of adults.* San Francisco: Jossey-Bass.

Cranton, P. (1996). *Professional development as transformative learning: New perspectives for teachers of adults.* San Francisco: Jossey-Bass.

Critoph, U. (1997). *Research Paper No. 4.* Canadian Labour Congress National Training Conference, June 25-27.

Cross, P. (1981). *Adults as learners.* San Francisco: Jossey-Bass.

Cross, P. (1989). The changing role of higher education in the United States. *International Journal of University Adult Education, 28*(1), 1-14.

Cruikshank, J. (1995). Economic globalization: Which side are we on? *International Journal of Lifelong Education, 14*(6), 459-470.

Cunningham, P. (1991). International influences on the development of knowledge. In J. Peters, P. Jarvis & Associates (Eds.), *Adult education* (pp. 347-383). San Francisco: Jossey-Bass.

Cunningham, P. (1993). The politics of workers' education: Preparing workers to sleep with the enemy. *Adult Learning, 5*(1), 13-17.

D'Anglejan, A. & De Koninck, Z. (1992). Educational policy for a culturally plural Quebec: An update. In B. Burnaby & A.

Cumming (Eds.), *Socio-political aspects of ESL in Canada* (pp. 97-109). Toronto: OISE Press.

Darkenwald, G.G. & Merriam, S.B. (1982). *Adult education: foundations of practice.* New York: Harper& Row.

Dassinger, J. (1997). *Introduction to the issues: A GLC survey of union attitudes towards training.* Research Paper No. 1. Canadian Labour Congress National Training Conference, June 25-27.

Davidson, H.S. (1995). An alternative view of the past: Revisiting the Mutual Welfare League (1913-1923). *Journal of Correctional Education, 46*(4), 169-174.

Delaney, I. (1985). *By their own hands: A field worker's account of the Antigonish movement.* Hantsport: Lancelot Press.

Delors, J. (1996). *L'éducation : un trésor est caché dedans. Rapport à l'UNESCO de la Commisssion internationale sur l'éducation pour le vingt et unième siècle.* Paris: Odile Jacob. Unesco.

Dennison, C.J. (1987). Housekeeper of the community: The British Columbia women's Institutes 1909-1946. In M.R. Welton, *Knowledge for the people.* Toronto: OISE Press.

Denton, F.T., Pineo, P.C. & Spencer, B.G. (1988). Participation in adult education by the elderly: A multivariate analysis and some implications for the future. *Canadian Journal on Aging, 7*(1), 4-16.

Department of Employment. (1989). *Development of assessable standards for national certification: Guidance note 1 on a code of practice and a development model.* Moorfoot, Sheffield: Training Education and Enterprise.

Department of Industry for Scotland. (1988). *Scottish enterprise: A new approach to training and enterprise creation* (Cm 534), Edinburgh: Scottish Education Department.

Deri, A. & Cooper, G. (1993). *Environmental education—An active approach.* Hungary: Regional Environmental Centre for Central and Eastern Europe.

DeRoo, R.J. (1995). The church as contemporary structure for adult religious education. In M.A. Gillen & M.C.Taylor (Eds.), *Adult religious education: A journey of faith development* (pp. 29-44). NY: Paulist Press.

Deshler, D. (1991). Social, professional, and academic issues. In J. Peters, P. Jarvis & Associates (Eds.), *Adult education* (pp. 384-420). San Francisco: Jossey Bass.

Desjardins, B. (1993). *Population, aging, and the elderly: Current demographic analysis.* Cat. 91-533E. Ottawa: Industry, Science and Technology Canada.

Devereaux, M.S. (1985). *One in every five: A survey of adult education in Canada.* Cat. SZ-139/1984E. Ottawa: Supply and Services Canada.

Devor, H. (1989). Teaching women's studies to convicted sex offenders. In S. Duguid (Ed.), *Yearbook of correctional education,* (pp. 129-154). Burnaby: Institute for the Humanities Simon Fraser University.

Dewey, J. (1933). *How we think.* New York: Heath.

DiCarlo, R.E. (1996). *Towards a new world view: Conversations at the leading edge.* Erie (Pa.): Eric Publishing.

Dirkx, J. (1997). Nurturing the soul in adult learning. In P. Cranton Transformative *learning in action, new directions for adult and continuing education.* San Francisco: Jossey-Bass (in press).

Dixon, N. (1993). *Report to the Conference Board of Canada on organizational learning.* Report prepared for the Conference Board of Canada, Ottawa.

Doane, J. & Hodges, D. (1987). *Nostalgia and sexual difference. The resistance to contemporary feminism.* NY: Methuen.

Dodaro, S. & Pluta, L. (1995). *The Antigonish movement: Past successes, current circumstances and future options.* Paper presented at the Rethinking the Antigonish Movement conference, October.

Doherty, N. (1992). Challenging systematic sexism in the National Language Training Program. In B. Burnaby & A. Cumming (Eds.), *Socio-political aspects of ESL in Canada* (pp. 67-76). Toronto: OISE Press.

Donegan, J. (1978). *Women and men midwives. Medicine, morality and misogyny in early America.* London: Greenwood Press.

Draves, W. (1980). *The free university: A model for lifelong learning.* New York: Association Press.

Drolet, M. & d'Amour, G. (1987, November). *Recognition of generic vocational competences: Results of a pilot-project with a group of welfare recipients.* Paper presented at the meeting of the Council for Adult and Experiential Learning, Baltimore, Maryland.

Drucker, P.F. (1994, November,). The age of social transformation. *The Atlantic Monthly, 274*(5).

Duguid, S. (1989). Preface. In S. Duguid (Ed.), *Yearbook of correctional education, 1989* (pp. vii-viii). Burnaby: Institute for the Humanities Simon Fraser University.

Duguid, S. (1993a). Planning for student success: A review of the character and objectives of prison education. In C. Eggleston (Ed.), *Yearbook of correctional education,* (pp. 177-188). San Bernardino: Center for the Study of Correctional Education.

Duguid, S. (1993b). Cognitive dissidents bite the dust—The demise of university education in Canada's prisons. *Convergence, 26*(3), 51-63.

Duguid, S. (1996). *Measuring the impact of education: Preliminary findings of the prison education research project.* Manuscript submitted for publication.

Dworkin, A. (1974). *Woman hating.* NY: Dutton.

Dworkin, A. (1983). *Right wing women.* NY: Perigree.

Ebel, R.L. (1978). The case for norm-referenced measurements. *Educational Researcher, 7*(11), 3-5.

Echeverria, L. (1983). Priorities in adult education in a world of crises. *Convergence, 16*(1), 36-39.

Edelson, P. (1992). Rethinking leadership in adult and continuing education. *New Directions of Adult and Continuing Education, 56,* 5-15.

Edwards, R. (1994). Really useful knowledge: Flexible accumulation and open and distanced learning. *Studies in Continuing Education, 16*(2), 160-171.

Edwards, R., Sieminski, S. & Zeldin, D. (Eds.). (1993). *Adult learners, education and training.* London: Routledge.

Edwards, R. & Usher, R. (1996). What stories do I tell now? New times and new narratives for the adult educator. *International Journal of Lifelong Education, 15*(3), 216-229.

Ehrenreich, B. & English, D. (1979). *For her own good: 150 years of the experts' advice to women.* New York: Anchor/Doubleday Press.

Einstein A. & Infeld, L. (1938). *The evolution of physics.* New York: Simon and Schuster.

Elderhostel Canada. (1996). *Spring catalogue: An educational adventure for adults.* Kingston, ON: Elderhostel Canada.

Elias, J. (1995). *Philosophy of education: Classical and contemporary.* Malabar, Florida: Krieger.

Elias, J.L. & Merriam, S. (1995). *Philosophical foundations of adult education.* (2nd edition) Malabar, FL: Krieger.

Elliot, T. (1995, December). Education programs in Tennessee. *The only voice, 6*(10), 1.

Ellsworth, E. (1992). Why doesn't this feel empowering? Working through the repressive myths of critical pedagogy. In C. Luke and J. Gore (Eds.), *Feminisms and critical pedagogy* (pp.90-119). New York: Routledge.

Ellsworth, J.H. (1992). Adults' learning: The voices of experience. *MPAEA Journal*, Fall, 23-34.

Employment and Immigration Canada. (1983). *Learning a living: Report of the task force on skill development leave.* Ottawa: Author.

Erikson, E.H., Erikson, J.M. & Kivnick, H.Q. (1986). *Vital involvement in old age.* New York: W.W. Norton & Company.

Evans, G. (1984). *John Grierson and the National Film Board.* Toronto: University of Toronto.

Evans, T. & King, B. (1991). *Beyond the text: Contemporary writing on distance education.* Geelong: Deakin University Press.

Evans, T. & Nation, D.E. (1987). What future for distance education? *International Council for Distance Education Bulletin, 14.*

Evans, T. & Nation D.E. (Eds.) (1989). *Critical reflections on distance education* (pp. 48-53). London: Falmer Press.

Evernden, N. (1992). *The social creation of nature.* London and Baltimore: John Hopkins University.

Ewems, T. (1979). Analyzing the impact of competence-based liberal education. In G. Grant, T. Ewens, Z. Gamson, W.Kohli, W. Neumann, V. Olesen & D. Riesman, *On competence: A critical analysis of competence-based reforms in higher education* (pp. 160-198). San Francisco: Jossey-Bass.

Excalibur Learning Resource Centre Canada Corp. (1996, February). *1995 Year-end report: Excalibur Learning Resource Centre Prairie Region* (Submitted to Prairie Region Chiefs of Education). Red Deer, AB: Author.

Faith, K. (1995). The Santa Cruz women's prison project. In H.S. Davidson (Ed.), *Schooling in a "total institution:" Critical perspectives on prison education* (pp. 173-192). Westport CT: Bergin & Garvey.

Faludi, S. (1991). *Backlash.* London: Chatto & Windus.

Faris, R. (1975). *The passionate educators.* Toronto: Peter Martin.

Fast, R. (1991). *The impact of sponsorship: The University of Manitoba's rural adult education program, 1936-1945.* Un-

published Master's thesis, University of Alberta, Edmonton, AB.

Fauré, E., Herrera, F., Kaddoura, A., Lopes, H. Petrovsky, A., Rahnema, M. & Ward, F. (1972). *Learning to be: The world of education today and tomorrow.* Paris: UNESCO

Federal Bureau of Prisons. (1991, May 1). PS5350.19 Literacy program (GED standard). Washington D.C.: United States department of Justice, Federal Bureau of Prisons.

Feeley, M.M. & Simon, J. (1992). The new penology: Notes on the emerging strategy of corrections and its implications. *Criminology, 30,* 449-474.

Feeley, M.M. & Simon, J. (1994). Actuarial justice: The emerging new criminal law. In D. Nelken (Ed.), *The futures of criminology* (pp. 173-201). London: Sage Publications.

Fenwick, T.J. (1996). *Women as continuous learners in the workplace.* Unpublished doctoral dissertation, University of Alberta, Edmonton, Alberta.

Ferguson, M. (1981). *Les enfants du verseau.* France: Calmann-Lévy.

Finger, M. (1966). Canadian Association for Adult Education (CAAE), *A White Paper on the Development of Adult Education in Canada.* Toronto: CAAE.

Finger, M. (1989). New social movements and their implications for adult education. *Adult Education Quarterly, 40*(1), 15-22.

Finger, M. (1991). Can critical theory save adult education from post-modernism? *Canadian Journal for the Study of Adult Education, 5,* 133-144.

Finger, M. (1995). Adult education and society today. *International Journal of Lifelong Education. 14,* 110-119.

Finger, M. & Woolis, D. (1994). Organizational learning, the learning organization, and adult education. *Proceedings of the Adult Education Research Conference* (pp. 151-156). Knoxville, TN: University of Tennessee.

Fiol, M.C. & Lyles, M.A. (1985). Organizational learning. *Academy of Management Review,*

Fischer, C.S., Hout, M., Jankowski, M.S., Lucas, S.R., Swidler, A. & Voss, K. (1996). *Inequality by design: Cracking the bell curve myth.* Princeton: Princeton University Press.

Fitzpatrick, A. (1920). *The university in overalls.* Toronto: Frontier College Press.

Flood, C. (1993). The learning organization. *The Worklife Report, 9*(2), 1-4.

Foran, T. & Reed, M. (1996). The correctional system. In L.W. Kennedy & V.F. Sacco (Eds.), *Crime counts: A criminal event analysis* (pp. 293-311). Toronto: Nelson Canada.

Fordham, P. (1992). *Education for all: An expanded vision.* Paris: UNESCO.

Forester, J. (1989). *Planning in the face of power.* Berkeley: University of California.

Forward, S. & Torres, J. (1986). *Men who hate women & the women who love them.* New York: Bantam.

Foucault, M. (1979). *Discipline and punish.* New York: Vintage Books.

Foucault, M. (1980). *Power/knowledge.* New York: Pantheon.

Foucher, R. & Tremblay, N. (1992). *Self-directed learning in the workplace: A framework for analysis.* Paper prepared for 7th International Symposium on Self-Directed Learning. West Palm Beach, California.

Fowler, J. (1981). *Stages of faith: The psychology of human development and the quest for meaning.* San Francisco: Harper & Row.

Fraser, L. & Ward, K. (1988). *Education from everyday living.* Liecester: NIACE.

Freire, P. (1970). *Pedagogy of the oppressed.* New York: Continuum.

Freire, P. (1974). *Pédagogie des opprimés.* Paris: Maspero.

Freire, P. (1994). *Education for critical consciousness.* New York, Continuum.

Freire, P. & Macedo, D. (1995). A dialogue: Culture, language and race. *Harvard Educational Review. 65*(3), 377-402.

French, V. (1989). Misogyny. In H. Tierney (Ed.), *Women's Studies Encyclopedia 3* (pp. 191-198). London: Greenwood Press.

Friesen, G. (1994). Adult education and union education: Aspects of English Canadian cultural history in the 20th century. *Labour/Le Travail 34,* 163-88.

Gagné, R.M. (1962). Military training and principles of learning. *American Psychologist, 17,* 83-91.

Gagné, R.M. (1970). *The conditions of learning.* New York: Holt, Rinehart, and Winston.

Galbraith, J.K. (1973). *Economics and the public purpose.* Boston: Houghton Mifflin.

Galbraith, M. & Sisco, B. (Eds.) (1992, Summer). Confronting controversies in challenging times: A call to action. *New Directions for Adult and Continuing Education, 60,* 13-20.

Gallagher, S. (1992). *Hermeneutics and education.* New York: SUNY.

Gamson, Z. (1979). Understanding the difficulties of implementing a competence-based curriculum. In G. Grant, P. Elbow, T. Ewens, Z. Gamson, W. Kohli, W. Neumann, V. Olesen & D. Riesman, *On competence: A critical analysis of competence-based reforms in higher education* (pp. 224-258). San Francisco: Jossey-Bass.

Gang, P. (1996). In R.E. DiCarlo (Ed.), *Towards a new world view: Conversations at the leading edge* (pp. 252-263). Erie (Pa.): Eric Publishing.

Garcia-Orgales, J. (1995). *Transition and difference.* Toronto: Communications Energy and Paperworks Union.

Garland, D. (1985). *Punishment and welfare: A history of penal strategies.* London: Aldershot.

Garland, D. (1990). *Punishment and modern society: A study in social theory.* Chicago: University of Chicago Press.

Garrison, D.R. (1989). *Understanding distance education.* London: Routledge.

Garrison, D.R. (1992). Critical thinking and self-directed learning in adult education: An analysis of responsibility and control issues. *Adult Education Quarterly, 42,* 136-148.

Garrison, R. & Baskett, M. (1989). A survey of adult education research in Canada. *The Canadian Journal for the Study of Adult Education, 3*(2), 32-46.

Gaucher, R. (1989). The Canadian penal press: A documentation and analysis. *Journal of Prisoners on Prisons, 2*(1), 3-24.

Gavin, D. (1993). The five practices of a learning organization. *Harvard Business Review,* July-August, 271-282.

Gayle, M. (1990). Toward the 21st century. *Adult learning, 1*(4), 10-14.

Gehring, T. (1995). Characteristics of correctional education instruction, 1789-1875. *Journal of Correctional Education, 46,* 52-59.

George, V. & Wilding, P. (1985). *Ideology and social welfare.* London: Routledge & Kegan Paul.

Gibbons, M., Bailey, A., Comeau, P., Schmuck, J., Seymour, S. & Wallace, D. (1980). Toward a theory of self-directed learning: A study of experts without formal training. *Journal of Humanistic Psychology, 20*(2), 41-56.

Gibson, F. (1991). Directions in parole—A Canadian perspective. In *International symposium on the future of corrections: Program.* Ottawa: Correctional Service of Canada.

Giddens A. (1990). *The consequences of modernity.* Stanford, CA: Stanford University Press.

Giddens A. (1991). *Modernity and self-Identity: Self and society in the Late Modern Age.* Stanford, CA: Stanford University Press.

Giddens, A. (1994). *Beyond left and right: The future of radical politics.* Stanford, CA: Stanford University Press.

Gildemeister, G.A. (1977). *Prison labour and convict competition with free workers in industrializing America.* New York: Garland.

Gilligan, C. (1988). *In a different voice: Psychological theory and women's Development.* Cambridge: Harvard University Press.

Giroux, H. (1992). *Border crossings, cultural workers and the politics of education.* London-New York: Routledge.

Glaser, R. (1963). Instructional technology and the measurement of learning outcomes. *American Psychologist, 18,* 519-521.

Goldin, C. & Thomas, J. (1984). Adult education in correctional settings: Symbol or substance. *Adult Education Quarterly, 34,* 123-134.

Gonczi, A. (1992). *An integrated competency approach to professional education and assessment: A consideration of arguments for and against.* (Discussion Paper). Sydney: University of Technology.

Gordon, E.E. (1997). The new knowledge worker. *Adult Learning, 8*(4), 14-17.

Gordon, P. (1990). Misogyny, dionysianism and a new model of Greek tragedy. *Women's Studies, 17,* 211-218.

Gosselin, L. (1982). *Prisons in Canada.* Montreal: Black Rose.

Government of Ontario. (1995). *People and skills in the global economy.* Toronto: Author.

Grace, A.P. (1995). The gospel according to Father Jimmy: The missions of J.J. Tompkins, pioneer adult educator in the Antigonish movement. *Convergence, 28*(2), 63-78.

Grace, A.P. (1996). Striking a critical pose: Andragogy—missing links, missing values. *The International Journal of Lifelong Education, 15*(5), 382-392.

Grace, A.P. (1997). Where critical postmodern theory meets practice: Working in the intersection of instrumental, social, and cultural education. *Studies in Continuing Education. 19*(1), 51-70.

Graham, D. (1994). *Loving to survive: Sexual terror, men's violence and women's lives.* NY: New York University Press.

Grant, G., Elbow, P., Ewens, T., Gamson, Z., Kohli, W., Neumann, W., Olesen, V. & Riesman, D. (1979). *On competence: A critical analysis of competence-based reforms in higher education.* San Francisco: Jossey-Bass.

Gray, C.W. (1973). *Movies for the people.* Montreal: National Film Board.

Griffin, D.K. (1978). *Ontario Institute for Studies in Education review of penitentiary education and training, Phase 1 report.* Ottawa: Education and Training Division, Canadian Penitentiary Service.

Griffin, R. (Ed.) (1988). *Spirituality and society.* New York: SUNY.

Griffin, V. (1988). Holistic learning/teaching in adult education: Would you play a one-string guitar? In T. Barer-Stein & J.A. Draper (Eds.), *The crafts of teaching adults* (pp. 105-131). Toronto: Culture Concepts.

Griffin, V. (1988). Learning to name our learning processes. *Canadian Journal for Studies in Adult Education,* 5(2), 1-16.

Groff, R. (1993). *Worker-driven training: A research report.* Toronto: Communications Energy and Paperworkers Union.

Group for Collaborative Inquiry. (1993). The democratization of knowledge. *Adult Education Quarterly, 44*(1), 43-51.

Grow, G. (1991). Teaching learners to be self-directed. *Adult Education Quarterly, 41*(3), 125-149.

Grow, G. (1994). Forum: In defense of the staged self-directed learning model. *Adult Education Quarterly, 44*(2), 109-114.

Gubar, S. (1994). Feminist misogyny: Mary Wollstonecraft and the paradox of "It takes one to know one." *Feminist Studies, 20*(3), 453-474.

Habermas, J. (1971). *Knowledge and human interests.* Boston: Beacon Press. Also see (J. J. Shapiro, Trans.) London: Heinemann.

Habermas, J. (1984, 1987). *The theory of communicative action.* Vol. 1: *Reason and the rationalization of society.* Vol. 2: *Lifeworld and system: A critique of functionalist reason* (McCarthy, T., Trans.). Boston: Beacon.

Habermas, J. (1984a). *Observations on the spiritual situation of the age.* Cambridge, MA: MIT Press.

Habermas, J. (1996). *Between facts and norms: Contributions to a discourse theory of law and democracy.* Cambridge: MIT Press.

Hager, P. & Gonczi, A. (1993). Attributes and competence. *Australian and New Zealand Journal of Vocational Education Research, 1*(1), 36-45.

Haggis, S.M. (1991). *Education for all I: Purpose and context.* Paris: UNESCO.

Halevy, E. (1956). *Thomas Hodgskin.* London: Ernest Benn.

Hall, B. (1979). Participatory Research: Breaking The Monopoly of Knowledge. In John Niemi (Ed.), *Viewpoints on adult education research.* Columbus, Ohio: ERIC Clearing House.

Hall, B. & Sullivan, E. (1994). *Transformative Learning: Contexts and practices.* In Awakening sleepy knowledge. Toronto: Transformative Learning Centre, OISE.

Hall, B.L. (1997). Transformative learning and democracy: Whose vision, whose planet, whose learning? Paper prepared for the *Crossing Boundaries, Breaking Borders 1997 SCUTREA International Conference.* University of London, London, England.

Hammerman, D. & Hammerman, W. (1973). *Teaching in the outdoors.* Minneapolis: Burgess Publishing Company.

Harasim, L. (1996). On-line education: The future. In T. Harrison & T. Stephen (Eds.), *Computer networking and scholarly communication in the twenty-first-century university* (pp. 203-214). New York: SUNY.

Harman, W. (1996). In R.E. DiCarlo (Ed.), *Towards a new world view: Conversations at the leading edge* (pp. 38-44). Erie (Pa.): Eric Publishing.

Harris, D. (1987). *Openness and closure in distance education.* Lewes: Falmer Press.

Harrison, T. & Stephen, T. (Eds.). (1996). *Computer networking and scholarly communication in the twenty-first-century university.* New York: SUNY.

Hart, M. (1993). Educative or miseducative work: A critique of the current debate on work and education. *Canadian Journal for the Study of Adult Education, 7*(1), 19-36.

Hart, M.U. (1992). *Working and educating for life: Feminist and international perspectives on adult education.* London: Routledge.

Haughton, G. (1993). Skills mismatch and policy response. In R. Edwards, S. Semisky & D. Zeldin (Eds.), *Adult learners, education and training.* London: Routledge.

Hawkesworth, M. (1990). *Beyond oppression. Feminist theory and political strategy.* NY: Continuum.

Hawkins, F. (1989). *Critical years in immigration: Canada and Australia compared.* Kingston and Montreal: McGill-Queen's University.

Heaney, T. (1993). Identifying and dealing with educational, social, and political issues. *New Directions for Adult and Continuing Education, 60,* 13-20.

Heberle, R. & Rose, W. (1994). Teaching within the contradictions of prison education. In M. Williford (Ed.), *Higher education in prison: A contradiction in terms?* (pp. 97-106). Phoenix: Oryx Press.

Held, D. (1993). Liberalism, Marxism and democracy. *Theory and Society, 22.*

Hester, M. (1992). *Lewd women and wicked witches: A study of the dynamics of male domination.* NY: Routledge.

Hiemstra, R.P. (1975). *The older adult and learning.* Lincoln, NE: University of Nebraska-Lincoln (ERIC Reproduction Document ED 117 371).

Hobsbawm, E. (1995). *Age of extremes: The short twentieth century 1914-1991.* London: Abacus Books.

Hodkinson, P. (1992). Alternative models of competence in vocational education and training. *Journal of Further and Higher Education, 16*(2), 30-39.

Holloway, J. & Picciotto, S. (Eds.) (1978). *State and capital: A Marxist debate.* London: Edward Arnold.

Holmberg, B. (1995). *Theory and practice of distance education*. New York: Routledge.

hooks, b. (1988). *Talking back*. Toronto: Between the Lines.

Houle, C. (1956). Professional education for educators of adults, *Adult Education, 6*, 3 (Spring).

Houle, C. (1960). *The inquiring mind*. Madison: Univ. of Wisconsin Press.

Houston, W.R. (Ed.). (1974). *Competency assessment, research, and evaluation: A report of a national conference*. Washington: American Association of Colleges for Teacher Education.

Houston, W.R. & Howsam, R.B. (Eds.). (1972). *Competency-based teacher education*. Chicago: Science Research Associates.

Hughes-Fuller, P. (1994). The theory and practice of Raymond Williams. *Proceedings of CASAE conference*. Vancouver: Simon Fraser University.

Hull, C. & Coben, D. (1991). The survival of the fittest? *Adults learning, 3*(1), 11-12.

Human Resources Development Canada. (1994). *Proposed research themes for a human resources development agenda*. (Applied Research Branch). Ottawa, ON: Author.

Huot, J. (1989). Keeping workers in their place: The role of the community college. In OFL/J. Davis (Ed.), It's *our knowledge: Labour, public education & skills training*, 31-38. Toronto: Our Schools/Our Selves.

Husén, T. (1992). The applicability of democratic principles and the mission of the university. *Interchange, 23*(1-2), 11-18.

Hutton, W. (1995). *The state we're in*. London: Jonathan Cape.

Hyland, T. (1994). Silk purses and sows' ears: NVQs, GNVQs and experiential learning. *Cambridge Journal of Education, 24*(2), 233-243.

Ibikunle-Johnson, V. & Rugumayo, E. (1987). *Environmental education through adult education*. Nairobi: African Association for Literacy and Adult Education.

Illich, I. (1970). *Deschooling society*. New York: Harper & Row.

Illsley, P. (1992). The undeniable link: Adult and continuing education and social change. In M. Galbraith & B. Sisco (Eds.), *New directions for continuing education, 54. Confronting controversies in challenging times: A call for action* (pp. 25-34). San Francisco: Jossey-Bass.

Immigration Canada. (1992a). *Annual report to Parliament: Immigration plan for 1991-1995: Year three-1993*. Ottawa: Minister of Supply and Services.

Immigration Canada. (1992b). *Questions and answers of the new Immigrant Language Training Policy*. Ottawa: Employment and Immigration Canada.

Iphofen, R. (1993). The hidden costs of open learning. *Adults learning, 5*(2), 42-43.

Isabelle R. (1994). *Survey of prior learning assessment in Canada*. Report for Human Resources Development, Canada.

Isabelle, R. (1995). *Prior learning assessment—A discussion paper*. Canadian Association of University Continuing Education (CAUCE/OCULL Wilfrid Laurier University, Kitchener/Waterloo.)

Isla, A. (1993a). The debt crisis in Latin America: An example of unsustainable development. *Canadian Woman Studies, 13*(3), (Spring) 65-68.

Isla, A. (1993b) Women, development and the market economy. *Canadian Woman Studies, 13*(3) (Spring).

Isla, A., Miles, A. & Molloy, S. (1996). Stabilization/structural adjustment./restructuring Canadian feminist issues in a global framework. *Canadian Woman Studies 16*(3) (Summer), 116-120.

Jansen T. & Wildemeersch, D. (1992). Bridging gaps between private experiences and public issues. In D. Wildemeersch & T. Jansen (Eds.), *Adult education, experiential learning and social change: The postmodern challenge* (pp. 5-17). Driebergen: VTA Groep.

Jansen, T. & Van Der Veen, R. (1992). Reflexive modernity, self-reflective biographies: Adult education in the light of the risk society. *International Journal of Lifelong Education, 11*(4), 275-286.

James, W. (1978). The divided self and conversion. In W.E Conn (Ed.), *Conversion: Perspectives on personal and social transformation*. New York: Alba House.

Jarvis, P. (1992). *Paradoxes of learning: On becoming an individual in society*. San Francisco: Jossey-Bass.

Jarvis. P. (1995, May). Educating the adult educator in an information society: The role of the university. A paper presented at the *International Conference on Educating the Educator: Role of the University*, Canmore, Alberta.

John Grierson Project. (1984). *John Grierson and the NFB*. Toronto: ECW Press.

Johnson-Riordan, L. (1994). In and against the grain of "new times" Discourses of adult education and the challenge of contemporary cultural theory. *Australian Journal of Adult and Community Education, 34*(1), 10-17.

Jones, D.B. (1981). *Movies and memoranda*. Ottawa: Canadian Film Institute.

Jung, C. ([1921] 1971). *Psychological types*. Princeton: Princeton University Press.

Kahn-Blumstein, A. (1977). *Misogyny and idealization in the courtly romance*. Bonn: Bouvier.

Kaplan, R. & Kaplan, S. (1989). *The experience of nature: A Psychological Perspective*. Cambridge: Press Syndicate of the University of Cambridge.

Kasworm, C. (1983). Self-directed learning and lifespan development. *International Journal of Lifelong Education, 2*(1), 29-46.

Keegan, D.J. (1980). On defining distance education. *Distance Education, 1*(1), 13-36.

Kegan, R. (1982). *The evolving self: Problem and process in human development*. Cambridge: Harvard University.

Kegan, R. (1994). *In over our heads: The mental demands of modern life*. Cambridge: Harvard University Press.

Keller, F.S. (1968). Goodbye, teacher. *Journal of Applied Behavior Analysis, 1*, 79-89.

Kelly, G.A. (1963). *The psychology of personal constructs*. (Vols. 1 and 2) New York: Norton.

Kennedy P. (1988). *The rise and fall of the great powers*. London: Unwin Hyman.

Kennedy, H. (1995). *Return to learn: UNISON's fresh approach to trade union education*. London: UNISON.

Kenway, J. & Modra, H. (1992). Feminist pedagogy and emancipatory possibilities. In C. Luke & J. Gore (Eds.), Feminisms and critical pedagogy (pp. 138-166). New York: Routledge.

Keough, N. (1995). Tales from the Sari-Sari: In search of bigfoot. *Convergence, 28*(4), 5-11.

Kerka, S. (1995). *Self-directed learning: Myths and realities*. (ERIC Document Reproduction)

Kidd, J.R. (Ed.). (1950). *Adult education in Canada*. Toronto: Canadian Association for Adult Education.

Kidd, J.R. (1952). A kind of partnership. *Food for Thought, 13*(1).

Kidd, J.R. (1953). *Pictures with a purpose*. Toronto: Canadian Association for Adult Education.

Kidd, J.R. (1960). *How adults learn* (revised edition). New York: Association Press.

Kidd, J.R. (1963). *Learning and society*. Toronto: Canadian Association for Adult Education.

Kidd, J.R. (1966). Organizing for lifelong learning. In J.R. Kidd & G.R. Selman (Eds.), (1978), *Coming of age: Canadian adult education in the 1960s* (pp. 78-85). Toronto: Canadian Association for Adult Education.

King, D.S. (1987). *The new right politics, markets and citizenship*. London: England, MacMillan Education.

King, P.M. & Kitchener, K.S. (1994). *Developing reflective judgment*. San Francisco: Jossey-Bass.

Klemp, G.O. (1979). Defining, measuring, and integrating competence. In P.S. Pottinger & J. Goldsmith (Eds.), *New directions for experiential learning: Defining and measuring competence* (pp. 41-52). San Francisco: Jossey-Bass.

Klemp, G.O. (1982). Assessing student potential: An immodest proposal. In C. Taylor (Ed.), New dimensions for experiential learning: Diverse student preparation: Benefits and issues. (pp. 37-48). San Francisco: Jossey-Bass.

Kneen, B. (1989). *From land to mouth*. Toronto: NC Press Limited.

Kneller, G. (1971). *Introduction to the philosophy of education*. New York: John Wiley and Sons.

Knowles, M. (1968). Andragogy, not pedagogy! *Adult Leadership*, April, 350-52, 386.

Knowles, M.S. (1970). *The modern practice of adult education: Pedagogy versus andragogy*. New York: Association Press.

Knowles, M. (1975). *Self directed Learning*. New York: Associated Press.

Knowles, M.S. (1980). *The modern practice of adult education: From pedagogy to andragogy*. Chicago: Follett Publishing Co.

Knowles, M. (1984). *The adult learner: A neglected species* (3rd edition). Houston: Gulf. (Original in 1973.)

Knowles, M.S. & DuBois, E.E. (1970). Prologue: The handbooks in perspective. In R.M. Smith, G.F. Aker & J.R. Kidd (Eds.), *Handbook of adult education* (pp. xvii-xxiii). New York: Macmillan.

Knowles, M. & Klevins, C. (1972). Resume of adult education. In C. Klevins (Ed.), *Materials and methods in adult education* (pp. 5-15). New York: Klevens Publications Inc.

Kolb, D.A. (1984). *Experiential learning*. Englewood Cliffs, N.J.: Prentice-Hall.

Koul, B.N. & Jenkins, J. (Eds.), (1990). *Distance education: A spectrum of case studies*. London: Kogan Page.

Kramarae, C. (1985). *A feminist dictionary*. Boston: Routledge & Kegan Paul.

Kuhn, T.S. (1962). *The structure of scientific revolutions*. Chicago: University of Chicago Press.

Kulich, J. (1991). Current trends and priorities in Canadian adult education. *International Journal of Lifelong Education, 10*(2), 93-106.

Labouvie-Vief, G. (1990). Wisdom as integrated thought: Historical and developmental perspectives. In R.J. Sternberg (Ed.), *Wisdom: Its nature, origins, and development* (pp. 52-83). Cambridge, UK: Cambridge University Press.

Laidlaw, A.F. (1961). *The campus and the community: The global impact of the Antigonish movement*. Montreal: Harvest House Limited.

Laidlaw, A.F. (Ed.). (1971). *The man from Margaree: Writings and speeches of M.M. Coady*. Toronto/Montreal: McClelland and Stewart.

Landry, C. (1992). Le champ d'études de l'andragogie/éducation des adultes dans les programs de certificat des universités Québécoises. *Revue canadienne de l'education permanente universitaire, 18*(1), 39-52.

Lauen, R.J. (1988). *Community-managed corrections*. United States: American Correctional Association.

Lave, J. & Wenger, E. (1991). *Situated learning: Legitimate peripheral participation*. New York: Cambridge University Press.

Laws, J. (1979). *The second X: Sex role and social role*. NY: Elsevier.

Layder, D. (1994). *Understanding social theory*. London: Sage.

Legere, B.J. (1914). The red flag in the Auburn prison. *The International Socialist review, 15*, 337-341.

Legge, D. (1989). Personal reflections on 'adult education' and the challenges of today and tomorrow. *Adult Education, 61*(4), 300-307.

Leirman, W. (1987). Adult education: movement and discipline between the golden sixties and the iron eighties. In W. Leirman & J. Kulich (Eds.), *Adult education and the challenges of the 1990s* (pp. 1-28). New York: Croom Helm.

Lesourne, J. (1988). *144education et sociétés, les defis de l'an 2000*, Paris: Ed. Le Monde/La Decouverte.

Levitt, B. & March, J.G. (1988). Organizational learning. *Annual Review of Sociology, 14*, 319-340.

Lewis, L. (1991). New educational technologies for the future. In S. Merriam & P. Cunningham (Eds.), *Handbook of adult and continuing education* (pp. 613-627). San Francisco: Jossey-Bass.

Lewis, R. (1966, July 1). Making a difference. *Maclean's, 109*(27), 2.

Lindeman, E.C. (1926). *The meaning of adult education*. New York: New Republic.

Lindeman, E.C. (1947). Methods of democratic adult education. In S. Brookfield (Ed.), *Learning democracy: Eduard Lindeman on adult education and social change*. London: Croom Helm, 1987.

Lindeman, E.C. (1961). *The meaning of adult education*. Montreal: Harvest House.

Linebaugh, P. (1995). Freeing birds, erasing images, burning lamps: How I learned to teach in prison. In H.S. Davidson (Ed.), *Schooling in a "total institution:" Critical perspectives on prison education*, (pp. 65-89). Westport, CT: Bergin & Garvey.

Little, D.J. (1991). Critical adult education: A response to contemporary social crisis. *Canadian Journal for the Study of Adult Education, 5*, 1-20.

Littlefield, J. (1993). History of Ohio central school system. In C. Eggleston (Ed.), *Yearbook of correctional education*, (pp. 44-58). San Bernardino: Center for the Study of Correctional Education.

Lotz, J. (1977). *Understanding Canada*, Toronto, NC Press.

Lotz, J. & Welton, M.R. (1987). Knowledge for the people: The origins and development of the Antigonish Movement. In M.R. Welton (Ed.), *Knowledge for the people: The struggle for adult learning in English-speaking Canada 1828-1973* (pp. 97-111). Toronto: Ontario Institute for Studies in Education.

Lovett, T., Clarke, C. & Kilmurray, A. (1983). *Adult education and community action*. London: Croom Helm.

Lowe, J. (1975). *The education of adults: A world perspective*. Toronto: Ontario Institute for Studies in Education.

Lucas, C.J. (1976). *Challenge and choice in contemporary education: Six major ideological perspectives*. New York: Macmillan.

Luke, C. & Gore, J. (Eds.). (1992). *Feminisms and critical pedagogy*. New York: Routledge.

Lund, B. (1994). Towards a theoretical framework for university community education. In M. Brooke & M. Waldron (Eds.), *University continuing education in Canada* (pp. 166-179). Toronto: Thompson Educational.

Lund, L. (1988). *Beyond business/education partnerships: The business experience*. Ottawa: Conference Board du Canada. no 918.

Lyons, N.P. (1987). Ways of knowing, learning and making moral choices. *Journal of Moral Education, 16*(3), 226-239.

MacInnes, D. & MacLean, J. (1992). *"What can women do?" The Antigonish movement and its program for women, 1918-1945*. Paper presented at the *Canadian Association for Studies in Cooperation*.

MacKeracher, D. (1994). Working women as relational learners. *Proceedings of the Canadian Association for the Study of Adult Education*. Vancouver, BC: Simon Fraser University at Harbour Centre.

MacKeracher, D. & McFarland, J. (1993/94). Learning working knowledge: Implications for training. *Women's Education Des Femmes, 10*(3/4), Winter, 54-58.

MacKeracher, D. & Mersereau, S. (1995). *Senior-friendly communities: Final report*. Report of a project funded by Health Canada through the Canadian Association on Gerontology. Fredericton, NB: The Third Age Centre.

MacLean, B.D. & Milovanovic, D. (Ed.), (1990). *Racism, empiricism and criminal justice*. Vancouver: Collective Press.

MacLellan, M. (1985). *Coady remembered*. Antigonish: St. F.X. University Press.

Magnesson, K. & Osborne, J. (1990). The rise of competency based education: A deconstructionist analysis. *The Journal of Educational Thought, 24*(1), 5-13.

Manpower Services Commission. (1981). *A new training initiative: An agenda for action* (HMSO Cmnd 8455). London: Manpower Services Commission.

Marchak, M.P. (1988). *Ideological perspectives on Canada*. (3rd edition). Toronto: McGraw-Hill Ryerson.

Marshall, J. (1992, October). Steelworkers' humanity fund education program. *Briarpatch*. 12-19.

Marsick, V. & Watkins, K. (1990). *Informal and incidental learning in the workplace*. London: Routledge.

Marsick, V. & Watkins, K. (1996). Adult educators and the challenge of the learning Organisation. *Adult Learning, 7*(4), 18-20.

Martin, D. (1995). *Thinking union*. Toronto: Between the Lines.

Maruani, M. & Reynaud, E. (1990). *Sociologie de l'emploi*. Paris: Editions de la Decouverte.

Mayo, P. (1994). A comparative analysis of the ideas of Gramsci and Friere from an adult education perspective. *The Canadian Journal for the Study of Adult Education, 8*(2), 1-28.

Mayo, P. (1994). Synthesizing Gramsci and Freire: Possibilities for a theory of radical adult education. *International Journal of Lifelong Education, 13*(2), 125-148.

McConnell, D. (1994). *Implementing computer supported cooperative learning*. London: Kogan Page.

McGhee, P. (1959). *The learning society*. Chicago: Center for the Study of Liberal Education for Adults.

McLaren, P. (1989). *Life in schools: An introduction to critical pedagogy in the foundations of education*. Toronto: Irwin.

Merriam, S. (Ed.). (1984). *Selected writings on philosophy and adult education*. Malabar, FL: Krieg.

Merriam, S. & Brockett, R. (1997). *The profession and practice of adult education: An introduction*. San Francisco: Jossey-Bass.

Merriam, S.B. & Caffarella, R.S. (1991). *Learning in adulthood: A comprehensive guide*. San Francisco: Jossey-Bass.

Merriam, S. & Lumsden, D.B. (1985). Educational needs and interests of older learners. In D.B. Lumsden (Ed.), *The older adult as learner: Aspects of educational gerontology* (pp. 51-72). San Francisco: Jossey-Bass.

Mezirow, J. (1978a). *Education for perspective transformation: Women's re-entry programs in community colleges*. Center for Adult Education: Teachers College. Columbia University.

Mezirow, J. (1978b). Perspective transformation. *Adult Education, 28*(2), 100-110.

Mezirow, J. (1985). Critical transformation theory and the self-directed learning. In Brookfield, S., *Self-directed learning: From theory to practice* (pp. 17-30). San Francisco: Jossey Bass.

Mezirow, J. (1989). Transformation theory and social action: A response to Collard and Law. *Adult Education Quarterly, 39,* 169-175.

Mezirow, J. (1991). *Transformative dimensions of adult learning.* San Francisco: Jossey-Bass.

Mezirow, J. (1994). Understanding transformative theory. *Adult Education Quarterly, 44*(4), 222-244.

Mezirow, J. (1996). Contemporary paradigms of learning. *Adult Education Quarterly, 46*(3), 158-173.

Mies, M. (1986). *Patriarchy and the accumulation of capital on a world scale: Women in the international division of labour.* London: Zed Books.

Miles, A. (1989). Women's challenge to adult education. *The Canadian Journal for the Study of Adult Education, 3*(1), 1-18.

Miles, A. (1996). *Integrative feminisms: Building global visions, 1960s-1990s.* New York and London: Routledge.

Miller, J.P. (1983). *The educational spectrum: Orientations to curriculum.* New York & London: Longman.

Miller, L. (1997). *The training situation in Quebec: A response to the national survey.* Research Paper No. 2. Canadian Labour Congress National Training Conference, June 25-27.

Mills, J. (1989). *Womanwords.* Harlow: Longman House.

Mohawk, J. (1996). A native view of nature, an interview by Charlene Pretnak in *Resurgence,* September/October 1996, 178, 10-11.

Montgomerie, C., Peters, F. & Ward, K. (1991). *Educational leadership in Alberta.* Edmonton: University of Alberta.

Moody, H.R. (1988). *Abundance of life: Human development policies for an aging society.* New York: Columbia University Press.

Moore, T. (1984). *Soul mates.* New York: Harper Collins.

Morin, T. (1993). L'Apprentissage Innovateur: un paradigme émergent en éducation des Adultes. Montréal, Thése de doctorat inédite, Faculté des études supérieures, Sciences de l'éducation, Département d'andragogie et de psychopédagogie; Université de Montréal.

Morin, T. (1996). Becoming a learning organisation. In *CASAE/CAAE Annual Conference: Rethinking Education, Training and Employment* (pp. 226-234). Continuing Education Division, University of Manitoba, Winnipeg: Manitoba.

Morin, L. & Cosman, J.W. (1989). Prison education: The need for a declaration of basic principles for the treatment of prisoners. In S. Duguid (Ed.), *Yearbook of correctional education,* (pp. 83-99). Burnaby: Institute for the Humanities Simon Fraser University.

Morrison, J.H. (1989). *Camps and classrooms.* Toronto: Frontier College Press.

Mott, V.W. (1994). The role of intuition in the reflective practice of adult educators. *Proceedings of the 34th Adult Education Research Council Conference,* University of Tennessee, Knoxville, TN.

Muir, J. (1950). Announcement for the CAAE. In J.R. Kidd Papers, Ontario Provincial Archives.

Myles, J. & Boyd, M. (1982). Population aging and the elderly. In D. Forcese & S. Richer (Eds.), *Social issues.* Scarborough, ON: Prentice-Hall Canada.

Naisbitt, J. (1983). *Les dix commandements de l'avenir.* Paris: Sand.

National Advisory Council on Aging. (1990). On lifelong learning. Position Paper no. 10. Ottawa: Author.

National Advisory Council on Aging. (1991). *Writings in gerontology #10: Mental health and aging.* Ottawa: Author.

National Advisory Council on Aging. (1993). Aging vignettes: A quick portrait of Canadian seniors (Vignette #17). Ottawa: Author.

National Advisory Council on Aging. (1996). *Aging vignettes: A quick portrait of Canada's retirement income system* (Vignettes #52, 56, & 64). Ottawa: Author.

National Institute of Adult Continuing Education. (1993). Learning for the future, a special issue on adult learning and the environment, in *Adults Learning, 4* (8), April.

Neumann, W. (1979). Educational responses to the concern for proficiency. In G. Grant, P. Elbow, T. Ewens, Z. Gamson, W. Kohli, W. Neumann, V. Olesen & D. Riesman, *On competence: A critical analysis of competence-based reforms in higher education.* (pp. 66-94). San Francisco: Jossey-Bass.

New Zealand Qualifications Authority. (1991). *Designing the framework: A discussion document about restructuring national qualifications.* Wellington: author.

Niemi, J. (1977-8). The meaning of lifelong learning. *Yearbook of adult continuing education.* Chicago: Marquis Academic Media.

Nietzsche, F. (1964). *On the future of our educational institutions.* New York: Russell & Russell.

Nixon, M. & Bumbarger, C.S. (1983, May). *Inmate education: Canadian education programs in provincial correctional centres.* Edmonton: University of Alberta, Department of Educational Administration.

Noble, D.D. (1990). High-tech skills: The latest corporate assault on workers. In S. London, E. Tarr & J. Wilson (Eds.), *The re-education of the American working class.* Westport, CT: Greenwood Publishing Group.

Norris, N. (1991). The trouble with competence. *Cambridge Journal of Education, 21*(3), 331-341.

Novak, M. (1985). *Successful aging: The myths, realities and future of aging in Canada.* Markham, Ontario: Penguin Books.

Novak, M. (1993). *Aging and society: A Canadian perspective* (2nd edition). Toronto: Nelson Canada.

Nussbaum, F. (1984). *The brink of all we hate. English satires on women 1660-1750.* Lexington: University Press of Kentucky.

Nyerere, J. (1988). Adult education and development. *Adult Education and Development, 30,* 7-18.

O'Connor, J. (1984). *Accumulation crisis.* Oxford: Basil Blackwell.

Oddi, L. (1987). Perspectives on self-directed learning. *Adult Education Quarterly, 38* (1), 21-31.

Ogilivie, J. (1990). *The National Film Board and the cold war: A learning tradition is lost.* Unpublished paper, OISE Department of Adult Education.

Ohliger, J. (1967). *Listening groups: Mass media in adult education.* Boston: Centre for the Study of Liberal Education for Adults.

Ohliger, J. (1974). Is lifelong education a guarantee of permanent inadequacy? *Convergence, 7,* 47-59.

Ohliger, J. (1989). Alternate images of the future in adult education. In S. Merriam & P. Cunningham (Eds.), *Handbook of adult and continuing education* (pp. 628-639). San Francisco: Jossey-Bass.

Ontario Federation of Labour. (1992). *Training: A labour perspective.* Toronto: Author.

Orner, M. (1992). Interrupting the calls for student voice in "liberatory education": A feminist poststructuralist perspective. In C. Luke & J. Gore (Eds.), *Feminisms and critical pedagogy* (pp.74-89). New York: Routledge.

Orr, D. (1992). *Ecological literacy: Education and the transition to a postmodern world.* Albany: State University of New York Press.

Orwell, G. (1948). *Nineteen eighty-four.* London: Martin, Secker, Warburg.

O'Sullivan, E. (1998) *The dream drives the action.* London: Zed Press.

Pal, L.A. (1993). *Interests of state: The politics of language, multiculturalism, and feminism in Canada.* Montreal and Kingston: McGill-Queen's University Press.

Pannu, R.S. (1996). Neoliberal project of globalization: Prospects for democratization of education. *Alberta Journal of Educational Research, XLII* (2), 87-101.

Paquette, J. (1995). Universal education: Meanings, challenges, and options into the third millennium. *Curriculum Inquiry, 25* (1), 23-56.

Parkin, A. (1996). *Building civil society "from the ground up": The Halifax People's Summit.* Paper presented at Centre for Studies in Democratization, University of Warwick, England, February 16-17.

Pasquier, J. (1978). Experience and conversion. In W.E. Conn (Ed.), *Conversion: Perspectives on personal and social transformation.* New York: Alba House.

Pearson, E. & Podeschi, R. (1997). Humanism and individualism: Maslow and his critics. *38th Annual Adult Education Research Conference Proceedings* (pp. 203-207). Stillwater, Oklahoma: Oklahoma State University.

Perry, W. (1970). *Forms of intellectual and ethical development in the college years.* New York: Holt, Rinehart, and Winston.

Peters, O. (1983). Distance teaching and industrial production: A comparative interpretation in outline. In D. Sewart, D. Keegan & B. Holmberg (Eds.), *Distance education: International perspective* (pp. 95-113). London: Croom Helm.

Phillipson, R. (1992). *Linguistic imperialism.* Oxford: Oxford University Press.

Pigou, A.C. (1933:1968). *The theory of unemployment.* Haarlem: Frank Cass & Co.

Pike, G. & Selby, D. (1988). *Global teacher, global learner.* London, Sydney, Auckland, Toronto: Hodder and Stoughton.

Plumb, D. (1993). Time and space in adult education: The dimension of domination and resistance in modern and postmodern times. In *Proceedings of the 12th Annual Conference of Canadian Association for the Study of Adult Education* (pp. 301-306). University of Ottawa, Ottawa.

Poggeler, F. (Ed.) (1990). *The state and adult education: Historical and systematical aspects.* Frankfurt: Verlag Peter Lang.

Pratt, D.D. (1988). Andragogy as a relational construct. *Adult Education Quarterly, 38*(3), 160-181.

Prawat, R.S. (1993, August-September). The value of ideas: Problems versus possibilities in learning. *Educational Researcher,* 5-16.

Prospectus. (1994, November 21). Consortium for Organizational Learning: An invitation to join. Centre for Public Management.

Pulp, Paper and Woodworkers of Canada. (1993). *Jobs, trees and us—the PPWC'S forest policy.* Ottawa: Author.

Quigley, A. (1991, October). Trials, traditions, and the twenty-first century. *Adult Learning,* 21-23.

Rachal, J. (1989). The social context of adult and continuing education. In S. Merriam & P. Cunningham (Eds.), *Handbook of adult and continuing education* (pp. 3-14). San Francisco: Jossey-Bass.

Raelin, J.A. & Cooledge, A.S. (1996). From generic to organic competencies. *Human Resource Planning, Winter,* 24-33.

Ransome, P. (1992). *Antonio Gramsci: A new introduction.* London, UK: Harvest/Wheatsheaf.

Raven, J. (1984). *Competence in modern society: Its identification, development and release.* London: H.K. Lewis.

Redding, J.C. & Catalanello, R.F. (1994). *Strategic readiness: The making of the learning organization.* San Francisco: Jossey-Bass.

Reiman, J. (1984). *The rich get richer and the poor get prison* (3rd edition). New York: Macmillan.

Rich, A. (1993). *What is found there: Notebooks on poetry and politics.* New York and London: W.W. Norton.

Richardson, B. (1981). Film in the service of people, *The Globe and Mail,* April 8, 7.

Ridington, R. (1995). Freedom and authority: Teachings of the hunters. In R.B. Morrison & C.R. Wilson (Eds.), *Native peoples: The Canadian experience* (pp. 232-259). Toronto: McClelland & Stewart.

Rigolot, F. (1994). Rabelais, misogyny and Christian charity: Biblical intertextuality and the renaissance crisis of exemplarity. *Progressive Modern Language Association, 24,* 225-237.

Rivera, J. (1992). A non-traditional approach to curriculum for prisoners in New York State. *Journal of Prisoners on Prisons, 4*(1), 29-34.

Roberts, W. et al. (1993). *Get a life: A green cure for Canada's economic blues.* Toronto: Get a life.

Robinson, R.D. (1996, March). The learning organization. *Adult Learning 7*(4), 16-17.

Robson, J. (1994). The New Zealand national qualifications framework: A basis for action? *Journal of Further and Higher Education, 18*(3), 63-73.

Rockhill, K. (1995). Challenging the exclusionary effects of the exclusive mask of adult education. In M. Collings (Ed.), *The Canmore Proceedings* (pp. 1-6). Saskatchewan: University of Saskatchewan.

Rodby, J. (1992). *Appropriating literacy: Writing and reading in English as a second language.* Portsmouth, New Hampshire: Boynton/Cook, Heinemann.

Rogers, C. (1972). *Le developpement de la personne.* Paris: Dunod.

Rogers, K. (1966). The troublesome helpmate: A history of misogyny in literature. London: University of Washington Press.

Rose, A. (1996). Examining the fascination with learning organization. *Adult Learning, 7*(4), 5-15.

Ross, E. (1995). Syphilis, misogyny and witchcraft in 16th century Europe. *Current Anthropology, 36*(2), 333-337.

Rose, J. (1991). *Worth fighting for: Selected speeches and articles, 1983-91.* Ottawa: Canadian Union of Public Employees.

Ross, R.R. & Fabiano, E. (1985). *Time to think: A cognitive model of delinquency prevention and offender rehabilitation.* Johnson City, TN: Institute of Social Science and Arts.

Roth, I. (1990). Challenging habits of expectation. In J. Mezirow and Associates (Eds.), *Fostering critical reflection in adulthood.* San Francisco: Jossey-Bass.

Rough, J. (1994). Measuring training from a new science perspective. *Journal for Quality and Participation*, October/November, 12-16.

Rubenson, K. (1992). Adult education: The economic context, in F. Cassidy & R. Farris (Eds.). *Choosing our future: Adult education and public policy in Canada.* Toronto: OISE Press.

Russell, D. (1925). *Hypatia or women and knowledge.* NY: E.P. Dutton & Co.

Ryan, T.A. (1995). Correctional education: Past is prologue to the future. *Journal of Correctional Education, 46*, 60-65.

Ryan, W. (1972). *Blaming the victim.* NY: Vintage Books.

Sardello, R. (1995). *Love and the soul.* New York: Harper Perennial.

Sass, B. (1996). NOVA looks up learning. *Edmonton Journal*, February 20, D1.

Saunders, R.M. (1965) Toronto *field naturalists' club its history and constitution.* Toronto: Toronto Field Naturalists' Club.

Sbarbaro, E. (1995a). Notes on prison activism and social justice. In H.S. Davidson (Ed.), *Schooling in a "total institution": Critical perspectives on prison education* (pp. 141-146). Westport, CT: Bergin and Garvey.

Sbarbaro, E. (1995b). Teaching "criminology" to "Criminals." In H.S. Davidson (Ed.), *Schooling in a "total institution:" Critical perspectives on prison education* (pp. 91-101). Westport, CT: Bergin & Garvey.

Schaie, K.W. (1977-78). Toward a stage theory of adult cognitive development. *Journal of Aging and Human Development, 8*(2), 129-138.

Schenk, C. & Anderson, J. (Eds.). (n.d.). *Re-shaping work: Union responses to technological change.* Toronto: Ontario Federation of Labour, Technology Adjustment Research Program.

Schick, C. (1994). *The university as text: Women and the university context.* Halifax: Fernwood.

Schon, D. (1995, November/December). The new scholarship requires a new epistemology. *Change*, 27-34.

Schon, D.A. (1983). *The reflective practitioner.* New York: Basic Books.

Schon, D.A. (1987). *Educating the reflective practitioner: Toward a new design for learning and teaching in the professions.* San Francisco: Jossey-Bass.

Schroeder, W.L. (1970). Adult education defined and described. In R.M. Smith, G.F. Aker & J.R. Kidd (Eds.), *Handbook of adult education* (pp. 25-43). New York: Macmillan.

Schultz, T. (1961). Capital formation by education. *The American Economic Review, 1*(2), 1-17.

Schultz, T.W. (1981). *Investing in people: The economics of population quality.* Los Angeles: The University of California Press.

Schuttenberg, E. & Saundra, T. (1987). The role of the adult educator in fostering self-directed learning. *Lifelong Learning, 10*(5), 4-6, 9.

Schutz, A. (1973). *Collected Papers, Volume 1: The problem of social reality.* The Hague: Martinus Nijhoff.

Schutz, A. (1975). *On phenomenology and social relations.* Chicago: University of Chicago Press.

Schutze, H. (1992) Human resource development: Education and the world of work. In L.E. Burton, *Developing resourceful humans.* New York: Routledge.

Schwass, R. (1972). *National Farm Radio Forum, the history of an educational institution in rural Canada.* Doctoral Thesis, University of Toronto, Toronto.

Scott, S. & Schmitt-Boshnick, M. (1994). Integrating the personal and social in transformation theory, *CASAE Proceedings* (pp. 380-385). Abbotsford, BC: University College of the Fraser Valley.

Scott, S.M., Chovanec, D.M. & Young, B. (1994). Philosophy-in-action in university teaching. *The Canadian Journal of Higher Education, 23*(3), 1-25.

Scottish Vocational Education Council. (1988). *Credit where credit is due: The report of the accreditation of work-based learning project.* Glasgow: Scottish Vocational Education Council.

Selman, G. (1975). Canadian adult educators on Canadian adult education, *Canadian Journal of University Continuing Education, 2*(1), 5-15.

Selman, G. (1981). *The Canadian Association for Adult Education in the Corbett years: A re-interpretation*, Vancouver: University of British Columbia/Centre for Continuing Education.

Selman, G. (1982). R. Kidd and the CAAE 1951-1961. *Occasional Papers in Continuing Education, 22.*

Selman, G. (1984). Stages in the development of Canadian adult education. *Canadian Journal of University Continuing Education 10*(1), 7-16.

Selman, G. (1987). Adult education and citizenship. In F. Cassidy & R. Faris (Eds.), *Choosing our future: Adult education and public policy in Canada*, Symposium Series 17 (pp. 36-49). Toronto: OISE Press.

Selman, G. (1989). 1972-Year of affirmation for adult education. *The Canadian Journal for the study of Adult Education*, 3(1).

Selman, G. (1991). *Citizenship and the adult education movement in Canada*. Vancouver: University of British Columbia/Centre for Continuing Education.

Selman, G. (1994). Continuing education and the Canadian mosaic. In M. Brooke & M. Waldron (Eds.), *University continuing education in Canada* (pp. 4-18). Toronto: Thompson Educational.

Selman, G. (1994). *Felt along the heart: A life in adult education*. Vancouver: Centre for Continuing Education, (UBC).

Selman, G. (1995). *Adult education in Canada: Historical essays*. Toronto: Thompson Educational.

Selman, G. & Dampier, P. (1991). *The foundations of adult education in Canada*. Toronto: Thompson Educational.

Selman, G. & Kulich, J. (1995). Between social movement and profession: A historical perspective on Canadian adult education. In G. Selman, *Adult education in Canada: Historical essays* (pp. 29-35). Toronto: Thompson Educational.

Senge, P., Ross, R., Smith, B., Roberts, C. & Kleiner, A. (1994). *The fifth discipline fieldbook: Strategies and tools for building a learning organization*. New York: Doubleday.

Senge, P. (1991). *The fifth discipline: The art and practice of the learning organization*. New York: Doubleday.

Sewart, D. (1983). Distance teaching: A contradiction in terms? In D. Sewart, D. Keegan & B. Holmberg (Eds.), *Distance education: International perspectives*. London: Croom Helm.

Shapiro, R. (1995). Liberatory pedagogy and the development paradox, *Convergence, 28*(2), 28-45.

Shaw, R.B. & Perkins, D.N.T. (1991). The learning organization: Teaching organizations to learn. *Organization Development Journal, 9*(4), 1-12.

Shiva, V. (1989). *Staying alive: Women, ecology, and development*. London: Zed Books.

Shor, I. & Freire, P. (1987). *A pedagogy for liberation: Dialogues on transforming education*. New York: Bergin & Garvey.

Shore, C. & Roberts, S. (1995). Higher education and the panopticon paradigm: Quality assurance as "disciplinary technology." *Higher Education Review, 27* (3), 8-17.

Shorter Oxford English Dictionary, (1987). Oxford: Clarendon Press.

Silver, H. & Brennan, J. (1988). *A liberal vocationalism*. London: Methuen.

Sim, A. (1943). Films for farmers. *CSTA Review* 36.

Sim, A. (1954). Canada's farm radio forum. In J.R. Kidd (Ed.), *Learning and society: Readings in Canadian adult education*. Toronto: CAAE.

Sim, A. (Ed.) (1954). *Canada's Farm Radio Forum*. Paris: UNESCO.

Simon, B. (1990). *The search for enlightenment: The working-class and adult education in the twentieth century*. London: Lawrence & Wishart.

Simosko, S. (1995). *PLAR: Prior learning assessment and educational reform: A vision for now*. Centre for Curriculum and Professional Development and The British Columbia Council on Admissions and Transfer, Victoria, British Columbia.

Singer, J.S. (1972). *Boundaries of the soul: The practice of Jung's psychology*. New York: Double Day.

Sinnott, J.D. (1994). The future of adult lifespan learning: Learning institutions face change. In J.D. Sinnott (Ed.), *Interdisciplinary handbook of adult lifespan learning* (pp. 449-465). Westport, CN: Greenwood Press.

Skinner, B.F. (1976). The free and happy student. In C.J. Lucas, *Challenge and choice in contemporary education* (pp. 219-225). New York: Macmillan.

Smith, D. (1995). *First person plural: A community development approach to social change*. Montreal: Black Rose Press.

Smith, E. & Norlen, R. (1994). Tele-distance education in women's studies: Issues for feminist pedagogy. *Canadian Journal for the Study of Adult Education, 8*(2), 29-44.

Smith, G. (1992). *Education and the environment: Learning to live with limits*. New York: Suny Press.

Smith, J. (1989). *Misogynies*. London: Faber and Faber.

Solicitor General of Canada. (1990). *Annual Report 1988-1989*. Ottawa: Minister of Supply and Services Canada.

Somerville, M.A. (1996, May). *Constructing a global community from new science and old values*. Convocation speech presented at St. Francis Xavier University, Antigonish, N.S.

Sorensen, A.B. & Kelleberg, A.L. (1994). An outline of a theory on the matching of persons to jobs. In D.B. Grusky (Ed.), *Social stratification in sociological perspective*. San Francisco: Westview Press.

Spear, G. & Mocker, D. (1991). The future of adult education. In S. Merriam & P. Cunningham (Eds.), *Handbook of Adult and Continuing Education* (pp. 640-649). San Francisco: Jossy-Bass.

Spencer, B. (1994). Educating union Canada. *Canadian Journal for the Study of Adult Education, 8*(2), 45-64.

Spencer, B. (1995). Old and new social movements as learning sites: Greening labour unions and unionising the greens. *Adult Education Quarterly, 46(1), 31-41*.

Spencer, B. (1995). Removing barriers and enhancing openness: Distance education as social adult education. *Distance Learning, 10* (2), 87-104.

Spencer, B. and Taylor, J. (1994). Labour education in Canada: A SoliNet conference. *Labour/Le Travail, 34,* 217-37.

Spronk, B. (1994). Distance learning for participatory development: A case study. *Canadian Journal of University Continuing Education 20*(2), 9-22.

Stabler, E. (1987). *Founders: Innovators in education—1830-1980*, Edmonton, University of Alberta.

Stalker, J. (1996). Women and adult education: Rethinking androcentric research. *Adult Education Quarterly, 46*(2), 98-113.

Stanage, S. (1994). Adult education as ethical and moral meaning through action. *Proceedings of the 35th Annual Adult Education Research Conference* (pp. 348-353). Knoxville, TN: College of Education, University of Tennessee.

Stanage, S.M. (1987). *Adult education and phenomenological research*. Malabar, FL: Krieger.

Statistics Canada. (1991). *Adult literacy in Canada: Results of a national study.* Cat. 89-525E. Ottawa: Industry, Science and Technology Canada.

Statistics Canada. (1992). *1991 Census of Canada: Age, race and marital status.* Cat. 93-310. Ottawa: Industry, Science and Technology Canada.

Statistics Canada. (1992). *Mother tongue: The nation.* Catalogue number 93-313. Ottawa: Statistics Canada.

Statistics Canada. (1993). *Aging and independence: 1993 overview of a national survey.* Cat. H88-3/13/1993E. Ottawa: Health Canada.

Statistics Canada. (1993). *Aging vignettes: A quick portrait of Canadian seniors* (Vignette #17). Ottawa: National Advisory Council on Aging.

Statistics Canada. (1993). *Ethnic origin: The nation.* Catalogue number 93-315. Ottawa: Statistics Canada.

Statistics Canada. (1993). *1991 Census of Canada: Educational attainment and school attendance.* Cat. 93-328. Ottawa: Industry, Science and Technology Canada.

Statistics Canada. (1993). *Population estimates by first official language spoken: Dimensions.* Catalogue number 94-320. Ottawa: Statistics Canada.

Statistics Canada. (1994). *Health and activity limitation survey's guide.* Cat. 82-602E. Ottawa: Industry, Science and Technology Canada.

Statistics Canada. (1995). *Women in Canada: A statistical report* (3rd edition). Cat. 89-503E. Ottawa: Industry Canada

Sternberg, R.J. (1988). *The triarchic mind: A new theory of human intelligence.* New York: Penguin Books.

Stewart, T.A. (1994). Your company's most valuable asset: Intellectual capital. *Fortune.* October 3, 68-74.

Stone, J. (1995). Jailhouse lawyers educating fellow prisoners. In H.S. Davidson (Ed.), *Schooling in a "total institution": Critical perspectives on prison education* (pp. 173-201). Westport, CT: Bergin and Garvey.

Stubblefield, H.W. & Keane, P. (1994). *Adult education in the American experience.* San Francisco: Jossey-Bass.

Swift, J. (1995). *Wheel of fortune: Work and life in the age of falling expectations.* Toronto: Between the Lines.

Tarnas, R. (1996). In R.E. DiCarlo (Ed.), *Towards a new world view; Conversations at the leading edge* (pp. 21-34). Erie (Pa.): Eric Publishing.

Taylor, J. (1996). The solidarity network: universities, computer-mediated communication and labour studies in Canada. In T. Harrison & T. Stephen (Eds.), *Computer networking and scholarly communication in the twenty-first-century university* (pp. 277-290). New York: SUNY.

Taylor, J.A. (1989). Transformative learning: Becoming aware of possible worlds. Unpublished master's thesis, University of British Columbia.

Taylor, M. (1987). Self-directed learning: More than meets the observer's eye. In D. Boud & V. Griffin (Eds.), *Appreciating adults learning.* London: Kogan Page.

Taylor, M. (Ed.). (1997). *Workplace education: The changing landscape.* Toronto: Culture concepts.

Taylor, R., Rockhill, K. & Fieldhouse, R. (1985). *University adult education in England and the USA.* Beckenham: Croom Helm.

Tennant, M.C. (1993). Perspective transformation and adult development. *Adult Education Quarterly, 44,* 34-51.

Tennant, M.C. & Pogson, P. (1995). *Learning and change in the adult years: A developmental perspective.* San Francisco: Jossey-Bass.

Tett, L. (1996). Community education, the "underclass" and the discourse of derision. *International Journal of Lifelong Education 15*(2), 19-31.

Thom, R. (1980). Modélisation et Scientificité. In P. Delattre P. & M. Thellier (Éds.), *Elaboration et justification des modéles. Application en biologie* (pp. 21-27). Paris: Maloine-Doin, T. I.

Thomas, A. (1961). The learning society. In. J.R. Kidd (Ed.). (1963), *Learning and society* (pp. 405-412). Toronto: Canadian Association for Adult Education.

Thomas, A. (1987). Government and adult learning. In F. Cassidy & R. Faris (Eds.), *Choosing our future: Adult education and public policy in Canada,* Symposium Series 17 (pp. 103-130). Toronto: OISE Press.

Thomas, A. (1991). *Beyond education: A new perspective on society's organization of learning* San Francisco: Jossey-Bass.

Thomas, A. (1991). Relationships and political science in adult education, evolution and achievements. In P. Jarvis & Associates (Eds.), *A developing field of study.* Oxford/San Francisco: Jossey-Bass.

Thomas, A. (1993). The new world of adult learning. *Learning Magazine, 6*(2), 5-8.

Thomas, A. (1994). The wonderful promise of chaos theory for adult learning and adult education. *CASAE Proceedings* (pp. 399-403). Vancouver: Simon Fraser University.

Thomas, A. & Klaiman, R. (1989). *An evaluation of the Ontario "equivalent standing for mature students" Policy.* Department of Adult Education, OISE/UT Toronto.

Thomas A. & Klaiman, R. (1989). *The utilization of prior learning assessment as a basis for admission and the establishment of advanced standing in education in Canada.* Department of Adult Education, OISE/UT, Toronto.

Thomas, A. & MacKeracher, D. et al. (1982). *Adult learning about Canada,* Ottawa, Department of Secretary of State.

Thomas, A.V. (1916). Address to Saskatchewan Homemakers' annual meeting. *Proceedings of the Saskatchewan Homemakers' Clubs.*

Thomas, F.G. (1935). Canadian adult education: A landmark. *The International Quarterly of Adult Education, 2*(2-3), 75-87.

Thomas, J. (1995). The ironies of prison education. In H.S. Davidson (Ed.), *Schooling in a "total institution:" Critical perspectives on prison education* (pp. 1-23). Westport, CT: Bergin and Garvey.

Thompson, J. (Ed.) (1987). *Education for a change*. London: Hutchinson.

Thompson, J.B. (1990). *Ideology and modern culture: Critical social theory in the era of mass communication*. Stanford, CA: Stanford University Press.

Thompson, J.H. & Randall, S.J. (1994). *Canada and the United States: Ambivalent allies*. Montreal & Kingston: McGill-Queens University Press.

Thompson, J.H. & Seager, E. (1985). *Canada 1922-1939*. Toronto: McClelland and Stewart.

Tilbury, D. (1994). The international development of environmental education: A basis for a teacher education model? In *Environmental Education and Information 13*(2), 1-20.

Tibbetts-Schulenburg, J. (1989). Saints. In H. Tierney (Ed.), *Women's Studies Encyclopedia, 3* (pp. 397-399). London: Greenwood Press.

Tierney, W.G. (1992). *Official encouragement, institutional discouragement: Minorities in academe—The Native American experience*. Norwood, NJ: Ablex Publishing Company.

Tierney, W.G. (1993). *Building communities of difference*. Toronto: OISE Press.

Tollefson, J.W. (1991). *Planning language, planning inequality: Language policy in the community*. London and New York: Longman.

Tompkins, J.J. (1921). *Knowledge for the people: A call to St. Francis Xavier's College*. Antigonish, N.S. (Privately printed).

Torton-Beck, E. (1991). Therapy's double dilemma: Anti-Semitism and misogyny. *Women and Therapy, 10*(4), 19-30.

Touchette, C. (1989). *L'aube de l'andragogie*. Montréal: Université de Montréal.

Tough, A. (1966, Autumn). The assistance obtained by adult self-teachers. *Adult Education, 17*(1).

Tough, A. (1979). *The adult's learning projects: A fresh approach to theory and practice in adult learning* (2nd edition). Toronto: OISE.

Tough, A. (1981). *Learning without a teacher: A study of tasks and assistance during adult self-teaching projects*. Toronto: OISE Press.

Tough, A. (1993). The future of adult learning. In T. Barer-Stein & J. Draper (Eds.), *The craft of teaching adults* (pp. 233-242). Toronto: Culture Concepts.

Touraine, A. (1981). *The voice and the eye: An analysis of social movements*. Cambridge: Cambridge University Press.

Towers, J.M. (1994). The perils of outcome-based teacher education. *Phi Delta Kappan, 75*(8), 624-627.

Toynbee, A. (1947). *A study of history*, New York: Oxford University Press.

Ulrich, D., Jick, T. & von Glinow, M. (1994). High-impact learning: Building and diffusing learning capability. *Organizational Dynamics*.

Unauthored (no author's byline) (1950), Canada as a filmmaker. *Food For Thought, 10*(6), 9-14.

UNESCO. (1985). *Declaration of the fourth international conference on adult education*. Paris: UNESCO.

University of Alberta. (1994). *Broader horizons: A report compiled by the extension function sub-committee for submission to the vice-president (academic's) advisory committee on restructuring*. Edmonton, AB: Author.

U.S. Department of Justice. (1994) *Bureau of Justice statistics: Sourcebook of criminal justice statistics*. Washington D.C.: Hindelang Criminal Justice Research Center.

U.S. Department of Justice. (1996). Correctional population in the United States 1980-1993. [http://www.ca-lyx.net/~...er/govpubs/corr93.html]. Washington D.C.: Office of Justice Programs.

Usher, R. & Edwards, R. (1994). *Postmodernism and education*. London: Routledge.

Usher, R. & Edwards, R. (1995). Confessing all? A "postmodern guide" to the guidance and counselling of adult learners. *Studies in the Education of Adults, 27*(1), 9-23.

van Vuuren, N. (1973). *The subversion of women as practiced by churches, witch-hunters and other sexists*. Philadelphia: Westminster Press.

Vantour, J. (Ed.), (1991). *Our story: Organizational renewal in federal corrections*. Ottawa: Correctional Service of Canada.

Verner, C. (1961). Basic concepts and limitations. In J.R. Kidd (Ed.), (1963), *Learning and society* (pp. 229-240). Toronto: Canadian Association for Adult Education.

Verner, C. (1964). Definitions of terms. In G. Jensen et al. (Eds.), Adult *education: Outlines of an emerging field of study*. Washington, DC: Adult Education Association.

Verner, C. & Dickenson, G. (1974). *Union education in Canada*. Vancouver: UBC/Labour Canada.

Vernon, F. (1969). *The development of adult education in Ontario, 1790-1900*, Unpublished Doctoral Thesis, Toronto: OISE.

Viezzer, M. (1986). Learning for environmental action. In *Convergence*, Special Issue *24*(2), 1992, 3-8.

Waldie, P. & Bourette, S. (1997, January 11). Good job news excludes youth. *The Globe and Mail*, p.B1.

Walker, G. (1995). Meaningful learning in organizations: Building on learning styles research. In *1995 Proceedings of the 14th Annual Conference of Canadian Association for the Study of Adult Education* (pp. 225-229). Montreal: Concordia University.

Wallace, M. (1993). Discourse of derision: The role of the mass media within the education policy process. *Journal of Education Policy, 8*(4), 321-337.

Waring, M. (1988). *If women counted: A new feminist economics*. San Francisco: Harper and Row.

Watkins, K. & Marsick, V.J. (1993). *Sculpting the learning organization*. San Francisco: Jossey-Bass.

Webster's Third International Dictionary (1986). Springfield, Mass.: Merriam-Webster.

Weir, D.J. (1973). A history of education in Canadian federal correction. In A.R. Roberts (Ed.), *Readings in prison education* (pp. 39-47). Springfield, IL: Charles C. Thomas.

Welton, M. (Ed.) (1987). *Knowledge for the people: The struggle for adult learning in English-speaking Canada, 1828-1973*. Toronto: OISE Press.

Welton, M. (1987). "Vivisecting the nightingale:" Reflections on adult education as an object of study. *Studies in the Education of Adults, 19*(1), 46-68.

Welton, M. (1991). What's new in the history of adult education. *HSE/RHE, 3*(2), 285-297.

Welton, M. (1993). The contribution of critical theory to our understanding of adult learning. In S. Merriam (Ed.), An update on adult learning theory. *New Directions for Adult and Continuing Education, 57,* Spring. San Francisco: Jossey-Bass.

Welton, M. (1993). Social revolutionary learning. *Adult Education Quarterly, 43*(3), 152-164.

Welton, M. (1994). Cathedrals and doghouses: A conversation. *International Journal of Lifelong Education, 13*(4), 281-289.

Welton, M. (1995). *In defense of the lifeworld: Critical perspectives on adult learning.* Albany, N.Y.: SUNY.

Werner, D.R. (1990). *Correctional education theory and practice.* Danville, ILL: Interstate Publishers.

West, G.W. (1994). Learning organizations: A critical review. *Proceedings of the Annual Midwest Research-to-Practice Conference in Adult, Continuing, and Community Education* (pp. 210-217). University of Wisconsin-Milwaukee, Milwaukee, Wisconsin.

Weston, J. (1995). Poll shows enivronmental issues a priority for most Canadians. *Alternatives, 21*(4), 12.

Wheeler, K. (1985). *International environmental education: An historical perspective. Environmental Education and Information, 4,* 144-160.

Whitaker, R. (1991). *Canadian immigration policy since confederation.* Ottawa: Canadian Historical Society and the Multiculturalism Program, Government of Canada.

Wick, C. (1993). *The learning edge: How smart managers and smart companies stay ahead.* New York: McGraw-Hill.

Wilbur, K. (1996). *A brief history of everything.* Boston: Shambhala.

Wildemeersch, D. (1992). Crossing borders in socio-cultural education with adults. In D. Wildemeersch & T. Jansen (Eds.), Adult *education, experiential learning and social change: the postmodern challenge* (pp.155-168). Driebergen: VTA Groep.

Wildemeersch, D. (1994). Life-world transformation and the issue of ecological responsibility. *Presentation in the 1994 International Experiential Learning Conference,* Washington.

Wildemeersch, D. (1995, November). Reconciling the Irreconcilable: Adult and continuing Education between private and public responsibility. *Discussion paper for Reconciling the Irreconcilable conference,* University Leuven, Belgium. Wilfrid Laurier University, Kitchener/Waterloo.

Wilkins, H. (1991). Computer talk: Long distance conversations by computer, *Written Communication (8),* 56-83.

Williams, R. (1990). *What I came to say.* London: Hutchinson Radius.

Williamson, G.L. (1992). Education and incarceration: An examination of the relationship between educational achievement and criminal behaviour. *Journal of Correctional Education, 43,* 14-22.

Wilson, A.V. (1991). *Epistemological foundations of American adult education, 1934 to 1989: A study of knowledge and interests.* Unpublished doctoral dissertation.

Winchester, I. (1992). Introduction. *Interchange, 23* (1-2), 1-17.

Windham, D. M. (1992). *Education for all: The requirements.* Paris: UNESCO.

Witter, S.R. (1979). *An historical study of adult education in two Canadian women's organizations.* Unpublished M.Ed. graduating essay, University of British Columbia.

Wittgenstein, L. (1958). *Philosophical investigations.* (3rd edition) New York: Macmillan.

Wolfe, A. (1995). *Competence-based assessment.* Buckingham: Open University.

Woodsworth, J.S. (1909). *Strangers within our gates.* Toronto: University of Toronto Press (Reprinted 1972).

Young, W.R. (1978). *Making the truth graphic: The Canadian government's home front information structure and programs during World War II.* Unpublished Ph.D. thesis, University of British Columbia.

Zuboff, S. (1988). *In the age of the smart machine: The future of work and power.* New York: Basic Books.

AGMV Marquis

MEMBER OF SCABRINI MEDIA

Quebec, Canada
2005